The Demon of the Continent

The
Demon of the Continent

Indians and the Shaping of American Literature

Joshua David Bellin

PENN

University of Pennsylvania Press
Philadelphia

10 9 8 7 6 5 4 3 2 1

Published by
University of Pennsylvania Press
Philadelphia, Pennsylvania 19104-4011

Library of Congress Cataloging-in-Publication Data

Bellin, Joshua David.
  The demon of the continent : Indians and the shaping of American literature / Joshua David Bellin.
    p.   cm.
  Includes bibliographical references (p.   ) and index.
  ISBN 0-8122-3570-3 (cloth : alk. paper); ISBN 0-8122-1748-9 (pbk. : alk. paper)
    1. American literature—History and criticism.   2. Indians in literature.   I. Title.
PS173 .I6 B45 2000
810.9'3520392—dc21   00-033799

For
Samuel Abraham and Pearl Rosenberg Bellin
Floyd Joseph and Norma Lengst Crowley

Contents

Introduction

Wherever I go, I tread in the tracks of the Indian. . . . Strange
spirits, dæmons, whose eyes could never meet mine; with another
nature and another fate than mine.

—Henry David Thoreau, *Journal*

In 1923, when the scholarly study of American literature was in its early
stages, D. H. Lawrence perceived at the heart of the literature a conflict
between the savage spirit of the land and the civilized texts that sought to
quell it. "Up till now," Lawrence writes, "the unexpressed spirit of America
has worked covertly in the American, the white American soul." But
"within the present generation," he prophesies, "the surviving Red Indians
are due to merge in the great white swamp," and a change will come about:
"A curious thing about the Spirit of Place is the fact that no place exerts its
full influence upon a new-comer until the old inhabitant is dead or absorbed. So America. While the Red Indian existed in fairly large numbers,
the new colonials were in a great measure immune from the daimon, or
demon, of America. The moment the last nuclei of Red life break up in
America, then the white men will have to reckon with the full force of the
demon of the continent."[1] This prediction was, of course, false on both
counts; the last nuclei of red life have not broken up, nor has their presence
been reckoned with. Indeed, offering the reckoning as a final one, Lawrence himself disguises the Indian presence even as he asserts it. The
demon of the continent works covertly in his soul as well, safe matter for
his literary judgments because it cannot interact with them.

Lawrence's paradigm—in which only the absent, imagined Indian is
of consequence to American literature—has, moreover, proved enduring.
As efforts to extend the literary canon have intensified, the study and
teaching of Native American oral and written art have flourished; similarly, there has been a growing recognition among historians, anthropologists, and ethnohistorians that Indians must be seen not as Lawrence's
"voiceless, nameless, and faceless" demon, but as "people who powerfully

affected the course of our historical development as a nation."[2] Yet literary critics have continued to overlook Indians as determinants of American— rather than specifically Native American—literature; though Indian authors have been revisited and revived, the notion that the presence of Indian peoples shaped American literature as a whole remains unexplored. (Indeed, one of the few essays to entertain such a notion concludes that "American writers . . . might have been profoundly influenced" by the presence of Indians, "but in fact weren't.") Roy Harvey Pearce's *Savagism and Civilization* (1953) set the agenda for the analysis of Indians in American literature: "Studying the savage," Pearce writes, "in the end [whites] had only studied themselves. . . . The Indian became important for the [white] mind, not for what he was in and of himself, but rather for what he showed civilized men they were not and must not be." Later critics have followed Pearce's lead: Richard Drinnon, for instance, traces the images of those "dark *others* that white settlers were not and must not under any circumstances become," while Robert Berkhofer asserts that "the Indian as an image was always alien to the White."[3] The study of Indians in literature, as distinguished from the study of Indian literatures, remains a study of images versus realities, white representers versus represented Indians.

Clearly, such analyses are invaluable; Pearce's concluding remarks— "it might be that there will always be somebody who needs to be subdued— men to play the part of Indians and so become savages standing in the way of civilization"—remain resonant as the parade of "savages"—Saddams, Serbs, Somalis—continues. Yet at the same time, if such studies alert us to the violence and inequalities of Indian-white contact, their focus on images of Indians threatens to update what they deplore. Image studies, that is, picture Indians as silent, ineffectual, and—most important—unnecessary to (white) history, (white) ideology, (white) literature. Indians remain immaterial, in two senses: it makes no difference what they were, for they could only have been constructed as savages; and it makes no difference that they were, for they were powerless to contest their construction (and destruction). Thus, to cite two examples, Lucy Maddox's *Removals* (1991), though it deplores the "failure [of literary critics] to take seriously the presence of the American Indians as a factor in the shaping of [American] literature," is itself interested not in the Indian presence but in the ways in which the *removal* of Indians gave birth to an imagined Indianness: "It is only the fully reconstructed and mythologized Indian—one who lives nowhere in nineteenth-century America—who can be assimilated into the civilized American text." Likewise, Susan Scheckel's *Insistence of the Indian*

(1998) is concerned not with the presence of Indians—repeatedly referring to an Indian "ghost" that "haunt[s] the nation and its narratives," she agrees with Lawrence that only in death could they acquire significance—but with the ways in which writers "reified 'the Indian' into an object of contemplation that both reflected and provided imaginative space for reflection on the meaning of national identity."[4] Despite their revisionist intentions, such studies ultimately agree with the literary tradition they critique that Indians, who lived everywhere in America—as opposed to the reconstructed, mythologized, ghostly, reified "Indian"—are no more relevant to the reader than they were, or are, to the nation and its literature.

The central assertions of this study are that the presence of Indian peoples in the land that is now the United States has been of profound significance to the shaping of American literature—not only to texts that overtly engage this presence, but to the whole body of literature produced in a nation itself produced by encounter—and that this presence must be "reckoned with" in our reading and teaching of the literature. As I hope to show, it is an error to take the images of Indians in American literature as the sole or salient measure of Indian peoples' significance. Rather, it is because American literature emerges from contexts of encounter, from the interaction and intersection of peoples, that the presence of Indians is central to the literature. I propose that no matter how vital images of Indians were (and are) in molding the destinies and writings of Indians and whites, such images cannot be divorced from what Betsy Erkkila terms "the material and cultural contexts and contests" within which they existed; I propose further that those "contexts and contests" cannot be evaluated without an acknowledgment that Indians played active, complex, subtle roles in them.[5] Pearce himself hinted at the direction my study is to take: "[*Savagism and Civilization*], were it to be the study in ethnohistory toward which it immanently aspires, would have had to do for the Red side of the story what it did for the White. It would have to have been an account of mutual acculturation, as it were."[6] In the following pages, I seek to answer this challenge, to examine how processes of "mutual acculturation" manifest themselves in America's literature. Thus, I consider numerous literary works, authored by Indians and whites from the seventeenth to mid-nineteenth centuries, in light of their position within a network of cultural conflict, negotiation, and interchange encompassing diverse material and ideological points of encounter: the economic, the spiritual, the geographic, the linguistic, and the aesthetic. To do so, I must emphasize, is neither to disguise nor to mitigate the violent facts of Indian-white encounter and of literary representation. It is dangerous to argue that violence can be compensated for by acts of sympathetic identification or creative appropriation. Moreover, as I show, the cultural interactions within which I claim American texts were forged are strenuously denied by most of those texts. To place cultural contact at the heart of American literature is to restore that literature to a history far more complex than has generally been admitted, to refuse to reduce Indians to static antagonists or fodder for a Euro-American imaginary but to view them as actors in dynamic processes in which America and its literature were (and are) inescapably embedded.

To frame my project in this way is to reconsider not only Pearce's conclusion but his premise; to interrogate not only the absence of the red "side," but the discourse of "sides" itself. For if it is this discourse that has shaped literary images of Indians, it is also this discourse that underlies the images approach to American literature. At the heart of image studies, that is, lies the assumption of white and red sides that clash at some Turnerian frontier, where the former claims the literal power to replace, and the literary power to repossess, the latter. Yet though this captures some of the emphases of Indian-white encounter—and of literary representations of it—it distorts in a number of ways: most plainly, by ignoring the creativity and resourcefulness of Indian peoples, but more subtly, by positing Indian and white peoples as monolithic, self-contained, necessarily opposed entities, who can only expand and wither, suppress and resist, represent and be represented. As ethnohistorian Richard White argues in his study of Indian-white encounter in the Great Lakes region, the second of these tenets is no less flawed than the first: in the "middle ground," White's term for the place of meeting between peoples, "no sharp distinctions between Indian and white worlds could be drawn. Different peoples, to be sure, remained identifiable, but they shaded into each other."[7] Again, this is not to deny imbalances of power or to suggest a harmonious resolution of differences. Rather, it is to suggest that differences are transformed through contact, such that the discourse of sides radically simplifies the processes of appropriation and accommodation, destruction and creation, that mark cultural encounter.

Thus what White and other ethnohistorians suggest is that not only must Indian peoples' significance to cultural encounter be recognized, but in so doing, past (and persistent) paradigms of encounter must be revised. Such a revision may require, as Alfonso Ortiz argues, that we "dispense with the notion of frontier altogether"; or at least, in the words of Arnold

Krupat, that we adopt an "ethnocritical frontier orientation," one that is "concerned with differences rather than oppositions, and so seeks to replace oppositional with dialogical models." For what cultural encounter illustrates is the inadequacy not only of fixed frontiers but of fixed cultures. Cultural encounter renders the view of culture as a "static, harmonious, and basically impermeable program or control mechanism, hermetically sealed off in peoples' heads from other cultural systems" and thus immune to contact, untenable.[8] Ethnohistorical studies bear this out; while it is sometimes possible to catalogue material possessions that Indians or whites "contributed" to or "borrowed" from the other,[9] debates over such matters as the Iroquois impact on United States republicanism, the origin of scalping, and the development of the Mother Earth concept suggest that contact is a matter neither of simple fusion nor of simple separation, where certain differences vanish while other differences remain inviolate.[10] What encounter shows, rather, is that cultures in contact are *intercultural*, consisting of the complex, intricate, and even indeterminate interrelationships among their diverse members.

An intercultural literary criticism, accordingly, views texts as taking shape through, and shaping in turn, these cultural interrelationships. An intercultural literary criticism maintains that encounter is far more than a background into which the literature can be inserted or against which it can be highlighted. On the contrary, an intercultural literary criticism argues that it is precisely through intimate, rich, dynamic interactions among multiple peoples that American literature exists at all. An intercultural approach to literature thus differs subtly but significantly from a multicultural approach, in which one forms alternate canons or places neglected works in an existing one; a comparative approach, in which, as Andrew Wiget explains, "currently canonical texts are read against texts from other American literary traditions, and each is allowed the privilege of illuminating the other"; and a "cosmopolitan" approach, in which, Krupat writes, one establishes a canon "constituted not only by the simple sum but by the complex interaction of national literatures."[11] Valuable though these approaches are in challenging an established canon, none questions the notion of a canon as the sum of its discrete components; all, that is, assume distinct texts, emanating from distinct traditions, that can only retrospectively, as a compensatory act, be brought into contact in the ideal space of the critical study or the classroom. An intercultural literary criticism, by contrast, maintains that American texts, canonical and non-canonical alike, have *themselves* been formed through the "complex interaction" of peoples. An intercultural literary criticism, that is, maintains that *any* American text, whatever the putative ethnicity of its author[12]— and I emphasize this, given the critical tendency to view "minority" texts as examples of cultural negotiation while treating "dominant" texts as if they are free from such concerns—has been forged by the processes of encounter within which it exists. In his collection of the works of William Apess, a Pequot orator and writer to whom I will return in the course of this study, Barry O'Connell phrases with admirable clarity the central tenet of an intercultural literary criticism: "Neither Euro-Americans nor Native Americans have available some culturally unmixed terrain on which to move or any pure medium free from the effects of the other." An intercultural literary criticism, in sum, sees texts as formed by, forming, and a form of encounter: fertile, contested, and multiply determined, they exist on the shifting borders, or in the indefinite field, between peoples in contact.[13]

There are, however, a number of problems an intercultural criticism raises, problems with which I will be occupied throughout this study. The most significant of these concerns the reconstruction of the Indians' words, beliefs, and positions within the intercultural field. It is neither by chance nor by preference that the majority of the texts I will explore were written and published by Euro-Americans. Throughout the period of this study, the vast majority of printed material on Indian-white encounter was authored by whites (though it may have been, as with treaties, ethnographies, or missionary tracts, mediated by Indian interpreters). Consequently, it is imperative to recognize that Indian "voices" in American texts exist in translation—by which I mean not only that they have been transmitted in an alien modality and languages, but that they have been shaped by the visions and ideologies of Euro-America. Nor is it possible absolutely to isolate these variables; if we do not know what needs Euro-American reporters brought to the encounter, what words they translated, or how suitable those words were for their supposed equivalents, neither do we know how these acts of personal, linguistic, and cultural translation intersect in the text. The texts themselves seldom inspire confidence; for example, though the works of John Eliot, the seventeenth-century Puritan missionary who figures prominently in my first chapter, invariably contain authenticating documents pleading his skill and probity as a translator— "the Interpreters," one such document reads, gave "a publick testimony to the truth of Mr. *Eliots* Interpretations" of the Indians' words—these interpreters, themselves converts and thus perhaps inclined to view their fellows' words through a Euro-American lens, would have been unlikely to burst Eliot's bubble in any event, given their reliance on Euro-American favor. (Nor, at that, were their testimonials particularly glowing; Eliot's translations, they hedged, were *"for the substance the same which the* Indians *answered, many times the very words which they spake, and alwayes the sense."*)[14] Perhaps, then, the "very words which they spake" survive, if at all, in a wholly subordinate relation to other concerns. Perhaps, indeed, their words were never spoken at all, but were crafted to achieve ends that either required falsification or that made fidelity irrelevant.

At the same time, the Indians' worlds, like their words, had been affected by contact, and mediated by textualization. There are a number of ways in which scholars have attempted to ascertain the realities of Indian existence during a period when few Indians possessed the ability or resources to publish written accounts; but leaving aside archaeological evidence—itself subject to the qualification that it does not speak[15]—these lead back to textual problems. One can, for example, collect a number of Euro-American reports, looking either for consistencies or for incongruities, either of which might be taken as proof of an elusive reality. Yet each of these qualities might represent nothing of the sort: consistency might merely reflect the grip of an accustomed schema, while incongruity might merely reflect an observer's idiosyncrasies, incompetence, or caprice. One can, then, decide to focus on those Indians who have left written works— though particularly in colonial times, one will find few indeed.[16] Yet Indian authors' works had been shaped by Euro-America both overtly— through the media of literacy and the European languages, the priorities of white editors, patrons, and sponsors, and the demands of a predominantly white audience—and covertly, through the fact that Indians had coexisted with Euro-America for years by the time they wrote. One can, finally, seek support not by multiplying past texts but by pursuing present ones; as ethnohistorians often do, one can look to works on living Native communities to uncover the lives of their ancestors. Yet far from bypassing textuality in this way, one confronts a new series of textual questions (a fact that ethnohistorians too seldom acknowledge): the extent to which ethnohistorical works have been shaped by a legacy of colonialism and by the older writings from which their conclusions, or preconceptions, are drawn; the validity of those works' interpretations of existing oral and material sources; the applicability of their interpretations, however valid, to the past; and so on.[17] Considering how a similar set of problems presents itself for a materialist literary criticism, Fredric Jameson summarizes the difficulties: "Since by definition the cultural monuments and masterworks that have survived tend necessarily to perpetuate only a single voice in [a] class dialogue, the voice of a hegemonic class, they cannot be properly assigned their relational place in a dialogical system without the restoration or artificial reconstruction of the voice to which they were initially opposed, a voice for the most part stifled and reduced to silence, marginalized, its own utterances scattered to the winds, or reappropriated in their turn by the hegemonic culture." If, as Jameson argues, textual archaeology is "artificial," then one must not imagine it to possess an extratextual legitimacy. Then, too, his warning about the reappropriation of stifled utterances is well heeded in this day of coffee-table Tecumseh quotes and Hollywood wolf dances. One cannot drape textual Indians in the mantle of authenticity even when the text portrays them in seemingly positive ways: as chaste ecologists, saintly underdogs, spiritual savants. This "sentimental romance of alterity," as Henry Louis Gates terms it, merely replaces one claim for textual authority with its reverse.[18]

All of these reservations, of course, apply to Euro-American "voices" as well. Though whites authored most of the texts in this study, the authors were not *in* their texts, and neither were they masters of or untouched by the material, linguistic, cultural, and personal forces of encounter through which their texts were shaped. Nonetheless, even if one could claim an equivalent textuality to all voices, the processes by which the textual Euro-American and textual Indian came into existence are instances of, and partners in, more visible hierarchies. And even if this were not so, the principal challenge to an intercultural *literary* criticism (for I do not deny the possibility of an intercultural criticism not reliant on the literary) would still be the fact that it must depend largely on Euro-American modes, media, and messengers. There is, to be sure, a danger in insisting on this fact: the danger, as David Murray puts it, that one will end up "textualising the Indians out of existence," thereby repeating the acts of erasure one means to critique.[19] Yet given that textualized Indians have almost invariably been employed to promote and justify violence against their real-life counterparts, to accept these textual portraits uncritically is not only naive but potentially deadly.

Yet at the same time, I would argue that this way of posing the problem—as a choice between "real" and "textual"—contributes to the problem; that if an intercultural literary criticism must resist claiming to speak for the "real" Indian, it must also avoid speaking in terms of a "realness" outside of the conditions of contact within which textualization operates. For all the problems an intercultural approach entails, Jameson's involves an "artificiality" of its own: schematizing the "hegemonic" voice and its "opposing" other, he fixes these voices beyond the contexts of their production (and thus beyond their textualization). An intercultural approach, conversely, argues that it is precisely because Indian and Euro-American voices exist within complex, problematic contexts of interaction that their textualization is itself complex and problematic; that the "text" and the "real" are not opposed but interrelated. This claim does not, of course, enable one to escape the text. Rather, this claim suggests that the text must *not* be escaped, for the text, if it obscures the processes that gave it birth, *is* those processes—including the processes of obscuring, which themselves take form through encounter. And if this is so, then American texts cannot be ransacked for a "real" Indian (or Euro-American) presence greater than encounter. If this is so, then the realness of the Indian or Euro-American, far from constituting some pure being beyond the text's warping influence, is inseparable from the varied contexts from which the text arose. Thus where Pearce has written that "Indian customs and traits" are "embodied," if one "looks hard enough," in "most" texts on Indians, I would argue that one can never distill a bodily Indian from the text—even when, I repeat, the text's author is a person whose ancestry, political affiliation, or self-representation (or any combination thereof) is Indian.[20] The reason for this is not, however, solely that Indians have been silenced by a textual (and literal) hegemony; it is also that Indians and Europeans alike (this need not mean equally, if, in fact, that could be quantified) have been shaped by processes that render the notion of an unmediated voice illusory. And accordingly, the realness of persons or cultures in contact cannot be seen as opposed, superordinate, or ancillary to the contact situation; the realness of persons or cultures in contact is inextricable from, and must be sought in, the discourses of conflict, accommodation, and interchange that characterize encounter and its texts.

In summary, though I will have ample occasion to draw on historical, anthropological, and ethnohistorical studies, I will insist as a literary critic that these works, however valuable or valid, are *texts*. I will insist in turn, as an *intercultural* literary critic, that texts must be viewed within contexts of encounter, that generative and destabilizing region in which cultures, peoples, languages, and literatures exist not singly but in relationship with their various others. The act of restoring Indians to America's texts and contexts, in this light, becomes not a project of acknowledging their presence in "our" literature, of identifying the discrete "influences" they have had, of rescuing "their" beliefs and practices from oblivion, or of constructing a model of America in which truth equals plenitude. The intercultural act, rather, emphasizes the indeterminacy of "presence," of "their" beliefs and "our" literature (and of their "their" and our "our"), of influence, truth, and the idea of America. Focusing, as Françoise Lionnet puts it, on the "process whereby all elements involved in the interaction [are] changed by [the] encounter," interculturalism suggests that no element can belong solely and eternally to one culture, for no culture is free from process, interaction, change.[21] And as such, the most profound consequence of interculturalism may lie in the shift from discrete elements to the encounters in which they—and the critic's vision as well as the vista of American literature—are changed.

This study is concerned with that shift. In pursuing the shift, I have found various elements of my own training and practice challenged, modified, discarded; I have found that a turn toward the dynamics of encounter has resulted in new linkages, categories, and readings. These serve, I hope, not only the specific purpose of illuminating particular moments of encounter, but the broader purpose of suggesting the paradigmatic changes that a focus on encounter institutes. Yet to propose such changes is clearly as much a polemical as an analytical move (not that every analysis is not a polemic); and it is proper to articulate not only my biases but, just as important, their repercussions. The reader, I trust, will take these comments not as disclaimers but as a guide to this study's intentions, an introduction to its self-reflections, and an invitation to enter into dialogue not simply over its formulations but over the nature of interculturalism itself.

So to begin: it may strike readers that the analysis offered here is too single-minded, as if interculturalism is not merely *a* means of exploring American literature but *the* means. I am, I hope, as suspicious of single-causation theories as any critic; and I will, I believe, illustrate that interculturalism is too multifaceted to be viewed as a single cause. Yet my decision to isolate Indian-white interaction is vulnerable to objection: not only do I overlook other peoples, but I dismiss other postulates regarding the sources of American literature. I have no wish to minimize or answer such objections; on the contrary, I wish to foreground them in order to foreground the fact that critical choices are motivated, not predetermined. In my case, the choice to single out Indian-white interaction was motivated by two convictions: first, that it is a valid, significant, and—frankly—central context for American literature; and second, that authors of past studies have not only paid far too little notice to this context but have felt far too little need to notice their lack of notice. I should clarify, then, that when I say I have disregarded other contexts, this is not a concession but a challenge; though *Walden* has been viewed through European Romanticism, liberal individualism, abolitionism, and so on, I am convinced that it can and should be viewed through Creek ceremonies of earth-renewal and the basket industry of the New England Indians.

This leads to a related issue. It may strike readers that in foregrounding interchange this study de-emphasizes difference, that my insistence that Indians and whites exist within contexts of interculturalism threatens to negate cultural traits that may *not* have been transformed by encounter. Again, this is a valid point: I am sympathetic to the argument that many productions survived encounter largely or wholly intact, and I am sympathetic as well to the argument that minimizing differences robs people of sources of pride, distinction, and identity. Yet again, if by emphasizing interchange over difference I am producing a selective portrait of the whole—as clearly I am—this should be seen as a critical position, one grounded in my distrust of definitive pronouncements as to which culture "owns" what and in my belief that difference is in little need of my support: in my desire, that is, to challenge the assumption that difference, even where it exists, is unproblematic. Was Romanticism, at least as it was elaborated by American Transcendentalists, unaffected by encounter? Did (as I suggest at a later point) the Emersonian turn to a "primitive" language of Nature owe at least some of its emphases, its power, and its anxieties to the presence of Indian peoples forced from their homelands? If such questions seem bizarre, I am convinced that this is because difference has held too long and unhealthy a monopoly on the study of American literature; and it is my hope that in hazarding the bizarre I may help our understanding of the normal to be interrogated.

There are, in addition to these theoretical issues, two practical aspects of my approach I would raise. First, as the authors to whom I have referred indicate, this work places considerable (though far from exclusive) emphasis on the East, and specifically New England. Once more, this was meant to challenge a persistent assumption: that Indians were literally absent from the East after the early years of contact and, in consequence, absent except as imagined Others from that small body of works by antebellum New Englanders that still constitutes the dominant American literary canon. Yet in making this choice, I have myself felt the absence of other, less well-known works; my focus threatens both to dissolve the numerous sites of contact that existed and to sequester, and thereby sim-

plify, what it does discuss. At the same time, I have felt that, if the geographic distribution of texts is too narrow, the volume might be too great.
Though I have made no attempt at coverage, that preposterous bugbear
and grail of the survey course, I have spanned centuries, locales, peoples in
an attempt to illustrate the pervasive links between encounter and literary
texts. Yet whatever the gain in doing so, the loss lies in blurring or short-
changing particularities; not only did various peoples differ in significant
ways, but, as Ramón Gutiérrez points out, individual communities "had
many voices that often spoke in unison, but just as often were diverse and
divisive."[22] I have attempted to honor this fact, to suggest the effects of
interculturalism not only between peoples (however defined), but within
any community; I have not, however, always been successful. (Along these
lines, I have relied on tribal names, despite evidence that the "tribe" was a
European invention or a result of the European invasion, but in either case
not a useful concept for grouping Indian peoples.) These matters are not,
perhaps, as weighty as the theoretical issues. They do suggest, however,
that if interculturalism resists fixity, fixity infects interculturalism—that not
all elements of my critical vision have been freed from conventional places.
And this suggests, in turn, that the study of encounter needs to inaugurate
even greater shifts than are evident here; that it needs to challenge all of the
categories by which American literature has been conceived—including
the category *of* American literature.

In making these comments, I mean to suggest how this study—any
study—is affected by the limits it questions. By the same token, however,
this study—any study—is affected by the questions it limits. Encounter, as I
portray it in the following pages, is provisional, not definitive; thus my
readings are provisional, not definitive. That being said, it should be obvious that this study cannot attempt to tell the full complexity of the
encounters between peoples in America. Indeed, the full complexity may
lie in the fact that intercultural encounter cannot be reduced to any number
of tellings, but must be seen as an informing principle of all tellings.

Something of the complexity I envision for the study of American
literature will be evident from the structure of this work, which proceeds
not in a linear fashion—a fashion too deeply infected by the frontier model
to be anything but a liability—but through a series of intercessions into
moments of intercultural activity, the series as a whole reflecting a deepening of intercultural critical practice. The introduction has established the
conditions for an intercultural literary study. The first chapter applies interculturalism to, or derives it from, a central dynamic in Indian-white

relations: the conversion of Native peoples. In this chapter, Indian conversion both exemplifies the attempts to erase interculturalism from American life and letters and, however paradoxically, forms an arena in which the intercultural gains expression. I next consider the relationships between literary texts and two prominent instances of intercultural encounter: the meeting of Indian and white economies, and the cross-pollination of Indian and white spiritualities. A short interlude follows; having examined some of the texts and contexts of interculturalism, I broaden my view to the physical and narrative shaping of America, asking not only how interculturalism marks particular texts but how it grounds the stories Americans tell about their land, nation, and literature. The fourth chapter traces interculturalism during the years immediately preceding and following the birth of the United States, noting the ties between Indian-white geographic and nationalist struggles and the particular form of storytelling known as history; the fifth chapter tracks a similar set of questions into the antebellum era, exploring how the Indians' presence makes possible an emergent form of storytelling—ethnologic science—that depends on the erasure of that presence. Chapter 6 is interested in how nation-building, geographic conflict, and scientific study play themselves out in the quest for an American literature, how the stories that have come to be honored as most characteristically American seek to assimilate yet eradicate the presence of the Indians. In my final chapter, I turn to the possibility of a critique of national identity, expansion, and literary history: I consider the efforts of Indian authors to retain a place in the American story, and retain their claims to American lands, against attempts to write, and force, them out of the nation. Each chapter, then, approaches interculturalism from a unique perspective, through a unique aspect of American life and literature, and with a unique set of questions. The whole, it is my hope, suggests at once the scope of American interculturalism, the variety of avenues for exploration, and the increasingly complex challenges that attend a deepening immersion in America's intercultural literature.

Chapter One

Indian Conversions

> Woe be to me if I call that conversion to God, which is indeed sub-
> version of the soules of Millions. . . . For it is not a forme, nor the
> change of one forme into another . . . that makes a man a convert.
>
> —Roger Williams, "Christenings Make Not Christians"

In 1850, Henry A. S. Dearborn, mayor of Roxbury, Massachusetts, proposed a monument to John Eliot, the seventeenth-century "Apostle" to the
neighboring Indians. The monument was to be an elaborate affair: "A
Corinthian column, surmounted by a Funereal Urn. . . . Whole height,
forty-two feet. The fence is supported by Doric columns . . . the pales
alternate Crosses and Arrows, as emblematical of Eliot's Christian office,
and of the Indians for whom it was assumed. On the front side of the
pedestal of the column, a basso-relievo of an open folio Bible, exhibiting
the title page of Eliot's translation; the letters in intaglio and gilded." None
of the posterity of Eliot's converts would, presumably, visit this shrine: the
Christian Indians of the town of Natick, once Eliot's showpiece, had been
pronounced "practically extinct" two years earlier, and when Dearborn
refers to "that much wronged, long suffering, yet unsubdued, undismayed,
energetic and persevering race," he is, however incredibly, speaking of his
own. Yet despite the ultimate failure of Eliot's mission, the monument
would testify to "the profound veneration which is entertained for the
FIRST and time-honored herald of the Christian Religion to the primeval
inhabitants of this vast Republic."[1]

Auspiciously, if astoundingly, a representative of these people had
recently arrived in Roxbury to view Eliot's tomb. This was Kahgegagah-
bowh[2] or George Copway, an Ojibwa convert who, "when informed of the
measures which had been adopted for doing honor to [Eliot's] memory . . .
expressed the deepest solicitude, that they should be crowned with success,
and volunteered his aid, so far as he was enabled to do so, in the accom-
plishment of that object." Copway sent a twenty-five-dollar contribution
and his compliments: "This will be a lasting memento before your children

and our children, what true greatness is; and would to God, that while they are under its shadow, the self-sacrificing spirit which was in Eliot, might be felt by them, for the moral elevation of man and glory to the Great Spirit." In return, Dearborn ordered that a figure be added to the engraving printed to fund the monument: a feathered Indian, draped in a blanket and holding a bow, who stands before the fence with its alternating crosses and arrows, pointing to the massive column in gratitude or devotion. Suppressing numerous ironies and worse—months earlier, President Taylor had ordered the removal of the Lake Superior Ojibwas; Copway, depicted in his autobiography as anything but a painted warrior, was boosting a removal scheme of his own on the tour that brought him to Roxbury; and Dearborn, in the 1830s, had helped draft fraudulent treaties for the removal of the Seneca Indians—this image condenses encounter to a single, symbolically charged moment: dwarfed by the pillar, shut out by the fence, and mute before the textual acts of Bible and proposal, the wild Indian has failed to enter the covenant of conversion that Eliot opened.[3]

This image illustrates an idea Roy Harvey Pearce termed "savagism" but, for reasons I will explore, I prefer to call "conversionism." It is an idea that speaks, as in the following quote from D. H. Lawrence, of absolute difference, absolute conflict, and absolute resolution to America's encounters: "The red life flows in a different direction from the white life. You can't make two streams that flow in opposite directions meet and mingle soothingly." It is an idea that has shaped conceptions of Indian-white encounter from Eliot's day to the present. Yet however compulsory or ironclad conversionism seems, encounter reveals its inadequacy; for as the experience of people such as Copway attests, conversionist claims of disparity and incommensurability fail to account for the amorphous, destabilizing process of conversion itself. As Victor Turner writes in his study of ritual transformation, the initiate's condition "is one of ambiguity and paradox, a confusion of all the customary categories. . . . This coincidence of opposite processes and notions in a single representation characterizes the peculiar unity of the liminal: that which is neither this nor that, and yet is both."[4] Viewed (as Turner sees it) as a mechanism for maintaining order, conversion can be defined only in relation to the oppositions between which it oscillates. Viewed, however, as the oscillation, conversion becomes instead an image of the indefiniteness of encounter. In this chapter, then, I argue that conversionism, whether as practice—a blueprint for the alteration of Indian souls—or representation—an ideal that mandated opposition as the grounds of homogeneity—cannot control the forces of encounter. Indian conversion is thus not only the subject of this chapter but a means of interrogating the subject, of exploring a conversion process that embraced individuals, peoples, a country, and its literature.

Conversion and Subversion

If Dearborn's temple of the apostle bordered on the vulgar, he was nonetheless correct in assigning Eliot a seminal role in the development of the ideology and practice of Indian conversion among American Protestants.[5] Commencing his ministry in 1646, Eliot managed during the next three decades to gather several hundred native hopefuls into internal colonies or "Praying Towns," where the converts pursued a twin emphasis: civilization and Christianity. As Eliot explained, only after the Indians had been "brought from their scattered and wild course of life, unto civill Cohabitation and Government" could they "be fit to be betrusted with the sacred Ordinances of Jesus Christ." Measured solely by numbers, Eliot's labors were largely unavailing. Yet the idea behind his program provided a touchstone for future efforts. Rooted in what Robert Berkhofer terms the "fusion of religion and lifestyle"—or the "confusion," in George Tinker's perhaps more apt term—Eliot's paradigm of conversion demanded that Indians renounce all aspects of their heritage, sacred and secular.[6] However unlikely Indians were to achieve, or Christians to accept, this revolution, in theory conversion anticipated the extirpation of Indians, as Indians, from the continent.

Given the central role Indian conversion played in shaping both the practical and the conceptual emphases of encounter, it is surprising how little has been done to investigate or, more properly, theorize it; critics have described its methods, makers, and martyrs, while taking its existence largely for granted. Two contradictory appraisals of conversion have emerged: while some see missionary enterprise as a sign of Christian benevolence—"Evangelization was simple in motivation: first, giving glory to God, and second, compassion for the ruined spiritual and physical state of the Indians"—others dismantle it as a vile and violent conspiracy, meant to "subdue a troublesome racial minority under the pretense of Christian paternalism."[7] The first of these analyses is plainly wanting: to laud evangelism is to slight not only its tragic consequences but its contexts, conflicts, and controversies. Conversely, if it is reductive to view missionary ardor as wholly disingenuous, it is no less false to view it as wholly duplicitous. For Eliot and his followers, the "confusion" of spirit and culture was no confusion: Indian "culture"—a term none would have used—was merely an elaboration of heathenism and was thus doomed perforce and providentially. However grievous the outcome of their convictions, one must not oneself "confuse" the results of missionary labors with the motivations.

Rather than viewing Indian conversion as separable from or a feint for other concerns, then, one must place it where its practitioners did: at the center of their belief system, where it both illuminates and draws from a range of activities. On the one hand, Indian conversion grew out of Christian ideals, aspirations, and fears. For instance, as Richard Cogley has shown, the opinion that the Indians were remnants of the Lost Tribes made their recovery a matter of some urgency, since many Christians held that the conversion of the Jews was a precursor of the millennium.[8] Then, too, conversion served more immediate spiritual needs. Missionary bulletins often seem less appeals than jeremiads: "Let these poor Indians stand up, incentives to us," Thomas Shepard wrote. "Who knows but God gave life to New England to quicken Old, and hath warmed them that they might heat us." Conversion, moreover, could be seen as a means of appeasing the deity in the here and now—"it is not to be wondred at, that the Lord hath afflicted us by the Indians," wrote Increase Mather during the 1675–1676 conflict that would come to be called King Philip's War, "*since the body of the present Generation hath no more of an heart to endeavour their Conversion*"—or of tempering the divine wrath to come: if Christians failed in their duty, one critic warned, "these poore Indians will certainly rise up against us, and with great boldnesse condemn us in the great day of our accompts."[9] If this is hypocrisy, it is of a particularly earnest strain; if it is benevolence, it is of a particularly self-serving sort. In either case, it is evident how literally Christians read the Indians' fate as inseparable from their own.

Not only, however, did conversion help satisfy divine mandates; at the same time, it took part in secular concerns. Eliot had written that he intended, in addition to broadcasting the gospel, to "bridle, restrain," and "also to humble" the Indians; and while he would likely have seen such bowing to authority as a universal ideal, in practice it seemed a means of breaking Indians to a temporal master. Whether one agrees with Francis Jennings that Eliot's ministry was but a smokescreen for a Puritan land-grab, or accepts Neal Salisbury's assessment that proselytizing followed settlement, helping to "clear the few Indians who remained," it is evident that missionaries contributed to dispossession in a variety of ways, even if they did not favor it: by pressuring Indians to relinquish lands, fomenting internal dissension, placing converts under colonial jurisdiction, and—least forthrightly but most pervasively—contesting Indian self-conceptions and allegiances.[10]

Indeed, missionaries often acknowledged, if covertly, their role in boosting worldly interests. Eliot, as usual, set the pattern, admitting that he must discredit native chiefs to make headway: "Since the [sachems] are cut off," he wrote, their people "do bow the Ear to hear, and submit to pray unto God." Less circumspect was Cotton Mather: "May the New-Englanders be so far *politick*, as well as *religious*," he counseled, "as particularly to make a *mission* of the gospel unto the mighty nations of the Western Indians[,] . . . lest those horrid pagans . . . [be] a scourge to us." In 1723, Solomon Stoddard posed a like solution to the region's ongoing Indian troubles: " 'Tis much better to convert them: Then they will do good, they will serve and glorify God, they will help to enlarge his Kingdom, and be a benefit to their Neighbours."[11] None of this proves that missions were mere pawns or props of colonial power; it does suggest, however, that the conquest of souls went hand in hand with the conquest of the continent.

Thus far I have focused on Indian conversion solely as it relates to Euro-America. To grasp conversion's scope, however, it is insufficient to separate preceptor from receptor. In saying this, I do not mean merely that one must recover the Indian "side"; rather, considering the convert reveals, among other things, the inadequacy of the discourse of "sides." This discourse has dominated depictions of converts, who have been slotted into a hierarchy based on the extent to which one side has been abandoned for the other. At the top are the model Christians, like the man who, "if any did abuse him . . . could lie downe at their feet, and if any did smite him on the one cheeke . . . would rather turne the other." Next are the "friendless outcasts, to whom the earth has denied a place beyond the extent of a grave—half-mingling with their people, from whose wretchedness and depravity they recoil, and half-mingling with the whites, where their bitterness of soul becomes not less intolerable." At the base are the cheats, backsliders, and dissemblers, reaping the rewards of civilization while luxuriating in the outrages of savagism: "There was [one] praying Indian," Mary Rowlandson recalls, "so wicked and cruel as to wear a string about his neck, strung with Christian's fingers."[12] Viewing conversion as a radical transfer from one steady state to its virtual opposite, commentators have relied on a positivist language of signs and tokens, tangible evidences of the real, the genuine, the pristine.

Such language, troublingly, lingers, preventing even works with revisionist aims from transcending the model of contrasting or opposing sides. Among the ethnohistorians who have sought to explode stereotypes of Indian converts, for example, James Axtell has led the way in arguing that one cannot focus on the converters alone, but must "ask whether the *Indians*, from *their* point of view, were successful or not in adopting or adapting Christianity." Axtell notes that conversion might represent an opportunity to manipulate hostile colonial conditions, to forge creative alliances between peoples, and to adopt effective, if unspectacular, measures of resistance and revitalization. Yet though Axtell's project would seem to encourage an intercultural approach, his desire—perhaps, as an ethnohistorian, his need—to identify the Indian "side" leads him to search for an essential Indian beneath the "protective coloration" of Christianity. Believing that conversion was a means by which converts guarded their "cultural integrity," Axtell must conclude that "Christianity often lay very lightly on the surface of their lives," that many were merely "paying lip service" to the Christian faith—that, in short, converts were chameleons who donned spiritual dazzle to conceal traditional practices, placate earthly overlords, and wheedle newfound privileges. There is, to be sure, some evidence for this, the most striking I know being one missionary's claim that Indian leaders wished to "get into the church" to "assert their own authority"—in effect, to use the church as the seat of tribal governance.[13] Yet however valid Axtell's portrait is in particulars, its twinned beliefs that one can readily distinguish genuine core from artificial accretions and that one can sift distinct, incarnate cultures from texts are hazardous on the whole.[14]

What is striking about the texts of conversion is that they make a shambles of such beliefs. Consider, for example, the works of Eliot, who sought as much as any to crop Indians to the conversionist frame: he was famous for levying fines on all lapses from a utopian cultural purity, from the residual (powwowing) to the trivial (hair length) to the bizarre (bestiality),[15] while the confessions and other supposed instances of Indian self-representation that pepper his writings are policed to ensure orthodoxy. Yet despite—or because of—his omnivorousness, Eliot could be slow to catch conversion experience pulling against conversionism. In 1654, for example, during a public catechism staged before the civil and ecclesiastical leaders of the colony, he posed a simple question and received, seemingly, a simple reply: "Q. *What is God?* A. An Ever-living Spirit."[16] Evidently satisfied, Eliot moved on; the catechumen, for his part, performed admirably, nailing the doctrines of the unity, ubiquity, and eternality of the ever-living spirit called God.

This moment that produces not a murmur in Eliot's text, however, opens a host of questions that Eliot did not think to ask, or perhaps knew better than to raise. For according to fellow linguist Roger Williams, the word translated as "spirit"—likely "manitou"—was patently *not* equivalent to the Christian "God": "There is a generall Custome amongst them, at the apprehension of any Excellency in Men, Women, Birds, Beasts, Fish, &c. to cry out *Manittóo*, that is, it is a God . . . and therefore when they talke amongst themselves of the *English* ships, and great buildings, of the plowing of their Fields, and especially of Bookes and Letters, they will end thus: *Manittôwock* They are Gods." In light of this suggestion that the Indian word stands less for a fixed thing than for a protean quality—in light, moreover, of the claim that textuality is the crowning example of *manittóo*—it seems that the translation of the word "God," or the word of God, cannot control the word's ambiguous, polysemous potential. Eliot himself ponders, though obliquely, this problem of multiplicity where there should be unity. Whether assuming a conventional humility or honestly uncertain of his fluency (or both), he habitually laments the incompleteness of translation: "Some things spoken I understood not, and some things slipt from me. . . . I requested the Assembly, That if any one doubted of the Interpretations that should be given of [the Indians'] Answers, that they would Propound their doubt, and they should have the words scanned and tryed by the Interpreters, that so all things may be done most clearly." That Eliot leaned heavily on catechisms was, perhaps, attributable to this anxiety; yoking answers to questions, the catechism seeks to squelch discursive latitude. Toward this end, though one of Eliot's works was titled *The Indian Dialogues*, each of the book's fictional "dialogues" ends with a missionary outmaneuvering his savage interlocutors, a process captured by one new proselyte's admission: "I yield to what you say."[17] This statement, of course, should remind one that Euro-America's power was not merely material ("I yield") but textual ("what you say"), or that the material and the textual were mutually sustaining; I do not wish to suggest that the Indians' words (or Roger Williams's, for that matter) are free from textualization or from the intercultural situation. On the contrary, I wish to argue that the Indian "spirit" undermines Euro-America's absolute power by *revealing* the material and textual conditions of appropriation and interchange, displacement and simultaneity, that encounter, like conversion, entails.

With this in mind, consider another figure whose life story, due to a conjunction of circumstances denied Eliot's converts and the vast majority

of their successors—an interested editor, a marketable story, and a racial history akin to that of most readers—was made accessible to Euro-
American audiences and has become newly popular among literary critics:
Mary Jemison, a captive who lived the majority of her long life with Seneca Indians and whose *Narrative of the Life of Mrs. Mary Jemison*, recorded
by James E. Seaver, appeared in 1824. Perhaps even more so than with
those who crossed the border in the other direction, discourse on people
like Jemison has emphasized irrevocable and irrecoverable difference; here,
for example, are the famous reflections of Benjamin Franklin, written five
years before Jemison's 1758 capture: "When white persons of either sex
have been taken prisoners young by the Indians, and lived a while among
them, tho' ransomed by their Friends, and treated with all imaginable
tenderness to prevail with them to stay among the English, yet in a Short
time they become disgusted with our manner of life . . . and take the first
good Opportunity of escaping again into the Woods, from whence there is
no reclaiming them." Evaluations of Jemison have continued to rely on the
discourse of "sides," though in a different way: by trying to sift the essential
Jemison from the corrupting influence of the text. Thus Annette Kolodny
laments that "what seems authentically to have been Jemison's story" only
rarely "breaks out of the molds to which Seaver . . . would consign it";
Susan Walsh, arguing that Jemison's story has been "mediated by the
interpretive agendas of assorted white male editors," seeks the "preliterate
Seneca traditions of self-telling" that exist in "conflict" or even "opposition" to editorial agendas; Susan Scheckel continues this theme, noting the
"conflict between Seaver's repeated struggles to impose narrative order and
Jemison's persistence in telling her story"; and June Namias, in her edition
of the narrative, frets that "Seaver's rendition is not pure" and thus decides
to omit much of the editorial apparatus in order to "recover Mary Jemison's own words."[18] What emerges from Jemison's text, however, is the
impossibility of attaining any such purity; the *Narrative* is marked by
intricate and ultimately unresolvable movements and moments across cultures. Jemison herself, as depicted in the introduction, symbolizes this:
though "her complexion is very white," her English perfect, her "industry"
undiminished, and her homestead manorial, "her dress" is "made and
worn after the Indian fashion," "her habits" are "those of the Indians," and
"her ideas of religion" are "those of the great mass of the Senecas." The
narrative proper further complicates the picture, as it fluctuates between
reciting Indian vices and praising their "kind, tender and peaceable" character; between longing for the "blessings of civilization" and finding com-

fort from the "many [Seneca] friends to whom I was warmly attached";
between bemoaning the "depredations" the Indians commit "upon the
whites" and condemning attempts to "civilize and christianize [the In-
dians]"; between sensationalizing Indian atrocities and depicting a white
man achieving the pinnacle of Indian brutality: "Holding [the infant] by
its legs, [he] dashed its head against the jamb." Even Seaver's appendix—a
detached, third-person summary of Indian manners and customs, virtually
mandatory at the time—extends rather than settles the ambiguity, decrying
the "premeditated cruelties" of the Indians on one page and commending
their "moral virtues" on another.[19] Jemison's narrative is thus another example that those who cross may shiver borders; that converts (and their
narratives) span worlds in ways too tangled and obscure to permit surefire
notions of cultural inviolability or, indeed, of infallibly identifiable worlds.

Yet what past and persistent renderings of such people suggest is that
it is precisely this threat of cultural ambiguity that conversionism existed
(and persists) to control; that if conversion forms a site in which the
equivocal energies of encounter are focused and figured, conversionism
erects a framework under which those energies can be defused. Thus it was
that conversionism played so vital a role not only in Indian affairs but
throughout American life: a manifestation of the desire for fixed terms,
static categories, impregnable boundaries, conversionism formed an um-
brella under which anything in need of definition, restoration, supplementation, or confirmation *as* a thing could seek shelter. And in situations of
encounter, everything *is* in need of such aid; in situations of encounter, as
traveler George Catlin, who had spent years "mingling with red men,"
sensed, the frontier was not a great divide but a "fleeting and unsettled
line" that could be crossed, complicated, and compromised. Thus Thomas
McKenney, the nation's first Superintendent of Indian Affairs, expresses
both the all-encompassing demand of conversionism and the anxieties it
held in check: "If we can comprehend the power that it would require to
unhinge all that *we* cling to, and introduce in its stead an entirely new
system of both faith and practice, overturning all that is lovely in our eyes,
in our social, political, and moral relations, we may form some tolerable
notion of what that system should be . . . to produce a reformation in the
Indians, lead them to cast aside their habits, remodel their modes of thinking, abandon their faith, and their hopes in the future, and adopt in their
places everything new, everything strange, and everything mysterious!"
Thus Indian converts, schooled on such conversionist homiletics and sent
out into a culture that practiced what it preached, often fulfilled the bleak-

est of caricatures: warned that "he had one of two things to do—either throw away all that belonged to the white race, and turn Indian; or quit being Indian, and turn white man," McKenney's personal benevolent enterprise, a Choctaw boy whom he christened James Lawrence McDonald, chose a third option: suicide. And thus Catlin, however responsive to the fluid currents beneath the crust of conversionism, took care to avoid suspicion of having become "*semi-Indianized*" by disavowing the frontier as a place "that offends Heaven, and holds in mutual ignorance of each other, the honourable and virtuous portions of two people, which seem destined never to meet."[20] Conversionism, in short, asserted the fixity of cultural things in the face of the intercultural possibility that things could not be fixed—the possibility that, as Eliot acknowledged (or tried not to), "things" slipped from one precisely because they no longer were things in a unitary discourse, but were the products of a conversion experience binding individuals, peoples, the country itself.

The "great Point of [Indian] *Conversion*," then (as Williams put it), was great because it provided a stable point in an unstable field. The great point I would make is that no matter how powerful conversionism is— powerful in shaping both encounter and reconstructions of it—it must not be taken as the truth or the whole. If one applauds, as a study of Indian converts does, that "when their old beliefs appeared to be failing them, the Indians reached out for new ones"; if one deplores, as a study of white captives does, that some "succumbed to the alien culture"; if one assumes, as I did in a paper that opens with the same anecdote as this chapter, that by the nineteenth century Indians had "long been strangers to the citizens" of the eastern United States; if, in short, one views peoples, cultures, beliefs as objects with fixed, integral, invariant outlines, one parrots the conversionist catechism: old beliefs are not new; an alien culture is not our culture; strangers are not citizens, for things are what they are, and what they are are things.[21] To suggest that an individual, nation, or culture can be at once Indian and white, that in situations of encounter the terms "Indian" and "white" (and, for that matter, "individual," "nation," and "culture") cannot exist beyond contact with their others, is to suggest that the texts native to such situations be read not as fixed positions but as records of conversion, of intimate and ongoing conflict, appropriation, accommodation, revelation. In the chapters that follow, I will apply this proposition to diverse sites of encounter, to diverse people who were involved in dramas of conversion and interculturalism, and to diverse texts that developed within these contexts. Before I do so, however, I would like to explore in a range of literary texts how profound and pervasive the impact of conversionism—and conversion—were. Here, I will be interested in how conversionism functions to assert the sanctity of cultural codes, and how, at the same time, those codes are unsettled by intercultural encounter.

Indian Demons, Christian Saints

The great point of Indian conversion was tested anew during the nineteenth-century era of Indian removals. Antebellum missions seemed poised to fulfill the promise of a Christian continent as they availed themselves of the wider field of action made possible by expansion and the broader means of support made possible by the federal Civilization Fund of 1819. Colonial missionaries were elevated to folk-hero status, with Eliot enjoying a near-cult revival in the literature of the time. Dearborn's proposal was restrained by the standards of this literature, which in the words of Martin Moore, Eliot's antebellum successor at Natick, foresaw the apostle's example inspiring "many such laborers" to "*go forth into all the world and preach the gospel to every creature.*"[22]

Yet no sooner was this missionary bark launched than it was assailed by those who doubted its course and chances. An early parody, Philip Freneau's "Indian Convert" (1797) ends with the nominal convert's rejection of heaven: "I cannot consent to be lodged in a place / Where there's nothing to eat and but little to steal." Later authors elaborated on this theme, investing it with greater seriousness and certainty; as one reviewer of Cooper's *Pioneers* (1823) wrote: "[Mohegan's] death scene, in which, notwithstanding his supposed conversion to Christianity, he is plainly relapsing into the faith of his fathers, looking forward to the happy hunting grounds where he shall rejoin the spirits of his tribe, is very well done; as are several other passages designed to exhibit the apparent incapacity of the red man to conceive the religion of the whites." By the 1830s, somber estimations of failure became the norm. George Bancroft mourned that "benevolence has, every where in our land, exerted itself to ameliorate the condition of the Indian," but all "in vain"; Lewis Cass, Jackson's first-term Secretary of War, paid tribute to missionaries' "ardent zeal and untiring labor," but pronounced their work "unavailing and unproductive," leaving "no permanent memorial." Even the most "ardent" of Eliot's followers found his efforts stillborn; Convers Francis concludes his *Life of John Eliot* (1836) with thanks that the apostle was spared seeing "that those for whom he labored were doomed to vanish before the white man, instead of sharing with him the blessings of civilization and Christianity."[23] The Word, it seemed, had fallen on deaf—or dead—ears.

As a whole, it is difficult to judge how accurate such appraisals were. Yet it is notable that the most widespread assault on missionary benevolence coincided with the years during which a sizable population of eastern Indians, the Cherokees, were proclaiming a resurgence.[24] Missionary work among the Cherokees had produced, apparently, the permanent memorials Cass found lacking: not only did prominent Cherokees bless their missionaries for "inculcating moral and religious principles into the minds of the rising generation," but one member of that generation, Catharine Brown, was so renowned for piety that, according to a mission-sponsored account of her life, many "were unwilling to believe she was an Indian." The extent of such christianization was perhaps exaggerated, as Theda Perdue points out, to "portray the Cherokees not as a tribe struggling toward 'civilization,' but as a society which had already reached that goal"; most commentators agree that fewer than ten percent of the Cherokees "belonged to Christian churches after over thirty years of proselytizing among them."[25] Yet such statistics, I would argue, reveal conversionism's ludicrousness—how, in thirty years, can a people swap one system for its supposed opposite?—and inadequacy: instead of reckoning the fund of meanings available to the Cherokees, one ticks plus and minus signs in the church ledgers.

The case of the Cherokees, however, shows on a regional or national level how conversion eludes, questions, restructures such absolutes. The Cherokees, if their most widely published (because English-literate) representatives are any indication,[26] desired neither to buck nor to embrace all aspects of the wider culture; though their leaders generally advocated Euro-American ideals (and, it seems, met with internal resistance as a result), they undertook these ideals on and in their own terms. This is suggested by a letter John Ross, principal chief of the Cherokee Nation after 1827, wrote to Secretary of War John Calhoun in 1824:

You say that we must be sensible, that it will be impossible for us to remain for any length of time in our present situation, as a distinct society or nation, within the limits of Georgia, or of any other state and that such a community is incompatible with your system and must yield to it. And that we must either cease to be a distinct community, and become, at no distant periods a part of the state within whose limits we are, or remove without the limits of any State. . . . It rests with the interests, the disposition and free consent of the nation to remain as a separate community or to enter into a Treaty with the United States for admission as citizens, under the form of a Territorial or State Government, and we can only say that the situation of the nation, is not sufficiently improved in the arts of civilized life, to warrant any change at present.

Ross' subtle—and at this early stage in the Cherokee Removal crisis perhaps somewhat playful—rejection of Calhoun's advice illustrates the borderland position he strove to occupy. Both options of his apparent concession to conversionism subvert what they seem to uphold: the Cherokees will either be an aboriginal nation or an Indian state. (And in any event, Ross points out, the Cherokees are not "civilized" enough to take action at present.) In 1830, Cass, wielding his access to the periodical press to publicize a quarrel with Ross, described the chief's nation as "an anomaly upon the face of the earth"; Georgia congressman (and, later, governor) Wilson Lumpkin termed the Cherokees' domain a "land of confusion" that, he hoped, would be "converted" from "a savage wilderness" into "the peaceful abodes of an enterprising and industrious population." Simultaneously Indian and Christian, the Cherokees showed that signs of opposition were not, as McKenney's ward despairingly wrote his benefactor, "mark[s] as deep and abiding as that which Cain bore," but were tools of power made to prevent the nation from recognizing its most cherished cultural codes as nothing more than made.[27]

The problems of conversion, and the practices of conversionism, are expressed variously in Removal-era literary texts, whether articulated as overt concerns or patterned into discourse. To say this is to suggest that, though a work may be, as Wayne Franklin writes of Cooper's *Wept of Wish-Ton-Wish* (1829), only "nominally concerned with 'conversion'" as a subject, it can be imbued in conversion as subtext. Thus, to select an even less likely work, Nathaniel Hawthorne's "May-Pole of Merry Mount" (1836) may not be about the southern conflicts in any explicit sense; indeed, as an assessment of Indians, the final word in Hawthorne's 1836 review of Francis's *Life of John Eliot* has the ring of finality: "extinct." And yet, in its critique of segregationist polities, its references to the mingling of religions—"an English priest, canonically dressed, yet decked with flowers, in heathen fashion"—and its use of what F. O. Matthiessen terms the "device of multiple choice" to break the link between object and essence, "May-Pole" is engaged with the problem at the root of conversionism and at the root of the Cherokees' 1836 removal order, the problem of the sanctity of cultural signs. To cite an intercultural context for "May-Pole" is not to reduce it to "an Indian story," something Hawthorne professed to "abhor"; quite the contrary, it is to suggest how reductive it is to label as Indian stories only stories populated by Indians—to take the "red symbol" (as Hawthorne termed Hester Prynne's stigma in his most famous work) for the whole.[28] It is important to emphasize, then, that if conversion is a figure by which antebellum writers explore cultural meaning, it is not merely a figure; the figure—like the culture—existed in situations of encounter, and works of the time, even when not based *on* the facts of interculturalism, are based *in* the fact of it.

Few texts of this period are more immersed in interculturalism than one that barely considers conversion at all: Robert Montgomery Bird's *Nick of the Woods* (1837), a novel that captures in bold, exaggerated strokes the fear that, uncontrolled, encounter "prostrates the strongest barriers" between peoples.[29] Like Cooper—who had described an America with no borders, only "borderers, for such by their frontier position they had in truth become"[30]—Bird envisions a world in which "strange things . . . loosed from the chains of association" run riot (86), a world in which things, unchained from a necessary association with signs, are not what they seem, or what they are. The device that sets *Nick* in motion, the arrival of two aristocratic Virginians, Roland and Edith Forrester, in the Kentucky borderlands, quickly takes a back seat to Bird's fascination with the cast of outcasts who violate their pure-bred culture, including the "Indian-like" servant, Telie Doe, whose "wildness" of feature contrasts with the "European tinge of her complexion" (53); her "Injunized" father (63), who has leagued with the region's "red niggurs" (48) to launch raids against the white settlements; and the rollicking frontier braggart Roaring Ralph Stackpole, a "demibarbarian" (111) who embraces "all critturs human and inhuman, Christian and Injun, white, red, black, and party-colored" (175). At the frayed edges of the nation, the boundaries between classes, cultures, and races waver; even the lily-white Forresters can be taken for "wild Indians" (113). The Indians, for their part, "fli[t] dimly along," "vague and indistinct" (134); seldom seen but always impending, they incarnate the pervasive threat of interculturalism.

For interculturalism, Bird suggests, is not out there in tangible form; rather, blurring form itself, interculturalism defies racial, cultural, and even individual purity and integrity. Thus the central figure of the novel, who gives *Nick* both name and shape—yet gives it neither—first appears as the embodiment of formlessness: "A figure stalking through the woods at a

distance . . . tall and gigantic in the growing twilight. . . . Distance and the
darkness together rendered the vision indistinct. . . . And now it was, that,
as it drew nigh, its stature appeared to grow less and less colossal and the
wild lineaments with which fancy had invested it, faded from sight. . . .
[T]he supposed fiend of the woods . . . suddenly presented to Roland's
eyes . . . the humble, peaceful, harmless Nathan Slaughter" (125, 126).
"Fancy," however, seems to have been more astute than reason; for this
man, a Quaker pacifist aloof from the settlers' genocidal wars, doubles as
the demonic Nick of the Woods, who haunts the dark and bloody ground,
preying on Indians and, as if in perverse relish of conversionist exactitude,
carving crosses into their chests. Slaughter's history explains, if it does not
justify, his actions: during what Nathan believed to be a friendly visit, he
handed his knife and gun to the Shawnee chief Wenonga, who turned
these weapons on the Quaker's family and scalped Nathan himself. Victim
and avatar of broken barriers, the Quaker Slaughter figures the most intimate threat of interculturalism: the loss of the ability not only to know
one's other but to name oneself.

Fittingly, then, Bird's border warfare builds to a confrontation between Nathan and Wenonga, where the white man, "daubing over his face,
arms and breast with streaks of red, black, and green paint," is "converted
into a highly respectable-looking savage" (263). Bird is at pains to draw
parallels between this newly made "convert" and his nemesis: a mirror
image of Wenonga, whose "grim countenance [is] hideously bedaubed"
with paint (320), Nathan accosts the man "in the Shawnee tongue, cor-
rectly and unhesitatingly pronounced" (321). In a final act of violent fraternity, Nathan cuts down his foe with the chief's tomahawk and scalps his
scalper, uttering a "wild whoop" of triumph (324). This bloody scene both
expresses and wards off the ruinous consummation of interculturalism; if
Nathan/Wenonga represents the culmination of intercultural mingling,
Bird crowns the possibility with a bloodbath that at once reveals and
contains his anxiety.

Paradoxically, then, it is through Nathan that *Nick* restores what
Nathan violates. For if Nathan is less a legitimate agent than the spawn of
those he slays, as a "madman" (233) he is safely distant from those his
sanguine deeds sustain. And if, as James Bryant writes, his blood lust bids
to expose the civilizing venture as "a mask of hypocrisy" under which
"malevolence is performed for personal gratification," the murder of his
family glosses his actions.[31] This paradox appears in the bloody crucifixes
Nathan scrawls with righteous ferocity; his impious zeal, Bird insists, is the

fruit of his "humanity" (150). The champion of that which he defiles, Nathan is at once reprehensible—born of an unthinkable breakdown of cultural coherence—and recuperable as a sign of that breakdown's tragic cost.

Bird, one could argue, is an extreme case. And yet, even "progressive" works—those that promote the assimilation of Indian peoples over antagonism—can be steeped in the fixed, opposing signs that breed the violence of *Nick*. One such work, Catharine Maria Sedgwick's *Hope Leslie* (1827), foregrounds conversion as a means by which to reflect on cultural, spiritual, and sexual intercourse. Set in New England after the Pequot War, *Hope Leslie* dramatizes encounter through paired narratives of border-crossing: the adoption of the Pequot princess Magawisca by the Fletcher family, Puritan guardians of Hope Leslie, and the marriage of Faith Leslie, sister of Hope, to the Pequot brave Oneco. In the critical revival *Hope Leslie* has enjoyed, this structure has been mined to show that Sedgwick "challenged the premises underlying" the Bird tradition; and to be sure, when contrasted with his nightmare of intercultural meltdown, the radical potential of her text is apparent.[32] Yet this potential may be more apparent than real: though *Hope Leslie* is, in many ways, a remarkable text—one of a very few antebellum texts, for instance, to include a stable Indian-white marriage[33]—even a text that challenges Bird's conclusion may accept its "premise." For though Sedgwick critiques conversionist practices, her critique acquiesces in its terms.

The influence conversionism holds over Sedgwick's text is evident as early as her preface: "The liberal philanthropist will not be offended by a representation which supposes that the elements of virtue and intellect are not withheld from any branch of the human family; and the enlightened and accurate observer of human nature, will admit that the difference of character among the various races of the earth, arises mainly from difference of condition" (6). Though overtly this passage critiques the discourse of sides, one detects a conversionist undercurrent in the metadiscourse of representation in which it is couched. Sedgwick continues: "In our histories, it was perhaps natural that [the Indians] should be represented as 'surly dogs,' who preferred to die rather than live, from no other motives than a stupid or malignant obstinacy. Their own historians and poets, if they had such, would as naturally, and with more justice, have extolled their high-souled courage and patriotism" (6). With its acknowledgment of Indian artists and questioning of the nation's Indian policies, this statement seems to reprehend the practices of conversionism. Yet it is at this point that conversionism intervenes; insisting that distinct means of representation belong "naturally" to the contestants, Sedgwick traces the incommensurability of cultures to a deep-seated difference, genetics as hermeneutics. And accordingly, though she credits the Indians with a common humanity, she does so only in the context of an abiding opposition, to reject which would be to nullify that which permits, indeed necessitates, her mediatory role.

This paradox, whereby the critique of conversionism accedes to the terms of conversionism, shapes both Sedgwick's investigation of Puritan-Indian conflict and her position toward its current repercussions. For all its promise, the novel's most famous episode—Magawisca's retelling of the Pequot War, which turns a just and holy defense against savage aggressors into a tale of Puritan barbarity and Indian heroism—is framed so as to mollify benevolent conversionism: "Magawisca's reflecting mind suggested the most serious obstacle to the progress of the christian religion, in all ages and under all circumstances; the contrariety between its divine principles and the conduct of its professors; which, instead of always being a medium for the light that emanates from our holy law, is too often the darkest cloud that obstructs the passage of its rays to the hearts of heathen men" (51). Viewed through this lens, Magawisca's narrative becomes less rebuke than plea; if, as Sandra Zagarell suggests, Sedgwick "challenges the official history" of encounter, that history has been risked to be revitalized. For there is little reason to doubt the exercises in hagiography in which Sedgwick engages: "In the quiet possession of the blessings transmitted, we are, perhaps, in danger of forgetting, or undervaluing the sufferings by which they were obtained. We forget that the noble pilgrims lived and endured for us. . . . What was their reward? Fortune?—distinctions?—the sweet charities of home? No—but their feet were planted on the mount of vision, and they saw, with sublime joy, a multitude of people where the solitary savage roamed the forest—the forest vanished, and pleasant villages and busy cities appeared—the tangled foot-path expanded to the thronged high-way—the consecrated church planted on the rock of heathen sacrifice" (72, 73). These lines, so clumsily soaring, may, of course, be read skeptically. What I would point out, however, is less content than form: cultural encounter emerges as a mechanism of oppositions, resolved through an appeal to progress yet held (physically so, thanks to the dashes) in eternal dissension. Here, the argument of the preface takes graphic form; here, the novel's representation of difference reproduces its thoughts on representation. Considering this passage, it is hard to agree with Christopher Castiglia that Sedgwick challenges a "tradition" that "opposes the wilderness to society"; it appears, rather, that opposition was, as for the tradition to which she belonged, central to her vision.[34]

In this light, it is notable that when Sedgwick addresses conversion itself, conversionist discourse mounts. Of Magawisca's mother, she records: "Many christian men and women laboured for her conversion but she would not even consent that the holy word should be interpreted to her. . . . She died . . . immoveably fixed in those sentiments" (22). This woman's "fixed" beliefs have, moreover, been transmitted to her daughter: "To [Christianity] her eye is shut and her ear is closed, not only with that blindness and deafness common to the natural man, but she entertaineth an aversion, which has the fixedness of principle" (32). Such passages, to be sure, are spoken not by Sedgwick but by her Puritans. Yet they are consistent with the self-representations of her Indian characters, who do nurture a fixed disdain for the gospel. And if, in Magawisca's case, aversion owes less to insensibility than to the baneful effects of encounter, it cannot be blamed solely on this. Sedgwick provides her every opportunity to embrace the Word, even calling the nation's most famous evangelist to her aid: "A man of middle age walked beside her [Magawisca]," a man "whose deep set and thoughtful eye, pale brow, ascetic complexion, and spare person, indicated a life of self-denial, and of physical and mental labour; while an expression of love, compassion, and benevolence, seemed like the seal of his Creator affixed to declare him a minister of mercy to His creatures" (282). In an endnote, Sedgwick writes of the Christian's current duty: "We cannot but hope, that the present enlightened labours of the followers of Eliot, will be rewarded with such success, as shall convert the faint-hearted, the cold, and the skeptical, into ardent promoters of missions to the Indian race" (353 n. g). Perhaps, then, if more Christians could convert to Eliot's fold, the Indians would not cling, as Magawisca does, to separatism: "The Indian and the white man can no more mingle, and become one, than day and night" (330). Yet in *Hope Leslie* itself, there is no such hope;[35] the Pequots' despite for Eliot's message makes past dispossession palatable, and present dispossession contemplatable, by suggesting that the tenets of opposition so forcefully modeled by the apostle are, truly, natural.[36]

In significant respects, then, *Hope Leslie* shows the limits of progressive thought, which could lament the excesses of conversionism while maintaining its grounds. Yet at the same time, such moments as Magawisca's oration contain the possibility of turning on themselves, making conversionism subject of critique as well as mode of representation. I focus now on a work that more overtly explores—though it never explodes— conversionism: Herman Melville's *Typee* (1846). Melville's first novel argues that conversionism supplies not only the impetus of policy but the conditions of discourse—indeed, it argues that conversionism supplies the conditions of *Typee*'s own discourse. As such, this novel reveals the inadequacy of imagining complicity and critique as simple opposites, a position adopted by those who see *Hope Leslie* as a text that, rather than "remaining subject to discursive constraints, becomes a commentary on those constraints."[37] And as such, *Typee* extends what *Hope Leslie* broaches: the argument that one cannot merely condemn the ideas or acts of conversionism, for to do so is to ignore how one's own critique is implicated in what one deplores.

The Empire of Interpretation

By Melville's time, Indian conversion in his homeland had reached its nadir. The Eliot idea had been so discredited that Cooper in *The Deerslayer* (1841) felt free to reduce it to absurdity: "Hetty held [the Bible] out towards [the Hurons], in triumph as if she expected the sight would produce a visible miracle. . . . Fortunately . . . most of that which to them seemed inconsistent and paradoxical, was accounted for by the fact that the speaker possessed a mind that was constituted differently from those of most of the human race."[38] A decade later, Hawthorne travestied the tradition in Arthur Dimmesdale's conversion at the hands of his heathenish mistress on the road home from conferring with "the Apostle Eliot": "Breathing the wild, free atmosphere of an unredeemed, unchristianized, lawless region," his "spirit rose, as it were, with a bound, and attained a nearer prospect of the sky. . . . 'I seem to have flung myself—sick, sin-stained, and sorrow-blackened—down upon these forest leaves, and to have risen up all made anew.'"[39] A swipe, perhaps, at conversionism, which assumed impermeable boundaries between minister and those ministered to, this passage acts largely as farce, an ungentle reminder of how laughable Indian conversion had become, or had always been.

Yet if the glow of the gospel had faded in the East, it beckoned still in the West—west of the Mississippi, west of the continent—and conversionism answered. In *The Life of John Eliot* (1847), Nehemiah Adams reveals both the thrill of a new stage and the sturdiness of old scripts: regretting that the tribes for whom Eliot toiled have "disappeared," he is cheered that "many a missionary bark may yet be, essentially, a May-flower to distant parts of the earth." Adams singles out for praise the missionaries of the Sandwich Islands, who will "have their names enshrined by a grateful posterity in those distant seas." On his last page, the old seal of the Massachusetts Bay Colony (an Indian imploring, "Come Over and Help Us") attests that all places are alike, and alike fair game, in the spread of a conversionist empire.[40]

This revamped conversionism not only shaped *Typee*, but has shaped thought on it since. In its own day, the forces of conversionism were evident from gestation to reception to revision: in William Ellis's *Polynesian Researches* (1829), one of Melville's sources, which celebrates the "new order of things" that has overturned "the essential characteristics" of the Polynesian islanders; in reviews that denounced Melville for alleging "that savage is preferable to civilised life"; in religious journals that, according to George Long Duyckinck, "haul[ed] [*Typee*] over the coals"; in the notorious American Revised edition, in which Melville excised tens of pages deemed sacrilegious by his publisher.[41] Conversionism tagged *Typee* into the next century, though with a difference: where contemporaries had found Melville an ingrate and apostate, revivalists insisted that, whether the Marquesas of *Typee* were a paradise or a parody, the author of *Typee* would not have civilized folk resorting there.[42] Later criticism has developed along two lines based on whether the critic sees Melville's narrator, Tommo, as the author's stand-in or straw man. Thus while Gorman Beauchamp, taking the former view, discusses *Typee* in strict conversionist terms—"Melville-Tommo must escape from the Typees, else his personality would decompose in the very placidity of their soft, undemanding paradise, which represents, at least for Western man, a kind of mind-death"— T. Walter Herbert argues that Melville submits beliefs of this sort only as a means of exploring how such rigid "schemes of interpretation make sense, make nonsense, and wreak havoc in Polynesia." In my view, neither reading is sufficient; while the former affirms conversionism's absolute power, the latter affirms Melville's absolute freedom. Tommo, of course, claims such freedom; but this freedom, and his claims for it, are saturated with conversionist discourse. As Mitchell Breitwieser writes, *Typee* argues that "the root of colonialism is so deep that even an apparent rebel may turn out to be an assistant"; yet if this is so, the same holds for *Typee*.[43] Melville's novel, then, neither wholly accepts nor escapes conversionism; rather, as was incipient in *Hope Leslie*, it takes the terms of its own discourse at once as the medium of representation and as the object of critique.

Accordingly, *Typee*'s representations both describe and reveal their role in constructing what they describe or desire. "The Marquesas!" Tommo muses on shipboard. "What strange visions of outlandish things does the very name spirit up! Naked houris—cannibal banquets—groves of cocoanut—coral reefs—tattooed chiefs—and bamboo temples; sunny valleys planted with bread-fruit-trees—carved canoes dancing on the flashing blue waters—savage woodlands guarded by horrible idols—*heathenish rites and human sacrifices*."[44] The phrasing of this soliloquy—rife, like Sedgwick's paean to the Puritans, with freezing dashes—is revealing of *Typee's* method: insisting that a name "spirits up" images unbidden, the passage takes exaggerated precautions to disguise its role as interpreter of what it conveys. Similarly, if the consuming question of first contact—"Typee or Happar?" (110)—illustrates the wish to restrict the islanders to the binary good/bad, the Typee or Happar "side of the question" (101), this binary is questioned even as it is proclaimed. For these sides may be less fixed than fixed on; viewing the Typees' valley, Tommo's companion will "have it to be Happar," for "nothing else than Happar can it be" (100). That the supposed Happars turn out to be Typees—and that this changes everything Tommo believes he needs to know—suggests not only how conversionism shapes encounter but that it exists precisely to manage the uncertainties encounter holds.

Indeed, in the near burlesque scene of Tommo's acceptance by the Typee community, with its glowering heavies conjured into kowtowing flunkies, conversionism itself is expressed in terms at once ecstatic and absurdist: "What a transition! The dark figures around us leaped to their feet, clapped their hands in transport, and shouted again and again the talismanic syllables [Tommo's having said 'Typee'], the utterance of which appeared to have settled everything" (116). These "talismanic syllables," like the Word Eliot (or his pale, frail surrogate, Hetty Hutter) held out to the natives of Melville's continent, should "settle everything," for they insist that every thing is reliably settled. Yet if the power of conversionism is such that it assures the interchangeability of the Eliot-function, if even the profoundly *un*reliable Tommo can, or must, assume this function, then conversionism is revealed as an implement of power, existing within and because of specific colonial contexts rather than standing outside as their necessary explanation. If, then, *Typee* hints that conversionism is only a scheme of interpretation, it shows that it is not only this; or that schemes of interpretation are schemes of power. The semiotics of conversionism—its denial of the instability of the sign—and its hermeneutic elaboration—the division of representer from represented—reproduce the rule of Euro-American imperialism at home and abroad.[45]

The movement of *Typee* demands, then, a critique of conversionism that touches not only its effects—for these effects may always be rationalized—but its roots, the inflexible structures of opposition that, for an outcast like Tommo as for an icon like Eliot, blunt the fear that encounter might reveal the talismans of civilization to be empty signs. Yet the problem facing *Typee* is how to muster a critique that is not itself laced with conversionist discourse. The famous disquisition on the word "savage," for example, shows accusation turned to defense: "Thus it is that they whom we denominate 'savages' are made to deserve the title. When the inhabitants of some sequestered island first descry the 'big canoe' of the European rolling through the blue waters towards their shores, they rush down to the beach in crowds, and with open arms stand ready to embrace the strangers. Fatal embrace! They fold to their bosom the vipers whose sting is destined to poison all their joys; and the instinctive feeling of love within their breast is soon converted into the bitterest hate" (63). This passage merely flip-flops conversionism; though it initially seems a critique of interpretation—of how discourse "makes" what it says it only details—it is redeemed, as the word "converted" shows, by opposition: childlike/native as opposed to rapacious/white. Such an opposition, moreover—a patent foil, with the Typees naive where Tommo is worldly, confiding where he is suspicious, abused where he thunders against abuse—manipulates the Typees just as he charges the missionaries do:

[Typee religion] had not at all corresponded with the horrible descriptions of Polynesian worship which we have received in some published narratives, and especially in those accounts of the evangelized islands with which the missionaries have favoured us. Did not the sacred character of these persons render the purity of their intentions unquestionable, I should certainly be led to suppose that they had exaggerated the evils of Paganism, in order to enhance the merit of their own disinterested labours. . . . For my own part, I am free to confess my almost entire inability to gratify any curiosity that may be felt with regard to the theology of the valley. . . . An unbounded liberty of conscience seemed to prevail. . . . As the islanders always maintained a discreet reserve with regard to my own peculiar views on religion, I thought it would be excessively ill-bred of me to pry into theirs. (234, 236)

Here tweaking of conversionism interweaves with truckling to it. Beginning with the insight about the missionaries—they would have it to be cannibalism, for nothing but cannibalism can it be—the passage ends by repeating their act: Tommo taps Typee belief to promote his own empowerment, itself expressed in the orthodox terms of Protestant church membership: "I am free to confess." In this respect, Tommo anticipates the Boasian ethnographers of Polynesia who, Christopher Herbert writes, demonized their missionary forebears in order to "distract attention from whatever [was] dubious in their own activities" and to "reinforce their deeply equivocal fictional image of themselves as both scrupulously 'objective' professionals and as bearers of a gospel of liberation—as missionaries, in fact."[46] This analogy is, indeed, particularly apt: buttressed by the interpretive latitude ostensibly valued by the Typees, the Gospel according to Tommo grounds an exegetical authority every bit as voracious and doctrinaire as that of its adversaries.

What *Typee*'s attacks on civilization and Christianity reveal, then, is that conversionist protocols cannot be rewritten by one outsider's remonstrance; that, indeed, pretended outsiders may be as much insiders as those they scorn. Tommo, that is, cannot unsettle conversionism, because Tommo refuses conversion: the state of being alienated from his own discourse. Thus it is that *Typee*'s crisis of representation comes to a head in a scene that suggests this possibility: the scene in which Tommo resists his tattooing. As critics have noted, the exceptionally vehement terms of this scene signal its significance: "Not knowing to what extremities [the tattoo artist] might proceed, and shuddering at the ruin he might inflict upon my figure-head, I now endeavoured to draw off his attention from it. . . . When his fore-finger swept across my features, in laying out the borders of those parallel bands which were to encircle my countenance, the flesh fairly crawled upon my bones" (293). Opinion is divided, however, over *whose* flesh is crawling: Leonard Cassuto believes that it is Tommo who is under critique, who "at first appears to be a modern cultural relativist out of place and time, but who [now] shows his true colors—or rather his 'true color'"; Samuel Otter, on the other hand, refuses the division of narrator from author: "Melville wishes to save his face. Relativism has its limits."[47] What I would argue is that the limits of relativism—or representation—are what are at issue here; the possibility of sustaining or even mounting a critique of conversionism is confronted with an awareness of what such a critique would mean for Melville's narrator, discourse, novel, and culture. Thus it is that tattooing is assigned an inverse, or perverse, Eliot-function: "The whole system of tattooing was, I found, connected with their religion; and it was evident, therefore, that they were resolved to make a convert of me" (295). However accurate this interpretation may be, it suggests that in situations of encounter, no system can claim sole power of representation, that multiple systems coexist, however unequally, within contexts of conversion. Melville, I imagine, was as unsettled as his narrator by this; for Melville's time, like ours, barely sensed interculturalism as a reality, much less an alternative. Yet in disturbing the certainty of its own representations, *Typee* enables this alternative to exist, betokening an intercultural world in which the signs of culture are mere "arbitrary codes" (271) rather than all-encompassing truths.

And to divine such a world was to suggest, exactly two centuries after Eliot's ministry began, that conversionism itself might be a mere arbitrary construct to which Melville's people anxiously and ruthlessly clung to ward off the threat that faced, or threatened to de-face, them. It was this, perhaps, that made *Typee* so distressing to readers; their belief that Melville wished, in the words of missionary William Oland Bourne, to "convert [Christians] to Typeeism" indicates their sense that they were being forced to view themselves as participants in the conversion process, and thus being deprived of any simple faith in the comfortable representations of conversionism. *Typee*, simultaneously raising and renouncing its own discourse, renders conditional not only the objects of representation but the fact of it; and as such, it suggests that the terms of civilization may, or must, coexist with their others. In Melville's most famous work, *Moby-Dick* (1851), this possibility takes tangible form in the person of Queequeg, who is, the narrator discovers, immune to his Eliot-like ministrations: "After all, I do not think that my remarks about religion made much impression upon Queequeg. Because, in the first place, he somehow seemed dull of hearing on that important subject, unless considered from his own point of view; and, in the second place, he did not more than one third understand me, couch my ideas simply as I would; and, finally, he no doubt thought he knew a good deal more about the true religion than I did."[48] Articulating self-consciously the issues of *Typee*—the multiple "points of view" with which reality may be named, the incompleteness of discourse, the possibility that the "true" may be no more than sign taken for essence—*Moby-Dick*, like its predecessor, both reflects and reflects *on* the intercultural world from which it arose, where no culture can claim to represent its others outside its encounters with them.

None of the works in this chapter, of course—except, in an inchoate way, *Typee*—explores the various cultures that constitute that world; interculturalism emerges in its attempted suppression, as a negation of order or, for Melville, a barely glimpsed order behind his own. What this chapter might seem to suggest, therefore, is that interculturalism is no more than discourse or representation itself, a *way* of talking about cultural encounter rather than an outgrowth and facet of cultural conflict, negotiation, and interchange. The next two chapters attempt to ground the discursive in the material: focusing on specific contexts of encounter—economic contact in the next chapter, spiritual in the one following—I explore at once their intercultural nature and the discursive strategies by which interculturalism was, and is, denied. What I seek is to illustrate the mutual, if often antagonistic, links between intercultural activity and discourse, to trace in material contexts the insight that underlies *Typee*: however interculturalism may be denied, the signs of discourse refute the possibility of a final word free of its origins in encounter.

Chapter Two

The Charm of the Indian

The charm of the Indian to me is that he stands free and uncon-
strained in nature. . . . But the civilized man has the habits of the
house. His house is a prison in which he finds himself oppressed
and confined, not sheltered and protected.

—Henry David Thoreau, *Journal*

Consider two early accounts of the Indians of New England. The first,
from Cotton Mather's life of John Eliot (1702), is a complete derogation of
Indian life: "These doleful creatures are the veriest *ruines of mankind*. . . .
These abject creatures live in a country full of mines . . . but our shiftless
Indians were never owners of so much as a knife till we come among
them. . . . They live in a country full of the best ship-timber under heaven:
but never saw a ship till some came from Europe. . . . No *arts* are understood among them, except just so far as to maintain their brutish conversation, which is little more than is to be found among the very bevers upon
our streams." How different is William Wood's account in *New England's
Prospect* (1634): "To enter into a serious discourse concerning the natural
conditions of these Indians might procure admiration from the people of
any civilized nations, in regard of their civility and good natures. . . .
[T]hese Indians are of affable, courteous, and well-disposed natures, ready
to communicate the best of their wealth to the mutual good of one another. . . . As he that kills a deer sends for his friends and eats it merrily, so
he that receives but a piece of bread from an English hand parts it equally
between himself and his comrades, and eats it lovingly."[1] Where Mather
sees depravity, Wood sees beneficence; where Mather sees an antisoci-
ety, Wood sees an edenic brotherhood. There are, to be sure, common
threads—both, for example, see little labor in Indian society—yet as a
whole, they seem impossible to reconcile.

Typically, critics have dealt with such discrepancies in one of two
ways, depending on the discipline they follow: literary criticism or ethnohistory. Thus Jane Tompkins suggests that it is futile to appeal to any

colonial text for an accurate depiction of Indian life, for these texts display a "point of view from which Indians, though present, do not finally matter": the colonists saw what they saw "by virtue of a *way* of seeing which they could no more consciously manipulate than they could choose not to have been born." By contrast, James Axtell argues: "While ethnohistorians should always be skeptical of the *interpretations* placed on the natives' words and actions, the outsider's *descriptions* of that behavior are usually indispensable and often trustworthy."[2] For Tompkins, the text shrouds reality; for Axtell, the text is a window, however cloudy, to that reality. For Axtell, description and interpretation are distinct; for Tompkins, description *is* interpretation, and thus textual evidence can lead only to itself.

Yet different though these approaches are, both rest on a common assumption: that discourse exists independently of its contexts. In Tompkins's approach, discordant records reflect the recorders' biases (Mather and Wood had different agendas), while in Axtell's they can be sifted for the real (perhaps over time, colonialism had reduced the Indians from bounteous hosts to pitiable beggars). In either case, these authors place discourse outside encounter; discourse is something that reflects or distorts encounter but is not bound up in it. The only question to ask, then, is: "Does discourse accurately capture encounter?" And this question, I believe, bars one more important: "What is the *relationship* between discourse and encounter?" To ask this is not only to deny the record (or recorder) autonomy from the encounter; it is, more important, to deny that the Indians "do not matter" to American texts—that they are passive objects of Euro-American activity and reflection—for it is to suggest that discourse evolves within the encounters it shapes in turn.

In this chapter and the one following, I take up the question I posed at the end of the last: that of the links between the texts and contexts of encounter. Such an exploration will, I hope, mediate literary-critical and ethnohistorical approaches, joining the literary critic's skepticism about language with the ethnohistorian's concern with cultural interaction. Though this project can be initiated through any number of instances of encounter, my focus in this chapter will be on an instance that, as my opening quotations suggest, was of considerable consequence to America and its literature: the nature and contact of Indian and Euro-American economic systems. I enter this subject via an avenue that may seem unlikely: the discourse (evident in Wood) of the Noble Savage. Yet I have chosen this discourse precisely because of its unlikeliness, its seeming simplicity and separateness from encounter. As I will show, this discourse illustrates not only the interrelationships between texts and contexts, but the intercultural nature of those contexts and the texts generated within them.

Cannibal Economies

"The theme of the Noble Savage," Hayden White remarks, "may be one of the few historical topics about which there is nothing more to say." Since this chapter is concerned with reorienting Noble Savagism toward encounter, I would like to review what has been said. The Noble Savage, to begin with, antedated the discovery of America; its outlines are evident in Greek tradition. From the first, Arthur Lovejoy and George Boas contend, the Noble Savage has been a protean figure, serving the needs of "differing types of would-be reformers": the Noble Savage is Montaigne's wily cannibal, exposing the Age of Exploration's unhealthy appetites; Freneau's stoical Tomo-Cheeki, forcing the Age of Reason to confront its irrationality; and Châteaubriand's passionate Atala, baring the Age of Industrialization's hollow soul.[3]

In no case, however, is this being real. Noble Savagism, for most critics, is no more than narcissistic, reactionary wish-fulfillment, offering "a return to 'Nature's simple plan'" as a bogus solution to cultural problems. In the case of America, critics emphasize not only the unreality of Noble Savagism but the ways in which it thrived on the destruction of those it ostensibly championed. White, for instance, believes that "idolization of the natives of the New World occurs only *after* the conflict between the Europeans and the natives had already been decided," while Richard Slotkin claims that "once the threat of real Indians was removed from proximity to American civilization and banished to the frontier, the mythicization of the Indians could proceed without the problems and complexities arising from the realities of Indian-white relations." Noble Savagism, then, is doubly disingenuous: it is a celebration of those Europeans have conquered, and it originates in the European psyche in the first place.[4]

There are strengths to this argument; the Ignoble Savage leads all images of the Indian,[5] and Noble Savagism is notable largely for its banality. I question, however, the broader claim that discourse can be divorced from intercultural contact, that it is imposed unilaterally on helpless, or nonexistent, but in any case inconsequential native peoples. For there are weaknesses to the standard chronology: when, precisely, had "the conflict between Europeans and natives been decided"? at what time had "real Indians" (as opposed, presumably, to the "unreal" ones who lingered) been "removed from proximity to American civilization"; when did the "realities" of Indian-white relations cease to be problematic and complex? If one defines "conflict" (or "reality") as warfare east of the Mississippi, perhaps these claims hold true. But this definition is both too narrow and too grandiose. Not only does it ignore the variety of local meetings contact embraced, but in the process, it duplicates what it critiques: it reduces Indians to a negative image of civilization into which civilization expands. I am far from claiming that the Noble Savage is "real"—any more than any image is. Rather, I am suggesting that images cannot be addressed outside their material and ideological contexts. And I am suggesting further that those contexts were shaped by the diverse peoples who existed in, who constituted, America.

The discourse of the Noble Savage is, in fact, an illustration of this. However fanciful and generic it seems, Noble Savagism arises within a matrix of contact, conflict, and negotiation both material and ideological; or, more properly, within the specific intersection of material and ideology that characterizes the economic. Thus when, in his initial voyage, Columbus describes the Taino Indians in terms that would become central to American Noble Savagism, he contrasts notions of economic value: "They are very simple and honest, and exceedingly liberal with all they have; none of them refusing any thing he may possess when he is asked for it, but on the contrary inviting us to ask them. They exhibit great love towards all others in preference to themselves: they also give objects of great value for trifles, and content themselves with very little or nothing in return." Stephen Greenblatt writes that such passages reveal "the European dream" of "the grossly unequal gift exchange: I give you a glass bead and you give me a pearl worth half your tribe." Yet though this may be true of the Columbian conception of encounter, to use Columbus's terms is to blur "exchange": a glass bead is worthless and a pearl precious only in systems of exchange-value. Whether those Columbus imagined he had fleeced viewed a pearl as "worth" half their tribe—whether they viewed "worth" through the same material/ideological lens as Europe—is far from clear. What is clear is that Columbus's project mandates that those he encounters be assimilated to European systems of exchange, made mere adjuncts to the "temporal prosperity" he envisions in his landfall/windfall.[6] To achieve this, to turn potential bane to bonanza, Columbus reads the Indian system of valuation (whatever it was) as an empty prefiguration of his own: the natives, who barter gold for gewgaws, represent naive consumers beyond Europe's wildest dreams. Noble Savagism thus enables Columbus to acknowledge yet erase encounter: though his discourse invokes the economic realm, it manages, by constructing Indian economies as "natural" and therefore absent, to present itself as independent of the intercultural context that spawned it.

I would argue, moreover, that it is not merely through its overt argument, but through the texture of its discourse, that Columbus's Noble Savagism denies the intercultural. The terms on which his fable of "primitive" accumulation depends, terms rooted in the opposition nature/culture—the "natural" Indians are simple, honest, charitable, the "cultural" Europeans complex, duplicitous, penurious—mirror the central construct of market valuation: the opposition of mine and thine, such that items in an exchange must be the indisputable property of one or the other. In this light, Columbus's Noble Savagism emerges not only as a means of anticipating dispossession—turning Indian economies into a negative space to be inhabited by the positive force of the market, he renders literal the expression "your loss is my gain"—but as a means of textualizing what he hopes to realize. In the differential calculus of Columbian economics, as in conversionism, no term or object can be "owned" by more than one. Such discourse, as Eric Cheyfitz writes, demands "univocality: the assertion of a single voice over others, the mastery of one voice by another." And if this is so, then to sever this discourse from its intercultural roots is not simply to privilege one side but, in so doing, to adopt its terms, terms that allow no ambiguity or multiplicity in the ownership of goods, meaning, the encounter itself.[7]

Conversely, to restore the intercultural is to suggest that the terms of the market are neither the sole actors in the encounter nor the sole model of encounter. These possibilities lie at the heart of Montaigne's "Of Cannibals" (1578–80), in which Noble Savagism ironizes the Columbian equation, your loss = my gain. Montaigne, like Columbus, renders the Indians principally through lack; they possess "no sort of traffic, no knowledge of letters, no science of numbers, no name for a magistrate or for political superiority, no custom of servitude, no riches or poverty, no contracts, no successions, no partitions, no occupations but leisure ones, no care for any but common kinship, no clothes, no agriculture, no metal, no use of wine or wheat. The very words that signify lying, treachery, dissimulation, avarice, envy, belittling, pardon—unheard of." For Columbus such negative ethnography clears the way for the positive term of the market; for Montaigne it serves as a foundation for rethinking the value-laden terms of market discourse. He writes: "Three of these men, ignorant of the price they will pay some day, in loss of repose and happiness, for gaining knowledge of the corruptions of this side of the ocean; ignorant also of the fact that of this intercourse will come their ruin (which I suppose is already well advanced: poor wretches, to let themselves be tricked by the desire for new things, and to have left the serenity of their own sky to come and see ours!)—three of these men were at Rouen." Here Noble Savagism takes the form of a canny reversal of maritime commerce: the Indians will "pay a price" for their ill-starred venture; their "loss" of one quality will be weighed against (though not recompensed by) their "gain" of another; their "ruin" (they are, after all, on the road to Rouen) is "well advanced"—a comment on their detrimental advance of cultural capital and thus a pun on the advance that is a decline. Yet if the Indians seem mere dupes to be converted to the seesaw ideal of the market, Montaigne challenges not only this ideal but its discursive armature, its resistance to multiple "owners" of verbal no less than material value. Thus he writes sardonically: "Truly here are real savages by our standards; for either they must be thoroughly so, or we must be; there is an amazing distance between their character and ours." "Our" either/or standards are, however, what the savages violate as they view the market through a possibility it denies and thus collapse the "distance" it enforces: "They have a way in their language of speaking of men as halves of one another," Montaigne writes, and "they had noticed that there were among us men full and gorged with all sorts of good things, and that their other halves were beggars at their doors, emaciated with hunger and poverty." This model challenges the inequality central to the market; moreover, it echoes the market's critique of the Indians: the beggars are defined by lack. The model thus confounds the distinction between savage and civilized, mine and thine; it refutes an imperious master discourse that reduces all others to paupers at its gate. Montaigne, in other words, does not merely trot out a trio of Noble Savages to oppose the market. Rather, the presence of the Indians complicates market terms themselves, making possible an other way of measuring value: not through opposition but through interaction.[8]

I have refrained from calling this other way "Indian" because, to begin with, we do not know what Taino and Tupinamba economies were. How much Montaigne and Columbus understood or cared of them is an open question;[9] not only did they have obvious interests in portraying the New World inhabitants as they did, but there were classical parallels, such as Tacitus's Germans, for their images of nonacquisitive cultures. My purpose, then, is not to pin down the Indian side to the encounter; on the contrary, my purpose is to suggest that encounter reveals the discourse of sides to be a dangerous reduction, the very one by which Europe sought, in word and deed, to erase interculturalism. Noble Savagism may itself take part in this erasure, may disguise exploitation as well as contesting it, or disguise exploitation *by* contesting it. Yet Noble Savagism, to borrow Lawrence Buell's reformulation of pastoralism, is too complex "to permit monolithic categorization of most texts either as consensual or anticonsensual documents."[10] And this complexity points, once again, to the complex contexts of intercultural encounter.

Uncommon Beggars

Founded by Columbus and confounded by Montaigne, the theme of the Noble Savage persists in colonial America. It does not, to be sure, outrank images of Indian savagery; nor does it form the basis, as in years to come, of a distinct genre. Rather, it emerges—and will continue to, even when it achieves apparent autonomy from its roots—in the discussion of Indian economic practices. As did the early explorers of the Caribbean, the settlers of the eastern seaboard write of economies based not on the accumulation of goods but in an ethic one might call, in contrast to individual acquiring, reciprocal relinquishing. Generally, these writings appear to be descriptive rather than prescriptive: "They are extraordinary charitable one to another," Daniel Denton writes of the Delawares, "one having nothing to spare, but he freely imparts it to his friends, and whatsoever they get by gaming or any other way, they share one to another, leaving themselves commonly the least share." In 1656, however, Adriaen Van der Donk drew out the element of critique implicit in such observations: "It is not with them as it is here in Holland, where the greatest, noblest, and richest live more luxuriously than . . . a common man; but with them meat and drink are sufficient and the same for all." In Thomas Morton's *New English Canaan* (1637), critique is manifest: "Since it is but foode and rayment that men that live needeth," he writes, recalling the ethnography of Montaigne and pointing toward the "Economy" chapter of *Walden*, "why should not the Natives of New England be sayd to live richly, having no want of either?" He continues: "They are indeed not served in dishes of plate with variety of Sauces to procure appetite; that needs not there. . . . A bisket cake given to one, that one breakes it equally into so many parts as there be persons in his company, and distributes it. . . . According to humane reason, guided onely by the light of nature, these people leades the more happy and freer life, being voyde of care. . . . They are not delighted in baubles, but in usefull things."[11] Here reciprocal relinquishing unfolds the discourse that will characterize Noble Savagism throughout its career: pitting exchange-value ("baubles") against use-value ("usefull things"), Morton opposes civilized artifice and avarice to savage wholesomeness; the ills of complex society to the joys of the simple life; the confusions of culture to the plain dictates of nature.

Of course, the fact that such reports rely on the oppositional terms of the system they critique should alert one to their biases, polemics, misunderstandings, and translations. Morton's native ascetics, for instance, are plainly meant to confront the Separatists at Plymouth with their forgotten articles of faith, while Denton's liberal, literal Indian givers are, perhaps, willing to hand over more than provisions. Given that the first explorers emphasized native generosity, the image of Indian openhandedness would rapidly have entered a popular lexicon (as the recurring references to the division of food indicate); given its haziness, this shorthand could support any number of conclusions, not least that improvident savages must be taught the love of gain. Then, too, to accept these images unreservedly is to abstract Indian economies from the dynamics of encounter. Even Indian sources, such as Mahican convert Hendrick Aupaumut's nineteenth-century abstract of ancient rules of hospitality, must be approached with caution: "If you see any one hungry you must give him something to eat; though you should have but little cake, give him half of it, for you [are] also liable to hunger. If you see one naked, you must cover him with your own raiment. For you must consider that some future time you will also stand in need of such help; but if you will not assist, or have compassion for the poor, you will displease the Good Spirit; you will be called Uh-wu-theet, or hard-hearted, and nobody will pity on you the time of your distress, but will mock at you."[12] This could, of course, be a traditional code of ethics; but the echo of Matthew 25:41–46 suggests that one must consider the contact situation before projecting this code into the precontact past.

Yet at the same time, if one must be wary of taking these images at face value, one must remember that the tendency to devalue (and deface) non-European economies—and dismiss their depiction as quirks of the Noble Savagist imagination—is characteristic of the European market, which fosters the illusion of self-evidence by transforming other economies into precursors or mirror-images of itself. This illusion governs an influential study of Indian economies, Marcel Mauss's *The Gift* (1950). "It has been suggested," Mauss writes, "that [Indian] societies lack the economic market, but this is not true; for the market is a human phenomenon which we believe to be familiar to every known society." Given this belief, Mauss must see Indian economies as brittle, thinly veiled arenas of conflict, actuated by a protocapitalist "spirit of rivalry and antagonism" all the more reckless for its lack of institutional controls. Yet in using market terms indiscriminately—"expenditure," "interest," "creditor," "debtor," "property," and "consumption" appear on a single page—while ignoring the market's actual impact on Indian societies, Mauss merely revives Columbus's project: Indian economies exist only insofar as, having been eclipsed by the European market, they confirm its power to represent all value on its sole terms.[13]

There are thus two approaches that must be avoided: on the one hand, taking reciprocal relinquishing as an unquestionably Indian practice antagonistic to the market; on the other, taking reciprocal relinquishing as a purely regressive construct of the market. Not only do both approaches rely on the terms of opposition, but, in consequence, both lift Indian and Euro-American economies from encounter, fixing them as extratextual, transhistorical, essential terms. Between these options, however, lies the possibility of viewing relinquishing as a discourse both produced by and reflective of the contact situation, a discourse that, indeed, mirrors the conditions of contact: rather than reducing its other to nonbeing, relinquishing defines persons, goods, and the acts that bind them relationally, such that none exists without its others. For example, John Lawson's account of the ritual enactment of reciprocity among the Tuscaroras defies the idea of unvarying boundaries: "They are very kind, and charitable to one another, but more especially to those of their own Nation; for if any one of them has suffer'd any Loss, by Fire or otherwise, they order the griev'd Person to make a Feast, and invite them all thereto, and . . . every Man, according to his Quality, throws him down upon the Ground some Present, which is commonly Beads, *Ronoak*, *Peak*, Skins or Furs, and which very often amounts to treble the Loss he has suffer'd." The peculiarities in this passage—the one who has nothing gives the feast, while the others offer gifts to the point that the bereft might surpass them—evoke a flexible economic field. "Quality," rather than being a fixed term for (or quality of) those able to bestow charity on the less fortunate, becomes a reflection of variable, situated interrelationships. A reciprocal perspective, as such, does not deny difference or even hostility within or between economies—as Robert Brightman writes, reciprocity is capable of "coercive and exploitative modalities"—yet it does deny that any modality can be severed from the contexts of its creation.[14] Adopting a reciprocal perspective, one that neither absolutizes nor erases difference, thus opens two possibilities: not only does recognizing Indian economies reveal the pluralism of the country's economic history, but considering their relationships with Euro-American economies affords an alternative model for describing that pluralism. And this model suggests that Noble Savagism, a discourse arising from economic encounter, should be seen neither as the market's hallucinatory self-inversion nor as an unadulterated Indian critique, but as a means of interrogating the notion that the country's economy, like its literature, must be the property of one or the other.

Thus in 1643, Roger Williams called on Noble Savagism not only to decry the abuses of the Puritan market but to place it in intercultural context. This project shapes *A Key Into the Language of America* both in its particulars and in its form; in keeping with its claim to be "*an Implicite Dialogue*,"[15] the *Key* textualizes reciprocity by revising a format, the word list, that missionaries and adventurers had used to reduce encounter to an archival cataloguing of exotic terms. For Williams, the lists that constitute much of the *Key* provide opportunities to view language as an active, evolving medium between peoples. In the chapter "Of Eating and Entertainment," for instance, he recreates Indian-European dinnertime rituals:

Cotchikésu assamme.	*Cut me a piece.*
Cotchekúnnemi weeyoùs.	*Cut me some meat.*
Metesíttuck.	*Let us goe eate.*
Pautiínnea méchimucks.	*Bring hither some victualls.*
. . . .	. . . .
Cowàump?	*Have you enough?*
Nowâump.	*I have enough.* (101–2, 103–4)

Pairing English and Narragansett terms, Williams's linguistic work suggests interaction, not opposition. Williams, moreover, locates Indian practices not, as writers such as Morton had, in some never-never land of Nature but in contexts of interculturalism: "Whomsoever commeth in when they are eating, they offer them to eat of that which they have, though but little enough prepar'd for themselves. . . . It is a strange *truth*, that a man shall generally finde more free entertainment and refreshing amongst these *Barbarians*, then amongst thousands that call themselves *Christians*" (104). As such, the Noble Savagism of the poem that follows is situated within the specifics of encounter:

Course bread *and* water's *most their fare,*
O Englands *diet fine;*

. . . .

Sometimes God *gives them* Fish *or* Flesh,
Yet they're content *without;*
And what comes in, they part *to* friends
And strangers *round about.* (104)

Williams, of course, had reason to rail against the Massachusetts Bay
Colony; a desire to censure how it "entertained" his religious and political
convictions, his "strange truths," animates his discourse, and one should
not conclude that the opposition of native simplicity and English vulgarity
is adequate. Indeed, Williams's depiction of the Indians, far from suggesting that they have cornered the market on social felicity, is plainly meant to
recall colonial precedents such as John Winthrop's foundational address
aboard the *Arbella*, "A Model of Christian Charity" (1630): "All the parts of
this body being thus united are made so contiguous in a special relation as
they must needs partake of each other's strength and infirmity; joy and
sorrow, weal and woe. . . . [L]ove and affection are reciprocal in a most
equal and sweet kind of commerce. . . . We must entertain each other in
brotherly affection, we must be willing to abridge ourselves of our super-
fluities, for the supply of others' necessities." As Stephen Innes points out,
Puritans envisioned charity as "a reciprocal responsibility rather than a
paternal obligation"; since all were theoretically equal before God, charity
could not be fixed. Yet despite or because of such "theological egalitarian-
ism," Puritan leaders were quick to assert economic privilege: "God Al-
mighty in his most holy and wise providence," Winthrop's address starts,
"hath so disposed of the condition of mankind, as in all times some must
be rich, some poor, some high and eminent in power and dignity, others
mean and in subjection." Notwithstanding his wish for his people to "entertain" a "reciprocal" commerce, Winthrop founds the commonwealth on
the differential commerce of the market.[16]

　　Williams invokes this model, then, not merely to censure it but to contextualize and demystify it; exposing Winthrop's self-interest, he contrasts
the charity of the Bay Colony, a charity that presupposes inequality, with
that of the Narragansetts: "There are no beggars amongst them, nor father-
lesse children unprovided for" (115); there is apparently no covetousness
either, for "their houses are open, their doore is a hanging *Mat*" (122). In
one sense, the Indians function here as negations of the Puritans' godless
materialism (or God as materialism): naked and artless, they reveal the per-
versity of accumulation. But if so, then their challenge to the market images

a cultural (and divine) order where none are reduced to beggars or fatherless children. Reading Puritanism through the Indian polity, Williams twists a staple of Noble Savagism, the opposition of nature and art(ifice), not only to show Winthrop's classist brotherhood to be artificial but to highlight and confuse the oppositionalism latent in the Puritans' utopian ideal.

Toward this end, though Williams does find market practices in Narragansett society, he undermines the belief that they are divinely ordained. The description of Indian houses concludes: "Yet many of them get *English* boards and nailes, and make artificiall doores and bolts. . . . Many of them begin to be furnished with *English* Chests; others, when they goe forth of towne, bring their goods (if they live neere) to the *English* to keepe for them, and their money they hang it about their necks, or lay it under their head when they sleepe" (122, 123). Similarly, he notes a telling addition to their vocabulary: "*Cuppáimish* I will pay you, which is a word newly made from the *English* word pay" (216). This newly "made" (or coined) word, like the new practices, is "artificial"; there is, as Williams insists at the conclusion of the chapter "Concerning Their Coyne," no inherent, natural "value" (213) in the coin of the human realm:

> *The* Indians *prize not* English *gold*,
> *Nor* English Indians *shell*:
> *Each in his place will passe for ought,*
> *What ere men buy or sell.*
> English *and* Indians *all passe hence*,
> *To an eternall place,*
> *Where shels nor finest gold's worth ought,*
> *Where nought's worth ought but Grace.* (214)

In one respect, this poem is utterly conventional; gaining the world while losing one's soul was a mainstay of Puritan exhortations. Yet as the following chapter, "Of Buying and Selling," indicates, Williams invests this topic with a specific, local application:

> *Oft have I heard these* Indians *say*,
> *These* English *will deceive us.*
> *Of all that's ours, our lands and lives,*
> *In th' end they will bereave us.*
>
> . . . .
>
> Indians *and* English *feare deceits*,
> *Yet willing both to be*
> *Deceiv'd and couzen'd of precious soule,*
> *Of heaven, Eternitie.* (220)

Here Williams reveals how the fusion of God and Mammon plays out in the colonial situation. The Puritans have indeed gained a world; but far from representing the God-favored evolution of the one legitimate economic system, their gaining a world reflects in action what Winthrop's address does in discourse: the erasure of other economies through the imposition of the market's soulless terms. As in his revision of Winthrop's model, then, Williams simultaneously invokes economic encounter as a figure in a theological meditation and employs it to critique the market. Or one might say that the fact that he adopts this dual, flickering focus, where the Bay Colony is held to account at once for denying a transcendent currency and for imposing its own economics of encounter, itself unsettles the binary logic of Puritan economic/spiritual discourse.

It is intriguing, moreover, that a Narragansett ceremony of relinquishing plays a role in Williams's critique: "Their chiefest Idoll of all for sport and game, is (if their land be at peace) toward Harvest, when they set up a long house called *Qunnèkamuck* . . . where he that goes in danceth in the sight of all the rest; and is prepared with money, coats, small breeches, knifes, or what hee is able to reach to, and gives these things away to the poore, who yet must particularly beg and say, *Cowequetúmmous*, that is, *I beseech you*: which word (although there is not one common beggar amongst them) yet they will often use when their richest amongst them would fain obtain ought by gift" (231). This passage calls into question not only the specifics of Puritan economic practice but the very idea of a colonial economy that flourishes through the erasure, literal and discursive, of its various peoples. As a reflection on the market, the passage mocks the appeal to charity, with the rich callously exploiting the ritual for gain. Yet the passage also explores the poetics of reciprocity, the blurring of class lines in an enactment of the circulation of goods, the shifting interrelations of agents, through the social body. And as such, the passage's equivocal status blurs not only class but race: existing, like the *Key* itself, on a border of economies, reflecting at once on Puritan and Indian practices, the ceremony refuses to be obviously or permanently any one's property. Reciprocal relinquishing, then, becomes not simply the natural opposition to the cultural ethic of mine and thine that drives the Puritan market and saturates the Puritan mind; rather, it undermines opposition itself, revealing the intimate interconnections among persons and peoples in the colonial economy and thus refuting the belief that your loss must be, or can be, my gain.

And if so, if this other economy restructures the market relation of difference, perhaps it restructures the relation Williams's text bears toward its other. In the act of representing the Indians, that is, the *Key* complicates the distinction between representer and represented; reciprocity becomes not merely a rhetorical figure, but a principle of the text's rhetorical figurations. As such—however this may have been beyond Williams's intention or control—his work joins the reciprocal field it describes; manifesting a shifting, various mode of constructing the entities in its economy, it cannot own itself outside of an intercultural network. Some scholars have suggested that reciprocity may be characteristic not only of Indian economies but of Indian personhood; as Arnold Krupat phrases it, the Indian self may "not [be] constituted by the achievement of a distinctive, special voice that separates it from others, but, rather, by the achievement of a particular placement in relation to the many voices without which it could not exist."[17] Yet to view such an identity as distinctively, specially Indian—and thus, in the present case, to suggest that Williams's *Key* not only represents a dialogue but owes its dialogism to habits or self-representations he "learned from the Narragansetts"[18]—is, I would argue, to reinstate the ethic of ownership and indebtedness, of simple oppositions or influences between or within cultures, that encounter refutes. Thus I would prefer to say that reciprocity in the *Key* evokes precisely the difficulty of tracing intercultural productions to one side or the other; it illustrates the intimate, dynamic, multiple relationships between peoples that render problematic mine/thine models of the text, the other, or the encounter itself.

One could, of course, argue that encounter is irrelevant to the *Key*. Williams composed his work while sailing to England, seeking charter to Rhode Island; his charitable Indians may be mere fantasies to justify, or disguise, or justify by disguising, proprietary interests.[19] This possibility is strengthened not only by Williams's willingness to naturalize the market—"Many of them naturally Princes," he writes, "or else industrious persons, are rich" (124)—and disdain reciprocity—"an *Indian* with great quant[it]ies of money about him," he gripes, will "beg a Knife of an English man, who haply hath had never a peny of money" (218)—but also by other accounts of Algonquian economies. Echoing Winthrop in his depiction of the Indians as equally "willing to part with their mite in poverty as treasure in plenty" and "love-linked thus in common courtesy," for example, Wood shows that Noble Savagism could function to portray colonization as a manifestation of, yet an evolution beyond, Indian reciprocity. Yet if Williams's Indians *are* Noble Savages, this does not mean one can disjoin Noble Savagism from encounter. Only by abstracting Puritan New England from the contact situation can one write, as Sacvan Bercovitch does, that "in

England, capitalism evolved dialectically, through conflict with earlier and persisting ways of thought and belief. It was an emerging force in a complex cultural design. Basically, New England bypassed the conflict." The *Key* appeared during a time of intense conflict, a time that saw the decline of the fur trade, the increase of Indian servitude, and the first stirrings of the resistance that would culminate in Metacom's revolt. Anne Keary's observation that deed claims of this period bear "the marks of ongoing negotiation between the two cultures" can be said of the *Key* itself. Roger Williams might have agreed with a more recent Williams: "In authentic historical analysis it is necessary at every point to recognize the complex interrelations between movements and tendencies both within and beyond a specific and effective dominance. It is necessary to examine how these relate to the whole cultural process rather than only to the selected and abstracted dominant system."[20] The interrelated movements that shaped the *Key*, or the "whole cultural process" of which it was a part, cannot absolutely be ascertained; but they must be entertained.

Noble Savagism and Civilization

The Noble Savage, who played on the edges of cultural consciousness throughout the colonial period, gained respectability in early national America. A number of reasons for this newfound prominence have been offered: the expansion of the market, the dawning of literary nationalism, and the removal of eastern Indians. In these altered conditions, Noble Savagism was subsumed under a broadly primitivist mantle: sickened by the "meagre utilitarianism," "low pursuits of avarice," and "gaudy frivolities" of their urban, industrial, overrefined society, Americans sought a "wild and uncultivated" Nature lately freed of wild, uncultured opponents. Accordingly, critics agree that the flight to Nature had less to do with Indians (less than nothing to do with Indians) than with white desires and distempers, wishes and worries over the shape the nation was taking.[21]

In one sense, this conclusion is unsurprising. By the antebellum period, the bases of Native autonomy—particularly in the states where Noble Savagism boomed—had been in freefall for centuries; eastern Indians had been confined to reservations and reduced to servitude and charity. In turn, the apparent insignificance of Indians to the economic life of America lends credence to Crèvecoeur's rebuke of Noble Savagists as sourpusses "inspired only by a spirit of censure," who "assumed a type of primitive man, whom they didn't know at all" to "satirize their contemporaries." Rousseau, whose "Discourse on the Origin of Inequality" (1755) popularized the idea of a utopian state of Nature, seems to have agreed: "The investigations we may enter into, in treating this subject, must not be considered as historical truths, but only as mere conditional and hypothetical reasonings, rather calculated to explain the nature of things, than to ascertain their actual origin."[22] If it is easy to see Williams's Noble Savages as mere negations of an ambivalent enterprise, it is far easier to do so when Indian peoples and economies had, evidently, been negated in fact.

Yet as in Williams's case, this model of a market venture indulging in visions of a simpler time does not—nor does any model of the market's aggressions and regressions that erases Indian peoples—go far enough. As a means of showing this, I would like to consider the *locus classicus* of antebellum Noble Savagism, Philip Freneau's turn-of-the-century "Tomo-Cheeki" essays. In typical fashion, these essays oppose pristine Nature to the deprivations, deceptions, and desecrations of culture: "Why have my countrymen sent me to solicit trifles they might well do without, or necessaries for which they have substitutes in abundance;—to make treaties that will end in our destruction, by bringing us into a more intimate connexion with the white men. . . . I dislike these pebbled ways, these little lazy channels of putrifying water, this cracking of whips: the anxious discontented countenances of all I meet; proving alas! too clearly, that all are the slaves of care—that clouds their best days, because they have turned aside from the walks of nature. . . . The more I consider the condition of the white men, the more fixed becomes my opinion, that, instead of gaining, they have lost much by subjecting themselves to what they call the laws, and regulations of civilized societies." These words are plainly modeled on Rousseau's history of capital, where "the equality which nature has ordained" yields to "property and inequality, [which] converted clever usurpation into unalterable right" and "subjected all mankind to perpetual labour, slavery, and wretchedness."[23] Given this pedigree, critics have agreed that Freneau's "Indians" are but phantoms enlisted to chide a nation that had no sooner gained independence than it had begun a process of imperial decline.

The reference to Indian treaties, however, reveals that Freneau draws as well on the intercultural clashes that marked the nation's early years, clashes that facilitated the nation's independence but that many feared might mean the nation's decline. His series appeared amidst a simmering conflict involving the federal government, the southern states, and the

Creek peoples of whom Tomochichi was, if anachronistically, a member;[24] dreading, as Creek agent Benjamin Hawkins wrote, that "we shall have an Indian war," the United States had invited Creek chiefs to the centers of American power in the 1790s to resolve land and trade disputes. The source of the Creeks' resentment, moreover, seems not to have been solely frontier rascalry, but the federal program of forced acculturation for which Hawkins was the front man. In his view, the Creeks resisted this plan because of its rigors: a "beging, spoiled, untoward race," they "demand anything they want from a white man, and feel themselves insulted, when refused. They think they confer a favour on the donor if they accept of clothes from him when naked, or provisions when hungry."[25] Yet the practices Hawkins deemed proof of the Creeks' unfitness for the market— except as beggars—may point as well to their resistance to the economy he saw as absolute, or to economic absolutism. This is suggested by the following passage from James Adair's *History of the American Indians* (1775), written shortly before Hawkins's new nation took over the task of "civilizing" the southeastern tribes:

They say we are covetous, because we do not give our poor relations such a share of our possessions, as would keep them from want. There are but few of themselves we can blame, on account of these crimes, for they are very kind and liberal to every one of their own tribe, even to the last morsel of food they enjoy. . . . They frequently tell us, that though we are possessed of a great deal of yellow and white stone, of black people, horses, cows, hogs, and every thing else our hearts delight in—yet they create us as much toil and pain, as if we had none . . . [and] therefore we are truly poor, and deserve pity instead of envy. . . . They say, they have often seen a panther in the woods, with a brace of large fat bucks at once, near a cool stream; but that they had more sense than to value the beast, on account of his large possessions: on the contrary, they hated his bad principles, because he would needlessly destroy, and covetously engross, the good things he could not use himself, nor would allow any other creature to share of, though ever so much pinched with hunger. They reckon, if we made a true estimate of things, we should consider the man without any false props, and esteem him only by the law of virtue.[26]

As with Freneau, the oppositions of Noble Savagism are abundant here: liberality/covetousness, freedom/enslavement, virtue/violence. Yet in Adair's work, as in the *Key*, these oppositions emerge from the contact situation, resonating with the crises of displacement and disruption that attended the Indians' assimilation to, or expulsion from, the market. As such, this critique militates against the market's absolute authority not only by contextualizing it but by suggesting an other means of "estimating" the inter-relationship of peoples and economies.

In Freneau's work, by contrast, however his Creek rationalist may object to the market, his objections rationalize its logic; for Tomo-Cheeki does not speak of economic conflict but of a transcendent, incontrovertible dualism: Nature—the absence of economy—versus culture, the presence of it. And if this opposition hints at economic conflict, it covers its tracks: there can be no *economic* conflict if there is only one economy. The Tomo-Cheekian musings Freneau attributes to Opothle Mico, one of the Creeks' delegates to the 1790 Treaty of New York, clarify how antebellum Noble Savagism turned critic to apologist: "The seeds of the different kinds of grass brought from the ancient countries of the white men, when sowed among the wild vegetation of the plains and meadows of America do not long subsist in a state of good neighbourhood. One is continually bent upon extirpating the other. One is pale and sickly while the other is strong and vigorous, and many years do not elapse till we perceive the one kind entirely displaced by the other, and not a single blade left as a token that it once existed."[27] Here (though the speaker favors "wild" plant over "pale" implant), the idea of conquest is wholly naturalized, converted from clever usurpation to unalterable right. This attempt to naturalize conquest can be traced to the earliest encounters. Yet in Columbus's time and the years after, the opposition animating Noble Savagism had not outstripped the economic field generating it. It is thus not merely that, by Freneau's day, the market had erased Indian economies; rather, in so doing or in order so to do, it had transformed Indian "economies" into a natural vacancy that merely awaited the imperatives of culture, economics, and capital.

If, then, antebellum Noble Savagism alleviated anxieties about the market, it simultaneously sidestepped the Indians' presence in the market by arguing that Indians were *homo naturalis*, not *homo oeconomicus*. Yet as such, if Noble Savagism justified the market's work, it provided an escape valve by turning Indians into exemplars of natural freedom: just as all might profit from America's economy, so might all remain unsullied by it. Accordingly, circling back on itself, this image of Indians as the antithesis of economic life ensured their absence from it: though some few might yet exist in the nation's economy, they were for that reason not Indians but artificial, imitation whites. (This conviction lingers; to this day, no com-prehensive study of Indian labor and industry in the postconquest East exists.) Thus it was that Indians enjoyed an artistic vogue at this time, for Nature could be preserved only by the art that destroyed it. Noble Savag-ists looked to the vastness of the West or the mists of the past while ignoring what Ralph Waldo Emerson termed the "squalid remnants" next door; for these interstitial figures, who as Catharine Sedgwick put it had "imbibed the dreg-vices of civilization, without in the least profiting by its advantages," had surrendered their distinctive virtue and thereby spoiled the promise of economic independence for all.[28]

And as such, it was only "natural" that Noble Savagism should peak during the 1830s, a decade in which the relationships among Indian and Euro-American economies assumed a particularly complex form. In one sense, the southern Removal crisis, like its colonial and federal forerunners, was driven by economic conflict. Yet even more so than before, the antebellum version underscores the fallacy of viewing conflict as opposition. In 1826, Elias Boudinot, soon to be editor of the *Cherokee Phoenix*, inventoried his people's economic achievements: "At this time there are 22,000 cattle; 7,600 horses; 46,000 swine; 2,500 sheep; 762 looms; 2,488 spinning wheels; 172 waggons; 2,943 ploughs; 10 saw-mills; 31 grist-mills; 62 Blacksmith-shops; 8 cotton machines; 18 schools; 18 ferries"; he could have added twelve hundred slaves.[29] Yet if, according to this review, the Cherokees' economy was comparable to that of the larger society, in 1830 soon-to-be Secretary of War Lewis Cass partitioned improvement along racial lines: "That individuals among the Cherokees have acquired property, and with it more enlarged views and juster notions of the value of our institutions, and the unprofitableness of their own, we have little doubt. And we have as little doubt, that this change of opinion and condition is confined, in a great measure, to some of the *half-breeds* and their immediate connexions." Cass, though seemingly far from Freneau, is faithful to his terms. Rife with economic lingo, his overview hinges on the opposition of real Indians—who, he writes in the voice of negative ethnography, have "no courts, no officers . . . no relative duties to enforce, no debts to collect, no property to restore"; who are, in short, "in a state of nature"—and half-breeds, whose unreality inheres in their cultural, that is economic, that is capitalist ways.[30] West the Cherokees must go; there, in a space without culture, they can reclaim their true and only nature.

Cass, interestingly, suggests that those who did celebrate the state of Nature had done much to damage the nation's interests; deriding the clap-trap foisted on the public by "Rousseau and the disciples of his school"—Cooper was his real *bête noire*—he urges his fellows to view the issue with "the soberness of truth and reality." Yet just as Cass accepted the premise of Noble Savagism, so did the easterners he reviled accept what he deemed truth and reality. In 1835, Massachusetts congressman Edward Everett, though he had stormed against the Removal Bill five years before, offered

an economics lesson cheering to those currently negotiating the Cherokees' removal: "We cannot perceive in what way the forest could have
been cleared, and its place taken by the cornfield, without destroying the
game; in what way the meadows could be drained, and the beaver-dams
broken down, without expelling their industrious little builders;—nor in
what way the uncivilized man, living from the chase, and requiring a wide
range of forest for his hunting-ground, destitute of arts and letters,—
belonging to a different variety of the species, speaking a different tongue,
suffering all the disadvantages of social and intellectual inferiority, could
maintain his place, by the side of the swelling, pressing population,—the
diligence and dexterity,—the superior thrift, arts, and arms,—the seductive
vices, of the civilized race."[31] The reference to seductive vices is no knee-
jerk reactionism; it reveals the function of the Noble Savagist gesture: vices
share with thrift and arts the distinction of being cultural attainments, and
if civilization is to enjoy the latter it must abide the former. There can be
no compromise between Nature and culture, forest and field, bow and
plow: their loss, as always, is our gain.

Antebellum Noble Savagism, in sum, attempted to ensure that Indians were not simply displaced by the economy but deprived of an economic
existence altogether—not merely the right to make a living but the right to
exist *as* economic beings. As such, if one is to avoid reproducing this
discourse, one must refuse the argument that Indians had vanished or, at
least, ceased to be "real" by this time; one must read antebellum economic
and artistic practice in light of the efforts of Indian peoples, from the
remarkable legal battles of the Cherokees to the unremarked activities of
New England's "squalid remnants," to maintain a foothold in the economic life of the nation. To illustrate this, I would like to position Henry
David Thoreau's *Walden* (1854) in this wider context. Thoreau's critique of
the market has received ample comment;[32] I wish to examine how this critique is informed by native peoples southern and northern, how its exploration of their lives and labor hints at an intercultural model of America's
economy. Yet I wish to show how, at the same time, *Walden* reveals the
limitations of antebellum Noble Savagism: seeing savage nobility as freedom from the market, Thoreau finally conceives his revision as a removal.

The Busk and the Basket

Though it is probably too much to say, as Roy Harvey Pearce does,
that "primitivistic thinking in America was always radical," it was capable

of unsettling those who endorsed the nation's fundamental oppositions. Thus Robert Montgomery Bird denounced Cooper's Indians as wholly "contrary to nature," while Cass gibbeted the creator of Leatherstocking for parlor-bound naivete: "The author of these novels" has failed to consult "the book of nature. He describes beings with feelings and opinions, such as never existed in our forests. . . . They may wear leggins and moccasins, and be wrapped in a blanket or a buffalo skin, but they are civilized men, and not Indians." It was not Cooper alone, however, who nettled; Sedgwick's Indians, for example, were skewered by Timothy Flint, who found in Magawisca and her kind not the slightest "resemblance to nature."[33] Whatever their actual clout, Noble Savagists were seen as troublemakers who falsely believed a buffalo skin could mask essential difference, and whose jaundiced views must be treated with a strong dose of "nature."

It is little wonder, then, that even in 1854, *Walden* should raise a few hackles. A handful of splenetic reviewers dismissed Thoreau outright as a "would-be savage"; yet even positive notices automatically Indianized his project. A "child of nature," he had retired into a "semi barbarous state" to live a "simple but noble life"; his style was "crude but forcible," an allusion to Indian oratory that backed another reviewer's recommendation that the text "be printed upon birch-bark." As Robert Sayre notes, "for any American to go live in the woods immediately calls to mind living like an Indian." Transcendentalist eremite though he seemed, Thoreau was at the same time flirting with the line between red and white, and this threatened to expose the material and ideological erasures at the root of the American economy.[34]

Thoreau was not the first of his time to do so. He was, however, perhaps the first to do more than flirt, and his project can be measured when it is juxtaposed with other such ventures. Thus, an obscure travel narrative entitled *A Pedestrious Tour, of Four Thousand Miles, Through the Western States and Territories* (1819), written by New Hampshire lawyer Estwick Evans, anticipates Thoreau's goals and groundwork: "Civil society is not without its disadvantages. Whilst it adds to the information, and polishes the manners of man, it lessens the vigour of his mind and the generosity of his heart. He no longer experiences the sublime inspirations of Nature. . . . [H]ow happy should we be if we could ingraft the instruction, and impress the polish of civilization upon the lofty virtues of untutored life. . . . I wished to acquire the simplicity, native feelings, and virtues of savage life; to divest myself of the factitious habits, prejudices and imperfections of civilization; to become a citizen of the world; and to find, amidst the solitude and grandeur of the western wilds, more correct views of human nature and of the true interests of man." Evans, however, seems intent on reducing such proclamations to parody; though garbed (like Cass's cartoon Noble Savage) in "buffalo skins," he lugs along the accouterments of civil society: "A pocket-compass, maps, journal, shaving materials, a small hatchet, patent fire works, &c." Couple this with the stilted romanticism of the endless "reflections" promised on his title page— verbal ramblings as tiring as his physical must have been—and one is left with Evans the popinjay, the very image of the "young gentleman of leisure" who, Henry Nash Smith writes, could afford "to indulge himself in the slightly decadent cult of wildness and savagery which the early nineteenth century took over from Byron."[35] Evans's frontispiece, which depicts a latter-day wild man swaddled in hides (but flawlessly coiffed), confirms this assessment; the jaunty attitude of this portrait shows that his foray into the realm of the Noble Savage is merely a pose.

The same costume-party primitivism crops up in more serious efforts to reconcile wilds and town. Thus the 1844 essay "Life in the Woods" by Charles Lane, one of Thoreau's acquaintances, sets out to "contemplate the sylvan man" and to "compare him with the civilian, and see to which the superiority must be awarded, both as respects nature and conditions." Predictably, if hypothetically, Lane hands the laurels to the sylvan man, who "holds an immediate intercourse with nature." Yet when forced to get down to cases, his confidence dissipates: "The experiment of a true wilder-ness life by a white person must, however, be very rare. He is not born for it; he is not natured for it. He lacks the essential qualities as well as the physical substance for such a life, and the notion of entering on it must be considered merely an interesting dream."[36] For Lane and Evans, the gap between ideal and real wilderness is absolute.

Thoreau's experiment can be seen, in part, as an attempt to expose such hoaxes. Yet it is important to note that, in so doing, he exposes not only the fact that the emperor has no buffalo robe but the assumption beneath this hide: the assumption of an essential difference in the way peoples are natured—or cultured—that prevents, in Lane's words, their "amalgamation."[37] Where Evans and Lane use the image of civilized sav-age to reassert dichotomy over paradox, Thoreau realizes that this image can reveal racial dichotomies to be (like Evans's hair shirt) *assumed*: put on and put-ons. And as such, the Walden experiment, unlike Evans's and Lane's Noble Savagist trysts, becomes a test of Noble Savagism itself, a test of the oppositions by which whites claimed ownership of culture, civiliza-tion, and economy while relegating Indians to a pristine, doomed Nature.

Accordingly, *Walden* posits a series of oppositions—Nature/trade, red/white, wild/home—yet proposes their interrelation. Walden Pond is an ideal spot for this: "Lying between the earth and the heavens," it is "intermediate in its nature between land and sky," at once rooted in a natural spot and expressive of a transcendent ideal.[38] In this locale, leading a "primitive and frontier life, though in the midst of an outward civilization" (12–13), Thoreau employs a number of devices to unsettle the opposition of primitive and civilized states. To begin with, by detailing his economic activities—house-building, bookkeeping—he makes the wild cultural; conversely, by reframing market terms—"My purpose in going to Walden Pond was not to live cheaply nor to live dearly there, but to transact some private business" (18)—he suggests that market definitions cannot comprehend the varieties of economic activity. Furthermore, if by reducing the "necessaries of life" (13) to four—food, shelter, clothing, fuel—he advances the Noble Savagist doctrine of simplicity, at the same time, by illustrating that "the improvements of ages have had but little influence on the essential laws of man's existence" (13), he places natural and cultural lives on a par. Thoreau's effrontery in titling his initial chapter "Economy" lies, then, not simply in its assertion of a natural space devoid of the "factitious cares" of economic life (9), but in its revision of Noble Savagist conventions to confound the distinction between a natural and a cultural/economic space.

This leveling effect takes the form of explicit critiques as well. In some cases, these rely on mere inversion: "We are all poor in respect to a thousand savage comforts, though surrounded by luxuries" (27). At other moments, Thoreau outstrips such predictable stuff: "Even in our democratic New England towns," he writes, "the accidental possession of wealth, and its manifestation in dress and equipage alone, obtain for the possessor almost universal respect. But they who yield such respect, numerous as they are, are so far heathen, and need to have a missionary sent to them" (20). To speak of class stratification as heathen was nonsense; missionaries were to inculcate notions of privilege in the heathen, not exculcate them from their own. Elsewhere, Thoreau impugns the "savage taste of men and women for new patterns," compared to which tattooing "is not barbarous merely because the printing is skin-deep and unalterable" (22). This distinction—bodily integrity versus the caprice of fashion—has deep roots in Noble Savagist thought; yet Thoreau suggests contrarily that, if fashion consciousness is savage, then perhaps the (savage?) practice of tattooing is civilized. By punning, moreover, on "skin-deep," he undoes the distinction between skin and skein; the practice is both superficial (skin-deep) and permanent (skin-deep), natural and cultural, turning the body into a figural document. The confusing syntax heightens the ambiguity; does Thoreau mean that tattooing is not merely barbarous but something else ("it is not barbarous merely, because"), that the mere fact of its being unalterable makes it not barbarous ("it is not barbarous, merely because"), that its being unalterable does not in itself make it barbarous ("it is not *barbarous* merely because"), or that it is not the lone thing that is barbarous ("*it* is not barbarous merely because")? Such ambiguity, indeed, is central to Thoreau's project, which in the tradition of Montaigne and Williams does not so much use "natural" savages to critique "culture" as use the critique to confuse it. Such ambiguity leads to a question Thoreau finds weighty enough to italicize: "*If the civilized man's pursuits are no worthier than the savage's, if he is employed the greater part of his life in obtaining gross necessaries and comforts merely, why should he have a better dwelling than the former?*" (28). If, that is, Nature and culture are not absolute but relative and interpenetrating, by what right does white culture lay claim to its towns or the country itself?

Having issued this challenge, Thoreau must confront the peoples whose natural dwellings have been claimed by the forces of culture. He writes in the chapter "The Bean-Field": "It appeared by the arrowheads which I turned up in hoeing, that an extinct nation had anciently dwelt here and planted corn and beans ere white men came to clear the land. . . . Mine was, as it were, the connecting link between wild and cultivated fields; as some states are civilized, and others half-civilized, and others savage or barbarous, so my field was, though not in a bad sense, a half-cultivated field" (108, 109). Thoreau's pun places him within, yet without, Noble Savagism: a half-cultivated field is intermediate between Nature and culture. Yet as the case of the Cherokees showed, such indeterminacy or intermediacy had become not merely anathema but unthinkable. Thus this passage—like the bean field itself—rests on an ambiguity. As agriculturalists, the Indians have staked their claim to culture, yet as "unchronicled nations" (109), they have become a silent part of the enduring culture of America: they have "exhausted the soil for this very crop" (108). That this very crop is the same crop they planted heightens the ambiguity: if on the one hand the bean field is a cultural intertext, on the other it is a palimpsest, the Indians' ancient tillage having been appropriated by the white farmer as "manure" (108).

It is notable, then, that Thoreau's bean field finds its counterpart in an Indian ceremony, one that in his view balances nature and (agri)culture, reaping the products of the soil to adduce spiritual truths. A passage from

William Bartram's account of the southeastern Indians (published, like Freneau's essays, during the Creek crisis of the 1790s) moved Thoreau to write: "The customs of some savage nations might, perchance, be profitably imitated by us, for they at least go through the semblance of casting their slough annually" (51). The passage follows:

When a town celebrates the busk . . . having previously provided themselves with new clothes, new pots, pans, and other household utensils and furniture, they collect all their worn out clothes and other despicable things, sweep and cleanse their houses, squares, and the whole town, of their filth, which with all the remaining grain and other old provisions they cast together into one common heap, and consume it with fire. After having taken medicine, and fasted for three days, all the fire in the town is extinguished. During this fast they abstain from the gratification of every appetite and passion whatever. . . . On the fourth morning, the high priest, by rubbing dry wood together, produces new fire in the public square, from whence every habitation in the town is supplied with the new and pure flame. (51)[39]

The "most important and serious" ceremony in the Southeast, according to Revolutionary-era Creek leader Alexander McGillivray, the "busk" (as whites translated the Native American word) proved, like the ritual of relinquishing Williams described, both fascinating and troubling to Euro-American observers. Though Hawkins worked tirelessly to convert the Creeks to the market, he surprisingly praised the busk: "This happy institution of the Boos-ke-tuh, restores man to himself, to his family and to his nation." In Thoreau's century, John Howard Payne was sufficiently impressed by observing the 1835 busk—the last to be performed by the Creeks before their removal—to pierce removalist rhetoric: "So much for the beautiful state of our national legislation and morals, as civilizers and protectors of the red-men. . . . [T]he persons hovering upon the frontier," he continues, "care nothing for the Indians" except "finding out how much cotton their grounds will yield, and in what way the greatest speculation can be accomplished with the smallest capital." In contrast to this reduction of all things to the material, Payne sees in the ceremony a "mystical idiom . . . utterly incomprehensible to the literal minds of mere trafficking explainers": "I never beheld more intense devotion. . . . It was strange to see this, too, in the midst of my own land. . . . And it was a melancholy reflection for ourselves, that, comparing the majority of the white and red assemblage there, the barbarian should be so infinitely the more civilized and the more interesting of the two."[40] As in Williams's remarks on the Narragansetts' ceremony, Payne's comments suggest that the performance of reciprocity could reveal cultural oppositions to be mere code for, and justification of, the market's assault on Indian persons and economies.

In *Walden*, the busk expresses, as it were, Payne's mystical idiom, variously inflecting Thoreau's intercultural vision. On the one hand, it personalizes the rhythms of Noble Savagism: withdrawal from everyday business, purging of baggage, spiritual rebirth. Yet as for Payne, Thoreau's busk complicates Noble Savagism itself. A ritual evidently far older than European culture, the busk subverts both the exceptionalism of white America's destiny and the evolutionary mandate of the market. Indeed, as in Adair's text (which Thoreau read after *Walden* was published, else he might have noted the similarity), it provides an ironic gloss on the terms in which it is conveyed: it is the town fire that "consumes"; indices of market valuation (wear, filth), recontextualized by the busk, reveal their provisional, uninherent nature. By contrast, Thoreau charges, his society has naturalized the market's calculus of price and profit: "We have no festival, nor procession, nor ceremony, not excepting our Cattle-shows and so-called Thanksgivings, by which the farmer expresses a sense of the sacredness of his calling. . . . By avarice and selfishness, and a grovelling habit, from which none of us is free, of regarding the soil as property, or the means of acquiring property chiefly, the landscape is deformed, husbandry is degraded with us, and the farmer leads the meanest of lives" (114). The Indians, Thoreau intimates, have been removed from the land only to be replaced by a people so wedded to market mechanisms and mentality that they too are removed from it.

The busk, then, might "be profitably imitated" because it contests the pecuniary sense of profit and restores (to the individual, family, and nation) the spiritual sense: "What does it profit if one gain the world but lose one's soul?" Indeed, the busk challenges this distinction too, for it suggests that one can materialize but not degrade spirit, an ideal Thoreau seeks as well: "Shall I not have intelligence with the earth? Am I not partly leaves and vegetable mould myself?" (97). But if the spiritual (cultural) is material (natural), so is the material spiritual; cultivating a balance between world and soul, the busk values natural products not as "mere provender" (119) but as the "finer fruits" of life (9). In the busk, Thoreau maintains, Indian practices mediate between a "higher, or, as it is named, spiritual life" and a "primitive rank and savage one" (143): building, equipping, and maintaining a space that shapes Nature for cultural ends, the Creeks appear to bridge an opposition Thoreau's era saw as absolute.

If, however, the busk reflects *Walden*'s radical potential, it also reveals an affinity with a conventional Noble Savagism. Toward this end, it is intriguing that Thoreau, though he writes that "I have scarcely heard of a truer sacrament" than the busk, feels that it may be but "semblance," the "idea of the thing" and not the "reality" (51). The contrast is unclear; it seems, however, to imply that the busk, lacking value in itself, must be redeemed to be transformed into cultural capital. Thoreau thus reproduces, if somewhat elliptically, the terms of the market: just as the lands on and from which the busk took place have been appropriated by white culture, so does the busk become a vacancy on which the white author's cultural critique founds itself.

What facilitates this, of course, is that Bartram's busk is, for Thoreau, both geographically and temporally distant. Thoreau's lone mention of the southeastern tribes' more recent history appears in a journal entry amidst a hodgepodge of ignoble savagism: "For the Indian there is no safety but in the plow. If he would not be pushed into the Pacific, he must seize hold of a plow-tail and let go his bow and arrow. . . . A race of hunters can never withstand the inroads of a race of husbandmen. . . . What detained the Cherokees so long was the 2923 plows which that people possessed; and if they had grasped their handles more firmly, they would never have been driven beyond the Mississippi."[41] Nestled within this lazy meditation, the "2923" indicates that Thoreau possessed more than a passing interest in the events of the 1830s; yet the entry as a whole suggests his belief that interest was unnecessary after the Indians' passing. No such claim can be made for the Indians of Concord; in their persistence lies the possibility of recognizing the interaction of peoples in the nation's economy. Yet Thoreau's critique of that economy, it emerges, refuses to tolerate the Indians' presence; and as such, it ultimately denies the reciprocal perspective toward which *Walden* points.

Nowhere is this clearer than in the tale of the Indian basket-maker. This episode has been read as a "parable" or even a "fable"; its significance is, however, far greater than these terms allow.[42] Thoreau writes:

Not long since, a strolling Indian went to sell baskets at the house of a well-known lawyer in my neighborhood. "Do you wish to buy any baskets?" he asked. "No, we do not want any," was the reply. "What!" exclaimed the Indian as he went out the gate, "do you mean to starve us?" Having seen his industrious white neighbors so well off . . . he had said to himself: I will go into business; I will weave baskets; it is a thing which I can do. Thinking that when he had made the baskets he would have done his part, and then it would be the white man's to buy them. He had not discovered that it was necessary for him to make it worth the other's while to buy them, or at least make him think that it was so, or to make something else which it would be worth his while to buy. I too had woven a kind of basket of a delicate texture, but I had not made it worth any one's while to buy them. Yet not the less, in my case, did I think it worth my while to weave them, and instead of studying how to make it worth men's while to buy my baskets, I studied rather how to avoid the necessity of selling them. (17–18)

I have quoted this passage at length because it is one of the few in *Walden* (save a couple references to roving Penobscots) in which Thoreau addresses the daily lives of New England natives. Indeed, this interlude is virtually unparalleled in Euro-American literature;[43] for reasons I have mentioned, antebellum authors focused on historical figures and western tribes. The basket-maker is simply a common worker, trying to get by; he might be one's neighbor.

And, in the journal entry from which Thoreau adapted this passage, he was just that. There are three significant differences between the journal entry (from late 1850) and the passage in *Walden*; the first is that Thoreau's identification with the Indian ("I too had woven a kind of basket") is absent from the journal, which ends, "It is n't enough simply to make baskets You have got to sell them." Second, the sardonic remark—"or at least make him think that it was so"—does not appear in the journal, which reads, "He has not discovered that it is necessary for him to make it worth your while to buy them—or make some which it will be worth your while to buy." Third, the man who refuses the Indian is identified in the journal as "Mr Hoar," or Samuel Hoar, one of Concord's wealthiest citizens.[44]

The result of these changes is to convert a highly charged racial and economic conflict into a sly meditation on the hazards and triumphs of economic independence. Like the busk, Indian basketry might have indicated to Thoreau something else; as the incident that triggered his memory of the basket-maker suggests, impoverished Indians were visible enough to cast doubt on the ethic of individual freedom: "A squaw came to our door today, with two pappooses—and said—'Me want a pie.' Theirs is not common begging—You are merely the rich Indian who shares his goods with the poor. They merely offer you an opportunity to be generous and hospitable." This begging that is not "common"—Williams also uses the term in describing the Narragansetts' ceremony—points to a discourse of reciprocity still available in Thoreau's day (though it is possible he had simply picked up the term from Williams).[45] In any event, Thoreau could have seen in such uncommon practices a local, absolutely current parallel to the busk: the begging that is not begging questions the distinctions that drive the engine of charity and fix petitioner in opposition to provider. Further, if it is true, as Russell Handsman and Ann McMullen argue, that Indian craftspeople's weaving of traditional emblems into woodsplint baskets provided "a coded language of resistance" and "a shared or social identity" for their producers, Thoreau could have seen in the basket industry an attempt to mediate between market demands, which put premiums on mass production and trendiness, and artistic vision.[46] The Indian basket-maker, in short, might have challenged not only the economy Thoreau upbraids, but the rhetoric that denied Indians a place in that economy.

To entertain this possibility, however, would have been, in Thoreau's view, to lose a space from which to launch his critique. "Our village life would stagnate if it were not for the unexplored forests and meadows which surround it," he explains. "We need to witness our own limits transgressed, and some life pasturing freely where we never wander" (211). Here the life of the wild is an anticulture that acts as home base for revitalizing attacks. Civilized life, on the other hand, is "an *institution*, in which the life of the individual is to a great extent absorbed, in order to preserve and perfect that of the race" (26). Seeking a position on the margins of his society, Thoreau cannot admit that Indians—however marginalized by that society—may live by institutions (such as the "happy institution" of the busk) of their own. He cannot, moreover, admit that (as with the basket-maker) the institutions of the market have had significant effects on the peoples he looks to as exemplars of freedom. As such, using the basket-maker to remark on his own freedom from such demeaning transactions, Thoreau reveals his partnership with that which he assails: profiting from the Indian's failure, he makes the basket-maker's loss the poet's gain. That Thoreau was not free from the desire or need to hawk his goods—that he was, like the basket-maker, attempting to reconcile sales and art—is patent; in the years during which he revised *Walden*, he submitted essays to periodicals and struggled to fulfill his debt for the unsold copies of his bomb, *A Week on the Concord and Merrimack Rivers* (1849). Yet to corner a site of pure freedom, he downplays his commercial concerns while dismissing the Indian of his environment for the Indian of the past, the West: anywhere but the house next door.

It is evident, indeed, that Thoreau feels a certain contempt for this Indian, as for the poor of whatever race. "I foresee that if my wants should be much increased the labor required to supply them would become a drudgery," he wrote. "I trust that I shall never thus sell my birthright for a mess of pottage." The basket-maker, by selling his birthright, forfeiting the freedom that is his heritage for the curse of trade that is the white man's, has defiled and degraded himself, made himself, in more ways than one, unnatural. Thoreau, indeed, enters the primitivist mainstream in another journal passage: "Still here and there an Indian squaw with her dog— her only companion—lives in some lone house—insulted by school children—making baskets & picking berries her employment You will meet her on the highway—with few children or none—with melancholy face— history destiny . . . weaving the shroud of her race—performing the last services for her departed race. Not yet absorbed into the elements again— A daughter of the soil—one of the nobility of the land—the white man an imported weed burdock & mullein which displace the ground nut." This naturalization of racial conquest suggests the extent to which Thoreau relies on what he critiques: if he sees the wild as a site of renewal, he sees it as removed from culture, and therefore—like the squaw, an unlikely, but necessarily, "noble" savage—fated to be removed by it. Thus that which might have critiqued the critique—the busk and the basket—must be denied their place in, and their interrelationships with, Thoreau's society; they must be bracketed outside his society even as, indeed to the extent that, they critique it. And yet, if the Indian critique is outside the market, it becomes a justification of the market, what Michael Gilmore terms "a distorted—and reified—reflection of the laissez-faire individualist pursuing his private economic interest": the basket-maker is free to sell his goods (or not), to prosper (or starve) untouched by societal restraints. Thoreau knew that such freedom was illusory; he knew, as he wrote in *Walden*, that individuals were bound in a network of privilege and disempowerment: "Perhaps it will be found that just in proportion as some have been placed in outward circumstances above the savage, others have been degraded below him" (28). Yet for all such insights, when Thoreau encountered this degradation, he fell back on an opposition that justified it. "Nature against almshouses," he wrote in 1851; that the exemplars of Nature had been subjected to almshouses was a fact he could not bear to admit.[47]

My purpose here, I should stress, has neither been to review Thoreau's ambivalence toward the wild and the market, both of which have been treated at length,[48] nor to charge him with hypocrisy for failing to extricate himself from the economy he critiqued. Quite the contrary, I have sought to examine how his desire to divorce himself from an economy in which he knew he played a part—not least through his publications—led him to view the Indians as beings free from a system that (he also knew) had irrevocably changed their lives. And I would argue, further, that this need to erase Indians from America's economic life has informed later evaluations of Thoreau and of the culture in which he wrote. This critical consciousness takes shape within the field that was hotly contested during Thoreau's lifetime: the uses and liabilities of Noble Savagism. If critics of his day suspected Thoreau of indulging in primitivist hijinks, twentieth-century critics have leaped to clear his name. Leo Marx, for example, writes that "Thoreau is not a primitivist. . . . In *Walden*, accordingly, he keeps our attention focused upon the middle ground," the compromise between the "opposing forces of civilization and nature." Edwin Fussell contends that "Thoreau recommends no return to nature, nor to savage conditions, but only a move in that direction," a move "not at all primitive but very highly civilized." Writing twenty years after these critics, Lawrence Buell can take Thoreau's position for granted: "Thoreau, as is well known, was no primitivist, though he did have leanings in that direction." These assurances are curious: either Noble Savagism has gotten such a bad rap it is necessary to rescue a classic writer from its clutches, or the threat of Thoreau's Indianization is still strong enough to provoke denials. That the former may be the case is suggested by Marx, who writes that the pastoral ideal "enabled the nation to continue defining its purpose as the pursuit of rural happiness while devoting itself to productivity, wealth, and power. It remained for our serious writers to discover the meaning inherent in the contradiction." In this formula, complex pastoralism, as opposed to its naive counterpart (primitivism), distinguishes the serious from the populist writer, the diviner of ugly realities from the (basket?) peddler of pretty falsehoods. Thus Thoreau cannot be a primitivist—and here the first option shades into the second—for had he returned to what Sherman Paul terms the "unconsciousness of primitive existence," he would be no more a cultural treasure than the primitive artifacts he luckily disdained.[49] The subtext to the recuperation of Thoreau is unfortunate: Thoreau cannot be a Noble Savagist, for savages have nothing to offer culture save removing themselves to make a clearing in which culture can grow.

Thoreau did make a clearing, where he cultivated beans, books, busks, and baskets. But if we accept his depiction of himself in *Walden* as "a first settler" (177), we not only follow his blindness but make him more blind than he was. Denials of Thoreau's Noble Savagism rest on the Noble Savagist distinction itself, a distinction between, as Marx puts it, "Concord and the wilderness"; they assume that had Thoreau lit out for Indian territory, forfeiting the concord of civilization for the wilderness of savagery (however noble), he could never have taken his place in *our* culture—nor would he have been much of a loss. But the relative value of cultures to Thoreau—as if this could be quantified—is not the question; the question is whether *Walden* can be understood outside the intercultural world in which it took shape.[50] If we believe it can, if we believe it was by transcending Indian lives, work, and cultures that Thoreau became the writer he was, then like good Noble Savagists, like Thoreau himself, we make their loss our gain.

Chapter Three

Radical Faiths

Myoxeo asking him how many Gods the English did worship, he
answered one God, whereupon *Myoxeo* reckoned up about 37. principal gods he had, and shall I (said he) throw away these 37. gods for
one?

—John Eliot, in Henry Whitfield, *The Light Appearing More
and More*

When, in 1805, Jacob Cram of the Massachusetts Missionary Society approached the Seneca Indians living on the Buffalo Creek reservation, he
stepped into a spiritual battle that had raged across the continent for
centuries. Cram's contribution began modestly enough; zealous if a bit
plodding, he offered a conciliatory gesture to lull the antimissionary sentiment that had intensified since the Reservation era: "I have not come to
get your lands or your money, but to enlighten your minds." His heart,
however, was not in this ceremonial introduction; eager to broach his real
business, he continued: "There is but one religion, and but one way to
serve God, and if you do not embrace the right way, you cannot be happy
hereafter." Perhaps sensing that he had forfeited his audience's good will,
Cram added: "I want you to speak your minds freely; for I wish to reason
with you on the subject, and, if possible, remove all doubts, if there be any
on your minds."[1] Cram was confident that reason and revelation were on
his side; the Senecas could pose no challenge that could not be, like their
physical selves, removed.

The Indians took time to craft a response. Then the leader of the
antimission party, Sagoyewatha, He Keeps Them Awake, or Red Jacket—
a nickname denoting the colors of his wartime British allies—rose to answer: "You have got our country, but are not satisfied; you want to force
your religion on us. . . . You say that you are right and we are lost. How do
we know this to be true? . . . We are told that your religion was given to
your forefathers, and has been handed down from father to son. We also
have a religion, which was given to our forefathers, and has been handed

down to us. . . . Brother—the great Spirit has made us all, but he has made a great difference between his white and red children. He has given us different complexions and different customs. . . . Since he has made so great a difference between us in other things, why may we not conclude that he has given us a different religion, according to our understanding?" Spurned, Cram refused to shake Red Jacket's hand at meeting's end, muttering that there could be "no fellowship between the religion of God and the works of the devil."[2]

In the years that followed, Cram's pique came to appear prophetic, as missionaries carved inroads into Red Jacket's reservation. In 1826, George Catlin reported that the old chief had lost both his fire and his following: "Like many other great men who endeavour to soothe broken and painful feelings, by the kindness of the bottle, he has long since taken up whiskey-drinking to excess; and much of his time, lies drunk in his cabin, or under the corner of a fence, or wherever else its *kindness* urges the necessity of his dropping his helpless body and limbs." Red Jacket's final indignity occurred after his death in 1830, when the local missionary read a Christian service over his body and had his remains interred in a Christian cemetery. Six years later, Thomas McKenney, past Superintendent of Indian Affairs, and James Hall, author of "The Indian Hater," recalled the chief in the opening vignette of *The Indian Tribes of North America*: "Red Jacket was the *last of the Senecas*: there are many left who may boast the aboriginal name and lineage, but with him expired all that had remained of the spirit of the tribe."[3] Recycled endlessly in the following years,[4] the tale of Red Jacket's vain resistance and ignominious end became conversionist allegory: just as the Christian "spirit" must best the individual Indian soul, so must the continental struggle of Indian and white spiritualities end in the extirpation of the former by the latter.

Incredibly, this allegory has yet to be substantially challenged. Few subjects have been as documented, dissected, and detailed as that of American religious diversity. Indian religions, however, have been left to specialized works, themselves trapped in an unsatisfying schema: "precontact" religion construed in static, totalizing terms, dynamism the sole property of a Christian juggernaut that radically alters when it does not eliminate its opponent.[5] When Indian religions appear in broader contexts, they are reduced to curiosities or afterthoughts: lumped together, confined to an initial chapter, referred to only in light of missionizing, these religions, as Joel Martin argues, are removed from "*creative contact with history.*"[6] On the rare occasion that a study suggests a more complex interaction, the suggestion is made to be disproved. Thus Sam Gill's *Mother Earth* (1987), which concludes that the Earth Mother was the brainchild of hack journalists, supports the idea that Indian religions were mercifully trivial to the national spirit.[7] So pervasive is this model that it affects even scholars sensitive to the intercultural; thus John Webster Grant, though he theorizes that "Christianity has not really taken root in [a native] community until it has fused with its culture sufficiently to make possible its appropriation in distinctively indigenous ways," can neither perceive mutual interaction nor conceive it without the terms his own prove inadequate: "If the measure of [missionary] success is that most Indians have become Christian, the measure of failure is that Christianity has not become Indian."[8]

To be sure, some critics have proposed more reciprocal models, notably in the work on the Jesuits of New France.[9] Persistent assumptions about Indians, Christians, and the cultures in which they met have, however, blocked sustained consideration of the varied, productive examples of religious contact from the English colonies and the United States. In this chapter, I will explore the merest fraction of these points of contact, and suggest some of the ways American literatures develop in conjunction with them. My hope is that this will suggest the need for an approach to spiritual/textual sites that *starts* from the premise that Indians and Christians shared and contested not only the material but the immaterial territory they traversed.

A Mixed Worship

Refuse the image of a monolithic Christianity whittling away a monolithic heathenism, and a new picture emerges, strange yet certain: encounter affected every believer in America. Beginning in the years of first contact, Christian explorers and divines catalogued what they understood Indian religions to be. With the racial diversification of Christian assemblies, a process always halting and never free of prejudice but picking up pace during eighteenth-century seasons of awakening, Native Americans gained positions not only to reflect on Christian interpretations but to practice, preach, and promulgate their own. That the Indians' heightened presence reflected structural changes in Christian faiths—the spread of populist denominations that empowered the outcast with their emphasis on mercy over judgment and spontaneity over scripture; the doctrinal controversies over such tenets as baptism, Christ's divinity, and innate depravity that elevated private conscience over ministerial or communal decree; the blurring of the God *of* Nature with the God *in* Nature that made the divine message more capacious, polymorphous, and accessible[10]—does not preclude the Indians' role in this greater expansiveness; on the contrary, it means that America's spiritualities were receptive to questioning and questing, change and interchange. Couple this with the yet more intimate varieties of religious encounter that had been from the start—ecstatic captivities such as Mary Rowlandson's, ecclesiastical apprenticeships such as Mohegan minister Samson Occom's tutelage under Eleazar Wheelock, partnered publications such as the catechisms, hymn books, and Bibles of John Eliot and his translators—and what amazes is not that osmosis should have followed from (or initiated) these points of contact but that so little should have been admitted then or now.

That this is so can, of course, be attributed to the power of conversionism to obscure, throttle, and exile cultural, and particularly spiritual, interaction. In the seventeenth century, Increase Mather commended Eliot for heading off his converts' tendency toward a "blended, mixed worship"; in the nineteenth, when John Greenleaf Whittier took advantage of liberalizing trends in New England theology to suggest that his ancestors' beliefs had "been modified, and if we may so speak, *acclimated*, by commingling with those of [America's] original inhabitants," Nathaniel Hawthorne was ready for him: "The forest-life of the first settlers, and their intercourse with the Indians, have really engrafted nothing upon the mythology which they brought with them from England—at least," he hedged, "we know of nothing."[11] Religious mingling threatens the very core of conversionism; it is the specter to be exorcized or, at least, the spoof to be exposed.

Conversionism, moreover, operated not only on religious interchange but on Indian religions. Most often reported by missionaries—some, like Roger Williams, reluctant to witness "Sathans Inventions and Worships" for fear of contamination—or by their proselytes—who, operating under taboos both internal and external, avoid dwelling on the "Heathenish Ways, Customs & Religion" they have renounced—Indian religions are known in written form principally through people ill-equipped to understand them, and strongly invested not only in denying but in dethroning them. (Nor, it seems likely, were Christians solely responsible for misconception; those less scrupulous than Williams reported that Indians, too, were guarded about sacred matters: "To pretend to give a true Description" of Tuscarora belief, John Lawson wrote, "is impossible; for there are a great many of their Absurdities, which, for some Reason, they reserve as a Secret amongst themselves . . . [and] never acquaint any Christian with the Knowledge thereof, let Writers pretend what they will.")[12] Then, too, conversionism did not exist solely at the level of the word. By the time they were taken down—recorded—Indian religions had been, in large measure, taken down, subjected to the material arm of conversionism: physical displacement, the erosion of networks of education and indoctrination, and the onslaught of Christian proselytizing itself. As such, even if Christian reporters had not been inclined to view other religions in terms of their own, postcontact Indian religions may in fact have resembled their own. Numerous critics, for example, have argued that the very constructs revivalist prophets used to combat Christianity—acts of atonement and redemption, works of written or iconographic scriptures, claims of religious exceptionalism—were in large part adopted from Christianity.[13] In sum, considering the many and severe inequalities between Indian and Christian religions—inequalities in practice, prescription, and publication—one must take care not to call religious interaction what may be pure appropriation.

As always, however, if one must be wary of conversionism, one must be equally vigilant not to reproduce it. For the preceding cautions, however valid, are at the same time consonant with conversionist discourse: the belief that Indian religions are "un-Indian" if they deviate from a precontact ideal; the view that only radical, visible evidences—say, liturgical innovations that can be flagged as "Indian"—count as interaction or syncretism; and most broadly, the position that in the struggle of Indian and Christian religions, only the latter were free to act, and to act with such impunity that Indian religions might just as well have been no more than Christianity's function or projection. If, then, it is imperative not to slight the textual—and material—violence of religious encounter, it is vital to recognize, as James Ronda writes, that to represent encounter as "a one-sided struggle between ossified Indian traditions and a vital European Christianity" is to revive the image by which violence was effected (and effaced).[14]

I would argue, then, that it is only by placing religions in their intercultural contexts that one can both compass and refute this violence. For there is evidence that neither Indians nor Christians experienced (however they might represent) religious contact as a unidirectional replacement; that diverse peoples—both curiously and combatively, and with both outsiders' and insiders' eyes—tested, interpreted, and (re)defined the beliefs of their others. Thus, for instance, the questions from unconverted Indians that Eliot placed in his texts, ranging from the personal—"*Can we see*

God?"—to the doctrinal—*"Doth God know who shall repent, and beleeve, and who not?"*—suggest a process of native readings of Puritan Christianity, some of them, perhaps, initiating a reciprocal process: "There have been many difficult questions propounded by them," Thomas Shepard writes, "which we have been unwilling to engage ourselves in any answer unto, until we have the concurrence of others with us." Converts, too, are quoted as experimenting with Christian beliefs and practices—*"turning doctrins into their own experience,"* as Eliot put it—as in the following fast-day exhortation translated by Eliot: "If any of you bury a child or a friend, then you will mourn, and fast too, for if we offer you meat, you will refuse it, yea you cannot eat, because your heart is so full of sorrow. . . . Now this day is a day of mourning, and what doe we mourn for? not for a child or a friend, but a greater matter; we must mourn for our sins."[15] In some respects, Eliot and his colleagues seem to have fostered such synthetic moments. For all their disdain for a Jesuitical "blended, mixed worship," their attempts to find terms with which to communicate recondite matters led them, as John Wilson wrote, to metaphor: "Wee studied to give as familiar an answer as wee could, and therefore in this as in all other our answers, we endeavoured to speake nothing without clearing of it up by some familiar similitude." Due, however, to its estranging function, similitude could muddy rather than clear; for example, Eliot's fellow missionary, Thomas Mayhew, tells of being asked, "if a Pawwaw had his Imps gone from him, what he should have instead of them to preserve him," and of answering, "if he did beleeve in Christ Jesus, he should have the Spirit of Christ dwelling in him, which is a good and a strong spirit." The impact such trade-offs had on the Indians' Christianity, much less the Puritans', is virtually impossible to gauge. For example, though it is intriguing in light of the powwow's story that Eliot's recordings of Indian speeches regularly include the honorific "Phisitian" for Christ—thus suggesting that the Indians had fused the heart of Christian mediation with the shamans Eliot's people considered the greatest threat to Christ's reign—there are too many layers of translation to pinpoint the contours, extent, or direction of religious interchange (even if to do so were one's goal). What one can say is that Eliot and company feared that their preaching was in danger of returning in forms at once like and unlike its source, that in Indian hands, as Henry Whitfield put it, the Gospel might be "made *another Gospel,* by strange Interpretations."[16]

And if this fear was justified, then the even more unsettling possibility existed for Eliot and his kindred that these "interpretations" might affect their own; that, as David Murray writes, encounter might "demand some converting, or at least adaptation, of the missionaries' own beliefs." Clearly, resistance to such a thought was so high that it could manifest itself, if at all, only in the guise of its opposite: in the Indians' apparent transformation to orthodoxy. Thus, for instance, Eliot and Mayhew's *Tears of Repentance* (1653) contains a description of Indian conversion accounts that seems, at first glance, at one with the licensed language of sacred self-expression: "Though [the Indians] spake in a language, of which many of us understood but little, yet we that were present that day, we saw them, and we heard them perform . . . with such grave and sober countenances, with such comely reverence in gesture, and their whol carriage, and with such plenty of tears trickling down the cheeks of some of them, as did argue to us that they spake with much good affection, and holy fear of God, and it much affected our hearts." Notably, however, because atypically, this passage figures the divine presence as physically rather than verbally evident; unable to understand what the Indians are saying, the audience is nonetheless captivated by what they are doing. Traditionally, Puritan evaluations of conversion narratives, like Puritan reading generally, emphasized verbal content, the words or Word. As Geoffrey Nuttall puts it, though the divine spark was the ultimate measure of legitimacy, "The Spirit speaks in, by, or through the Word. Dissociation of the two is condemned."[17] Shepard adheres to this distinction in his comments on an Indian's address: "Expressed in many words in the Indian language, and with strong actings with his eyes and hands, being interpreted afterwards to the English, [it] did much also affect all of them that were present at this lecture." The term "lecture," and Shepard's syntax, make clear that until gestural language is made literal, the discourse is all affect with no effect. The danger of religious expression divorced from verbal referents is, moreover, expressed by Eliot: "One of our *Indians* did (as we are wont) exercise, which [the English] took so much notice of, and were so farre affected with, as that it pleased the Governour to advice me to write the substance of that which he spake"; plainly troubled that effect has preceded substance, Eliot is at pains not only to translate the discourse but to point out its miscues: "[The Indian's] second Question was, What is this pearle of great price? now in answer to this Question he did not pitch it on Christ alone, and shew the worth and price of Christ: but he did pitch it on faith in Jesus Christ, and repentance for sinne, and stood upon the excellency and necessitie thereof. And this was the greatest defect I observed in his Exercise, which seeing I undertake to relate that which none but my selfe understood, I dare not but truely relate, because the Lord heard all, and I must give an account of this relation before him." In light of such tremulous injunctions against inspiration unchastened by explication, it is fascinating that the note conveyed so guardedly above—that of act supplementing or even overriding word, sound outstripping or even defying sense—is heard throughout Puritan missionary writings, as in these remarks by John Endecott: "I could hardly refraine teares for very joy to see [the Indians'] diligent attention to the word first taught by one of the *Indians*, who before his Exercise prayed for the manner devoutly and reverently (the matter I did not so well understand) but it was with such reverence, zeale, good affection, and distinct utterance, that I could not but admire it." Even more revealing is Wilson's account of a convert's sermon:

This man . . . did begin with prayer very solemnely, standing up for some halfe quarter of an houre, then sitting downe spake unto them of the two Parables, concerning the Feild wherein the treasure hid, and the wise Marchant selling all for the pearle; wee understood him not (save Mr *Eliot*) excepting now and then a word or two, he discoursed to them some three quarters of an houre at the least, with great devotion, gravitie, decency, readines and affection, and gestures very becomming . . . and the rest of the *Indians*; diverse old men and women, and the younger did joyne and attend with much Reverence, as if much affected therewith; then he ended with prayer as he beganne. Then Mr *Eliot* prayed and preached in the *Indian* Language for some houre more, about coming to Christ, and bearing his yoake.[18]

After the Indian's spirited, though to the writer impenetrable, performance, Eliot's tidy, polite discourse appears flat: text unequal to speech. The Indians, according to Whitfield, found Puritan religion alienating precisely because of its obsessive verbalism: they "strongly stood for their own meetings, wayes and customes, being in their account more profitable then ours, wherein they meet with nothing but talking and praying."[19] I do not want to draw an absolute distinction here; I do not presume to know the shape of religious performance for seventeenth-century Algonquian Indians, and I do not wish to rehash the dated image of Puritanism as a purely scriptural, bloodless creed. At the same time, however, I want to suggest that Indians may not have merely benefitted from the post-Calvinist shift toward emotive/participatory religions, but may have played a role in calling them into being.

There are, at that, a variety of currents leading from early Indian-Christian encounters to the religious diversity of the eighteenth and nineteenth centuries. A particularly strong current, indeed, involves the very issue of diversity, the flexibility and forbearance that were proclaimed, if not always pursued, by a host of developing religions. Beginning in Eliot's time, Indians are quoted adopting positions of what might be called, if anachronistically, religious relativism, the opinion that disparate religions need not supplant, cancel, or subsume their others; sometimes in the context of missionizing, sometimes in exchanges between Indian and Christian partisans, and sometimes in overt critiques of Christianity (sometimes, as Red Jacket's speech suggests, in all three), Indians emerge as both adamant about their own faiths and clement toward the faiths of others. Roger Williams, for example, reports that the Narragansetts "have a modest Religious perswasion not to disturb any man, either themselves *English*, *Dutch*, or any in their Conscience, and worship, and therefore say: Aquiewopwaúwash, Aquiewopwaúwock. *Peace, hold your peace.*" Eliot, meanwhile, reconstructs the voice of a powwow, who insists, "we have Gods also, and more than [the English]. . . . Let us alone, that we may be quiet in the ways which we like and love, as we let you alone in your changes and new ways." Later, as missionary efforts and the related colonialist complex—expansion, the entrenchment of the market, and other threats to Indian self-determination—intensify, religious confrontations escalate to what Ronda terms "genuine theological debates"—or, perhaps, debates about whether any theology can be the genuine one.[20] Such debates were recorded with particular frequency in writings on the eighteenth-century revivalist movements among Indian peoples of the middle states and Midwest.[21] Thus missionary John Sergeant reported receiving the following rebuff from the Shawnees: "The Indians have one way of honoring and pleasing [God], and the white people have another; both are acceptable to him. . . . Christianity need not be the bond of union between us." A more militant relativism was recorded among the Delawares by Moravian missionary David Zeisberger: "In their sermons [the prophets] endeavor to preach what the Indians would like to hear. They say, for example, that there are two ways to God, one for the whites and one for the Indians. Thus it is easy for them to rid themselves of the teaching of the whites." Zeisberger may, of course, have been right about the immediate end of prophetic revitalism or relativism. Yet there are cases in which the meeting of religious rivals generates an experience more strange, more equivocal, than baldly functionalist explanations can satisfy. Consider, for example, a moment in David Brainerd's diary in which his mission to the Delawares is stalled by a devout and zealous reformer, or rather restorer, of what he supposed was the ancient religion of the Indians. . . . I discoursed with him about Christianity, and some of my discourse he seemed to like; but some of it he disliked entirely. He told me that God had taught him his religion, and that he never would turn from it, but wanted to find some that would join heartily with him in it. . . . It was manifest he had a set of religious notions that he had looked into for himself, and not taken for granted upon bare tradition; and he relished or disrelished whatever was spoken of a religious nature, according as it either agreed or disagreed with his standard. . . . I must say, there was something in his temper and disposition that looked more like true religion than anything I ever observed amongst other heathens.

Unlike most of his encounters with Indian prophets—as when he writes of one, "I have often thought 'twould be a great favor to the design of gos-pellizing the Indians if God would take that wretch out of the world"—here, it seems, Brainerd has found a religious figure whose persuasions match his in intensity and intention. That he professes admiration for the man may, indeed, reflect his recognizing a fellow missionary. It is intriguing, too, that Brainerd, a staunch advocate of a fading Calvinist authority, redacts the prophet's beliefs in terms that would be embraced by both revivalist and rationalist religions into the next century. "I call that mind free," William Ellery Channing wrote in 1830, "which jealously guards its intellectual rights and powers, which calls no man master, which does not content itself with a passive or hereditary faith, which opens itself to light whencesoever it may come," and which "follow[s] fearlessly the best convictions of [its] own understandings."[22] Whether Brainerd meant to cast doubt on the prophet's teachings or whether he was himself affected by them cannot be ascertained.[23] Yet if, as Richard White argues, run-ins "between missionaries and Indians could yield converts, but they were also grist for the syncretic mill," it may be that these processes were more related, and reciprocal, than his phrasing allows—that converts might have arisen from these sites precisely because "conversion" consisted less in yielding than in meeting in a place where both participants could adapt the other's religion to their own, and their own to the other's.[24]

A further, and yet more fertile, example will help illustrate this. Scholars commonly cite New York state as a hotbed of the religious generativeness of the post-Revolutionary period. Parallel to the Christian awakenings that swept the region, however, was a development among the state's Iroquois populations that gained Euro-American attention both locally and nationally: the religion founded at the turn of the century by the Seneca prophet Handsome Lake.[25] From all written accounts—eyewitness

versions by missionaries, late nineteenth- and early twentieth-century renderings by Seneca ethnographers and practitioners—Handsome Lake
preached of an abiding difference between Indian and Christian deities,
rituals, and ways to salvation. And yet, an intriguing moment in one
version of his Code—in which Christ himself warns the prophet's people
"that they will become lost when they follow the ways of the white man"—
suggests that Christian concepts helped foster and uphold this division.[26]
Such separatist syncretism, according to missionary Asher Wright, was far
from a new thing in Seneca religion:

It is extremely difficult to separate the purely Indian portion, from that which was
introduced by the early Jesuit Missionaries. . . . Our present pagan population,
[who] regard the White man's religion as never intended for the Indians, still
notwithstanding retain the rosary in their belt of wampum, and the mass for the
dead under the name of the funeral feast; the notion of purgatory in the temporary
punishment in hell for various sorts of sins, and the Confessional, in their yearly
assemblies, where the penitent recites his sins, fingering over the strings of Wampum. . . . Some of them also wear little silver crosses among their ornaments,
probably handed down from their ancestors, though they appear to have lost all
religious regard for them. But there are certain little female images, very probably
the copies and successors of the images of the virgin put into their hands by the
Jesuits, which are regarded with great veneration, if not actually worshipped.[27]

If Wright's wish to separate the "purely" Indian "portion" from the whole
reveals his adherence to conversionism, his admission that this wish is unlikely to be fulfilled reveals conversionism's insufficiency: that the Senecas
might have assimilated yet repudiated Christian beliefs, symbols, and even
deities is emblematic of the complexity of intercultural religious encounter.

And in this light, what is fascinating about the Handsome Lake
revival are not only its various meanings for the Senecas, but the ways it
informs the Christian texts that seek to explain (and contain) it. The
earliest Euro-American commentators on the trances, visions, and utterances of Handsome Lake were the Quakers who had begun ministering to
the Senecas shortly before the revival took hold (a coincidence that helps
explain why the revival took hold). One of these men, Halliday Jackson,
recorded the originary moment in his journal: "Now it came to pass in
these days that one of the Heathen [Handsome Lake] . . . lay upon his bed
sick and he fell . . . into a trance from the seventh untill the third hour of
the day, and was [as] it were caught up into Heaven, and saw wonderful
things which are not meet to be uttered—Howbeit he saith, he talked with

Men like Angels, who spoke unto him of things that should come to pass hereafter." The biblical diction appears, on first reading, an unabashed perversion of whatever Handsome Lake might have experienced. Jackson, it seems, means to impose on his sojourn among the heathen a heavy-handed scriptural framework, complete with golden calf: "And moreover it came to pass on the Seventh Day of the Feast that they Slew a dog and hung him on the image which they had set up, and put a String of Beads about his neck, and adorned him with Ribbons and fine apparel, and looked thereon and worshiped."[28] By these terms, the purpose of Jackson's discourse would seem to be to align himself with the true prophets of old, and thus to discredit the false prophet who, he perhaps saw, had arisen to challenge him for Seneca souls.

Yet by these terms, it must be counted odd that, given an opportunity to denounce Handsome Lake—two opportunities: one during a meeting with Seneca chiefs, one in the recording of it—Jackson hedges: "The rulers and counsellors of the people collected together and the[y] called me to the Village of Cornplanter the Chief, and Connudiu [Handsome Lake] de-clared the Vision before the people and the interpretation thereof was made known unto me and I wrote all the saying thereof in a Book—And after I had written these things they said unto me 'Now declare unto us thy opinion of that which thou hast written and thy Judgement of the Vision whether it be true or whether it be false[']—and not being willing openly to offend them (for they had great confidence in the vision) I answered and said I could not tell." Jackson's reticence may be mere diplomacy. Like all missionaries, he and his brethren were on uneasy terms with at least a seg-ment of those among whom they lived, and in this case—Cornplanter was not only Handsome Lake's brother but a favorite of the federal govern-ment—he needed to be particularly discreet. Jackson, in fact, presents his moves as sheer pragmatism: "I answered them warily, and forasmuch as I could not say the Vision was false, neither could I tell them that it was true, but when I enquired more particularly concerning the matter & the man-ner of the Vision, and perceived that the sayings were calculated to turn them from the evil of their ways, I told them they would do well to observe the sayings." His words, however, suggest something more disorienting about the Handsome Lake religion, something that, in turn, suggests another reading of his words. Jackson's oracular discourse, it may be, was not solely a corruption of or an effort to one-up Handsome Lake's visions, but an attempt, unconscious or not, to find language adequate to his experience of Handsome Lake's: whether the prophet had indeed adopted

Christian notation—sevens, threes, heavenly hosts—or whether Jackson performed this for him, what the biblical diction registers is a Christian's sense that he is in the presence not of another chaotic, transitory heathen quirk but, however foreign to the only terms he knows for sacred expression, of another religion. In this light, Jackson's text seems to echo the relativist response that, he wrote elsewhere, the Senecas employed when questioned on sacred matters: "It is our way of worship, and, to us, solemn and serious, and not to be made light of, however different it may be from your mode." Intriguingly, Jackson produced a transcript of Handsome Lake's visions—the version, presumably, to which he refers when he reports writing "all the saying thereof in a Book"—that suggests exactly this possibility of equivalence in difference. Told in the first person, free of King James English, and unframed by editorial commentary, this version literalizes the missionary's statement that "I could not tell" the truth or falsehood of the prophet's visions, for the conceit is that the teller is Handsome Lake himself, whose notions as recorded here—however unlike Jackson's mode—are left as another gospel, neither a paltry imitation of nor a threat to the one true Gospel.[29]

Indeed, to a second of the Senecas' missionaries, Henry Simmons, the teachings of Handsome Lake were not merely comparable to but confirmatory of Gospel promises. For Simmons, the revival among the Senecas was precisely that, an outpouring of the Spirit "wherein I felt the love of God flowing powerfully amongst us." Even more so than Jackson, then, he was inclined to take a relativist stance: "They requested me to tell them whether I believed [the visions] to be true. I told them there had been Instances of the same kind amongst White people even of the Quakers, falling into a Trance, and saw both the good place, and bad place, and seen many Wonderful sights, which I did believe. And told them I could see no reason why it should not be the case with them, as we are all of one Flesh & Blood made by the great Spirit." A commitment to tolerance was, of course, a strong part of the Friends' self-image. Indeed, their initial approach to the Senecas—as opposed to that of, say, Jacob Cram—stressed, with whatever degree of sincerity, the multitude of roads to God: "We do not wish to force upon you any of our performances in religion. We think it right that every man should follow the teachings of the Good Spirit, in his own heart, which, if attended to, would always lead him in the right path."[30] Thus as always, I would not want to suggest that Simmons "learned" tolerance from the Senecas, or (worse) was "converted" to the Indians' systems of belief. Quite the contrary, I would argue that Simmons's encounters, like Jackson's, illustrate the ways in which religious experience and expression elude conversionism, the ways in which, like the Senecas, the Quakers were balanced between separatism and syncretism, conviction and contingency.

Fifty years after the birth of the Handsome Lake religion, a similar indeterminateness marks the prophet's appearance in a work dedicated, more so than to anything else, to determinateness: Lewis Henry Morgan's *League of the Iroquois* (1851). Morgan's views of Iroquois religion, like his views of their politics, economics, and prospects, fluctuate; at one moment the Iroquois are no better than any people "shut out from the light of revelation," at another they surpass the ancient philosophers in "those luminous principles which lie at the foundation of sound theology."[31] These shifts in interpretation, however, are reconciled by Morgan's insistence on his authority *as* interpreter; indeed, seeming contradictions add to his authority as the one capable of recognizing and reconciling them. What *League* represents is the conversionist dream of total control; Iroquois religion, like all aspects of Iroquois existence, will be comprehended entirely through the Christian text.

Yet it is precisely this regal capacity that the Handsome Lake religion dethrones. The book's chapter on the prophet resists reconciliation with earlier statements such as the following: "The worship of the Iroquois, it is believed, has undergone no important change for centuries. . . . It is still the same, in all essential particulars, that it was at the period of their discovery. Some slight additions, ascribable, doubtless, to missionary instructions, will be detected, but they are too inconsiderable to change the form, or disturb the harmony of the whole." What *League* makes clear is that Handsome Lake's religion is not only a change but a considerable one; that it is an outgrowth of Seneca worship and not of missionary instruction; that it is important both to the Senecas and to any (like Morgan) who would study them; and that it is, for these reasons, inconsistent with any attempt (like his) to grasp the "essential particulars" or harmonious "form" of Iroquois belief and practice. As such, his chapter on the prophet is notably unsure of itself. Beginning with a headnote on Handsome Lake's "pretended" revelation and moving on to the self-contradictory statement that "the motives by which Handsome Lake claimed to be actuated were entirely of a religious and benevolent character"—a sentence that could be read either as verifying ("the motives . . . were entirely benevolent") or casting doubt ("claimed to be . . . entirely benevolent")—the chapter concludes with a move so unlike Morgan that one's first impulse is to ignore or dismiss it. Giving credit in a footnote to his principal Seneca source, Ely S. Parker, Morgan steps aside for the remaining twenty-five pages of the chapter and makes way for Parker's translation of the prophet's successor, "an eminently pure and virtuous man," preaching the new word.[32] As in Jackson's translation of the prophet's visions, Morgan is not available to editorialize, moralize, compromise, or anesthetize; he does not return at chapter's end or, for that matter, return substantially to the subject of religion in the remainder of the book. The effect, then, is of the prophet's words concluding the discussion of Iroquois religion; the effect, strangely, is less of the white interpreter having co-opted the prophet to subserve his own agendas than of the prophet having gained a new forum for the dissemination of his beliefs. And these beliefs, while they may please in their emphasis on sobriety, pacifism, and obedience, also convey a more radical message of land rights, racial equality, and, most pervasively, solidarity in difference: "It has grieved [the Great Spirit] that [the Senecas] are now divided by separate interests, and are pursuing so many paths. It pleases him to see his people live together in harmony and quiet."[33] In Morgan's text, as in the Quakers', the new religion is a vital and valid force, a faith that cannot be fully captured by its Christian counterpart because, in the act, it pushes against the form that seeks to hold it.

It is of course a mistake to believe that, when Morgan or Jackson appear to step aside, the words that follow are reliably those of the Senecas. As with Eliot, Brainerd, and the other sources I have cited, one is not dealing directly with Indian voices; Morgan himself confesses to having undertaken "some slight alterations" to Parker's discourse—a boilerplate phrase that could mean anything from the addition of a word to the fabrication of the whole—while Jackson does not provide even that much. As always, then, one must be alert to the agendas within Christian accounts of Indian religion. Relativism, for example, could be taken, however oddly, as a plea for a unified missionizing front; few Christians— teethed on the lives of martyrs and plighted to the evangelization of the globe—could resist the thought that Indian religion was too wishy-washy to pronounce itself the one and only. Moreover, it is possible that Indian relativism itself reflects either the impact of, or the textual shaping of, Christian religions, for whose followers, particularly during the years on which I have focused, questions of religious tolerance were urgent and central. And if this is so, neither can one deny the impact of conversionism on these texts; their themes—incompatible deities, racially determined paths to salvation—are as amenable to intolerance as to the reverse. It is even possible that this discourse serves purposes wholly beyond the inter-cultural. Indian relativism may, as in James Seaver's account of Seneca religion, be a means of shaming Christians into a more complete unifor-mity: "They [the Senecas] say that Jesus Christ had nothing to do with them, and that the Christian religion was not designed for their benefit; but rather, should they embrace it, they are confident it would make them worse, and consequently do them an injury. They say, also, that the Great Good Spirit gave them their religion; and that it is better adapted to their circumstances, situation and habits, and to the promotion of their present comfort and ultimate happiness, than any system that ever has or can be devised. They, however, believe, that the Christian religion is better calcu-lated for the good of white people than theirs is; and wonder that those who have embraced it, do not attend more strictly to its precepts, and feel more engaged for its support and diffusion." Or relativism may, as in Sauk rebel Black Hawk's cheeky, pugnacious (and translated) creed—"I have no faith in [other] paths—but believe that every man must make his own path!"—be useful to Christians as they struggle, with increasing hardship precisely because of the spread of religious diversity, to balance individual faith with institutional structures or strictures. Lack of palpable motives may make a text particularly mouth-watering. Southern trader Alexander Long's 1725 essay on Cherokee religion, for instance, contains not only an account of Indian-Christian parley but a hint of Indian sarcasm: baiting a Cherokee holy man by drawing out his theology only to ask whether his people would be willing to renounce it, Long receives the answer, "Yes wee would Gladly for then wee should be as wise as yo[u] and Could doe and [make] All things as yo[u] doe . . . and peradventure the grate god of the Inglish would Cause us to turn white As Yo[u] are."[34] The fact, however, that Long sent his account to the London Society for the Propagation of the Gospel—and that sarcasm, as indirection, is complicated by a text itself indirect—limits one's enthusiasm for this seemingly artless work.

The most obvious point here is that one should not seek unmediated Indian religions in textual sources. The more essential point, however, is that mediated does not equal inauthentic. If textualized Indian religions are not "real"—any more, for that matter, than are textualized Christian religions—neither can "real" religions be separated from the often baffling intercultural processes from which they arise, and of which they are a part. What my examples suggest is that religions do not merely define them-selves (rhetorically) in relation to others but that, in material ways—fore-most through conflict yet also through assimilation, inversion, extension, and many other forms of interchange—religions, as they are believed, practiced, and lived, come into existence in contact with their others. In saying this, I must reiterate, there are a number of things I am *not* saying. I am not proposing to draw absolute conclusions about Indian (or Christian) religions; in support of these conclusions, to insist on the validity of textual evidence; or in pursuit of these conclusions, to minimize the violence of Indian-Christian religious encounter, violence that has yet to be adequately recognized or, more importantly, resolved. I do, however, want to argue against any notion of set, opposed religions, and to argue instead for a focus on the multiple, local, even individual ways in which various religions, as they were lived and as they emerge in writing, existed, and persisted, interculturally. A final, more extended example will thus deal less with churches and movements than with a single antebellum Indian Christian whose faith and works testify—speak to and speak for—this view of American religious encounter: William Apess, a writer and speaker who sought to grasp and to wield the forces of contact, conflict, and negotiation from which America's religious experience and expression were forged.

The Word Made Fresh

From Deism to Unitarianism to Transcendentalism and beyond, New England's legacy of religious dissent has been, and continues to be, seen as central to the revolutionizing of American Christianity. The provocative nature of the region's theology is evident not only in ministerial but in lay literature. As much as any of her clerical contemporaries (including her brother, Convers Francis, who authored, among other works, a laudatory biography of John Eliot), Lydia Maria Child devoted her life to attacking the exclusivity and bigotry of established Christianity. Convinced, as she wrote in *The Progress of Religious Ideas* (1855), that "the religious sentiment [is] always and everywhere sacred," she argued that "when *religion* can utter itself freely, worshippers sing a *harmony* of many different parts, and thus make music more pleasing to the ear of God, and more according to the pattern by which he created the universe." A decade later, she wrote that if Christianity was "better adapted for a universal religion than any other, is it not simply because Christianity is an accretion of all the antecedent religious aspirations of mankind? . . . All the world being represented in the system, it may well be better adapted for a universal religion than any of its component parts. But it is still receiving accretions from present inspirations, and so it will go on." Toward the close of her life, in an article on "The Intermingling of Religions," she anticipated an "Eclectic Church, which shall gather forms of holy aspiration from all ages and nations, and set them on high in their immortal beauty, with the sunlight of heaven to glorify them all."[35] To Child, Christianity rebukes its own insularity and intolerance; owing its existence and vitality to spiritual diversity, the Christian religion commits itself to the destruction of other religions at the peril of destroying itself.

Yet if Child's writings reflect the extent of antebellum New England's religious daring, they also reveal one of its most prominent drawbacks: the failure to see Indians in the tapestry of spiritual diversity. In her first work, *Hobomok* (1824), Child adopts the liberal position that "spiritual light, like that of the natural sun, shines from one source, and shines alike upon all; but it is reflected and absorbed in almost infinite variety," yet she refuses to allow her heroine to "mingle her prayers with a heathen"; in her final work, *Aspirations of the World* (1878), she gathers excerpts from world religions to "show that the primeval impulses of the human soul have been essentially the same everywhere" and "to enlarge and strengthen the bond of human brotherhood," but she offers nothing from the literature, widely available (if not reliable) by this time, on Amerindian religions.[36] Even more tellingly, though Child wrote *The First Settlers of New-England or, Conquest of the Pequods, Narragansetts and Pokanokets* (1829) to condemn the impending southeastern removals and to advocate an alternative policy of racial and religious integration, she denies such a possibility in her own region. The mingling of religions could have benefitted both parties—"the primitive simplicity, hospitality, and generosity of the Indians would gradually have improved and softened the stern and morose feelings" of the Puritans, while "the pure religion of Jesus would have strengthened and confirmed [the Indians'] innate convictions" of the deity—yet this was not to be. If the past has any meaning for the present, then, it lies not in the hope of religious interaction in New England, but in the chance that the nation might be roused to the religion of simplicity, hospitality, and generosity the Indians had practiced before they were, as Child writes of the Pequots, "utterly destroyed."[37]

Child's elegy for the Pequots was particularly ill-timed (or well-timed, depending); for it was in 1829 that William Apess, a Pequot convert to Methodism, published the autobiographical *A Son of the Forest*, the first of his several works to consider the ongoing interaction of Indian and Christian peoples and beliefs in his native region.[38] Three years Child's senior,

Apess was, like her, exposed to the various forms of dissenting Christianity that percolated within the young republic; like her, though he chose Methodist populism over Unitarian skepticism as his means to this end, he was drawn to the tenets of equal rights, antiauthoritarianism, and self-rule preached by the fringe religions that ultimately surpassed the reputable in numbers and sway. Yet though Apess supports Nathan Hatch's claim that "religious outsiders" had "little sense of their limitations" during this period—and though revival-inflected religions did, as William Simmons illustrates, attract Indians who perhaps found therein "some basis in experience for believing that the new world in the making would include them"—Apess's life and writings announce that limitations still pertained, not only to the Indians' entrance to Christianity but to the recognition of their equality, indeed their existence, once they were in.[39] Thus where Child speculates that Christianity draws strength from outside "accretions," Apess puts this to the test, offering his life as an example of the interanimation of religions in the individual and nation. As a self-consciously Indian voice operating within a religion that denied such voices, Apess proposes a faith multiple and inclusive, a Native American Christianity.

This proposal is all the more remarkable, and urgent, given his multiply disenfranchised status. The son of a Pequot (or perhaps African) woman and mixed-blood Pequot man, removed from a Pequot community that whites denied existed when, at age four, he was taken from his abusive maternal grandparents and placed in a succession of apprenticeships with white families, Apess seemed a marginal figure who, like Thoreau's basket-maker (an occupation Apess's family did, in fact, pursue), had lost the "former, proud, heroic spirit" of savage nobility and "shrunk into the tameness and torpor of reasoning brutism."[40] Apess himself, it seems, had internalized such images: refusing the term "Indian" as "a slur upon an oppressed and scattered nation" (10), he cannot adopt what was presumably the only alternative: "Christian." A "cast-off member of the tribe," so "weaned from the interests and affections of my brethren that a mere threat of being sent away among the Indians into the dreary woods had a much better effect in making me obedient to the commands of my superiors than any corporal punishment" (10), Apess feels himself "nothing more than a worm of the earth" (4).

Such self-portrayals were, of course, encouraged not only by evangelical Christianity but by Indian conversion: only by admitting the utter depravity of one's soul and, in the case of the Indians, one's people could one be reborn in Christian civilization. Yet it is by adopting (and adapting) the conversionist call that Apess molds an identity embracing, though in constantly evolving tension, his cultural and religious heritages. In his eighth year, Apess attends the services of a barnstorming sect he identifies only as "the Christians" (12). Roused by their emphasis on individual ability and responsibility, he begins to claim an active role in his spiritual well-being: "I was led to make many serious inquiries about the way of salvation" (12–13). At the same time, he gains confidence to critique the Presbyterian to whom he is indentured, Judge Hillhouse: "I did not believe or, rather, had no faith in his prayer, because it was the same thing from day to day, and I had heard it repeated so often that I knew it as well as he" (15). In similar fashion, Apess dismisses the Sunday observances of General Williams, his next master: "The general attended the Presbyterian church and was exact in having all his family with him in the house of God. . . . I observed and felt that their ways were not like the ways of the Christians. It appeared inconsistent to me for a minister to read his sermon—to turn over leaf after leaf, and at the conclusion say 'Amen,' seemed to me like an 'empty sound and a tinkling cymbal'" (17). These are, to be sure, conventional caricatures: an exact but lifeless church religion is opposed to, and by, a felt religion of private conscience. In Apess's hands, however, the individualism of the Christians not only mocks the rote teaching of Scripture but exposes scriptures of power as rote, not right: pairing the Presbyterians, whom he sums up in three figures of institutional authority—judge, general, minister—with those who "had possession of the red man's inheritance and had deprived me of liberty" (18), Apess argues that the fixed, unchanging creeds of the orthodox formalize, as it were, relations of power. As he writes in a later work, *The Experiences of Five Christian Indians of the Pequot Tribe* (1833), orthodox preaching is "a selection of fine sentences," "read off in an elegant style, which only seemed to please the ear and lull the people to sleep" (125). In the house of God, the Presbyterians—whose "fine sentences" and "elegant style" mirror and justify the privileges they enjoy—soothe their sense of entitlement, winking at the oppression that, asleep in sin, they are pleased to call righteousness.

Revivalism, then, helps Apess to overturn doctrines of dispossession, to imagine an identity not dictated by his oppressors. As such, the *"perfect freedom"* (21) of his conversion to Methodism registers at once on a religious scale (the soul's freedom from sin), a social scale (the servant's freedom from harsh masters), and a racial scale (the Indian's freedom from Euro-American might). Galvanized by the Methodists' egalitarian vision—"I felt convinced that Christ died for all mankind—that age, sect, color, country, or situation made no difference" (19)—Apess is emboldened to give voice to his experience: "I felt moved to rise and speak. I trembled at the thought; but believing it a duty required of me by my heavenly father, I could not disobey, and in rising to discharge this sacred obligation, I found all impediment of speech removed" (41). As in the writing of the autobiography, Apess turns himself into the text he reads, and thus refuses his position in Euro-American readings. He insists that God speaks through him, a member of a despised race, and that institutional sanction can only strangle his voice: "In former days holy men spoke as they were moved by the Holy Ghost. I think this is right and believe more in the validity of such a call than in all the calls that ever issued from any body of men united" (43). As in his thoughts on formalism, Apess invokes a key term of religious dissent— private judgment—not only to deride bureaucratized religion but to argue that the words and deeds of a national "body of men united" issue not from heavenly necessity but from earthly expediency.

Thus far, it is possible to read Apess as a mouthpiece for the Methodist party line; the connections he draws between religious and cultural oppression were implicit in their discourse. Yet for Apess, these connections ground a more revolutionary move, one meant to fuse traditions that dissenting, no less than orthodox, Christians saw as irreconcilable. Toward this end, it is intriguing that all of Apess's writings appeared after he was expelled from the Methodist church for exhorting without a license. Though on the one hand his works suggest that he was the most faithful of converts, duty-bound to turn private conscience against its spokespeople, on the other his belief that the Methodists refused "to hear the Indian preach" (44) may have led him to identify the voice they had stifled as an Indian one. Indeed, the word "voice" is critical to this identity. If the power of revivalism lay largely in its emphasis on the spoken word, which encouraged the unlettered to forego clerical exegesis and, more broadly, to revise readings that sanctified their subordination, in Apess's writings the language of revivalism moves him beyond revivalism, indeed beyond writing, toward a language of Indian oral belief and expression.

How much Apess knew of oral culture is uncertain. (He was, however, aware of it, for he quotes passages on Indian eloquence in the appendix to *A Son*.) To stress voice over text was risky: not only was literacy seen as one of the abiding differences between savage and civilized, but it could take on religious overtones as well, as in Thoreau's observation in *Walden* that one must be "born again" to grasp the written word. Even more tellingly, though the following passage from Child seems to liken Indian and

Christian religions, her textual image scotches that resemblance: "Voices from the world of spirits spoke into [the Indian's] heart, and stirred it with a troubled reverence, which he felt, but could not comprehend. To us, likewise, they are ever speaking through many-voiced Nature; the soul, in its quiet hour, listens intently to the friendly entreaty, and strives to guess its meaning. All round us, on hill and dale, the surging ocean and the evening cloud, they have spread open the illuminated copy of their scriptures—revealing all things, if we could but learn the language! . . . Should I have learned more of the spirit's life . . . the soul of Nature's child might have lisped, and stammered in broken sentences, but it would not have muttered through a mask." As in *Hobomok*, where Child calls Creation "God's library" and "the first Bible he ever wrote," this passage separates the merely inchoate veneration of the Indians from the mature, because literate/literary, reflections of the author; whatever her desire to contact "many-voiced Nature," voices emerge as gaps, "broken sentences," in the "scriptures" of Creation. Interestingly, the textual image appears even in passages attributed to Indian relativists. The Senecas, for instance, were quoted spurning Christian instruction by invoking the "Big Book" that God has opened "to all men," while missionary Samuel Kirkland reported one Indian's speech to his people: "This white man . . . brings with him the white peoples *Book*. . . . Brothers, you know this book was never made for *Indians*. Our great Superintendent Thaonghyawagon *ie Upholder of the Skies* gave us a *book*. He wrote it in our heads & in our minds & gave us rules about worshipping him."[41] Whether Indians had adopted this figure of speech (the book as divine revelation) or whether Christians put it in their mouths is unclear. What is clear is that figures of *speech* (orality) were viewed as another heathen trait sentenced to fall on the road to redemption. If, as Apess came to believe, dissenting Christians had overturned biblical hierarchies only to make of their own words a scripture equally compulsory, their negation of an Indian presence derived not just from the silencing of particular Indian speakers but from a model of faith and calling that denied Indian discourse altogether.

Apess himself would seem to fulfill this model: born again into literate Christianity, he should mark any traces of the oral as "transitory" and "brutish" relics (to invoke Thoreau again) he has left behind. What is striking about his works, however, is their refusal to separate oral/Indian from written/Christian—their refusal, in fact, to identify either mode absolutely with either people. Arnold Krupat has argued that "whatever [Apess] may or may not have known and remembered of aboriginal orality, his commitment to a Christian tradition of 'exhorting' and 'preaching' provides a continuity with Native modes of communication." It is perhaps better to say that for Apess, Christian exhorting and preaching are the means of reconstructing the native modes that Christians had pronounced incompatible with their own. It is, then, through the acts that define him as Christian that Apess asserts his difference from Christianity; as David Murray puts it, he refuses to "accept white assumptions, even while using the language in which they are encoded."[42] Apess's works can be seen, then, as efforts to enact and enunciate religious interconnections that, I have argued, existed but were resisted all along. Invoking Indian orality as a living mode within the Christianity that meant to snuff it out, he seeks to make obvious what most thought odious, the mingling of religions in the souls, and soul, of the nation.

In this light, if the places in which Apess juxtaposes voice and text accord with the revivalist hierarchy, at the same time they seek to revive an oral language that Christian texts denied. Let me consider an old passage in this new light: "It appeared inconsistent to me for a minister to read his sermon—to turn over leaf after leaf, and at the conclusion say 'Amen,' seemed to me like an 'empty sound and a tinkling cymbal.' I was not benefited by his reading. . . . I could plainly perceive the difference between the preachers I had formerly heard and the minister at whose church I attended. I thought, as near as I can remember, that the Christian depended on the Holy Spirit's influence entirely, while this minister depended as much upon his learning. I would not be understood as saying anything against knowledge; in its place it is good, and highly necessary to a faithful preacher of righteousness. What I object to is placing too much reliance in it, making a god of it, etc." (17). The concluding lines of this passage continue Apess's critique of how power is constructed, and may be restructured: the codified inequalities of the Bible are "learned," not ordained, and are susceptible of invalidation by the experiences to which individual speakers bear witness. Yet these lines suggest further that inequality is not merely sanctioned by the Good Book, but resides in the sanctioning of books: if Christians project their readings as divine necessities, this is because they have "made a god" of textuality. Apess might have known of the belief that Indians at first contact had "made a god" of books;[43] he seems, at least, to be arguing that Christians, convinced that they have God's ear, are only reading their own releases. Apess is faithful to dissenting discourse by revealing the narrowness of any one reading; yet by using such discourse to reclaim an unread, oral alternative, he rebukes dissenting Christianity's own narrowness while illustrating how religions emerge in relation to one another.

In a variety of ways, moreover, Apess's own discourse enacts this interplay. To begin with, his works abound in figures of speech; in the quotidian as in the sacred world, the voice carries extraordinary and various power. For example, he writes: "Mrs. Furman," wife of his first master, "gave me a great deal of wholesome advice. This had a much better effect than forty floggings—it sunk so deep into my mind that the impression can never be effaced" (11). Conversely, words can be misused for ill: "The great fear I entertained of my brethren was occasioned by the many stories I had heard of their cruelty toward the whites. . . . If the whites had told me how cruel they had been to the 'poor Indian,' I should have apprehended as much harm from them" (11). In one sense, such examples simply support Apess's project of de-authorizing stereotypes: in his environmentalist psychology, people are what they are told. But at the same time, he invests the spoken word with a potency and ineffaceability equal to that generally reserved for print. "I always disliked to hear anyone swear," he explains, "but one day when I was angry I swore a horrid oath, and the very instant that it passed my lips my heart beat like the pendulum of a clock, my conscience roared despair and horror like thunder, and I thought I was going to be damned right off. I gave utterance to the word without thinking what I was doing; it could not be recalled, and afterward I thought I would not have said it for all the world. This was the *first* and the *last* time that I ever used so awful an expression, and I thought this of itself sufficient to sink my soul to the shades of everlasting night" (39). If Apess's dread appears excessive, it is in keeping both with his belief in one's ability to pronounce one's own fate and with his claim for the "sufficiency" of the oral. Exposing the prejudices of the Word while locating power in a modality Christian texts ignore, dismiss, or disfigure, Apess denies not only the preeminence of those texts' readings but the absoluteness of textuality itself.

Even more significantly, Apess not only exalts orality but exercises it, introducing into the Christian text that which Christians felt was foreign to the text. This is best apprehended from the whole of his work; as a point of departure, I select a passage from *An Indian's Looking-Glass for the White Man*, his 1833 manifesto on racism, with oral elements emphasized: "*I would ask* if there cannot be as good feelings and principles under a red skin as there can be under a white. *And let me ask*: Is it not on the account of a bad principle that we who are red children have had to suffer so much as we have? *And let me ask*: Did not this bad principle proceed from the whites or their forefathers? . . . I presume *this kind of talk* will seem surprising and horrible. . . . *And I can tell you* that I am satisfied with the manner of my creation, fully—whether others are or not" (156, 157). Impressive as this rhetoric is, there is perhaps nothing in its style to distinguish it from that of any orator. To say this is, however, to miss how the oratorical style is Apess's vehicle for asserting an Indian identity: appended to *The Experiences of Five Christian Indians*, the *Looking-Glass* proclaims, through the orality he terms his "proper element" (41), an Indian experience within a Christian nation that believed a red skin to be incommensurable with a state of grace. As such, just as Apess's writings insist on the oral legacy Christianity refuses to read, so do they use that legacy to make visible the presence of Indian Christians—to make visible, in fact, the presence of an Indian Christianity.

The body of the *Experiences* emphasizes this. In this text, Apess, almost certainly playing off the works of Eliot, collects the conversion-narratives of Pequot Christians, offering them "in [their] own language; it is broken, but you can understand it" (151). For writers like Child, such "broken" sentences were incomprehensible by and inadmissible to Christianity; for Apess, this "broken" language constitutes the substance of Christianity. Each convert tells his or her sorrows and speaks his or her salvation, while the author gathers these testaments to build a sacred society that exists in the text through the medium of speech, just as native voices survive in Christianity though read out by Christian texts. And just as Apess performs this act for his text, a similar act is performed in his text. As he says of his Aunt Sally George, who "could not read" but "could almost preach" (40): "Her organic power of communication, when tuned with heavenly zeal and burnt with heavenly love, was delightful, charming, and eloquent. I never knew her to speak unless the congregation was watered by an overwhelming flood of tears. She feared not to warn sinners to repentance while she lived. She was no sectarian; she would go among all orders of Christians and worship God with them, and was entirely free so to do. And I believe that she felt as much for her white neighbors as for her own kindred in the flesh" (150). Unlike those who oppose text to voice, white to Indian, Sally George mates talk with book to heal people of all races harmed by scriptures of oppression. An Indian minister preaching an oral bible, she illustrates how, as in Apess's texts, different traditions may infuse one another to the greater strength of all.

It appears, however, that Apess was unable to sustain his aunt's faith. Further experiences—notably with the Mashpee Indians' revolt against their reservation overseers—may have convinced him that directly political action was the only route to liberty. Thus in his last work, *Eulogy on King Philip* (1836), Apess damns Christian discourse altogether: "How have [the Indians] been destroyed? Is it by fair means? No. How then? By hypocritical proceedings, by being duped and flattered; flattered by informing the Indians that their God was a going to speak to them, and then place them before the cannon's mouth" (285). Against such murderous vocalizations he sets Philip, "the greatest man that ever lived upon the American shores" (290); and it is, significantly, Philip's oratory he praises: "It does appear that every Indian heart had been lighted up at the council fires, at Philip's speech, and that the forest was literally alive with this injured race" (296). A native preacher, exhorting Indian salvation—but not through the gospel—Philip rallies those of his injured race who remain; just as his words roused his people to resist Christian power, so does the recovery of those words resist the oblivion into which Christian texts have cast his call to arms. In Philip, Apess summons an ancestral voice (he does, in fact, claim descent from "the royal family of Philip" in *A Son* [3]) to vindicate an increasingly militant identity, one based in his final years more on revolution than reconciliation.

Yet if Apess finally takes a separatist stand, his writings as a whole reject the notion that any tradition can be fully separated from its others. Thus where Krupat, unable to assign a "Pequot sense" to Apess's works, argues that he fashions himself "the licensed speaker of a dominant voice that desires no supplementation by other voices," I would argue that it is through the dominant voice that the Pequot sense emerges. Conversely, where Murray, critiquing Krupat's handling (one that Krupat himself interrogates elsewhere), finds Apess's voice patently ironic—"it is precisely the ruling out of bounds by [Apess] of a natural or unmediated Indianness as a resource to fall back upon which is the most interesting thing in his writing"—I would argue that this is to overlook how Apess's creation of Indianness within the religion that had supposedly done away with Indians supports his case against that religion. As Barry O'Connell sums up, Apess "employed his Christian identity so as to assert, more forcibly and coherently, his identity as a Native American" (xlvii). Refusing either to submerge the Indian fully in the Christian or to differentiate the Indian fully from the Christian, Apess reveals the Indian and the Christian to coexist with, in, and through one another.[44]

As a final illustration of this, I would like to consider a particularly suggestive moment in which Apess alludes to the intersection of Christian and Indian beliefs. At the age of nineteen or twenty, during the process of advances and backslidings on the road to conviction, Apess "went among my tribe at Groton," where his aunt held prayer meetings. He reports: "These seasons were glorious. We observed particular forms, although we knew nothing about the dead languages, except that the knowledge thereof was not necessary for us to serve God. We had no house of divine worship, and believing 'that the groves were God's first temples,' thither we would repair when the weather permitted" (40). In this muted, oddly abstract idyll, Apess stages a stale tableau—Indians worshiping in the woods—to further his exploration of spiritual freedom. The features of this worship, however, elude the reader. Apess does not list the affiliations of his wilderness congregants, does not say what their "particular forms" were, does not state—goes out of his way not to state by quoting Bryant's "Forest Hymn"— whether, as he wavered on the verge of Christian conversion, he had met with other forms of spirituality, and whether his soul was shaped by them. Perhaps Apess, like Child, had determined that Indian voices could not be articulated. Yet his portrait is more complex than this. An Indian restored to a tribe Christians deemed utterly destroyed, using Christianity's image of a silenced Indian religion—using, moreover, the text of a Christian poet—to make that silence speak, Apess occupies here, as throughout, the nebulous region where Indian religion emerges equivocally from Christian rhetoric, and Christianity emerges enigmatically through Indian faith. With his own life a prominent and painful example, Apess envisioned an American religion that in his time had virtually no advocates, and since then has had all too few: a religion at once Indian and Christian, impossible without and inseparable from their mutual experience.

Interlude

Every image of the past that is not recognized by the present as one of its own concerns threatens to disappear irretrievably.

—Walter Benjamin, "Theses on the Philosophy of History"

"What do our anniversaries commemorate but white men's exploits?" Thoreau asked rhetorically in his journal. "For Indian deeds there must be an Indian memory—the white man will remember his own only." Whether he was troubled by this or not, Thoreau was certain that Indian history neither could nor would have a place in American history. "Our Indian races having reared no monuments," Hawthorne mused similarly, "when they have disappeared from the earth, their history will appear a fable, and they misty phantoms."[1] Unrecorded by whites and unrecordable by Indians, their deeds, their very existence, would fade—so the story went—from history to myth.

However just this story may be, it underscores a critical problem in the construction and reconstruction of American interculturalism. I have examined some of the ways in which the presence of Indians informs American texts; I have explored some of the contexts of encounter in which American literature takes form. Yet as I indicated at the outset, in doing so I have limited myself largely to texts that deny the Indian presence that I have claimed is central to them. An intercultural criticism must thus confront not only attempts to erase Indians from the historical record, but the lopsidedness of the record itself. An intercultural criticism must interrogate, along with the Indians' enforced absence from America's stories, the enforced absence of Indian stories from America.

To put it this way, of course, is to suggest that the absence of Indian stories has a story behind it as well. The question, accordingly, becomes not the veracity of statements such as Hawthorne's and Thoreau's but the conditions for them, conditions under which a story called history is enshrined while other stories are dismissed, or not heard at all. For as Michel de Certeau suggests, these processes are linked; it is by reallocating what they refuse to hear in accordance with what they desire to hear that histories constitute themselves yet portray themselves as unconstituted: "The other is the phantasm of historiography, the object that it seeks, honors, and buries. . . . A structure belonging to modern Western culture can doubtless be seen in this historiography: *intelligibility is established through a relation with the other*; it moves (or 'progresses') by changing what it makes of its 'other'. . . . [Thus] unfolds a problematic form basing its mastery of expression upon what the other keeps silent."[2] A licensed history, de Certeau argues, makes itself present, in both senses, by making something else past/absent. What this suggests for the study of Indian-white encounter is that it is through the active absence of certain stories that Euro-American history asserts itself: that the white man wills to remember his own deeds only by *making* Indian story appear a fable. And it is this, I believe, that accounts for the Indians' invisibility in the annals of encounter: constructed as tellers of myths and as peoples of myth, they are denied a place in the national story and a voice in recounting it.

Such a statement might seem odd, given prevailing views of myth. According to these views, myth is in essence all that history is not: fixed, compulsive, biased, illusory, as opposed to fluid, active, objective, real. As Richard Slotkin explains, myths "always represent the ideology of the moment as if it were the embodiment of divine or natural law. . . . Myth is 'fictional' in a double sense: It is an artifact of human intelligence and productive labor (although it may be made to appear as a 'fact of nature'); and it is a 'falsification' of experience—a partial representation masquerading as the whole truth." Roland Barthes, in a famous passage, defines myth precisely as history's antithesis: "Myth is constituted by the loss of the historical quality of things: in it, things lose the memory that they once were made." If, then, myth is at once an evasion and a violation of history, "the antidote," in Slotkin's words, lies in "rehistoricizing the myth," exposing it to, and through, the history it denies.[3]

Scholars have specified any number of features that both follow from and prove this opposition: myth is circular, history linear; myth is magical, history logical, and so on.[4] Yet however robust the opposition (or any of its features) appears, the fact that it has come to seem "too obvious to require definition"—has come to be founded on the very thing that presumably makes myth inferior to history, the representation of ideology as law— suggests its limitations. Myth itself, that is, has been "mythicized"; it has been transformed into a capacious, impenetrable blank against which any putatively historical analysis can be set.[5] In his study of theories of myth,

Ivan Strenski asks "why we *would* want to call something—if anything at all—a 'myth'"; the answer, I believe, is that doing so makes it possible to write myth and its peoples out of history.[6]

As an alternative, I propose that both myth and history be viewed as *stories*[7]—"stories of power," in Paula Gunn Allen's usefully ambiguous phrase—that contain, convey, and compel the temporal paradigms, explanatory and educative ideals, and expressive or artistic traditions of a people.[8] To use the word "story" is not to connote falsehood; it is to argue that all stories can be seen as true or false depending upon the systems in which they are placed. Nor do I mean to suggest that myth and history are identical; if both are stories, they could be stories "rooted," as Raymond DeMallie suggests, "in radically different epistemologies."[9] The purpose of viewing myth and history as stories is neither to censure nor to mystify; rather, it is to recognize both as forms of human creativity, and thereby (to recur to Barthes' imperative) to retain the memory that things were made. This is important, I feel, not only because it questions a naive faith in narrative objectivity or universality, but because it calls attention to the involvement of story itself in encounter: "myth" and "history," in this view, are not essential terms but operators within specific contexts of interculturalism. And if this is so, then to debate the relative value of myth and history is to disguise their *relation*, the fact that the coexistence and interaction of stories make possible, make visible, make up (constitute and fabricate) America.

This interlude, then, marks a broadening of concerns. The first chapter introduced the discourse of interculturalism; the next two explored discourse in action and reflection. The remaining chapters will investigate not only the relationships between encounter and stories *in* America but the relationships between encounter and stories *of* America—as physical place, resource, national idea, ground of identity, and source or object of narrative art. Yet if imagining America as a site and product of multiple stories requires a reconsideration of the stories that have (historically) been endorsed as history, there are limitations to this project. Most obviously, though I question the truth or adequacy of history, I am indebted to the historical systems and assumptions I question. In an attempt to break free from the limits of Western historiography, critics have applied the lessons of ethnohistory to history itself, seeking materials, methods, and models that reflect the philosophies as well as presence of Indians. The words of one scholar may stand as the motto of this "New Indian History" and as a rebuke of my study: "It is not enough to include native-white encounters in the revision of American history and culture or to question the monolith (the truth) of History. And it is not enough to find resistance and revision within narratives of colonial encounters. If we are truly to decolonize the representation of indigenous peoples and not simply locate them in positions of reaction to Western history, then we must allow ourselves to discover their actual and original contributions to the telling of history."[10] This point cannot be overstated: reliance on a certain way of "doing" story is at best an implied violence toward those who "do" story in other ways. I cannot pretend that I have avoided this violence. Yet at the same time, I must make clear that I am not concerned with restoring Indian stories to "our" history, for to do so—to recover Indian "contributions" that have been "left out of" a national narrative—would be to approve the notion that history *is* a unified, unitary object out of which something can be left. What I intend, rather, is to explore how the coexistence, conflict, and negotiation of American stories—Indian and white—complicate the notion of story (and America) as fixed, original, single, the inalienable property of any one people. I intend, in other words, to pursue the workings of interculturalism into the stories of America, to suggest that, just as the interaction of diverse cultures questions the idea *of* opposing cultures, so does the interaction of diverse cultural stories question the notion that one story can be separated from a complex field.

To say this, it should be clear, is not to insist that *all* stories are *wholly* products of encounter. It is, however, to say that stories usually divorced from encounter—especially "history" and "myth"—*are* involved in, even if they are not entirely created by, encounter; that the form, features, and functions of such stories are unimaginable without encounter; and that absolute claims for such stories' autonomy from encounter are precisely the means by which certain stories have been spurned as myth, others extolled as history. The story of America, I maintain, is in large part the story of stories contesting, reinterpreting, and interpenetrating one another. And believing this, I am interested, finally, in how the Indian stories without which America could not have existed should have become invisible in the story of America's literature.

* * *

To speak of "literature," however, is to suggest a provisional reason for the invisibility of Indian stories: the Indians' "telling of history" was (and is) primarily told, not written. As such, not only have Indian stories in writing been transmitted mainly by whites, but the oral nature of much Indian narrative has been taken to explain both the Indians' irrelevance to history—for what could illiterates offer?—and their inability to remember and record it. In 1915, anthropologist Robert Lowie summed up the previous century's attitude: "I cannot attach to oral traditions any historical value whatsoever under any conditions whatsoever."[11] Many scholars have reconsidered this assessment; while some have claimed that oral stories register real events,[12] others have urged, in Bernard Cohn's words, that such stories be read not to "sift historical fact from mythical fancy, but to try to grasp the meanings of the forms and contexts of these texts in their own cultural terms." Each approach, however, poses a problem: while the former resumes the search for the one true story (a story, moreover, whose realness is defined in Euro-American terms), the latter may shade into a dismissal of Indian stories, as when one scholar proposes that we study Hopi narrative because "we want to understand history in Hopi terms as well as in those of the objective world." Textual critics have had similar difficulties opening literary analysis to oral narratives (or the reverse): some study Native American, primarily oral, stories, some study Euro-American, primarily written, stories, some study both; but the relationships between the two have just begun to be broached. Thus, though critics have called for a "comparative studies" between "the narrative and poetic art" of Indians and whites, the conceptual difficulties such an undertaking implies cannot be dismissed.[13]

These difficulties are compounded by the fact that most Indian stories are not simply spoken, but performed: as Karl Kroeber explains, the oral story "never exists as text, only as act." The complexity of such acts has been of concern to folklorists: performance, Elizabeth Fine notes, may involve visual, aural, verbal, kinesic, artifactual (material), proxemic (spatial), tactile and even olfactory channels, not to mention the contextual factors that surround it. Nor are these features neatly separable, or even specifiable. As Robert Georges puts it, to "isolate any one aspect of a storytelling event . . . and to disregard or consider as subordinate or incidental all other aspects of a storytelling event is to give that one aspect an independence and a primacy it simply does not have."[14] Yet if there is broad consensus that these polyform narratives must be understood and recorded holistically, there is little consensus on how to do so, much less on how to treat oral performances in relation to the written narratives with which they coexisted.

Nor, to add a final complication, do such relationships emerge clearly

from the period of this study. "Performance originals," as Richard Schechner points out, "disappear as fast as they are made"; and if this is true of
all performance, those who took down Indian performances prior to the
twentieth century failed to consider, much less treat, any of the originals'
components adequately.[15] To begin with, the structure of the languages
was almost invariably ignored; though studies of Indian tongues commenced in the seventeenth century, Europeans were seldom interested in
the languages as such. For some, such as John Eliot, facility in Indian
speech was a means to converting Indian speakers; for others, including
Thomas Jefferson, language mapped Indian origins, migrations, and gene-
alogies, subjects of importance both to natural philosophy and to national
policy.[16] None of these linguists, however, supposed that language might
be integral to narrative; though they sometimes provided transliterations,
glossaries, or parallel texts, their belief that Indian languages were "clumsy
mechanism[s]," "defective" in form and "destitute" of refinement, left little
reason to investigate their workings. Modern ethnolinguists, however, argue that "interpretation of myth must be grounded in philology"; that
linguistic and paralinguistic features are central to meaning in oral narrative. Though it is an exaggeration to claim that philology is *the* key to
Indian story, one can agree with Judith Berman that "the meaning of a
myth," as in any story, "lies within the narrator's use of language, not
outside it."[17]

At the same time, most recorded Indian stories fail to satisfy the
criterion *of* story. To be sure, abundant narratives exist, either sprinkled
through travel and missionary writings or amassed in scientific treatises,
but disregard for source is evident throughout. As William Clements
remarks, white translators, believing that they must "enhance their texts'
literary features," produced texts "whose Native qualities were usually obscured beneath a heavy veil of Euroamerican accretions"; and while it is
risky—given the uncertainty of what the original texts were, the fact that
the idea of an "original" may itself be a Euro-American accretion, and the
complexity of encounter—to dismiss translations summarily, neither can
one overlook, even if one cannot specify, the lapses of comprehension, editorial decisions and excisions, and intentional misrepresentations brought
to the material.[18]

Finally, the treatment of contextual factors, though somewhat fuller
than the treatment of language and story, is perhaps even more dispiriting,
considering how far-reaching such factors are. Context embraces everything from the setting in which a tale is performed to the state of its people;

and while written accounts often sketch such details in, there is seldom any effort to relate the linguistic content of the performance—much less any other feature—to context. Most often, Indian stories serve as sidelights, "local color," or breathing places in narratives preoccupied with other matters; in the case of compilations specifically dedicated to the study of Indian myth, as we will see, the suppression of context is a distinguishing trait of, and a central clue to the function of, such works. Yet performance scholars have stressed the embeddedness of oral art in a nonreplicable milieu; as Georges puts it, "the total message of any given storytelling event is generated and shaped by and exists because of a specific storyteller and specific story listeners whose interactions constitute a network of social interrelationships that is unique to that particular storytelling event." As such, to replace one context (the event) with another (the report) is to create new tellers, listeners, interactions: a new story.[19]

Taking these considerations as a whole—or singly—it is plain that one must exercise extreme caution in attempting to bring Indian and Euro-American stories into their proper relation. The Indian stories with which I am concerned have been translated—recklessly—into English; they have been isolated in surroundings at best unfamiliar and at worst hostile; their speakers and auditors have seldom been identified; their performative aspects, social settings, location in time, and position in native repertoires have largely been effaced; indeed, their status or existence in actual native traditions is often uncertain. Translation, in other words, has taken place on a number of fronts; and to offer static, abstracted traces—what Victor Turner calls "the shucked off husks of living process"—as authoritative documents or timeless native wisdom, as some modern anthologies do, is absurd. But to accept the problems as authoritative or timeless is no less so; overwhelming as these problems appear, one must treat them as problems, rather than as givens prior to or greater than the encounter. For as I will argue, though Indian story (due to its performative nature) overtly demands awareness of contextual factors, it is imperative to place *any* story in its contexts, and in so doing to deny any story—even a story calling itself history—the status of the universal, the real, the only. And as I will further argue, this is so not only because the contexts within which America's stories were forged involved numerous peoples and stories, but because, as I intimated above, it was precisely by suppressing context—thereby turning history and myth to essential terms preexisting, overarching, and determining encounter—that Euro-Americans attempted to remove Indian stories from the nation. (Such attempts, moreover, can themselves be

traced to specific contexts: the physical removal of Indians, the multiplica-
tion of Indian writers and historians, and other factors to which I will
return.) The difficulties that attend the study of Indian story arose within
an arena of which Indian story was a part; and accordingly, if the problems
touched on in this interlude cannot be ignored—for they go hand-in-hand
with the development of Indian and Euro-American stories—neither can
they be naturalized, for the same reason. To understand these problems is
to understand the contexts of the stories; for the problems, and one's
understanding of them, derive from those contexts. And to understand
these contexts is to perceive, as Michel Foucault writes in a parallel track,
the extent to which Indian and white stories are "inextricably involved . . .
existing for each other, in relation to each other, in the exchange which
separates them."[20]

Chapter Four

Stories of the Land

"Are you wiser than our fathers? May not we rather think that *English* men have invented these stories . . . that they might wipe us out of our lands?"

—John Eliot, *The Indian Dialogues*

One of the earliest European recordings of an Indian story occurs in Thomas Harriot's *A Briefe and True Report of the New Found Land of Virginia* (1588). Scientist of the 1585 Roanoke expedition and an ethnographer in the Columbian mode, Harriot defines the Indians by lack: "They are a people poore, and for want of skill and iudgement in the knowledge and vse of our things, doe esteeme our trifles before thinges of greater value. . . . And by howe much they vpon due consideration shall finde our manner of knowledges and craftes to exceede theirs in perfection, and speed for doing or execution, by so much the more is it probable that they shoulde desire our friendships & loue, and haue the greater respect for pleasing and obeying us." The myth that follows is thus to be understood as yet more evidence of the poverty of Indian possessions: "They beleeue that there are many Gods which they call *Mantóac*, but of different sortes and degrees; one onely chiefe and great God, which hath bene from all eternitie. Who as they affirme when hee purposed to make the worlde, made first other goddes of a principall order to bee as meanes and instruments to bee vsed in the creation and gouernment to follow. . . . For mankind they say a woman was made first, which by the woorking of one of the goddes, conceiued and brought foorth children: And in such sort they say they had their beginning." The materialism that governs Harriot's lead-in to the myth governs his telling of it as well: the Indian god is an enterprising god, who, "purposing" to make a world, devises and deputizes all manner of "instruments." Nor are his worshipers any less the incipient entrepreneurs, with an eye for the main chance: "This is the summe of their religion," Harriot writes, "which I learned by hauing special familiarity with some of their priestes. Wherein they were not so sure grounded, nor gaue such credite to their traditions and stories but through conuersing with vs they were brought into great doubts of their owne."[1] The Indians, Harriot speculates, are eager to swap goods—and gods—for ones that offer a better return on investment; and their pragmatic Creator, one guesses, could only approve.

Harriot's text is thus an early instance of European history writing itself over, or through, myth—of European history turning stories *into* myth in order to write its own story as history. Harriot's proprietary history of origins, that is, strives to deny its genesis in encounter, to eliminate/ assimilate all other stories and thus present itself as prior to, greater than, and determinative of encounter. Critics have read texts like Harriot's in precisely these terms: to Gananath Obeyesekere the Indians are mere pawns in a story of "conquest, imperialism, and civilization," while for Stephen Greenblatt their voices are "produced by the power that ulti- mately denies" them. Eric Cheyfitz sums up: since "we have only English reports," texts such as Harriot's do not truly convey stories of encounter to begin with.[2]

And yet, for all its value in warning us not to view textualized Indian stories outside the contexts of their making, such a position is limited insofar as it abstracts Harriot's story from those contexts. Denying, in other words, the situations of contact within which Harriot's story was generated, this approach makes his story *the* story, and thus no story. Carolyn Porter's critique of Greenblatt is vital here: "The problem lies . . . in being limited to one set of discourses—those which form the site of a dominant ideology—and then reifying that limit as if it were coterminous with the limits of discourse in general."[3] What Porter suggests is that, though it is a mistake to divorce the Indian story from Harriot's—to view it as a reliable account—it is equally a mistake to divorce Harriot's from the contact situation—to grant his story the autonomy and self-evidence it claims. A middle ground would insist on seeing his story as inseparable from the contact situation; it would insist that no one story can be consid- ered superior to or wholly explanatory of that situation, for it is within the contexts of encounter that all such stories take particular shape. In these terms, Harriot's story would be seen as just that: a story, one that exists within (indeed exists because of) local intercultural relations, rather than a truth beyond telling or tellers. As such, the meeting of stories—however conflictual or unequal—unsettles any one story's absolute claim to the encounter or the ground on which they met.

I phrase it this way, moreover, to draw attention to the fact that the stories, the "claims," are not merely linguistic but physical: Harriot seeks to naturalize his story in order to monopolize the land. The Indians, he writes, were "not so sure grounded" after having heard him. This picture of myth as rootless reveals the link between Euro-American history and expansion, their joint work in displacing Indian claims. In what follows, I explore this link during a critical period in the constitution of America: the years surrounding the birth of the United States. Yet if in focusing on this period I tread familiar territory, I hope to defamiliarize it by emphasizing the place of Indian peoples and stories in the physical and narrative foundings of the nation.

Settling America

History was born of holocaust. As Anthony Kemp explains, the era of European exploration saw a static church history yield to a history of "supersession that divides the present from the past"; during the Enlightenment—that perhaps undefinable shift marked by secularism, republicanism, and the consolidation of colonial power—the concept of history as a non-replicable stream of events, each of which displaces what came before, became not only an article of faith but a mode of analysis.[4] Though it would be too neat to see eighteenth-century history as a complete break from the past, it would not be inaccurate to claim that the eighteenth century saw it as such. Modern history was that which supplanted superstition, tradition, and ritual: in a word, myth.

The significance of myth (or, to use the contemporary term, fable) for historians of this period can be measured by the fact that few begin without confronting it. In *The History of England* (1754), David Hume asserts that "the fables, which are commonly employed to supply the place of true history, ought entirely to be disregarded"; in *Letters on the Study and Use of History* (1752), Lord Bolingbroke argues that "what may have happened, is the matter of an ingenious fable: what has happened, is that of an authentic history"; in the *Encyclopédie* (1751–1776), Voltaire writes: "History is an account of events given as true; as opposed to fable, which is an account of events given as false."[5] For Enlightenment-era history to happen, something had to change, something had to submit, and myths provided that something. Myths were conceptualized as corrupt versions of history that would in time be exposed, and replaced, by the real: the "history of the errors of the human mind," as Bernard Fontenelle termed them in "Of the

Origin of Fables" (1724), myths presaged a historical telos that, surrendering to it, they fulfilled.[6]

Nor was this forecast of displacement merely abstract. If European *philosophes* predicted that the "Remains of ancient Superstition" would "dwindle away in proportion as the World becomes more enlighten'd," those Europeans who set foot in the New World were determined that this prophecy about myth—and the "gross and ignorant Nations" who adhered to it—should be realized. Thus on the one hand, explorers, scientists, and missionaries confirmed of Indian myths what historiography already knew: mercurial, fugitive, internally dissonant, such tales were defenseless against the solidity and surety of the one true history. Iroquois origins, Pierre de Charlevoix complains, are "so very uncertain, and almost always contradict themselves so grossly, that it is almost impossible to pick out any thing certain or coherent"; they are "a tissue of absurd imaginations, of fables so ill contrived, of systems so ill digested and so wild, that it is impossible to give any regular or just account of them." Joseph François Lafitau, in *Customs of the American Indians* (1724), agrees: "One cannot elicit anything from the Indians in general concerning their origin. . . . [T]radition, passing from mouth to mouth, changes as it is passed on, and degenerates into myths so absurd that one can only very reluctantly report them." Nicolas Perrot concurs in his comments on the Ojibwas: "All their history of ancient times proves to be only confused and fabulous notions, which are so simple, so gross, and so ridiculous that they only deserve to be brought to light in order to show the ignorance and rudeness of those peoples." And David Zeisberger, writing of the Delawares, asserts: "Concerning their origin no trace of tradition is to be found among the Indians. From some old Mingoes I heard that they believed themselves to have come from under the earth. . . . Others say that they came from under the water. . . . Others, again, claim that the first human being fell from heaven."[7] Issues of translation aside, these depictions of Indian stories as sloppy and wavering serve a definable purpose: if the Indians cannot settle on how they came to the land, they cannot settle on it.

If, moreover, such stories offered rhetorical justification for expansion, material backing came in the form of stories that denied the Indians' physical claims to the continent. One such story, devised by Locke at the close of the seventeenth century, supplied an evolutionary hierarchy of land-use: "God, who hath given the World to Men in common, hath also given them reason to make use of it. . . . 'tis the taking any part of what is common, and removing it out of the state Nature leaves it in, which *begins the Property*; without which the Common is of no use. And the taking of this or that part, does not depend on the express consent of all the Commoners. . . . *As much Land* as a Man Tills, Plants, Improves, Cultivates, and can use the Product of, so much is his *Property*." According to this model, the despoilers of God's bounty are not the colonizers, who obey a drive toward individual ownership, but the "wretched inhabitants" of the "uncultivated wast of America," who cling to a view of land as communal handout rather than alienable property.[8] Whether Indians were, in fact, communalists in the Lockean (or any) sense is, of course, open to question;[9] the influence of the paradigm, however, was enormous, allowing eighteenth-century writers less to deny Indian land-use outright—as some earlier reporters had[10]—than to deny Indian land-use even while admitting it. In Robert Beverley's 1705 account, Indian landholding appears as natural, even animal foraging, and thus an invitation to dispossession: "They claim no property in Lands, but they are in Common to a whole Nation," he writes. "Living without Labour, and only gathering the Fruits of the Earth when ripe, or fit for use . . . they need [not] quarrel for room, where the Land is so fertile, and where so much lyes uncultivated." So entrenched was this model by century's end that Timothy Dwight, though as a minister he might have named a more orthodox distinction, christened "*love of property*" the conversionist philosopher's stone: "Wherever this can be established, Indians may be civilized; wherever it cannot, they will still remain Indians."[11] Here, then, one sees in concrete terms how Euro-American stories assaulted Indian claims. Just as myths, the avatar of evanescence, were fated to be displaced by Europe's true history, so was communalism, the feeble precursor of property, doomed to be uprooted by the course of (non)human events.

This, at least, was the story. And yet, as critics have long recognized, Revolutionary-era America resembled less the tranquil, triumphal march such theories foretold than the "heterogeneous, incoherent, distracted mass" Thomas Jefferson feared. Historians have traced the anxieties of this period to sectional crises, factionalism, and the specter of foreign intrigue; literary critics, meanwhile, have argued that the doubts found in the writings of the founders suggest their disorienting sense that "there simply was no history of established authority to limit those who set about constituting the new nation."[12] To say this, however, is to overlook the presence of Indian peoples, whose "histories" posed precisely such "limits"; though Charles Brockden Brown, for one, insisted that "we have a *right* to the possession" of the land, he recognized the Indians as a "terrible militia" poised to defy that right.[13] The America of the time was, in more ways than one, unsettled; it was tenanted by native and European peoples, but the former had not relinquished, nor the latter gained, complete claim to the land. As such, though Indian claims might be imaged as relics superseded by a living history, those claims revealed the falsity of this story; in act—through resistance to colonization—and word—through stories of the land—Indians challenged the historical/territorial enterprise that sought to displace them.[14]

Indeed, some scholars, turning the colonizers' terms against them, have argued that the ways in which Indians held, defended, and narrated land challenged not only the act but the ideal of displacement. Such arguments hinge on the intriguing fact of a single ethic underlying Euro-American land claims and story claims, an ethic, indeed, based on singularity (singleness and uniqueness). Just as private property decrees that each space be occupied by only one legal owner, so does Enlightenment history dictate that each event be rendered by only one legitimate story. Yet Indian land claims, as Cheyfitz contends in the most theoretically astute rehabilitation of the communal, "do not naturalize, or absolutize, cultural places"; rather, they make possible, or necessary, the interrelation of claims: "The more flexible boundaries of [Indian] societies are grounded in a relation to the land (as place) that is opposed to that contained in the term *property*, which is grounded in a notion not of shifting and open boundaries, but of fixed and closed ones, both of the self and physical property."[15] Similarly, critics have argued that if multiple, even contradictory versions of myths exist, this reflects not incoherence or incompetence but a view of story as copious and approximate rather than unique and absolute: "While there might be differing stories on the same topic within any given native community, and families and individuals may differ in opinion about those stories," Angela Cavender Wilson maintains, "there is acknowledgment that there may be more than one 'right' version, that stories differ according to perspective, that people's interpretations change along the way, and that some individuals may be more adept than others in relaying specific stories."[16] According to these critics, Indians contested not simply Euro-American geographic and narrative absolutism but the very idea that land claims or story claims could be absolute.

There is, as I see it, great value in these arguments—if, that is, they are not themselves absolutized. Cheyfitz's intervention, for example, is seminal in its demand that geographic conflict be seen in terms of diverse ways of claiming and naming the land. And yet, to convert individualism and communalism to sheer rivals—as Cheyfitz does when he finds Indian claims "opposed" to Euro-American—is to reinscribe not only Euro-American strategies for claiming the land but the conceptual and legal oppositions Cheyfitz himself identifies with the ideal of property. And this is particularly problematic because, as Cheyfitz argues, communalism resists projecting claims as absolute oppositions beyond the places in which they operate; communalism, like reciprocity, connects any one claim to the others with which it coexists, and thereby shows the dependence of specific claims on the local and particular. Likewise, if Indian myths differ from Euro-American histories in their greater flexibility and multivalency, for this reason it is risky to argue, as in Albert Lord's influential comments on oral poetry, for a strict dichotomy: "Our real difficulty arises from the fact that, unlike the oral poet, we are not accustomed to thinking in terms of fluidity. We find it difficult to grasp something that is multiform. It seems to us necessary to construct an ideal text or to seek an original, and we remain dissatisfied with an ever-changing phenomenon. . . . The truth of the matter is that our concept of 'the original' . . . simply makes no sense in oral tradition."[17] To apply this distinction rigidly is to overlook the fact that *all* stories—even those "we" embrace—are fluid, multiform, mutable precisely because they are reliant on human productivity, and thus on the contexts of their making. Indian stories, because they are told and not written, may highlight this fact: such stories necessarily encode (even when they disclaim) the local nature of their production. Yet if written stories foster the illusion that they are beyond local contexts, such stories, as I have shown in the case of Harriot, themselves encode these contexts. What Indian stories illustrate, then, is that the "concept of the original" makes no sense in any tradition; that stories, like land claims, emerge within various, particular sites. And accordingly, restoring Indian land claims and story claims to the encounters of which they were a part does not mean renaming oppositions; quite the contrary, it means refusing to enshrine any claim as categorically legitimate or pristine, and thus reenvisioning any claim in light of the many that circulate and clash in the intercultural arena.

As a means of suggesting how such a reading might modify the landscape of the early republic, let me consider a figure whose acts and works pertaining to the Indians have been discussed widely but not interculturally: Thomas Jefferson, the first president to broach a systematic plan of Removal and one of the first Americans to take on the study of Indian lore.[18] On entering the presidency, George Washington had engaged Moravian bishop John Ettwein to prepare a report on the traditions of the northwestern tribes; yet if he sensed such intelligence would help him size up the peoples on whom he would shortly wage war, his interest seems not to have gone any further.[19] Jefferson, on the other hand, made it an affair of state to collect whatever material on Indian land and story he could. Thus, for instance, he commissioned Meriwether Lewis to ascertain "the extent & limit of [Indian] possessions" and "their language, traditions, monuments." If, as James Ronda writes, Jefferson wished in this way to "gather material" for "the empire of the mind," he was sure the empire of the mind would buttress that of the continent.[20]

His research taught Jefferson, first, that to corral Indian lands he must combat Indian landholding. In 1803, he ordered William Henry Harrison to ensure that Indian leaders "run in debt, because we observe that when these debts get beyond what the individuals can pay, they become willing to lop them off by a cession of lands." The same year, however, he saw signs of resistance to division and conquest: "The Indian tribes residing within the limits of the United States have for a considerable time been growing more and more uneasy at the constant diminution of the territory they occupy, although effected by their own voluntary sales, and the policy has long been gaining strength with them of refusing absolutely all further sale on any conditions, insomuch that at this time it hazards their friendship and excites dangerous jealousies and perturbations in their minds to make any overture for the purchase of the smallest portions of their land. A very few tribes only are not yet obstinately in these dispositions." Such alliances had, in fact, been building since the dawn of the republic; invoking communalism not simply as a tribal ideal but as a pantribal policy, Indian confederacies had disrupted desires that the land, and the story of it, be held in a way that could brook no alternatives, no contesting or contextualizing of the nation's claim. In 1786, for instance, the Iroquois, Delawares, and others instructed "that any cession of our lands should be made in the most public manner, and by the united voice of the confederacy; holding all partial treaties as void and of no effect." The following year, Creek leader Alexander McGillivray condemned a land cession negotiated by two chiefs, writing that his people "denied the right of any two of their country, to making any cession of land, which could only be valid by the unanimous voice of the whole, as joint proprietors, in common."[21] More threateningly, in 1793, the northwestern tribes, who had greeted the federal army's first campaigns with lopsided defeats in 1790 and 1791, met efforts to slip settlement through the backdoor with an alternative story about the lands "you say are settled":

BROTHERS: Money, to us, is of no value, and to most of us unknown: and as no consideration whatever can induce us to sell the lands on which we get sustenance for our women and children, we hope we may be allowed to point out a mode by which your settlers may be easily removed, and peace thereby obtained. . . . We know that these settlers are poor, or they would never have ventured to live in a country which has been in continual trouble ever since they crossed the Ohio. Divide, therefore, this large sum of money, which you have offered to us, among these people . . . and, we are persuaded, they would most readily accept of it, in lieu of the lands you sold them. If you add, also, the great sums you must expend in raising and paying armies, with a view to force us to yield you our country, you will certainly have more than sufficient for the purposes of re-paying these settlers for all their labor and their improvements. . . . You have talked to us about concessions. It appears strange that you should expect any from us, who have only been defending our just rights against your invasions. We want peace. Restore to us our country, and we shall be enemies no longer.[22]

The northwestern tribes, if this translation can be trusted, were not only powerful but canny adversaries, burlesquing concepts—"labor and improvements," for instance—that they realized would resonate with whites. In similar fashion, joining "proprietors" with "common" landholding, McGillivray employs these terms to unsettle them; likewise, the united Indians reject the "partiality"—self-interest and self-sufficiency—of any one claim. Literally and rhetorically, then, the claims of these Indian confederates suggested to Jefferson's people that their own were merely that: *claims*, neither universal nor manifest.

Jefferson's strategies for overcoming Indian claims were numerous, and force always waited in the wings. Yet as an address to Hendrick Aupaumut, representative of the Delawares and Mahicans, indicates, he preferred to shroud force beneath narrative, to meet story with story: "You have lived by hunting the deer and buffalo. . . . The whites, on the other hand, are in the habit of cultivating the earth. . . . Let me entreat you, therefore, on the lands now given you to begin to give every man a farm; let him enclose it, cultivate it, build a warm house on it, and when he dies, let it belong to his wife and children after him. Nothing is so easy as to learn to cultivate the earth; all your women understand it. . . . The only way to prevent [further sales] is to give to every one of your people a farm, which shall belong to him and his family, and which the nation shall have no right to take from them and sell; in this way alone can you ensure the lands to your descendants through all generations, and that it shall never be sold from under their feet."[23] In this story—told to a man who, during the wobbly first years of the republic, had been dispatched by Washington's

Secretary of War to negotiate with the northwestern tribes[24]—Jefferson plays a number of variations on the communal theme: he denies Indian landholding absolutely; admits Indian agriculture, though only as an improperly gendered and thus unproductive activity; and seeks to institute practices that, as his letter to Harrison reveals, tended to make Indian lands more vulnerable to encroachment rather than less. Jefferson, in short, portrays the communal as a decadent ruin rather than, as the confederates did, a vital part of the nation's geographic history. When, therefore, he prophesies to the Indians that if they follow his word, "you will unite yourselves with us" and "spread with us over this great island," this glimpse into futurity, like the sketch of the past, seems calculated to eliminate Indian claims so that a single claim may cover the continent.[25]

In this light, it is suggestive that Jefferson devoted himself not only to covering Indian land but to discovering Indian story. He regrets "that we have suffered so many of the Indian tribes already to extinguish, without our having previously collected and deposited in the records of literature, the general rudiments at least of the languages they spoke"; he envisions "a perpetual mission" among the Indians, one function of which would be to "collect their traditions." Again, philanthropy shelters self-interest; Jefferson may wish to preserve Indian voices, but only as mute myths in a living history. Yet the obstacles to this project emerge in his description of an Indian ossuary, whose silent contents have still the power to unsettle: "I first dug superficially in several parts of it, and came to collections of human bones, at different depths, from six inches to three feet below the surface. These were lying in the utmost confusion, some vertical, some oblique, some horizontal, and directed to every point of the compass, entangled, and held together in clusters by the earth. Bones of the most distant parts were found together, as, for instance, the small bones of the foot in the hollow of a scull, many sculls would sometimes be in contact, lying on the face, on the side, on the back, top or bottom, so as, on the whole, to give the idea of bones emptied promiscuously from a bag or basket, and covered over with earth, without any attention to their order."[26] Rummaging in southern tumuli, Jefferson unearths the heterogeneous, incoherent, distracted mass that underlies (and belies) the "superficial" calm of the nation: the mound is atomistic, ligatured as tenuously as his comma-spliced sentence. As such, this passage reveals the geopolitical anxiety beneath his attempts to appropriate Indian traditions for the national archives.

For the dead were the least of Jefferson's worries. In a letter to Handsome Lake after the latter's visit to Washington, for instance, Jefferson resorts to another story of the land to explain the necessity of further sales:

"You remind me, brother, of what I said to you, when you visited me the last winter, that the lands you then held would remain yours. . . . The lands were your property. The right to sell is one of the rights of property. . . . I hope, therefore, that on further reflection, you will see this transaction in a more favorable light." Yet unlike the dumb boneyard, the man to whom Jefferson told this story countered with another. Though the prophet seems to have touted Jeffersonian agrarianism, urging his people to "farm a little," his program as a whole was, in the view of the missionaries to the Senecas, "very inimical" to the goal of freeing lands for settlement. One record of his teachings indicates as much: "The Great Spirit when He made the earth never intended that it should be made merchandise, but His will is that all His creatures should enjoy it equally." Like McGillivray, the United Indians, and the northwestern tribes, Handsome Lake affronted the prescription that land—and the idea of it—be held exclusively. Proclaiming stories of the land that would mobilize a decade later around Tecumseh, who was quoted as asserting that "the Great Spirit intended [the land] as the common property of all the tribes" and thus that "no tribe has a right to sell, even to each other, much less to strangers, who demand all," Indians challenged not only the nation's claim but the notion that any claim, physical or narrative, could be the inalienable property of one nation, under God, indivisible.[27]

The settling of America, in short, was far from a settled matter. If Euro-Americans make it appear settled, one must read their works in relation to that which they disguise, deny, or distort; for it was by doing so that the nation sanctified its own claims. I turn now to two texts of this period, Benjamin Franklin's "Remarks Concerning the Savages of North-America" (1783) and William Bartram's *Travels* (1791), that reveal the ways in which Euro-Americans sought, in the literal and the literary, the Indians' dispossession. Yet I argue that if one reads these texts not through a proprietary history of expansion, with one claim necessarily and unproblematically displacing another, but through a model in which diverse land claims and story claims interact, vie, negotiate, the two show that the land from which they arose was a space of multiple configurations and conceptualizations, unassimilable to a single, expansive unity.

Founding Fables

"Remarks" appeared in the year the Treaty of Paris formalized United States sovereignty, the year before the Treaty of Fort Stanwix extended it over the Iroquois. Despite assurances of good will, the Six Nations of the Iroquois, it seems, had an inkling of how the One Nation of the United States would proceed: "We are now Masters of this Island," the Seneca chief Cornplanter's words read as he reported the words of the Americans, "and can dispose of the lands as we think proper or most convenient to ourselves." Such fears proved well founded; reeling after the war, the Iroquois were bullied into ceding lands and accepting the status of vassals. The Fort Stanwix treaty, ratified without the League's full consent, was ultimately renegotiated; in the meantime, the Iroquois sought a measure of self-determination by recruiting opposition to "partial" treaties. Like Franklin's people, the Iroquois were trying to secure political and symbolic unity amidst a host of forces threatening disintegration.[28]

This context renders suspect Roy Harvey Pearce's dismissal of "Remarks" as a mere "game, a case of good old Ben Franklin" pointing out that "things with high society are perhaps not quite as fine as they might seem."[29] If this is a game, it is a deadly one; if Franklin has cooked up a stock Injun to lampoon the *beau monde*, his timing is singular. Ironic frippery notwithstanding, "Remarks" is more than ludic Noble Savagism: a postbellum meditation on national union, it explores the dual acts by which Indians were removed from the nation and its story.

As such, from the first Franklin underscores, and upsets, the ways in which peoples organize national ideals: "Savages we call them, because their manners differ from ours, which we think the Perfection of Civility; they think the same of theirs." By way of example, he recounts how, at the 1744 treaty of Lancaster, the representatives of Virginia offered to educate six young Iroquois. The Indians respond: "Different Nations have different Conceptions of things; and you will therefore not take it amiss, if our Ideas of this Kind of Education happen not to be the same with yours." The opening aphorism and vignette recall the efforts of early national leaders and educators to mandate a common national history: "As soon as he opens his lips," Noah Webster wrote, every child "should rehearse the history of his own country; he should lisp the praise of liberty, and of those illustrious heroes and statesmen, who have wrought a revolution in her favor." Such appeals to a coherent past, a corporate identity, and a corps of luminaries implied that a unified nation could be engineered by idealizing exemplary precedents. As Benjamin Rush put it, canonical history was calculated to "render the mass of the people more homogenous," to "fit them more easily for uniform and peaceable government"—in short, "to convert men into republican machines." Franklin seems to have recognized in such discourse that America's history-in-the-making was just

that; that—as in the Indians' return offer to "make *Men*" of Virginia's
sons—citizens are "made," not born.[30] Playing off the nation's founding
document, he thus suggests that truths are selected, not self-evident, authorized by foundational stories (however unfounded), not by the will of
God, the laws of nature, or, to use Jefferson's sublime means of invoking
while denying agency, the course of human events.

Having undermined the idea of nationalism, Franklin next upends its
founding stories. He tells of a minister who, "having assembled the Chiefs
of the Sasquehanah Indians, made a Sermon to them, acquainting them
with the principal historical Facts on which our Religion is founded, such
as the Fall of our first Parents by Eating an Apple, the Coming of Christ to
repair the Mischief, his Miracles and Suffering, &c. When he had finished, an Indian Orator stood up to thank him. What you have told us,
says he, is all very good. It is indeed bad to eat Apples." Crafting sly savages
to drag Christianity from its pedestal was a familiar deist prank, and it
seems to be Franklin's as well when his chief offers a story "in Return":

In the Beginning our Fathers had only the Flesh of Animals to subsist on, and if
their Hunting was unsuccessful, they were starving. Two of our young Hunters
having killed a Deer, made a Fire in the Woods to broil some Parts of it. When
they were about to satisfy their Hunger, they beheld a beautiful young Woman
descend from the Clouds, and seat herself on that Hill which you see yonder
among the blue Mountains. They said to each other, it is a Spirit that perhaps has
smelt our broiling Venison, & wishes to eat of it: let us offer some to her. They
presented her with the Tongue: She was pleased with the Taste of it, & said, your
Kindness shall be rewarded. Come to this Place after thirteen Moons, and you
shall find something that will be of great Benefit in nourishing you and your
Children to the latest Generations. They did so, and to their Surprise found Plants
they had never seen before, but which from that ancient time have been constantly
cultivated among us to our great Advantage. . . . The good Missionary, disgusted
with this idle Tale, said, what I delivered to you were sacred Truths; but what you
tell me is mere Fable, Fiction & Falsehood. The Indian offended, reply'd, my
Brother, it seems your Friends have not done you Justice in your Education; they
have not well instructed you in the Rules of common Civility. You saw that we who
understand and practise those Rules, believed all your Stories; why do you refuse to
believe ours?[31]

Most critics read this ingenuous story as a chiding reminder that there are
no "common" rules of civility, only vanity and bigotry. At the same time,
however, the episode of the Indian chief draws out deeper, material connections between storytelling and geographic conflict. In his career as a

printer of, and later delegate to, Indian treaties, Franklin had reported the tenacity of Iroquois stories in recording intercultural events. "As we are old," one speech read, "it may be thought that the Memory of these things may be lost with us, who have not . . . the Art of preserving it by committing all Transactions to Writing: we nevertheless have Methods of transmitting from Father to Son, an Account of all these Things, whereby you will find the Remembrance of them is faithfully preserved, and our succeeding Generations are made acquainted with what has passed, that it may not be forgot as long as the Earth remains." (A passage in "Remarks" seems based on this speech: "They preserve Tradition of the Stipulations in Treaties a hundred Years back, which when we compare with our Writings we always find exact.") The reference to "the earth" suggests, moreover, that the Iroquois perceived a tie between custody of the past and command of the country. This impression is strengthened by the fact that origin stories, far from being "idle tales," were routinely recited during disputes over land. Thus, during the 1744 treaty referred to in "Remarks," when the Onondaga orator Cannasatego (himself featured in "Remarks") took issue with deeds Pennsylvania produced to settle claims to Maryland, his protest was registered as such a story: "When you mentioned the Affair of Land Yesterday, you went back to old Times, and told us, you had been in Possession of the Province of *Maryland* above One Hundred Years; but what is One Hundred Years in Comparison of the Length of Time since our Claim began? since we came out of this Ground? For we must tell you, that long before One Hundred Years our Ancestors came out of this very Ground, and their Children have remained here ever since."[32] These incidents reveal conflict over stories to be a conflict over the land, a narrative battle with grave material consequences.

Reading "Remarks" through Indian treaties makes clear that its players are not bantering, but bargaining over lands and lives. The answer to the chief's question is obvious: to believe his story is to grant his claims to divine favor, intimacy with the land, agrarianism, and the coexistence *of* stories, while to dismiss his story as (in the missionary's fulsome phrase) "fable, fiction and falsehood" is to deny those claims. Yet at the same time, by juxtaposing origin tales, Franklin applies the proposition of "Remarks" to the "affair of land": all claims, however compelling and necessary to their people, may be flaccid and nugatory to others. If, then, the minister believes the "historical Facts on which our Religion is founded" ensure his claim, Indian stories reveal these "facts" to be "founded" solely on stories taken—like the found(ed) lands—to be self-evident.

At the same time, Franklin's experiences with Indian treaties clarified the links between origin stories and the specific act in which his people were engaged: that of nation-building. For the Iroquois, it seems, the assertion of origins was not merely a means of countering objectionable treaty provisions; rather, origin stories contextualized treaties within the broader story of the League. Negotiations, Franklin observed, invariably began "agreeable to the *Indian* Custom" with the "Condolances," or the Ritual of Condolence. This ritual was performed when a sachem died to comfort the clans the deceased had represented and to elect a new leader; its basis for doing so, at least so far as one can tell from recorded versions, was an invocation of the League's founding. Emphasis on revitalization seems to have suited the Condolence, moreover, for the diplomatic functions in which Franklin witnessed it. At a 1753 treaty, for instance, an Iroquois speech to their western allies was translated: "We must let you know, that there was a Friendship established by our and your Grandfathers; and a mutual Council Fire was kindled. In this Friendship all those then under the Ground, who had not yet obtained Eyes or Faces (that is, those unborn) were included. . . . We therefore now come to remind you of it, and renew it; we re-kindle the old Fire, and put on fresh Fuel." Representative and preservative, the Condolence, in Matthew Dennis's words, "provided the Iroquois an explanation of their past and a practical guide for their present and future."[33] As such, it highlights the constitutional role of origin stories: like Franklin's people, the Condolence suggests, the Iroquois were invested in recalling (or inventing) an originary template, compelling obedience to its dictates, and resisting its fragmentation or displacement.

One can see, then, how Iroquois stories of union animate Franklin's essay. As a parable of the nation's founding, or of how parables further the founding, written at a time when his nation was turning Indian stories into "fable, fiction, and falsehood" to create an origin free of rival claims, "Remarks" restores Indian stories—and thus Euro-American stories—to their intercultural contexts and conflicts. The chief's tale emerges as both counterpart to and an attack on the Euro-American foundational story, which exists through its displacement of others. Catching history in the act, Franklin implies that the most sacred of national stories—the sacredness of the story of nation—is no more God-given than the land on which it takes place. It is, rather, by taking the place of stories it holds to be fables that the nation holds its own fable as truth.

This reading makes possible, moreover, a means of rethinking an ongoing dispute over American interculturalism. Considerable scholarly and popular attention has been focused on the question of the Iroquois League's impact on the Constitution; basing their argument in part on Franklin's encounters, historians, many of whom are of native ancestry, have argued that America's founders "wove an intellectual blanket out of history as they knew it, including their perceptions of the native confederacies with which they lived."[34] This thesis has occasioned a debate more rancorous than reasoned; the complex issue of Indian involvement in American republicanism has been reduced to a question as laughable (for most) as the chief's myth: was the Constitution copied from the Iroquois? Bearing in mind that Iroquois constitutionality, whether it shaped that of the United States, was likely shaped by that of the United States, I would repeat that Franklin's experiences enabled him to *see* Iroquois and American foundings as related. Thus in a letter of 1751 central to the Iroquois Founders theory, he wrote of colonial union: "It would be a very strange Thing, if six Nations of ignorant Savages should be capable of forming a Scheme for such an Union, and be able to execute it in such a Manner, as that it has subsisted Ages, and appears indissoluble; and yet that a like Union should be impracticable for ten or a Dozen English Colonies, to whom it is more necessary, and must be more advantageous; and who cannot be supposed to want an equal Understanding of their Interests." Franklin's verbs (the Iroquois have "formed" and "executed" a union), his statement that the League "appears" indissoluble, and his confession that union is not natural but "advantageous" to certain "interests," reveal his sense that union is at bottom a story hatched to serve specific ends. Thus when some stories are termed myths—when critics dismiss the Iroquois Founders theory as a myth or, in an unfortunate reversal, when advocates of the theory term its dismissal "a colossal myth"—this is to take as essence the product of what one is critiquing.[35] That is to say, "Remarks" shows how certain stories are made myths by a story of Union, or unitary story, called history. In this respect, Franklin anticipates Peter Hulme's critique of colonialist historiography: "One of the ways in which ideologies work is by passing off partial accounts as the whole story. They often achieve this by representing their partiality as what can be taken for granted, 'common sense,' 'the natural,' even 'reality itself.' This in turn often involves a covering of tracks: if something is to appear as simply 'the case' then its origin in historical contingency must be repressed. Generally speaking this repression can take two forms: the denial of history, of which the most common version is the argument to nature; or the historical alibi, in which a story of origins is told."[36] The real myth, Franklin attests, is this history of origins, with its delusion that its own story is the one and only.

Yet if Franklin's intercultural situation led him to a strikingly modern exposé—led him, that is, to *recognize* his intercultural situation—it also led him to take part in what he exposed. It is more than happenstance that he attributes the chief's story to the "Sasquehanah," or Susquehannocks, Iroquoian speakers who, by the time of the Revolution, had ceased to exist as a people: the tribe was shattered during the seventeenth century—perhaps by the Iroquois, though this story has been questioned[37]—while the few to retain a tribal identity were massacred near Conestoga, Pennsylvania in 1763. In *A Narrative of the Late Massacres* (1764), Franklin styles the Conestogas a "Remains of a Tribe of the Six Nations," but whether he means a member or a dependent is uncertain; nor is it certain if he knew their genealogy.[38] However, in the speech of Cannasatego from which I have quoted, the orator's claims hinge on the status of the Susquehannocks, who, he asserts, are tributaries of the Iroquois and therefore have no say over the lands in question. Thus Franklin would likely have seen the Susquehannocks as a people ousted by those on whom his nation, at the time of "Remarks," was performing a similar act.

If so, his choice of the Susquehannocks seems a means of containing, if not condoning, the appropriations of land that fostered, fed, and followed the late war: as aggressors and empire-builders, the Iroquois can hardly object now that their history of usurpation has come home to roost. Franklin does not say this is right, but he does not say it is wrong; indeed, if there is no right—only rites—then judgment becomes a luxury, and all that matters is which story possesses the power to possess the land. Such cynicism does not, however, square with his agonized reflections in *Late Massacres*: "Their Fathers received ours, when Strangers here, with Kindness and Hospitality. Behold the Return we have made them! When we grew more numerous and powerful, they put themselves under our *Protection*. See, in the mangled Corpses of the last Remains of the Tribe, how effectually we have afforded it to them!" (*Late Massacres* can, in fact, be seen as a pre-text to "Remarks"; the ravage of a "little Common-wealth"—and the "numberless Stories," "pure Inventions" "contrived" to justify it—broach what "Remarks" explores on a national scale.) Franklin's temporizing thus suggests a more conflicted, and limited, man than I have sketched thus far, one who, for all his insights into the partiality of history, is unwilling to view Indian stories as equivalent to or belonging with his own. Franklin cannot fully commit to a story unifying and mollifying; he is unable to forget the mangled corpses that the Revolution, no less than the late massacre, has left; and he remains aware that it is violence, not verity, that ensures Indian peoples and stories will be rendered inert and mythic. Yet as in the Constitutional Convention, when he urged ratification as a show of "our real or apparent unanimity," he accepts, and suppresses, his savage remarks in the name of Union.[39]

Wicked Instruments

If "Remarks" deems the matter of land settled for the Iroquois, it was far from settled for the southeastern tribes among whom William Bartram traveled from 1773 to 1778. The Revolutionary period proved critical for these peoples; though their territory was, as R. S. Cotterill puts it, "theoretically undiminished" by war, the southern Indians experienced an "epidemic of land cessions" in the next decade. At the same time, resistance to land sales, particularly among the Creeks, estimated at a strength of 6,000 warriors, placed the fledgling nation in a bind; land was needed to boost the economy, but southern states refused to relinquish western lands until their demands for Creek territory had been resolved. In 1790, the year before the *Travels* appeared, a treaty favoring the Creeks was drafted (and broken); in 1792, agent Benjamin Hawkins warned: "While we contemplate the going into their country, we may bid adieu to peace; their attachment to their native soil is such that they will part with it but with their lives."[40] If, under these circumstances, Bartram's text could be seen as something of a military intelligence manual—"when there is at least a probability of war, with a part of the tribes, among whom Mr. Bartram resided," one reviewer wrote, "some traits of their character, will be pleasing, if not instructive"—it also highlighted traits that, if instructive, were far from pleasing: the Indians, Bartram corroborates Hawkins, "are ready always to sacrifice every pleasure and gratification, even their blood, and life itself, to defend their territory and maintain their rights."[41] The *Travels* appeared when competing claims dramatized the factitiousness of the nation's founding, and the flimsiness of its foundation; whatever truths were held self-evident, it was less evident who would hold the truths—or the lands.

As with "Remarks," then, it is inadequate to read Bartram's intercultural vision as it traditionally has been read: as mere "sentimental exoticism," Noble Savagism for a guilt-ridden victor.[42] Bartram's views cannot be lifted from the intercultural world in which they took shape; indeed, as a record of travels over a land that was itself taking shape through the exaggeration of some, and suppression of other, relationships to the land its peoples maintained, his narrative is an exploration not only of land but of narrative, of "the symbolizing process," in Priscilla Wald's terms, that "converts a changing land mass into a nation, making its shifting boundaries seem coherent."[43] The unsettled state of the country, that is, alerts Bartram to the ways his text constructs meaning from the many the land contains. And further, by encoding diverse claims, Indian and white, the *Travels* undermines its own claim to absolute control of the land.

It is in this light that one should regard the aspect of the *Travels* that has commanded the most attention: the discourse of natural history, according to which the land can be catalogued and comprehended under a single capacious design. Bartram's narrative begins: "The attention of a traveller should be particularly turned, in the first place, to the various works of Nature, to mark the distinctions of the climates he may explore, and to offer such useful observations on the different productions as may occur" (15). Christopher Looby notes that the "stiff and immutable world" posited by natural history expressed "an intensely desired end to the flux of revolutionary social-historical change"; if, as I have argued, this desire reflected intercultural anxieties, one can see natural history seeking to settle those revolutionary energies as well.[44] Though the naturalist, as Mary Louise Pratt writes, "extracts all the things of the world and redeploys them into a new knowledge formation," this appears an impartial act: naturalism "strives to make [its] informational orders natural, to find them there uncommanded, rather than assert them as the products/producers of European knowledges or disciplines." This rhetoric of "anti-conquest," by which explorers "secure their innocence in the same moment as they assert European hegemony," emerges when Bartram portrays himself as "the Flower hunter" (163), an inoffensive man-child the Indians—though "extremely jealous of white people travelling about" their country (270)—permit to roam at will.[45] Such expansionist naturalism can, too, be overt: "This vast plain, together with the forests contiguous to it, if permitted (by the Siminoles who are sovereigns of these realms) to be in possession and under the culture of industrious planters and mechanics, would in a little time exhibit other scenes than it does at present, delightful as it is" (199). The final, offhand phrase discloses the naturalist's peculiar immunity; like Jefferson, in whose research imperialism passes for empiricism, Bartram is most likely to plumb the meaning of the land and least likely to seem as if that act of speculation is anything more than speculative.

As the most striking feature of his work, natural history appears to map a privileged terrain over which Bartram holds sway. Yet if naturalism straitens the *Travels*, it is to erect limits even more binding to argue, as Pamela Regis does, that Bartram can "record only what the rhetoric has devised formulas to represent."[46] Such a reading is possible only if one confirms what naturalism seeks: to occupy all places yet deny that its dominion is built on other places. Yet Bartram's naturalism, far from exulting in its certain claim, reveals that, if it seems one must record only what the rhetoric has devised formulas to represent, the formulas were devised to make it seem that way. Thus Bartram regularly calls attention to his failure of authority: "How shall I express myself so as to convey an adequate idea . . . to the reader, and at the same time avoid raising suspicions of my veracity?" (118). On the one hand, this plea of incompetence reflects humility before God's "consummate artifice" (22); yet on the other, it registers a sense of the text's own artifice. As he writes elsewhere: "Although this [scene] may seem to exhibit a just representation of the peaceable and happy state of nature which existed before the fall, yet in reality it is a mere representation" (151). The unified world naturalism posits—its unitary claim to posit that world—is a "mere representation"; the reality is a world in which any eye must see itself legislating the order it desires in defiance of the multiple orders that exist with it.[47]

It is, then, the coexistence of claims that accounts for the tension in Bartram's discourse, its doubt whether it is a singular system under which the land must be narrated or but a single system of narrating the land. The presence of other systems introduces uncertainty into civilized discourse, an uncertainty, indeed, into the discourse of civilization: "Such is the virtue of these untutored savages; but I am afraid this is a common-phrase epithet, having no meaning, or at least improperly applied; for these people are both well-tutored and civil; and it is apparent to an impartial observer, who resides but a little time amongst them, that it is from the most delicate sense of the honour and reputation of their tribes and families, that their laws and customs receive their force and energy. This is the divine principle which influences their moral conduct, and solely preserves their constitution and civil government in that purity in which they are found to prevail amongst them" (111). Bartram's dismantling of the savage/civilized dualism is remarkable not only for its avoidance of bathos but for its suggestion that the terms falter in an alien context. His conviction in this regard is not, to be sure, firm; he retreats from his pronouncement that the terms "have no meaning," and his quizzical relativism is compromised by the very language he judges inadequate: civil, honor, reputation. His text, then, reveals the strain of attempting to see the unconventional with conventional terms, or the strain of seeing its conventions as tools of mastery rather than truths; thus it is unsurprising that the last sentence restores a universal "divine principle." Yet the possibility that cultures consist of networks of signifiers with no final significance remains; in a letter to a fellow natural-ist, Bartram writes with self-defeating circumspection: "If adopting or imitating the manners and customs of the white people is to be termed civilization, perhaps the Cherokees have made the greatest advance."[48] In this impossible statement, which has a people advancing into something that is, perhaps, no thing, schemes for fixing the other unambiguously are shown their ambiguity by the other. There is, it seems, no natural lan-guage, no single means of naming the peoples who inhabit the land.

And if there is not, neither can there be any one means of claiming the land those peoples inhabit. For it is, finally, conflict over land that drives Bartram's exploration of Nature; the soil of the continent, which he end-lessly checks and critiques, is, he senses, the source from which conflict springs. Unsettling the language of naturalism, or the naturalness of lan-guage, Bartram is able to envision competing claims to the land; or, more accurately, it is those claims that unsettle a language designed to identify the land with one people, use, idea. Thus in his account of a land cession, diverse views of the land ground the conflicts naturalism denies: "Just as [the surveyor] had determined upon the point, the Indian chief came up, and observing the course he had fixed upon, spoke, and said it was not right; but that the course to the place was so and so, holding up his hand, and pointing. The surveyor replied, that he himself was certainly right, adding, that that little instrument (pointing to the compass) told him so, which, he said, could not err. The Indian answered, he knew better, and that the little wicked instrument was a liar; and he would not acquiesce in its decisions, since it would wrong the Indians out of their land. This mis-take (the surveyor proving to be in the wrong) displeased the Indians" (58). Straining for levity, Bartram attempts an ironic reversal of first-contact parables in which Indians were portrayed worshiping European wonders: here, natural intuition outfoxes civilized gadgetry.[49] Yet if this episode contains an admission of science's inability to maintain order, it likewise reveals scientific discourse—the maintenance of order—to be an "instru-ment" of power, which no amount of naturalism can naturalize. This does not make Bartram a champion of Indian claims; he insists that this is "our" land (58), and he is gratified when, after the brief unpleasantness, the Indians withdraw their complaints. Nor does he deem Indian perceptions definitive; the chief "proves" right, but this does not prove his unqualified right. Quite the contrary, this episode suggests that any claim is, like any discursive claim, inadequate; since, in fact, the land is open to diverse renderings, any claim must *be* merely discursive, and therefore a "liar" to the extent that it takes itself as unimpeachable. Indian claims reveal white claims to be, like the opposition savage/civilized, signs that can be meaningful but that possess no certain meaning.

When, therefore, Bartram turns to Indian landholding, it is notable that he conveys their system not only as an opponent to Euro-American claims but as an alternative to the ideal of opposition. Here, for example, he describes Creek agriculture: "The whole town is summoned, by the sound of a conch shell, from the mouth of the overseer, to meet at the public square, whither the people repair with their hoes and axes; and from thence proceed to their plantation, where they begin to plant, not every one in his own little district, assigned and laid out, but the whole community united begins on one certain part of the field, where they plant on until finished; and when their rising crops are ready for dressing and cleansing they proceed after the same order, and so on day after day, until the crop is laid by for ripening" (400–401). This exemplary portrait of order, it must be said, resembles primitivist paeans such as Beverley's, where "[the land] did still seem to retain the Virgin Purity and Plenty of the first Creation, and the People their Primitive Innocence." Moreover, it recalls Bartram's own image of the pastoral slave estate: "The sooty sons of Afric forgetting their bondage, in chorus sung the virtues and beneficence of their master" (257). Yet where most writers saw such unconscious Arcadianism as the extent of Indian (or African) abilities, Bartram's passage complicates its roots. Grasping diurnal and seasonal rhythms while shaping them to human productivity, the Creeks are not merely of Nature, but users of Nature. At the same time, their uses complicate the proprietary ethic that upheld the appropriation of land and labor: "It has been said by historians," Bartram comments, "concerning the customs and usages of the aborigines of America, that they have every thing in common, and no private property; which are terms in my opinion too vague and general, when applied to these people" (400). Like the disgruntled reviewer who groused that "the savage alone might be expected to lament the loss of his hunting grounds; and if he be thus driven to betake himself to any kind of agriculture, he is made a more sociable and useful being by the alteration," historians are unable to see that "usage" is itself determined by usage; instead, they isolate a communalism that must be translated into the single useful mode of property.[50] But the Indians, Bartram indicates, use the land in their own terms, terms lost in translation: "This is their common plantation, and the whole town plant in one vast field together; but yet the part or share of every individual family or habitation, is separated from the next adjoining, by a narrow strip, or verge of grass, or any other natural or artificial boundary" (400). To be sure, Bartram seems unaware that such forms might reflect intercultural developments; in this regard, he abstracts Creek agriculture from context.[51] Yet his naturalization of land-use jars with his portrait of it as a cultural system, one that—like naturalism—creates order from and imposes order on the land. Finding the Indians engaged in acts of union, Bartram finds unifying discourses to be inadequate precisely because they appropriate Indian acts to their own ends.

But Bartram does not make this find on his own. He discovers, rather, that the finding—and owning—are themselves unifying fables. And it is the presence of Indian stories that reveals this, that reveals any claim to be a construct that achieves a coherent, satisfying, but not inherently true or false picture of the land. As such, Bartram's text is structured by two stories of the land and its use. One finds him and a companion happening upon a "most enchanting" vision (288): "A vast expanse of green meadows and strawberry fields . . . [where] young, innocent Cherokee virgins, some busy gathering the rich fragrant fruit, others having already filled their baskets, lay reclined under the shade of floriferous and fragrant native bowers . . . whilst other parties, more gay and libertine, were yet collecting strawberries, or wantonly chasing their companions, tantalising them, staining their lips and cheeks with the rich fruit" (288, 289). This scene of "primitive innocence"—an echo of Beverley—is, Bartram confesses, "too enticing for hearty young men long to continue idle spectators" (289). Accepting the maidens' basket, he and his crony "regaled [themselves] on the delicious fruit, encircled by the whole assembly of the innocent jocose sylvan nymphs" (289–90). Here, Bartram indulges in a conceit Annette Kolodny has termed the "lay of the land": a feminized wilderness, coy and lascivious, tempts the white man, while the fruits of the earth are offered in a soothing ritual that cloaks violent conquest.[52] This is an America naturalized to fetish, a yielding land that silently surrenders to its rightful owner.

Yet there is another story in the *Travels*, one qualifying the desire for absolute ownership. It is, Bartram writes, a Creek story of the land:

This vast accumulation of waters, in the wet season, appears as a lake, and contains some large islands or knolls, of rich high land; one of which the present generation of the Creeks represent to be a most blissful spot of the earth: they say it is inhabited by a peculiar race of Indians, whose women are incomparably beautiful; they also tell you that this terrestrial paradise has been seen by some of their enterprising hunters, when in pursuit of game, who being lost in inextricable swamps and bogs, and on the point of perishing, were unexpectedly relieved by a company of beautiful women, whom they call daughters of the sun, who kindly gave them such provisions as they had with them, which were chiefly fruit, oranges, dates, &c. and some corn cakes, and then enjoined them to fly for safety to their own country; for that their husbands were fierce men, and cruel to strangers: they further say, that these hunters had a view of their settlements, situated on the elevated banks of an island, or promontory, in a beautiful lake; but that in their endeavours to approach it, they were involved in perpetual labyrinths, and, like enchanted land, still as they imagined they had just gained it, it seemed to fly before them, alternately appearing and disappearing. They resolved, at length, to leave the delusive pursuit, and to return; which, after a number of inexpressible difficulties, they effected. When they reported their adventures to their countrymen, their young warriors were enflamed with an irresistible desire to invade, and make a conquest of, so charming a country; but all their attempts hitherto have proved abortive, never having been able again to find that enchanting spot. (47–48)

This story resembles Bartram's wishful vision, yet marks it as delusory: the daughters of the sun offer the products of the land, but the land itself is not to be possessed. Interestingly, Hawkins found Creek views of property delimited on just these lines: "I have explained the mode among civilized people, of taking property of every description, even land, to satisfy just claims. They are pleased with the mode, so far as it respects personal property, but land they say should not be touched."[53] It may be, then, that this story is of intercultural origin; the jealous husbands could embody responses to the fantasies and actualities of European aggression. As a warning, the story gives the lie to Bartram's peaceable kingdom; as another reading of human being in nature, it unsettles the tale of mastery, revealing it to be but one relationship to the land.

One could argue, of course, that Bartram, in casting these stories as opposing monoliths, affirms the story of mastery. Indeed, since the Creek story—despite its similarity to other recorded examples[54]—appears only in the *Travels*, it could be that he altered (or created) it to suit his agenda, one that appears when he concludes that, whether the Creeks are up to it or not, their land is "well worth contending for" (48). Thus their story, in one respect, symbolizes what it seems to disown: the pursuit of an absolute claim unmarked and unmarred by competitors. Yet as in the description of

Creek agriculture, this absolutizing tendency wars with a relativizing one: including this story with the other, the *Travels* enables both stories to emerge as stories, each a possibility, and neither one necessary or complete. If, then, Bartram takes the Creek story to prove his people's claims, the story renders his claim uncertain, revealing it to be—like all claims—a story, one that arises from specific contexts of encounter and thus cannot disguise its role in constructing what it desires. Illustrating what Bruce Greenfield terms the "local" mode of travel-writing, which recognizes America as "a mosaic of inhabited lands whose peoples have their own senses of history and destiny," the Creek story "implies another basis" for "imagining the Euro-American relationship with the western continent"; it suggests the multiple nature of America's story (and the multiple stories of America's nature), revealing how constellations of meaning are selected and actuated in a land that contains any number of such constellations.[55]

I do not want to be misunderstood at this point. Whatever alternatives Bartram, or Franklin, sensed, their texts, far from ushering in an era of enlightenment, stand at the gateway of spiraling land cessions, tribal dislocation, and human disaster. To say this is not, however, to portray them as token voices of sympathy redeeming a legacy of violence. Such a representation would fail on all counts: though in a minority, they were not tokens; though sympathetic, they were only intermittently so; and though it must be remembered, violence may not be redeemed. My point is that whatever stories Bartram's and Franklin's people told—and enforced—they cannot be taken as the whole story. To tell the whole story, one must recognize that wholeness is itself a story; that no claim is absolute; and that, even in the texts that record their dispossession, the Indians engage their dispossessors in debate over the meanings and uses of the land.

Chapter Five

Mind out of Time

Ask not the red sage to tell you how, or when, or where. He knows
it not, and if he should pretend to the knowledge, it would be the
surest possible evidence, philosophically considered, that his responses were fabulous.

—Henry Rowe Schoolcraft, *Notes on the Iroquois*

In 1800, naturalist Joseph-Marie Dégerando lectured at the Paris meeting
of the Société des Observateurs de l'Homme on the topic "Considerations
on the Various Methods to Follow in the Observation of Savage Peoples."
Conscious of the moment at the dawn of a new century, the featured
speaker was not content to pitch a mere field guide to explorers and commercial venturers; rather, he set out to define a science yet to be named:
anthropology. "The Science of Man," he begins, "is a natural science, a
science of observation, the most noble of all." Believing that opportunities
for observation have been squandered due to lack of systematic precepts,
Dégerando launches into a critique that could be found (minus the word
"savage") in a modern textbook: "Often explorers have based the accounts
that they bring us on incorrect or at least on dubious hypotheses. For
example, they habitually judge the customs of Savages by analogies drawn
from our own customs, when in fact they are so little related to each
other. . . . They make the Savage reason as we do, when the Savage does
not himself explain to them his reasoning. . . . It were wiser to gather a
large number of facts, before trying to explain them, and to allow hypothesis only after exhausting the light of experience." Having dealt with pro-
cedural tactics, Dégerando moves to hermeneutics: "The terms used to
pass on to us the results of [explorers'] observations are often in our own
language of vague and ill-determined meaning. Consequently, we are in
danger of taking their accounts in a way which they did not intend."
Dégerando faults past observers' "lack of impartiality" as one cause of
misinterpretation; but he admits that observation itself may skew the evidence, as it is "bound to be a natural source of fear, defiance, and reserve."

He concludes with a pronouncement that has pressed and plagued ethnographers ever since: "The first means to the proper knowledge of the Savages, is to become after a fashion like one of them."[1]

It is fair to ask, of course, how one is to become "like" those one terms "savages." Despite his warning against false analogies, Dégerando himself wonders whether savages hold property, whether the influence of their "priests" is "salutary," and so on.[2] Like those he chastises, he "makes the Savage reason as we do"; for all his incipient relativism, for all his methodological qualms, he is sure the other will turn out to be what he already believes.

And yet, his suspicion that savages do not reason as "we" do is arresting. By midcentury, this hunch will harden into an absolute that grounds not only the growing profession of anthropology but a pervasive anthropological mentality. In antebellum America, the first anthropologists (or ethnologists, as they called themselves) collected a vast hodgepodge on Indian cultures. Yet though this sloppy assemblage might have led to the view, in Christopher Herbert's words, that "all combinations of customs are possible for human societies, and that no one arrangement can claim after all to possess more logical coherence than any other," though it might in consequence, as Lee Clark Mitchell writes, have promoted "respect, tolerance, even cultural relativism," it tended, quite the contrary, to buttress the belief in a distinctive, immutable, expendable savage mind.[3] To understand this curiously particularist absolutism, one must uncover the opposition that impelled and upheld ethnology: the opposition of history and myth.

In *Time and the Other*, anthropologist Johannes Fabian critiques the central trick of his trade: the "denial of coevalness," the "persistent and systematic tendency to place the referent(s) of anthropology in a Time other than the present of the producer of anthropological discourse." This tendency is evident in Dégerando's lecture: "The philosophical traveller, sailing to the ends of the earth, is in fact travelling in time; he is exploring the past; every step he makes is the passage of an age. Those unknown islands that he reaches are for him the cradle of human society." What Fabian does not note is the way in which such chronological distancing was undergirded by the concept of myth: it was indigenous peoples' supposed inability to conceive, create, or transmit history that rendered them of no consequence to the peoples of history, the study of history, or the stuff of history. Constructing Indians as, in George Catlin's words, "a dying nation, who have no historians" and "never can speak in the civilized world," or in Lewis Henry Morgan's reckoning, a people who "would have passed away, without leaving a vestige or memorial of their existence behind, if to them had been intrusted the preservation of their name and deeds," ethnology speaks for or about mythic peoples who are, in two senses, out of time.[4]

Such discourse is undeniably powerful; to this day, most scholars discuss the birth and spread of ethnological science as if Indian peoples were mere objects of study rather than actors in the contexts of ethnology's creation. More: scholars routinely argue that ethnology was made *possible* by the Indians' defeat, deterioration, and disappearance. As Mitchell phrases it: "Ironically, acknowledgment of the viability of indigenous cultures . . . gained acceptance just as Americans finally undermined most of those cultures." Studies of American ethnology, then, focus on prominent practitioners—Benjamin Smith Barton, E. G. Squier, George Hamilton Cushing—or institutions—Charles Willson Peale's American Museum, the American Ethnological Society, the Smithsonian. Depending on the critic's sympathies, these men and monuments may earn praise or scorn. Yet in accepting the independence of ethnology from encounter, even those who question whether "irony" is the best way to describe the bond between removal and recovery must conclude that "real" Indians needed to vanish for "science" Indians to be fabricated.[5]

The aim of this chapter is to question the "absence" of Indians from ethnological texts and contexts—to show, indeed, that ethnology exists precisely to deny the conditions under which, and under which alone, it can exist. To fulfill this aim, I focus on one of ethnology's central figures: Henry Rowe Schoolcraft, whose founding work on oral narrative helped legislate, arbitrate, and execute the idea of a mythic Indian mind removed from history, the nation, and ethnology itself. In what follows, I attempt neither genealogy nor biography;[6] my interest lies specifically in challenging ethnology's discourse of myth. Yet to challenge this discourse, I argue, it is insufficient merely to unmask ethnology's representations—to point out that the Philadelphian Catlin had surely heard of, if not witnessed, Cherokee spokesperson Elias Boudinot's tour of the East, or that Morgan knew, having aided the Iroquois in fighting fraudulent treaties, why their "deeds" were so tenuous—for this is to overlook how ethnology is implicated in its contact with those it represents. To interrogate ethnology, one must go beyond "recovering" myths that would else be "lost"—a goal in keeping with ethnology's own principles. Rather, one must recover what ethnology denies: the intercultural contexts within which its own stories and storytellers are shaped, and within which Indian stories and storytellers, far from being what Morgan termed the "passive and silent spectators" of white science, are active, vocal participants and competitors in its creation.[7]

The Mythic Mined

The term "myth" did not exist until the nineteenth century. Previously, Robert Richardson reveals, "When a single myth was referred to, it was always as a 'mythological fiction,' a 'poetical fiction,' a 'tradition,' a 'poetical history,' or, most commonly, a 'fable.'" Even without the term, as the previous chapter attests, historians had little trouble decreeing what was true history and what was false. To the extent, however, that idiomatic consensus marks a profession's self-recognition, the birth of the term myth is significant, for it marks the birth of ethnology. In the eighteenth century, historians and scholars of myth had considered their tasks comparable. Both, in fact, had seen their subjects to be historical or diachronic; both studied records that charted, though in considerably different ways, the development (or decline) of peoples. In the words of the Abbé Banier, whose *Mythology and Fables of the Ancients, Explain'd from History* (1738) was the most influential mythographic treatise of its century: "This Principle must be deeply rooted in the Mind, that Fables are not wholly of the nature of Fictions; that they are Histories of the Times furthest back, which have been disfigured, either through the Ignorance of the People, the Artifice of the Priests, or the Genius of the Poets."[8] Clearly enough, Banier and his colleagues had no intention of claiming that myths were *reliable* histories. They did, however, believe that myths, however unreliable, *were* histories, and could accordingly be "explain'd" in terms of historical change, loss, and corruption.

Ethnology, on the other hand, was founded in the view that myth was essentially different from history, that it could not be comprehended—embraced or assessed—by historical means. It was futile, accordingly, to study the evolution of myth, its relation to history; myth had no evolution—could not, being myth, evolve—and bore no relation to history. Myth was to be viewed, rather, synchronically: as a self-referential sign system divested from historical settings, encounters, effects. Thus Schoolcraft, identifying the unique scope and challenge of his nascent profession, writes that the Indians were "under a kind of self-reproach, to reflect that they had indeed no history. . . . Ages have dropped out of their memory," leaving "an entire blank." He concludes magisterially: "Few of the Indians are qualified, by habits of reflection, to state that which is known or has occurred among them in past years; and those who attempt to supply by invention what is wanting in fact, often make a miserable jumble of gross improbabilities. History cannot stoop to preserve this. It must be left as the peculiar province of allegory and mythology."[9]

Schoolcraft was one of the first, and by midcentury the foremost, of a breed of journeyman ethnologists who strove to fill the blanks. Typical of workers in this young science, he fell into it by accident. A bankrupt glassmaker from New York state, he was lured west by the mineral riches of Missouri; his travel account caught the eye of Secretary of War John Calhoun, who was preparing an expedition to the Upper Mississippi under Lewis Cass. In 1822, in the first of many preferments he owed Cass, Schoolcraft gained the post of Indian agent at the Sault Ste. Marie station on Lake Superior. There he met trader John Johnston, whose wife, Susan, an Ojibwa woman "celebrated for her stock of traditional lore," introduced him to her people's oral narratives. Shortly after, the young agent married the Johnstons' daughter Jane. At the time, he gushed that "I have in fact stumbled, as it were, on the only family in North West America who could, in Indian lore, have acted as my 'guide, philosopher, and friend.'" Failing to realize a return on the region's natural resources, Schoolcraft had discovered an untapped resource—a "fund of fictitious legendary matter," as he termed it—that would prove equally precious to him, his field, and his nation.[10]

A growing investment in this cache of mythic matter convinced Schoolcraft that he had, indeed, hit the mother lode. As early as 1822, he hinted at myth's import: "Who would have imagined that these wandering foresters should have possessed such a resource?" he gaped. "This curious trait . . . lifts up indeed a curtain, as it were, upon the Indian mind, and exhibits it in an entirely new character." In quest of a distinctive "Indian mind" from the first, Schoolcraft was yet unsure of its source; in 1825, he speculated that "their customs and imaginative tales have alternately acted as cause and effect" on each other, yet concluded that "to trace the history of [myth's] operation upon the savage mind, would be impossible, if it were attempted." What is interesting here is that, however vain he feels the search would be, Schoolcraft argues that there *is* a "history" linking myth to mind. In 1827, however, in an experimental probe into "The Unchangeable Character of the Indian Mind," he took the first step toward abolishing history: pondering the anomaly of "a race, who have existed in contact with a people differing from them in all that constitutes physical and intellectual distinction, without having embraced, in any visible degree, manners and opinions urged upon them by the precept and example of centuries, or without having lost any of the distinguishing traits, which mark them as a peculiar people," he posited "a principle in the Indian mind" itself, an inherency for or beyond all time.[11]

Years later, he would discover what that principle was—or, more precisely, he would discover that it had been under his nose all along. In his inaugural collection of myths, *Algic Researches, Comprising Inquiries Respecting the Mental Characteristics of the North American Indians* (1839), he named myth as the quintessence of the Indian mind: "Hitherto our information has related rather to their external customs and manners, their physical traits and historical peculiarities, than to what may be termed the philosophy of the Indian mind. . . . It was found necessary to examine the mythology of the tribes as a means of acquiring an insight into their mode of thinking and reasoning, and the probable origin of their opinions and institutions. . . . Nothing in the whole inquiry has afforded so ample a clue to their opinions and thoughts, in all the great departments of life and nature, as their oral imaginative tales," the "strong belief in which furnishes the best clue to their hopes and fears, and lies at the foundation of the Indian character."[12] Here myth not only expresses but shapes the Indian mind; it is not a result of the Indians' environment but a sign of the environment of Indianness. A conceptual language "characteristic of the mental habits of these tribes" (18) and "everywhere the same" (7), myth thus bars not only progress but the chance of change; tinkering with the trivia of Indian existence cannot touch the existential Indian. Schoolcraft did not, then, ever unravel myth's history; instead, he removed myth from history. As he summed up in a retrospect of his career, myth had proved the royal road to "the dark cave of the Indian mind," showing it to be, first, a dark cave, and second, a primordial—and eternal—mind.[13]

It would, of course, be foolish to name Schoolcraft as sole progenitor of ethnology. His work was in some ways the articulation of theories that had simmered since the early years of contact—theories, heretical in the seventeenth century but gaining ground thereafter, of the radical diversity of human types[14]—while ideas analogous to his bubble up throughout the antebellum human sciences. Philologists such as Peter S. Duponceau, for example, concluded from the "peculiar" form of Indian languages that "the same mind presided over their original formation," while archaeologists including Ephraim George Squier reasoned from the shape of Indian burial mounds to the "unity of elementary beliefs" that "lie at the basis of all the primitive mythological systems" of America.[15] It had taken but a small step, meanwhile, for post-Enlightenment historians to conclude that Indians were not merely doomed by history but incapable of contributing to history either as record or as event. Adopting Johann Gottfried von Herder's late eighteenth-century view that each people possesses a "genetic spirit . . . ancient as the nation, ancient as the country it inhabits," nineteenth-century historians, foremost of whom was Herder's countryman Leopold von Ranke, argued that "there is . . . but one system of populations among mankind which takes part in [the] general historical movement, while others are excluded from it." The debt ethnology and historiography owed each other can be seen in the third volume of George Bancroft's *History of the United States*, published the same year as *Algic Researches*: "The copper-colored men are characterized by a moral inflexibility, a rigidity of attachment to their hereditary customs and manners. . . . This determinateness of moral character is marked, also, in the organization of the American savage. . . . This inflexibility of organization will not even yield to climate: there is the same general resemblance of feature among all the aboriginal inhabitants, from the Terra del Fuego to the St. Lawrence."[16] The crossover between sciences was tangible as well; snippets of Bancroft's sentences graced a work parallel to Schoolcraft's in content, akin to his in significance, and also published, like his, in 1839: Samuel George Morton's *Crania Americana*. Morton's work followed a presidential precedent in scavenging Indian graves to argue the impracticality of racial mingling: "However much the benevolent mind may regret the inaptitude of the Indian for civilisation, the affirmative of this question seems to be established beyond a doubt. His moral and physical nature are alike adapted to his position among the races of men, and it is as reasonable to expect the one to be changed as the other. The structure of his mind appears to be different from that of the white man, nor can the two harmonise in their social relations except on the most limited scale."[17] Morton, though cold to myths, had much to say about the brain that contrived (or was contrived by) them; Schoolcraft, though disinclined to chart the protrusions of Indian crania, had located the rootstock of these superficial features. For both, the white mind—which had thought to unearth savage skulls and stories—and the Indian mind—whose arcane secrets had lain dormant for eons—were separated by a span no history could express or bridge.

If, however, Schoolcraft was far from the lone laborer he sometimes claimed to be, his weight should not be underestimated. In practical terms, his reputation and connections placed him at the center of a variety of endeavors: Bancroft and Morton applied to him while preparing their works; Lewis Henry Morgan, having heard a lecture in which Schoolcraft termed America "the tomb of the Red man," set out to discover their burial places; poets, most famously Henry Wadsworth Longfellow, rooted through his writings; journals solicited his meditations on Indian mythology and policy; he was a vice-president of the American Ethnological Society, bowing only to elder statesman Albert Gallatin; and in the 1850s, it was Schoolcraft whom the federal government commissioned to prepare the encyclopedic *Historical and Statistical Information Respecting the History, Condition and Prospects of the Indian Tribes of the United States* (1851–1857), which hammered home for thousands of folio pages that those in a prehistoric condition had no prospects.[18] Moreover, if Schoolcraft could give, he could also take away. If nothing else, he was expert at finagling federal perks and was a tireless defender of his fiefdom, making sure that those who failed to show him the proper deference found the doors of opportunity slamming in their faces. Perhaps for this reason, he has fared particularly ill among those who have succeeded him. Though grudgingly saluting him as a pioneer, workers in his field have avidly itemized his flaws—narrowness of his own mind, vagary and contradiction, pedantry and pettiness—and deemed his methods at best laughable, at worst lamentable. "A man of deficient education and narrow prejudices, pompous in style, and inaccurate in statement," as Daniel Brinton terms him, he has, Stith Thompson chastises, distorted Indian tales "almost beyond recognition"; his myths, Elémire Zolla concludes, are no better than "simplistic, jog-trot" adaptations.[19] Yet despite such attacks, Schoolcraft's theory of a mythic mind in thrall to its own symbolic code shaped anthropology into the next century, materializing in Lucien Lévy-Bruhl's concept of "prelogical" mentality, where the "representations" of mythic peoples are "bound up with preperceptions, preconceptions, preconnections"; Ernst Cassirer's critique of a "mythically bound and fettered" psyche that pines in self-imposed "bondage to things"; the Sapir-Whorf hypothesis that a people's language imposes "inexorable laws of pattern of which [the speaker] is unconscious" and by which the speaker is "constrained completely" within "unbreakable bonds"; and Claude Lévi-Strauss' famous image of the "bricoleur" who, "pre-constrained" by the materials available, is "restricted by the fact that they are drawn from the language where they already possess a sense which sets a limit on their freedom of manoeuvre." In sum, whether one views

Schoolcraft as revolutionary intellect or providential clod, his theories, fusing the story of the Indians' defeat with the defeat of the Indians' stories, lent defeat the cachet of destiny. "The great question of the removal of the Indians," he wrote in 1830, "is, as I conceive, put to rest. Time & circumstance have decided it against them." Conceiving a mind unmoored from time and immune to circumstance, his work justified the past, codified the present, and piloted the future of this great question.[20]

The ways in which *Algic Researches* seeks to remove myth from history are evident from its broadest outlines to its smallest detail. In Schoolcraft's text, myths appear, as Kenneth Roemer writes of modern anthologies, "in a vacuum": arranged randomly, abutting but bearing no obvious relation to each other, and bereft of context except what little is provided by their titles, they are severed from the conditions of their production (and reconstruction). The editorial apparatus with which Schoolcraft equips his work—"general considerations" on myth; "preliminary observations" on the tales; footnotes sprinkled throughout—similarly frames myth as object of study rather than speaking subject. Where writers such as Bartram had remarked on Indian stories when they appeared in the narration, and thus had implicitly suggested their origin in contexts of encounter, in Schoolcraft their significance lies in their appropriation as "specimens" (15) of science, of that which presumably has an authority independent of context. Albert Lord's comments help gloss these formal innovations: "Ironically enough, it was the collector and even more those who used his collection for educational, nationalistic, political, or religious propaganda who presented the oral society with a fixed form of its own material . . . [and thus] the oral process is now nearly dead." The connection, however, is far from ironic. The reduction of oral tradition, a "living, changing, adaptable artistic creation," to the "ossified cliches" of *Algic Researches* served the nationalistic purpose of removing myth from the nation—of constructing Indian story as if, rather than participating in the varied contexts of America, it had always been absent from a singular history.[21]

When one descends from the form of Schoolcraft's work to its contents, a similar picture emerges. Indeed, given his belief that the myths are "homogeneous," that their "general features coincide" (18), it could hardly have been otherwise. (Though he often attributes tales to their tribe of origin, the "generic" title "Algic" [5] is equally popular.) A fairy-tale diction enhances the myths' timelessness; "there lived a celebrated hunter" (27) and "there was an old man" (34) are typical frames.[22] When Schoolcraft provides the stingiest of temporal gestures, these throw the myths into remote antiquity, into an "era of flint arrow-heads, earthen pots, and skin clothes" (20). "Many years ago," he writes (41), or "in times past" (58). To emphasize that the Indians, like their stories, remain stuck in a "primitive" period (23), Schoolcraft populates the myths with hunters, warriors, and jugglers; at the same time, he steeps the tales in a tone of loss. "The Red Lover" ends with the heroine "pin[ing] away, until that death she so fervently desired came" (45); "Bokwewa" follows an Indian unable to save his brother from the "dissipations into which he had fallen"(86); the central character of "Iena" is "a poor man," "forlorn" and "almost helpless" (87); "Sheem" tells of a child abandoned in a "bleak and barren" place (94). Hunger, cold, and privation mark the Indians' physical world; and though Schoolcraft proclaims himself taken by "the moral often conveyed" in their social world (23), the overriding impression is of a people "who live in fear, who wander in want, and who die in misery" (19).

Thus far, I have presented Schoolcraft's myths *as* his. To a large extent, my choice has been dictated *by* his: he does not say on what basis he picked these stories, and he offers few hints as to his translating principles, writing that he has left the tales "in their original forms of thought and expression" (19), only excising "vulgarity" (174). With one notable exception, to be discussed shortly, and two brief references,[23] he acknowledges only white translators (26), not native tellers. As such, just as he wrenches the tales from time, he denies them a lived presentation: though he notes the emphasis Indian performers place on "repeating the conversations and speeches, and imitating the very tone and gesture of the actors" in their tales (19), when, midway through his gallery of third-person narratives, a stray oral tag—"our people" (106)—slips in, it comes as a shock. Moreover, when Schoolcraft refers to storytelling events, it is in the most derisive of terms; he writes of "the belief of the narrators and listeners in every wild and improbable thing" (19) and devotes one tale to belittling the teller: "He had so happy an exemption from both the restraints of judgment and moral accountability, that he never found the slightest difficulty in accommodating his facts to the most enlarged credulity. Nor was his ample thirst for the marvelous ever quenched by attempts to reconcile statements the most strange, unaccountable, and preposterous. Such was Iagoo, the Indian story-teller, whose name is associated with all that is extravagant and marvelous, and has long been established in the hunter's vocabulary as a perfect synonym for liar" (230). As such passages indicate, the denial of the performative acts—those of his sources—and reconstitutive acts—his own—from which his tales derive is of considerable importance to Schoolcraft.

It would not, indeed, be too much to say that the reason for his text's existence is its refusal of the contexts that gave it birth. Such is, as James Clifford comments, characteristic of ethnographic discourse, which ensures its authority by depicting living peoples as "lost, in disintegrating time and space, but saved in the text. . . . It is assumed that the other society is weak and 'needs' to be represented by an outsider (and that what matters in its life is its past, not present or future)." This "ethnographic allegory" is, of course, but one story and may, therefore, be placed in contact with its others; for instance, Scott Michaelsen has coupled the works of Lewis Henry Morgan and Ely S. Parker to explore how "the subaltern voice, collaborative and countertextual, is lodged at the very sites of invention of the various anthropological discourses." Yet as Richard Bauman argues, such an exploration must not lead one to believe that the "primordial essence" of the oral performance can be distilled from "such other agendas and framings as may secondarily be imposed upon it"; on the contrary, ethnographic agendas are "*constitutive*" of the text as it is shaped "in the recording encounter and through every rendering thereafter."[24] And in the case of Schoolcraft, these agendas function explicitly to suppress collaboration, to annul acts of textual reshaping and therefore, however paradoxically, to augment the shaper's power. As the learned ethnologist ranges myths before him, dividing and measuring to suit his own, unstated aesthetic, myth appears at once as the distinctive language of the Indian and as ethnology's creation, or as a language that, because myth, can occupy history only as a dead artifact of ethnology's discourse.

Nonetheless, if it is difficult to reconstruct the collaboration on which Schoolcraft relied, much less the tales from which he worked, it is possible to restore, in some measure, his activity of turning Indian story to myth, and thus to deny his own story-making the illusion that it is not made. Schoolcraft's lifelong efforts, in Brian Dippie's words, to "monopolize Indian subjects" should alert one not only to the fact of scientific rivals but to the refusal of his Indian "subjects" to be monopolized by the science to which they were subjected.[25] These subjects were many: translators and interpreters, speakers and writers, the famed and the forgotten. All, however—due to social or sexual position, lack of literacy or audience, or Schoolcraft's interference—have been nearly imperceptible in studies of *Algic Researches* or of ethnology as a whole. In Chapter 7, I discuss two Indian writers who, though not immediately involved with Schoolcraft, contested theories such as his; for now, I would like to consider several figures whose close or distant connections with Schoolcraft help restore the material and narrative contacts he labors to eclipse.

The most conspicuous case of an Indian "subject" silenced by Schoolcraft is that of John Tanner, a white man who had been captured by Indians in childhood but had resumed sustained contact with his birth society in 1828 when he took a position as Schoolcraft's interpreter. Fired after a short and apparently rancorous relationship, Tanner published one of the earliest collaborative Indian autobiographies: *A Narrative of the Captivity and Adventures of John Tanner* (1830), written by doctor, explorer, and part-time ethnologist Edwin James and issued three years before Black Hawk's famous *Life*.[26] If, however, the *Narrative* provided Tanner a forum in which to construct his subjecthood, it also roused Schoolcraft's hunger for Indian subjection. In print and in private, the ethnologist mocked Tanner's autobiography as "a mere pack-horse of Indian opinions" with zero "fidelity" and maligned Tanner as "a very savage in his feelings, reasonings, and philosophy," a perfect "realization of Shakspeare's idea of Caliban."[27] Having served as Schoolcraft's voice for a time, and having voiced his own life later, Tanner was ultimately portrayed by Schoolcraft in the terms of ethnologic discourse, by which the Indian could have no voice, or life, without the intercession of the white interpreter.

Those few critics who have studied the Tanner-Schoolcraft relationship have ignored this discourse, favoring personal grudges as the rationale for Schoolcraft's vendetta: he was displeased by Tanner's work habits, annoyed by Tanner's attempts to recover back pay after his dismissal, or miffed by the letters Edwin James wrote on Tanner's behalf.[28] Not only, however, do these interpretations fail to explain either the content or the severity of Schoolcraft's animus, but in overlooking the relation Tanner and his narrative bear to Schoolcraftian ethnology, they help further ethnology's illusion. Erasing the conflictual foundations of ethnology, that is, such conjectures verify a discourse that derives its potency from its claim to originate not in specific contexts of encounter but in the necessary, the natural, the real.

In this light, what is initially striking about Tanner's *Narrative* is not its rejection but its apparent acceptance of that discourse, its anticipation, in form and precept, of the culminating statement of *Algic Researches*. To begin with, like Schoolcraft's narratives, Tanner's is framed by a white interpreter, who provides an introduction, footnotes, and reams of material on Indian vocabulary, place names, and so on; beneath this baggage, Tanner seems, indeed, a mere "pack-horse" for an ethnologic excursion. James's commentary, moreover, foreshadows Schoolcraft's theories (and characterizations of Tanner) in its insistence on deep-seated difference: the prototype of "the solitary savage, with his own habits and opinions," James writes, Tanner "returns to the pale of civilization, too late in life to acquire the mental habits which befit his new situation." To be sure, James departs from Schoolcraft in positing that "mental habits" are acquired, not innate; then, too, he presents these remarks to enlist sympathy for one whose "modes of thinking" are "so different from ours."[29] Yet not only is his editorializing conformable to the ethnologic story of the voiceless Indian, but as Schoolcraft's work makes clear, it was the belief in separate "modes of thinking" that gave this story shape and warrant.

The *Narrative* itself, furthermore, seems to corroborate ethnology's assessment of the Indians as "a race" who are "so destitute, so debased, and hopeless" that they are no longer audible, and whose "uniform and rapid depression and deterioration" will in no time seal their lips for good. Tanner's years in the wild form a litany of drunkenness, disease, and decline: "The men were often drunk, and whenever they were so, they sought to kill me"; "we soon began to fall sick"; "thus we lived for some time, in a suffering and almost starving condition"; "we found our condition too desolate and hopeless." On the rare occasions that an influx of food and shortage of alcohol permit other activities, Indian life in the *Narrative* is a stupefying round of gambling, war-partying, and horse-stealing, with the occasional outbreak of unordinary violence: self-amputation, Tanner's attempted suicide, a brawl ending in the loss of one man's nose to another's teeth.[30] The extent to which Tanner was responsible for these details is, of course, uncertain; though James, like Schoolcraft, swears ethnologic impartiality—Tanner's "narrative, as nearly as possible, [is given] in his own words," the "sentiments expressed" being "exclusively his own"—it is, as always, hazardous to guess what belongs to the speaker and what to the amanuensis. Tanner himself was reported to complain that James "put down a great many . . . things that I never told him"; the disreputable air Schoolcraft had cast over his narrative, however, makes it possible he was attempting to disown the book, and in any event, his statement (itself recorded by a white editor) does not specify where truth ends and lies begin.[31]

Given the *Narrative*'s seeming compliance with ethnologic discourse, it is tempting to argue, as Gordon Sayre does, that "the animosity that Schoolcraft expressed toward James and Tanner may thus reflect not ideological differences, but rather fundamental similarities between Schoolcraft's ambitions and the life and work of two potential competitors."[32] If, however, Schoolcraft felt threatened by James's prior claim to ethnologic territory, it is vital to note the ways in which the pioneer ethnologist and his subject/collaborator diverge from Schoolcraft's methods and conclusions. The most obvious difference is that the *Narrative* presents itself *as* a record of a specific, contemporary Indian person's life, rather than as a review of anonymous tales lost in the mists of antiquity and of their tellers' clouded minds. Tanner was, unlike Schoolcraft's spectral sources, known to people of his time and capable of continuity in ways that the abstracted Indian of *Algic Researches* was not.[33] In the Tanner narrative, then, a dialectic emerges between the distant voice that is subject *to* ethnology and the insistent voice that is the subject *of* its own life; indeed, this dialectic points to the asymmetrical yet joint contexts that make ethnology possible, contexts *Algic Researches* forcefully suppresses. It is in this sense that, though I disagree with John Fierst that James did not "take possession of" the *Narrative*, I would argue that he calls attention to the acts of possession inherent but seldom acknowledged in ethnology, and thus renders local and provisional his own act.[34] That Schoolcraft should seek to dispossess the *Narrative* is thus understandable, for with the example of ethnology's cooperative nature already before the public, his attempts to present his method as the sole option of, and his translations as the sole creation of, ethnology could never be total.

Along these lines, it is notable that the *Narrative* announces not only the individual but the cultural contexts of (dis)possession within which and through which ethnology operated. Indian removal, James argues in the introduction,

manifests, more clearly than volumes of idle and empty professions, our intentions toward [the Indians]. . . . Our professions have been loud, our philanthropic exertions may have been great, but our selfish regard to our own interest and convenience has been greater, and to this we ought to attribute the steady decline, the rapid deterioration of the Indians. We may be told of their constitutional indolence . . . destining them to be forever stationary, or retrogradant; but while remaining monuments and vestiges, as well as historical records of unquestionable authority, assure us, that a few centuries ago they were . . . a great, a prosperous, and a happy people; we ought not to forget that injustice and oppression have been most active among the causes which have brought them down to their present deplorable state.

Written in 1830, the year in which Schoolcraft was pinning the Indian Removal Act on "time and circumstances," this passage reveals that the ethnologic story of the Indians as a "race, doomed by *inscrutable destiny*" belongs not within the canons of invariable law but within a legacy of acts aimed at the Indians' "utter extermination." Indeed, James takes on

Schoolcraft directly in his introduction. Referring to an article of School-craft's that reads, "we are among those who think that [Indian] customs and manners, laws and observances, have not materially changed, at least since the days of Cabot and Hudson," James counters such "Unchangeable Character of the Indian Mind" logic with his own explanation of Indian decline.[35] Moreover, James's sentence reading "we may be told of their constitutional indolence, destining them to be forever stationary," leads one to believe he also intends to contextualize the words of a main force behind both ethnologic research and Indian removal: Schoolcraft's patron, Cass, who had portrayed the Indians in April 1827 (scant months before the Tanner-James collaboration began) as a people wholly "stationary," who pass their lives in "listless indolence" and are "destined to disappear." (That James may have meant to indict Cass is strengthened by an episode in the *Narrative*, one of the few to finger individual evildoing, in which Tanner reports that Cass plied him with rum to test whether he had inherited his adoptive race's supposedly constitutional intemperance—a bitter commentary on governmental encouragement of the alcohol trade and on ethnology's discourse of genetic determination.) The Tanner nar-rative, in sum, is concerned both with the politics of its own fashioning and with the political landscape within which ethnology could seem to tran-scend such considerations. Schoolcraft's reaction against it—his portrayal, in particular, of Tanner as a man so overcome by "Indian notions" as to fit rather than fight the paradigm of *Algic Researches*—can thus be traced to his intolerance of any story that might expose his own.[36]

And in this respect, the most tantalizing aspect of the Tanner-Schoolcraft relationship is the prospect that the stories Schoolcraft called his own were themselves forged from that relationship. As Sayre points out, it is reasonable to think that Schoolcraft's interpreter in the late 1820s may have "aided in the collection and translation of Ojibwa tales." One might even wonder if Schoolcraft's dismissal of his interpreter—and how painful it would have been to be indebted to an Indian's "interpretations" of myth!—had anything to do with his fear that, at the moment he had begun to gauge the value of a publication on myth, Tanner and James (the latter of whom had prepared a manuscript as early as 1826 on Algonquian mythology) might beat him to the punch. Schoolcraft is largely silent on the matter, writing only, and in a sentence that disguises Tanner's possibly active role, that "I drew out of [Tanner] some information of the Indian superstitions"; Tanner's narrative, meanwhile, is largely silent on Indian story, containing only a page or two of tales. One such tale, however, hints

at, if not Tanner's collaboration with Schoolcraft, the ways in which competing stories shape ethnologic discourse: "A baptized Indian, . . . after
death, went to the gate of the white man's heaven, and demanded admittance; but the man who kept watch at the gate told him no redskins could
be allowed to enter there. 'Go,' said he, 'for to the west there are the villages
and the hunting grounds of those of your own people'. . . . So he departed
thence; but when he came to the villages where the dead of his own people
resided, the chief refused him admittance. 'You have been ashamed of us
while you lived; you have chosen to worship the white man's God'. . . .
Thus he was rejected by both parties."[37] Beyond its mordant commentary
on conversion—and the tempting thought that the man who bars "redskins" from glory is Schoolcraft himself—this tale is notable for its tracing
of racial incompatibility to existing prejudice, and not, as ethnology had it,
to eternal law. Indeed, one can view Tanner and Schoolcraft's possible
collaboration in just these terms: that the shadowy scenario is conceivable
suggests the intercultural contexts from which ethnology arises; that it
remains so shadowy reveals how ethnology strives to blot out human contexts at all.

If Tanner's part in the production of *Algic Researches* can only be
speculative, another Indian speaker and interpreter with whom Schoolcraft was on intimate terms does receive credit, however passing, in his
work's pages. First among those he "deemed important to name" as a
translator is "Mrs. Henry R. Schoolcraft" (26); and though he does not say
which tales he took from his bicultural, bilingual wife,[38] a number of the
myths in *Algic Researches* had appeared the year before, spoken (so it was
said) by Jane's mother, Susan Johnston, and translated by Jane, in British
traveler Anna Brownell Jameson's *Winter Studies and Summer Rambles in
Canada* (1838). Exceptionally rare during this period, the fact of related
stories having been recorded in two cases and (perhaps) from the same
speaker and translator is notable in itself. At the same time, this coincidence provides the opportunity Tanner does only by implication: contrasting a story in *Winter Studies*, "The Allegory of Winter and Summer," with
its counterpart in *Algic Researches*, "Peboan and Seegwun, an Allegory of
the Seasons," offers insight into Schoolcraft's shaping of Indian narrative
and thus into the contexts within which ethnology was shaped.

Jameson's "Allegory" tells of "a man from the north, gray-haired,"
who meets a fellow traveler, "a young man, very beautiful in his appearance, with red cheeks, sparkling eyes, and his hair covered with flowers."
This unlikely pair builds a fire and sits to "converse, each telling the other

where he came from, and what had befallen him by the way." Yet in the midst of their dialogue, the young man feels a chill, the source of which is soon apparent: "The old man spoke and said, 'When I wish to cross a river, I breathe upon it and make it hard and walk over upon its surface. I have only to speak, and bid the waters be still, and touch them with my finger, and they become hard as stone. The tread of my foot makes soft things hard—and my power is boundless.'" The young man, "growing tired of the old man's boasting," discloses his own powers: "I have seen [the earth] covered with snow, and the waters I have seen hard as stone; but I have only passed over them, and the snow has melted; the mountain streams have began to flow, the rivers to move, the ice to melt: the earth has become green under my tread, the flowers blossomed, the birds were joyful, and all the power of which you boast vanished away!" The young man, it turns out, is Spring. The tale closes with the other, Winter, "vanishing away: but each, before they parted, expressed a hope that they might meet again before many moons."[39]

"Peboan and Seegwun" follows this version in the main, but varies in particulars. The old man now sits "alone in his lodge," "very old and very desolate": "Day after day passed in solitude, and he heard nothing but the sounds of the tempest, sweeping before it the new-fallen snow" (39). Spring is no longer "very beautiful," but "a handsome young man" (39); where in *Winter Studies* the "red cheeks" and "sparkling eyes" invoke the protagonists of women's periodicals, in *Algic Researches* they project the cocksure bravado of the frontier hero: "His cheeks were red with the blood of youth, his eyes sparkled with animation, and a smile played upon his lips" (39). Unlike the Jameson version, in which the two sit by the hearth to share the day's gossip, this version frames the contest as a warrior's ritual, with the lighting of pipes preceding a recital of "prowess and exploits" (39). Moreover, the tension between the men is exacerbated, the duel becoming an exercise in one-upmanship wherein the two counter each other blow for blow: "'I breathe,' said the young man, 'and flowers spring up all over the plains.' 'I shake my locks,' retorted the old man, 'and snow covers the land'" (39). Once again, Spring bests Winter: "The tongue of the old man became silent. . . . As the sun increased, he grew less and less in stature, and anon had melted completely away" (40). Yet there is a finality to this conquest missing in *Winter Studies*, where "each expressed a hope that they might meet again before many moons."

If these differences are suggestive, one should be cautious what one makes of them. To begin with, it is not known whether Henry relied on

Susan, Jane, an unnamed speaker, or even Jameson as his source. At the same time, though Jameson follows form in disclaiming responsibility for her version, stating that it was "written down from [Susan's] recitation, and translated by her daughter," she surely subjected Jane's words to shaping of her own. It is thus risky to venture which version is most faithful to a conclusive oral account; even if the domestic tints of the Jameson version are not hers—and they probably are, given her efforts throughout *Winter Studies* to make Indian women accessible to her readers—Jane, who despite her frontier life was educated in the canons of white womanly propriety, might have contributed these embellishments herself.[40] This being said, it is still intriguing that the Jameson telling offers a reconciliation unavailable in the Schoolcraft; along with the homey touches that mitigate the tale's violence, the ending offers a tentative harmony, the seasonal cycle—a linear progression for Schoolcraft—hinting at interdependence. The Jameson version, like Tanner's *Narrative*, manifests to an extent the collaborative nature of its production; as each man "tells the other where he came from, and what had befallen him," the possibility of a mutual relationship between transmitter and receiver, informant and interpreter is, if provisionally, entertained. And as such, the story's concern with the circumstances of story-making suggest the impossibility of fixing any one telling *as* the "conclusive" account, the fact that each telling, being context-specific rather than the final word, must continually encounter its other(s).

Conversely, the Schoolcraft version seems to pursue a vision of solitary authority, of conclusiveness: just as, by erasing his sources and thereby denying their stories' placement in a temporal or temporary milieu, he claims uncontested curatorship of Indian myth, so are the men in his telling more obviously bent on the assertion of a single voice over the other. (Where the Jameson version emphasizes the sharing of stories, the Schoolcraft version ends with the silencing of Winter's tongue.) Whether it is racial allegory—with aged Winter, "frozen" in time and unable to adapt to the fresh winds blowing, succumbing to the figure identified with both the fluidity of progress and the bright dawn of the risen Son—an indictment of warrior life, or a personification of the myth/history split, Schoolcraft's version bases its authority to present Indian myth on an image of myth as un-present, a relic and an absence that can be made present only at his behest and by his leave.

Toward this end, and as a final illustration of the intercultural contexts within which Schoolcraft was, however unwillingly, enmeshed, it is instructive to consider the one myth in *Algic Researches* that does foreground its presentation. Briefly mentioned in the introduction as one "of the modern class of Indian fictions" (24), this myth, which appears at the end of the book's first volume under the title "Paradise Opened to the Indians," is headed by a "Historical Note": "The following is a literal translation of the story related by the noted Algic chief Pontiac, to the Indian tribes whom he wished to bring into his views in forming his general confederacy against the Anglo-Saxon race in the last century. It is taken from an ancient manuscript journal now in the possession of the Michigan Historical Society. This journal . . . appears to have been kept by a person holding an official station, or intimate with the affairs of the day, during the siege of the fort of Detroit by the confederate Indians in 1763" (116). This myth is thus flagged as a departure: it is located in a prominent spot in the text, is accessible to others, and is taken from a speaker who played a central role in a drama of intercultural conflict. Pontiac's myth tells of a Delaware who dreams of touring the afterlife. Reaching heaven, he is greeted by the Creator, who counsels individual, social, and continental change: "I hate you to drink as you do, until you lose your reason; I wish you not to fight one another. . . . The land on which you are, I have made for you, not for others: wherefore do you suffer the whites to dwell upon your lands? . . . Drive them away; wage war against them. I love them not. They know me not. They are my enemies, they are your brothers' enemies. Send them back to the lands I have made for them. Let them remain there" (118, 119). The tale ends with the newly appointed prophet delivering the divine laws to his people.

This story, though in ways different from those of Schoolcraft's bosom acquaintances, might contest his discourse of myth, might foreground the narrative interplays from which the nation—and ethnology—arose. For one thing, its context questions the homogenizing power of his work; here myth—both as spoken and as recovered—exists *in* history. The contents, moreover, witness a dependence on encounter: merging what it casts as a traditional cosmogony with elements drawn from Christianity and European folklore (a glass mountain, for instance), this story announces itself to *be* a story, a situated act rather than a given truth. And, indeed, this story exists in a tradition of multiple-origins tales recorded beginning in the mid-eighteenth century, one example of which comes from Timothy Dwight's contact with the Oneidas:

Before man existed, there were three great and good spirits, of whom one was superior to the other two, and is emphatically called the Great Spirit and the Good

Spirit. At a certain time this exalted being said to one of the others, "Make a man." He obeyed, and taking chalk formed a paste of it, and molding it into the human shape infused into it the animating principle, and brought it to the Great Spirit. He, after surveying it, said, "This is too white."

He then directed the other to make a trial of his skill. Accordingly taking charcoal, he pursued the same process, and brought the result to the Great Spirit, who, after surveying it, said, "It is too black."

Then said the Great Spirit, "I will now try myself"; and taking red earth he formed a human being in the same manner, surveyed it, and said, "This is a proper (or perfect) man."[41]

These stories, according to reports of the time usually alarmist in tone, were adaptable to—or arose in the context of—nativist resistance to conversion and expansion. In such cases, the original racial separatism was pursued to an eschatological "Vission of Heaven where there was no White people but all Indians."[42] A particularly intriguing instance of such an apocalyptic story was recorded in 1824 by another protégé of Lewis Cass, budding ethnologist C. C. Trowbridge, who translated from the Shawnee prophet Tenskwatawa a version of the story that, perhaps, this speaker had told Tecumseh's followers the decade before: "When the Great Spirit made this Island he thought it necessary to make also human beings to inhabit it, and with this view he formed an Indian. . . . The Great Spirit then opened a door, and looking down [the Indians] saw a white man seated upon the ground. . . . The great Spirit told them that this white man was not made by himself but by another spirit who made & governed the whites & over whom or whose subjects he had no controul. That as soon as they reached their Island and had got comfortably situated, this great white spirit would endeavour to thwart his designs." Here, it seems, is an alternative reading of the ethnology meant to silence such readings. Cass, then governor of the Michigan Territory, had heard rumors of a renewed Indian uprising and had thought it prudent to contact the primary spiritual force behind the contests of the previous decade. Under these circumstances, one might hazard that Tenskwatawa—who his opponent in the earlier contest, William Henry Harrison, owned was a man of "considerable talents"—saw through the sudden outpouring of interest and used his role as ethnographic informant to proclaim what ethnology denied, the fact of Indian stories of America's destiny: "If it be foreordained that every thing is to belong to the whites, in four years the [Indians' sacred] fire will become visible to all the world. Then the Indians grown desperate by a consciousness that their end is approaching will suffer the fire to burn and to destroy the whites, upon whom they will call, tauntingly, to quench it."[43] I do not claim that such stories are evidence of precontact Indian "racial" thought, for to deny the stories' existence within sites of encounter might suggest that racial discourse and difference are, as ethnology urged, absolute and universal. I do not, for that matter, claim that such stories, however wide-spread, can be accepted without reference to the politics of the texts in which they appear.[44] On the contrary, I wish to suggest that like Tanner's and Jameson's texts, such stories, precisely because they call attention to their location in contexts of encounter, contest ethnology's claim that myth and history are independent of such contexts. Where Schoolcraft insists that his text fully and necessarily contains the nonspeech of myth, these tales construct Indian and Euro-American stories as contemporaries, com-batants, collaborators that must account for one another in the ongoing story of America. And as such, they make visible not only the features of Euro-American colonialism—land hunger, religious bigotry, and so on—but the work of ethnology itself; they expose ethnology's efforts to present itself, and the colonialism it sustains, as divinely decreed truth.

Applying such stories to *Algic Researches* thus reveals how Schoolcraft cloaks the local facts of textual and scientific politics. For Pontiac's myth, contained within a manuscript that seems to have imbibed myth's evanes-cence—several words are "obliterated" (116)—can, Schoolcraft maintains, come to light only through him, and only then to depict a struggle that, his appropriation of the myth is meant to prove, has long been settled. School-craft's terms, moreover, strive to remove all doubt as to why myth has so meekly rolled over; historical note or no, he depicts the myth as a "curious specimen of Indian fiction" that announces the Indians to have been, time out of mind, dupes of "mythology": "No stronger proof could, perhaps, be adduced of . . . the prevalence, at that time, of oral tales and fanciful legends among the tribes" (116). As such, Pontiac emerges not as a chal-lenger to ethnology's domain but as its aide, for he preaches an illusory, mythic "paradise" that prevents the Indians from ascending to the real heaven or haven of historical progress. In Schoolcraft's crowning *Historical and Statistical Information*, a passage suggesting that Cass and Trowbridge had shared Tenskwatawa's story with Schoolcraft reverts to the myths of the prophets: "The opinion that prior times had attained all that was worth attainment, one of the dogmas of Pontiac, has had the most paralyzing effect upon the progress of the hunter tribes. Elksquatowa [Tenskwatawa], the Shawnee Prophet, had a powerful effect in confirming [this opin-ion]. . . . [T]he wild-wood tribes of A. D. 1850 are, mentally, physically, and characteristically, identical with those of A. D. 1500." The "historical inter-est" (116) *Algic Researches* ascribes to Pontiac's myth does not, then, inhere in the myth, but in the fact that the only myth to present Indians known to history contesting their removal confirms their inability to present themselves, and thus to remain in history. A reviewer of *Algic Researches*, perhaps recalling this tale, summed up the spirit of the whole: "The scene is changing with each year, and the past, with respect to the Savages, does not recur. They fall back with no hope to recover lost ground; they diminish with no hope to increase again; they degenerate with no hope to revive in physical or moral strength. . . . After observers will find mere fragments, or a heterogeneous mass"; but this "chaos of aboriginal facts will be reduced, under [Schoolcraft's] hand, to some degree of order." Reducing the "heterogeneous mass" by turning the voices by which it was upbraided and upraised into the "scattered bones" of the past (as Schoolcraft wrote in another echo of Jefferson), *Algic Researches* is a testament not, as its named author had it, to the vanished Indian but to the ages-long effort to remove competing stories, remove the fact *of* story, from America's ground.[45]

And in this respect, Schoolcraft's work finally reveals (or conceals) that at the heart of ethnology lies not mental but material speculation, conflict over America's ground. For as Fabian argues, expansion requires not only space but time: "Time to accommodate the schemes of a one-way history: progress, development, modernity (and their negative mirror images: stagnation, underdevelopment, tradition). In short, *geopolitics* has its ideological foundations in *chronopolitics*."[46] Theories such as Schoolcraft's peaked precisely when Indians were most publicly fighting for their place on the land and in history, and thereby threatening geographic hegemony; *Algic Researches* appeared the year after the Cherokees had been consigned to a territorial distance as total as the temporal one Schoolcraft decreed. I do not wish to make too much of this date, which may be a mere coincidence of the calendar; I do not wish to see a conspiracy in a conjunction. Yet as I have insisted, ethnology, if it is neither identical to nor inseparable from extrascientific concerns, does arise from the very intercultural contexts it most seeks to obscure; and if my examples have been drawn from Schoolcraft's life and work, his life and work cannot—as the stories of Pontiac and Tenskwatawa suggest—be permitted to obscure the larger, continental contexts within which they operate. Schoolcraft himself, mineralogist turned mythographer, bridges the geographic and narrative seizure of Indian materials; indeed, one of the first myths he offered his country, published in his 1821 account of the mining tour that set in motion his mining of the Indian mind, speaks to the literal and ideological control of the land:

The Indian related, that passing in his canoe during the afternoon of a beautiful summer's day, across Winnebago lake . . . he espied at a distance in the lake before him, a beautiful female form standing in the water. Her eyes shone with a brilliancy that could not be endured, and she held in her hand a lump of glittering gold. He immediately paddled towards the attractive object, but as he came near, he could perceive that it was gradually altering as to its shape and complexion; her eyes no longer shone with brilliancy—her face lost the hectic glow of life—her arms imperceptibly disappeared; and when he came to the spot where she stood, it was a monument of stone. . . . [H]e ventured to lay his hand upon the statue, and finally lifted it into his canoe. Then sitting in the other end of the canoe, with his back towards the miraculous statue, he paddled gently towards the shore, but was astonished, on turning round, to find nothing in his canoe, but the large lump of copper, "which," he concluded, taking it carefully from a roll of skins, "I now present to you."

In this myth, Schoolcraft finds the "fund" of "material" he would claim myth to be, and (as he had written of myth in 1822) takes "possession" of this "resource." The myth is, just as it describes, an object science can turn to its account. Casting the myth as a mere product that, like the copper that forms its content, "cannot fail, both to augment our sources of profitable industry, and to promote our commercial independence," Schoolcraft asserts his and the nation's independence from all other claims.[47] Indeed, that the myth describes the metamorphosis of a living spirit to dead stone heightens the illusion of monologue: just as the "European race [has] overspread the land, and the Indians [have been] driven before them" (16), so are Euro-American researchers now to claim the deposits, mineral and mythological, the Indians have left behind.

The transformation of Indian narrative to myth, in sum, represented an attempt to build a nation on the rocks and bones of peoples excluded from the nation. In a similar vein, the subordination of myth to literary history represented an effort to turn Indian claims into the absent foundation of an original literature, to create a national story out of Indian myth that left Indian myth out of the national story. The following chapter turns to this project. Yet like the chapter now coming to a close, the next maintains that it is insufficient to consider in isolation the stories antebellum writers told; that one must place these stories in contact with the Indian stories against which—and from which—America's literary origins were forged.

Chapter Six

Myth and the State

It seems that our first business is to supervise the production of
stories, and choose only those we think suitable, and reject the rest.

—Plato, *The Republic*

A generation after its war for national independence, America's war for literary independence was waged. Having laid to rest its colonial past, the
nation, wrote patriots like Henry Schoolcraft, wanted a literature to contest
the tyranny of British letters: "It is time, in the course of our national developments, that we begin to produce something characteristic of the land
that gave us birth. No people can bear a true nationality, which does not
exfoliate, as it were, from its bosom, something that expreses the peculiarities of its own soil and climate. . . . And where! when we survey the
length and breadth of the land, can a more suitable element, for the work be
found, than is furnished by . . . the free, bold, wild, independent, native
hunter race?" This equation of native peoples with a native literature was
common; thus in a review of James Eastburn's *Yamoyden* (1820), John Palfrey praises the author's use of "the antiquities of the Indians. Whatever in
their customs or superstitions fell within the scope of the plot, is seized on
with an admirable tact, and made available for the purposes of poetry. . . .
Whoever in this country first attains the rank of a first rate writer of
fiction," he predicts, "will lay his scene here." Similarly, R. C. Sands urges:
"If faith in wild predictions, and entire submission of the soul to the power
of ancient legends and visionary prophecies, are useful to the poet or
romancer, here they may be found in abundance and endless variety." And a
third critic, fearful of "colonizing our minds" to Europe, holds that if "a
writer of this country, wishes to make its history or its traditions the subject
of romantic fiction, . . . he must go back to the aborigines."[1]

Antebellum literary nationalism has captivated scholars since its re-
appearance, a century later, in efforts to create a uniquely American literary
criticism.[2] Traditionally, however, such studies have ignored the relationship of literary nationalism to that which the nation rejects—the relation-

ship of myth to the state. Most have treated the quest for a literary Columbus as the flowering of a long dormant impulse; since, as Benjamin Spencer writes, "from the beginning" Americans cherished "a sense of distinctive nationality," and since the Indians were America's "distinctive literary possession," their artistic discovery was only a matter of time.[3] Yet such an argument reproduces an odd ellipsis: if the Indians furnish materials for a national literature, then literary identity is founded on that which the nation excludes. In the previous chapter, I considered a similar paradox in antebellum ethnology; in this chapter, I wish to uncover the acts of physical and ideological removal to which literary nationalism owed its existence and to suggest the ways Indian peoples informed and contested the literature that sought their erasure.

Though not one to advocate explicitly the literary use of Indians, Ralph Waldo Emerson provides a point of entry into these issues. To Emerson, the central problem of his generation was its failure to develop a mode of seeing and being adequate to the present. Thus *Nature* (1836) begins: "Our age is retrospective. It builds the sepulchres of the fathers. . . . The foregoing generations beheld God and nature face to face; we, through their eyes. Why should not we also enjoy an original relation to the universe? Why should not we have a poetry and philosophy of insight and not of tradition, and a religion by revelation to us, and not the history of theirs? . . . [W]hy should we grope among the dry bones of the past?" *Nature* is thus an attempt to find a language that confronts/creates the essence of America without the intervening dross of age. And, in keeping with Friedrich Schlegel's turn-of-the-century pronouncement that "one could summarize all the essentials in which modern poetry is inferior to the ancient in these words: We have no mythology," Emerson concluded, however paradoxically, that for the nation to realize a language suited to America's revolutionary history, it must reclaim a traditional language of myth: "Because of this radical correspondence between visible things and human thoughts, savages, who have only what is necessary, converse in figures. As we go back in history, language becomes more picturesque, until its infancy, when it is all poetry. . . . By degrees we may come to know the primitive sense of the permanent objects of nature, so that the world shall be to us an open book, and every form significant of its hidden life and final cause." Here mythic language constitutes rock-bottom reality, the union of sign and signified. To regain it, to "pierce this rotten diction" between object and utterance and "fasten words again to visible things," is thus to secure an original relation to the universe.[4]

Or, more important, to the country. Thirty years after *Nature*, Emerson repeated his masterwork's theme: "Our debt to tradition," he writes, "is so massive, our protest or private addition so rare and insignificant . . . that, in a large sense, one would say there is no pure originality. . . . Our country, customs, laws, our ambitions, and our notions of fit and fair,—all these we never made, we found them ready-made; we but quote them."[5] First in Emerson's list is "our country"; and while he could mean simply that the land was there from the first, the word "our" suggests otherwise. For "our" country (nation or land) was not given; rather, it became "ours" through the taking. Repositioning Emerson in an intercultural context, it becomes clear that his sense of interloping, unoriginating, reflects the fact that "our" country was "theirs," that the "traditions" of the first peoples mediate between word and thing, verbal claim and physical. As such, to assimilate those traditions to an "original" literature is to "seize" (Palfrey's word) an unmediated relationship to the land; turning myth to the (im)material of poetry grounds a continental hegemony free of Indian peoples.

It must be stressed, however, that this appropriation was not merely "retrospective." For if in 1836 references to the "sepulchres of the fathers" and "dry bones of the past" invoked ethnological researches into those whose traditionalism had supposedly fated them to vanish, it simultaneously echoed Indians who continued to insist on their place in "our" country. "The land on which we stand we have received as an inheritance from our fathers," the Cherokees wrote in 1829, in one of many memorials sent to Congress. "It is our fathers' gift; it contains their ashes; it is the land of our nativity, and the land of our intellectual birth." It was, then, by transforming such utterances into dead vestiges that writers denied the ongoing interaction of stories, the multiple claims to space, in America. As an example, though Thoreau took up his mentor's quest for an "American mythology," when his Penobscot guide during his *Maine Woods* travels, Joe Polis, offered a story expressing his own claim, Thoreau was quick to disclaim it:

The Indian repeated the tradition respecting this mountain's having anciently been a cow moose,—how a mighty Indian hunter, whose name I forget, succeeded in killing this queen of the moose tribe with great difficulty, while her calf was killed somewhere among the islands in Penobscot Bay, and, to his eyes, this mountain had still the form of the moose in a reclining posture, its precipitous side presenting the outline of her head. He told this at some length, though it did not amount to much, and with apparent good faith. . . . An Indian tells such a story as if he thought it deserved to have a good deal said about it, only he has not got it to say, and so he makes up for the deficiency by a drawling tone, long-windedness, and a dumb wonder which he hopes will be contagious.[6]

However sketchy, this story accords with later accounts that name the hunter as Gluskabe the Transformer, an Abenaki figure who, like Emerson's "Namer or Language-maker," was credited with turning natural facts to human symbols—"Glus-gahbé," Charles Leland quotes one source, "gave names to everything"—and was consequently associated with the features of the Abenaki people's homeland: "Over all the Land of the Wabanaki there is no place which was not marked by the hand of the Master."[7] One can only speculate why (or even if) Polis told this story; perhaps he was merely swapping hunting tales. It is possible, however, to place this story in contact with Thoreau's: showing how, "to his eyes," Gluskabe's acts are manifest in the landscape, Polis's story indicates that Indian "tradition" is not an absence to be assimilated but a living presence that both prefigures and authorizes Indian claims to the land.

And as such, Thoreau's ho-hum reaction reveals less his indifference than his refusal to allow other "eyes" to perceive that land. As Robert Richardson comments, "Thoreau did not in any way adapt existing myth to his literary needs. . . . Instead, and the point is important, he tried to recover for himself the original conditions in which the early creators of the great myths found themselves."[8] The point is indeed important, though not solely for what it says of Thoreau's method. The absence of "existing myth" for Thoreau is inseparable from his attempt to find/found an "original" myth; if he is to present appropriation as origination, he must re-cover, cover over or up, the stories of the land's original inhabitants. Thus, though this was, as far as Thoreau let on, his lone firsthand encounter with Indian story,[9] he preferred to rhapsodize over Indian words that could not interfere with their reinscription:

There can be no more startling evidence of their being a distinct and comparatively aboriginal race, than to hear this unaltered Indian language, which the white man cannot speak nor understand. . . . It was a purely wild and primitive American sound, as much as the barking of a *chickaree*, and I could not understand a syllable of it. . . . These Abenakis gossiped, laughed, and jested, in the language in which Eliot's Indian Bible is written, the language which has been spoken in New England who shall say how long? These were the sounds that issued from the wigwams of this country before Columbus was born; they have not yet died away. . . . I felt that I stood, or rather lay, as near to the primitive man of America, that night, as any of its discoverers ever did.

Like Polis's story, the Indians' speech is, so far as Thoreau is concerned, dumb; indeed, their speech *is* the mythic language he seeks, a "natural" language that acquires meaning only when—comparable to Eliot's work on Indian souls—the poet converts it to his literary needs. Like School-craft, then, Thoreau abstracts Indian words from context in order to turn them to timeless myth, the distinctive possession of America's original literature.[10] For Thoreau, as for his fellows, Indian myth is "the stuff out of which Genius weaves her best fabrics,—those which are most truthful, and most enduring, as most certainly native and original—to be wrought into symmetry and shape with the usual effects of time and civilization."[11] To ensure the nation a "native" and "original" claim, myth, by itself, can be no more than mute, brute "stuff." Time and civilization must tell the tale.

The campaign for literary nationalism, in sum, was fought not only against Europe's courtly muses but against America's native mythos. Seeking to expose the ideological roots of this campaign, critics have begun to explore the role key texts of literary nationalism played in erasing the Indians' presence; interestingly, however, they have employed the very terms by which that erasure was effected. Robert Clark, for example, writes that in *The Last of the Mohicans* (1826), James Fenimore Cooper constructs a "mythological" image of Indian-white conflict to "assuage [his] anxieties over the White possession of Indian lands," while Helen Carr writes that in *The Song of Hiawatha* (1855), Henry Wadsworth Long-fellow creates "a myth for one culture" from "the myths of another" to justify "the displacement of the Indians."[12] Yet in both cases, the act of displacement is naturalized: Indians, and their myths, are necessarily absent from literary history. In what follows, accordingly, I am interested not only in how these authors convert "traditions" to their own "origin," but in how the stories they make myth prove, as Thoreau feared, "contagious," interacting with their own. In Joe Polis's words: "You see 'em my tracks."[13]

The Graves of the Fathers

Cooper's *Last of the Mohicans* appeared two years after James Monroe presented a formal plan of Indian removal to Congress and four years before Andrew Jackson signed act into law. In Cooper's state, 1826 was the year the Senecas ceded most of their two main reservations. The question that Cooper, himself an inheritor of Oneida land, posed in *The Pioneers* (1823) was thus pressing: "Whence came these riches, this vale, and those hills, and why am I their owner?"[14] *Pioneers* appeals to the law of property to answer this question; *Mohicans* delves into Indian claims, the stories of the Delawares and Mahicans (whom Cooper, joining these peoples with the unrelated Mohegans, termed the "Mohicans"). Critics have, in fact, taken the shift from history to myth as the novel's structuring device; in Richard Slotkin's words, at its midpoint "we leave the stage of 'history' and firmly enter the world of myth."[15] As the quotation marks around "history" indicate, however, this dichotomy must be qualified; and though Slotkin feels that myth, as an essential term, can do without ironizing, it is precisely the process by which such terms are essentialized that *Mohicans* illustrates. Cooper is far from confident of where the stage of history and the world of myth are to be found; rather, he labors to found the two, to erect history's stage on a mythic world and thereby claim that myth, and world, as history's own.

Toward this end, it is instructive to consider the genre *Mohicans* helped define: the historical romance. To critics of the time, the fusion of history and romance was fraught with risk. Just as, in Schoolcraft's words, the "boundaries between truth and fiction are but feebly defined among the aborigines," who weave the "scattered incidents and landmarks of their history into the web and woof of their wildest tales," so could a historical romance destabilize historical truth: "History cannot be studied to advantage in romance, because this mixture of truth and falsehood confounds the mind, renders it at length incapable of distinguishing the facts from distortions or embellishments, and finally weakens that salutary reliance upon the reality of the past, on which no inconsiderable portion of our reverence for truth itself is founded." Cooper confided to his literary club his ambivalence about the form he had popularized: "If there be a man in this community who owes a debt to the Muse of History, it would seem to be the one who has now the honor to address you. No writer of our country has invaded her sacred precincts with greater license or more frequency. Sir, I have not been unmindful of the weight of my transgressions in this particular, and I have long and seriously reflected on the means of presenting an expiatory offering before the altar of the offended Goddess." Though speaking with tongue in cheek here, Cooper would turn earnest when reviewers picked apart his later novels as self-serving autobiographies. "In a work *professing* to be a fiction," he shot back, "no one has a right to suppose any part true, that can not be *shown* to be true. Writers of fiction do, certainly, often introduce circumstances more or less true, but an intelligent reader understands that an ingenious blending of fact and fancy contributes to the charm of this species of composition. . . . Even known *historical events are* allowed to be perverted, to aid [writers] in rendering their works more interesting."[16] Whether this satisfied Cooper—and, given that he crossed out "truth" and substituted "fact," he seems to have been only "more or less" certain of the terms he was juggling—it reveals his feeling that romance might be history "perverted."

Thus it is intriguing that Cooper argues that *Mohicans* is not a romance after all: "The reader, who takes up these volumes, in expectation of finding an imaginary and romantic picture of things which never had an existence, will probably lay them aside, disappointed. The work is exactly what it professes to be in its title page—a narrative. As it relates, however, to matters which may not be universally understood, especially by the more imaginative sex, some of whom, under the impression that it is a fiction, may be induced to read the book, it becomes the interest of the author to explain a few of the obscurities of the historical allusions" (1). Cooper's dig at female readers was a time-honored way of cordoning history off from the lightweight, untrustworthy novel. Yet if histories are masculine/true and novels feminine/false, what is the sexual and ontological status of "narrative"? That Cooper resorts to this omnibus term suggests that his sexist distinction represents an effort to draw a line his novel will not support. And by referring to the "obscurities" of history, he himself erases what he draws—for this is the charge he levels against myth: "There is so much obscurity in the Indian traditions, and so much confusion in the Indian names, as to render some explanation useful" (5). His explanation, however, merely restates the problem: "Whites have assisted greatly in rendering the traditions of the Aborigines more obscure by their own manner of corrupting names" (6). The narrative itself does little to clear up the obscurity; on the contrary, it misses no opportunity to render a world as impenetrable and unreliable as myth: "Their anxious and eager looks were baffled by the deceptive light" (63); "every trace of their footsteps was lost in the obscurity of the woods" (131). In his fine study of these recurring images, Thomas Philbrick can be pardoned for an understatement: "The world of the novel is one that is rarely seen clearly and known with certainty."[17] The only certainty, rather, is the lack of it.

Or the only certainty is what one makes of it, using narratives that conceal as much as, or to the extent that, they reveal. Thus Cooper's novel contains a variety of narratives, each with a distinctive take on reality. There is rumor: "More substantial evils were preceded by a thousand fanciful and imaginary dangers . . . nor was there any ear, in the provinces, so deaf as not to have drunk in with avidity the narrative of some fearful tale of midnight murder, in which the natives of the forests were the principal and barbarous actors" (13). There is romance: "The young man sunk into a deep sleep, dreaming that he was a knight of ancient chivalry, holding his midnight vigils before the tent of a re-captured princess, whose favour he did not despair of gaining, by such a proof of devotion and watchfulness" (129). There is salvationism: "My feet would rather follow the tender spirits intrusted to my keeping, even into the idolatrous province of the Jesuits, than take one step backward, while they pined in captivity and sorrow" (224). These narratives are more than idle constructs; they shape reality, are reality, for their tellers. None, however, can claim to be reality, for reality permits any number of tellings, all of which obscure. As Natty comments: "One moccasin is no more like another, than one book is like another; though they who can read in one, are seldom able to tell the marks of the other. . . . Let me get down to it, Uncas; neither book nor moccasin is the worse for having two opinions, instead of one" (186). Get down to it Natty does; but his opinion mediates what "it" is.

This is not to say that Cooper doubts there is an "it." As his thoughts on the massacre at Fort William Henry show, he honors a sovereign truth beneath layers of obfuscation: "It is now becoming obscured by time . . . and, as history, like love, is so apt to surround her heroes with an atmosphere of imaginary brightness, it is probable that Louis de Saint Véran will be viewed by posterity only as the gallant defender of his country, while his cruel apathy on the shores of the Oswego and of the Horican, will be forgotten. Deeply regretting this weakness on the part of a sister muse, we shall at once retire from her sacred precincts, within the proper limits of our own humbler vocation" (180). Clearly, however history (as record) diverges from what it depicts, Cooper would blanch at the notion that history (as event) is merely the sum of its "imaginary" depictions. And yet, if history can be told through any number of narratives, then all are inchoate history. Not all will serve one's ends with equal efficacy and dispatch—Gamut's effete psalmistry and Heyward's moony medievalism prove inexpedient during times of intercultural war, and they are sent packing by Natty's frontier machismo—but this is precisely Cooper's point: no narrative "is" history until from an array of incipient histories the one that enforces a certain, though of necessity uncertain, truth is crowned, while the others are displaced.

In this regard, it is critical that Cooper stages the first encounter between his main white and Indian characters as a debate between narratives—narratives, moreover, of displacement. First is Natty's recital, keyed to justify white claims: "Your fathers came from the setting sun, crossed the big river, fought the people of the country, and took the land; and mine came from the red sky of the morning, over the salt lake, and did their work much after the fashion that had been set them by yours; then let God judge the matter between us, and friends spare their words!" (30). Yet if this Franklinesque story, adapted by Cooper from Moravian missionary John Heckewelder's history of the Delawares, constructs dispossession as cyclical, Cooper knew another story from the same source. According to this story—which, Heckewelder asserts, the Indians preserve "on the tablets of their memories"—the Delawares had been displaced "by fraud or by force," most infamously by the Walking Purchase of 1737, in which a specious deed and map devised by William Penn's proprietary agent, James Logan, deceived the sachem Nutimus. The Delawares, according to Heckewelder, regularly "go over this ground"; refusing to spare their words, they tell another story, one that traces Euro-American claims to violent duplicity, not natural right.[18]

Indeed, it is precisely the question of whose claim will gain the appearance of the natural that the opening dialogue dramatizes. And notably, Natty's comments suggest that Indian narrative has the upper hand: "I am willing to own that my people have many ways, of which, as an honest man, I can't approve. It is one of their customs to write in books what they have done and seen, instead of telling them in their villages, where the lie can be given to the face of a cowardly boaster, and the brave soldier can call on his comrades to witness for the truth of his words. In consequence of this bad fashion, a man who is too conscientious to misspend his days among the women, in learning the names of black marks, may never hear of the deeds of his fathers. . . . But every story has its two sides; so I ask you, Chingachgook, what passed, according to the traditions of the red men, when our fathers first met?" (31). Natty's misogynist illiteracy picks up the argument of the preface, but broadens it; the confusion of names is now chargeable to writing itself, which (as Emerson held) aggravates the gap between word and deed. Oral discourse, on the other hand, heals the breach: "'Tis what my fathers have said," Chingachgook declares, "and what the Mohicans have done" (31). Similarly, where the names of black marks hold an attenuated relationship to their objects, Chingachgook claims an immediate, hereditary knowledge of the land: "Does not this stream at our feet, run towards the summer, until its waters grow salt, and the current flows upward. . . . [T]he fathers of Chingachgook have not

lied!" (31). For Natty, who admits that "your traditions [of the land] tell you
true" (31), the only recourse is to suggest peevishly, "Know you any thing of
your own family, at that time?" (33). This phase of the debate, intriguingly,
resembles an exchange recorded during the Walking Purchase negotiations; challenged by Logan to declare how he knew "how much land was
sold as he was very Young at the time [and] as the Indians had no Writings," the sachem was said to have retorted: "He had it from his Father."[19]
The land, and the story of the land—the "it" Nutimus had—are one;
Logan must summon written documents to break that unity. Yet if written
words, as Natty remarks, "fall far below savage customs" (57), where sign
equals thing, then all the deeds on earth cannot naturalize white claims.

Cooper, of course, was no groper among the dry deeds of the past;
there is little chance he knew the Walking Purchase proceedings. My
purpose in recounting this episode is not, in any event, to revive the debate
over Cooper's grasp of colonial times.[20] On the contrary, my purpose is to
point out that it is a mistake to read Cooper solely in relation to a colonial,
and thus extinguished, Indian presence; that his interest in Indian traditions should alert one to ongoing conflicts. Cooper's fascination with Indian fathers in *Mohicans* has been noted by many; while Stephen Railton
ascribes this to the oedipal drama, Mark Patterson tracks it to revolutionary anxiety: the "conflict in Cooper's work is between historical change—
the movement away from an origin—and the possibility of permanence—
the presence of that origin in succeeding generations." This may be. The
custom, however, of seeing Cooper's Indian fathers as figures solely of
individual and Euro-cultural angst is of a piece with his own efforts to
make Indians subserve his claims; that is, when critics find in Cooper's
Indians only Cooper's people, they repeat the act by which literary nationalism sought to turn living, vocal Indians to the silent, imaginary
origin of the nation. And this tendency to, as Eric Cheyfitz puts it, see
"Indians and Indian history in the Leatherstocking Tales [as] merely a
rhetorical ornament to an essentially European content" is particularly
damaging here because it overlooks the central role paternal discourse
played in the physical counterpart of literary nationalism: the effort to turn
vocal, living Indians from their lands.[21] The imagery of the United States
as Great White Father is well known; at the same time, the discrediting of
Indian fathers took various forms in Removal-era Indian policy.[22] In 1805,
for example, Thomas Jefferson identified Indian leaders as one of the
greatest impediments to federal initiatives: "The endeavours to enlighten
[the Indians] on the fate which awaits their present course of life, to induce

them to exercise their reason, follow its dictates, and change their pursuits with the change of circumstances have powerful obstacles to encounter; they are combated by the habits of their bodies, the prejudices of their minds, ignorance, pride, and the influence of interested and crafty individuals among them who feel themselves something in the present order of things and fear to become nothing in any other. These persons inculcate a sanctimonious reverence for the customs of their ancestors; [teach] that whatsoever they did must be done through all time . . . and exert all their faculties to maintain the ascendancy of habit over the duty of improving our reason and obeying its mandates." In 1827, Lewis Cass took a different tack, using paternal imagery to picture Indians as congenitally incapable of change: "A principle of progressive improvement seems almost inherent in human nature. . . . But there is little of all this in the constitution of our savages. Like the bear, and deer, and buffalo of his own forests, an Indian lives as his father lived, and dies as his father died." More direct was Wilson Lumpkin, who seethed during the debates over the Removal Bill that "those [Cherokees] who have emigrated are delighted with their new homes, and most of their brethren who remain in the States would gladly improve their present condition by joining them: but their lordly chiefs, of the white blood, with their northern allies, 'will not let the people go.'"[23] A composite develops of Indian fathers as those most responsible for the death-grip of tradition, most resistant to healthy change (in the form of removal), and most answerable for the doom resistance calls down upon their people.

If, however, paternal discourse availed removalist interests, Indians used it as well—though for quite different ends. Cherokee petitions to Washington display numerous runs on this discourse; for example, the image I quoted before of the Indians as faithful sons is paired with a more pointed figure that challenges the nation's attacks on Indian fathers, disputes the nation's assumption of fatherhood of its Indian peoples, and goads the nation's Christian conscience: "It is not the fear of chiefs that has forced upon them this determination to remain," they write, but a desire to live "where their Great Father alone placed them." Then, too, some Indians seem to have found uses other than the conventional one. In an address published during his eastern tour of 1826, for instance, Elias Boudinot announced: "You here behold an *Indian*, my kindred are *Indians*, and my fathers sleeping in the wilderness grave—they too were *Indians*. But I am not as my fathers were—broader means and nobler influences have fallen upon me." Here Boudinot, rather than asserting allegiance to his fathers' graves—an image that could be taken to disprove current title—invokes the image to repudiate it, to portray the Cherokees' land claims as pressing and present, not antiquated and obsolete. Whether or not it is true, as Cooper's daughter maintained, that her father prepped for his Indian novels by tailing the "deputations to Washington from the Western tribes" that were "quite frequent at that moment," their frequency argues both for continued conflict between Indian and white fathers and for Cooper's consciousness of it.[24]

And what this suggests is that Cooper's narrative, and mistrust of narrative—his suspicion that written words do not sustain an original relation to things—are informed by the Indian claims that coexist with his own. The multiple narratives of *Mohicans*, that is—each manifesting rupture between word and deed, story claim and land claim—reflect not just an ideological burden, the conquerors' sense that the "original owners of the soil" mock "the origin of [the] nation" (304 n). More important is the fact that the ideological—and actual—battle for America went on, showing that the traditions the Indians had from their fathers, far from being groundless myth, continued to ground the Indians' presence and resistance. Thus if, as Steven Blakemore writes, Cooper doubts "the power of language to finally order the discordant tensions of the new world," this is because intercultural conflict proved the nation's inability to claim and name the land unequivocally: in ways both tangible—through legal, journalistic, literary, even armed combat—and intangible—through their illustration that any claim is situated, contextual, local; in short, a narrative—Indians introduced discord into the nation's power over the "new" world.[25]

Cooper's solution is to return to Indian claims—to "go back to the aborigines"—and make them, as Natty's first words imply, his own: "Even your traditions make the case in my favour, Chingachgook" (30). Throughout the novel's second volume, Cooper undermines Indian narrative in precisely the way he fears it undermines his, by severing word from deed: where Chingachgook drew a "natural" link between act and utterance, his narrative is gradually displaced by the narratives of others who cannot claim his faith or fidelity. As in *Algic Researches*, then, *Mohicans* disowns the intercultural nature of its production; if it is the coexisting narratives of the Indian fathers that shape Cooper's narrative, it is by converting them to myth that he denies their ability to engage his.

This strategy appears most plainly in Cooper's treatment of a figure who scorns sober oratory for words meant to inveigle: the dem(on)agogue

Magua. Magua can be (and has been) read as a precursor of the populist orators Cooper would go after in *The American Democrat* (1838); like them, the wily Huron possesses the skill to make each listener believe "the hidden meaning was precisely such as his own faculties enabled him to understand, or his own wishes led him to anticipate" (283).[26] Once again, however, to place Magua in this camp is to overlook parallels with Native orators such as Red Jacket—who in 1826 was stripped of his tribal voice as part of the machinations by which speculators forced Seneca land sales[27]—and Tenskwatawa, who had speech enough the year of Monroe's Removal plan to preach a nonwhite destiny for the nation. Yet if, as the multiple-origins myth he tells the Delawares indicates, Magua arises from this tradition, it is through Magua that Cooper disparages the tradition. For however legitimate Magua's charge that the white man "stops the ears of the Indians" in order to "enclose the land" (301)—however accurate, that is, his critique of Cooper's stifling of Indian speakers to naturalize white claims—Magua's word is wholly illusory, a myth wielded to further a personal vendetta. Placing Indian tradition in the mouth of a man who sunders what is said from what is so, Cooper follows Jefferson and company in portraying Indian leaders as self-interested scoundrels who enforce submission to myth.

Yet there is another orator and prophet in *Mohicans*, whose part in the mythicization of Indian narrative is less obviously damning, though more ultimately damaging, than Magua's. Tamenund's significance to the novel's ultimate direction is evident in his first appearance: "His frame, which had once been tall and erect, like the cedar, was now bending under the pressure of more than a century. . . . His dark, wrinkled countenance, was in singular and wild contrast with the long white locks, which floated on his shoulders, in such thickness, as to announce that generations had probably passed away, since they had last been shorn" (293). With his sepulchral bearing and legendary pedigree—rumors float that he held "secret communion with the Great Spirit" (293)—Tamenund seems a living antiquity, "who belonged rather to another world than to this" (294). Known in Cooper's time as a Delaware demigod, the father of agriculture and the clan system, Tamenund was known also as the first to sign away his people's land: "His name was first presented in writing, to the civilized world, on June 23, 1683, when he affixed his mark to a deed of that date, granting to William Penn, Proprietor, 'all my Lands Lying betwixt Pemmapecka and Nessaminehs Creeks . . . for yᵉ Consideration of so much Wampum, so many Guns, Shoes, Stockings, Looking-glasses, Blanketts

and other goods as he, ye s^d William Penn shall please to give unto me.'"
Years later he was said to have clinched the deal by relinquishing all "Land
claimed by us from the beginning of the World to the day of the date
hereof."[28] However reliable these white deeds, the story was current in
Cooper's day; Tamenund, to him, was the Indian "patriarch" (293) who
had entered history only to cede claims stretching back to "the beginning
of the world."

Indeed, it is as a patriarch that Tamenund ushers Indian story fully
into myth. Magua, a renegade telling tales he knows to be lies, cannot
achieve this; Tamenund, the "father" of the Indian "nation" (305), can.
From his first expression, Tamenund reveals the return to ancestral memory to be nothing but compulsive flight from the present: "Who speaks of
things gone! Does not the egg become a worm—the worm a fly—and
perish! Why tell the Delawares of good that is past?" (302). To Tamenund,
time telescopes into a frozen moment: "It was but yesterday . . . that the
children of the Lenape were masters of the world!" (305). This is, clearly, a
perversion of Chingachgook's invocation of the fathers; rather than forge a
link between present and past, Tamenund collapses the two, turning he-
redity to predestination, tradition to prescription. Accordingly, though
his apocalyptic myth resembles stories attributed to revivalist prophets—
"when the whites shall have ceased killing the red men, and got all their
lands from them," Heckewelder reports one such story, "the great tortoise
which bears this island upon his back, shall dive down into the deep and
drown them all," and "when he again rises, the Indians shall once more be
put in possession of the whole country"[29]—this story is, like all Tamenund's words, a mere "incoherent burst" (308), hallucinatory "images" with
no connection to "the visible objects of the world" (303). Read through
Tamenund, Chingachgook's fusion of word with world thus comes to
signify not the legitimacy of his story but its self-referential nature, its utter
uncoupling from what it claims.

And as such, when Uncas lets himself be read into Tamenund's myth,
he forfeits his place in history; what was in Chingachgook an admirable,
indeed inimitable, fealty to the fathers becomes the mark of fatality. Uncas's
relapse into myth is signaled by his war-song, a "natural" language now
defined, like that of Thoreau's Abenakis, as meaningless sound: "The notes
were in the extremes of human sounds; being sometimes melancholy and
exquisitely plaintive, even rivalling the melody of birds—and then, by
sudden and startling transitions, causing the auditors to tremble by their
depth and energy" (319). If, then, the battle held under Uncas's command

aborts the promise of Indian revival, as revolutionary agency yields to an-cestral codes of vengeance, it simultaneously resurrects a yet more ancient code: occurring in a world so prehistoric "it seemed as if the foot of man had never trodden" there (326), a world in which the principals seem torn from "the legends of ancient poetry" (335), the ritualized slayings that claim two differently, but equally, unreliable prophets—Uncas and Magua—return the Indians to their traditional beginning to finalize their historical end. Donald Darnell argues that "the bright destiny legend has predicted for him" makes Uncas a mythic hero; yet as a mythic hero, Uncas's destiny must be death.[30]

Tamenund's redemptive myth thus becomes a history of the Fall; the circular vision of the Delaware patriarch turns out to be ironically pro-phetic, as creation leads ineluctably to destruction. The novel's closing likewise circles back to its start, with the Mohican father's "natural" lan-guage now converted to barren sound:

Then a low, deep sound was heard, like the suppressed accompaniment of distant music, rising just high enough on the air to be audible, and yet so indistinctly, as to leave its character, and the place whence it proceeded, alike matters of conjecture. It was, however, succeeded by another and another strain, each in a higher key, until they grew on the ear, first in long drawn and often repeated interjections, and finally in words. The lips of Chingachgook had so far parted, as to announce that it was the monody of the father. . . . [I]t was apparent, by the manner in which the multitude elevated their heads to listen, that they drunk in the sounds with an intenseness of attention, that none but Tamenund himself had ever before com-manded. But they listened in vain. The strains rose just so loud, as to become intelligible, and then grew fainter and more trembling, until they finally sunk on the ear, as if borne away by a passing breath of wind. (345)

Of the original owners of the soil, Tamenund alone retains a voice; but his speech, as Cooper reveals when the patriarch pronounces his children's doom, is as powerless as Chingachgook's babble:[31] " 'It is enough!' he said. 'Go, children of the Lenape; the anger of the Manitto is not done. Why should Tamenund stay? The pale-faces are masters of the earth, and the time of the red-men has not yet come again. My day has been too long. In the morning I saw the sons of Unâmis happy and strong; and yet, before the night has come, have I lived to see the last warrior of the wise race of the Mohicans!' (349–50). This famous elegy must be read ironically. For all its beauty—or because of it—it is, like Magua's seductive fable, a myth ordained, dictated, as history. However free of mercenary aims, Tamenund is guilty, as Jefferson charged, of convincing his people that "whatsoever they did must be done through all time"—or outside all time. Displacing Indian fathers by transforming their traditions to myth, Cooper thus creates an original claim for his nation while creating himself as the father, the originator, of a literary tradition.

Yet throughout *Mohicans*, Cooper remains aware that the mythicization of Indian narrative is itself a narrative, one that must be actively made and monitored. Even images that proclaim the "mythic" nature of the Indians' world harbor uncertainty. "It would not have been difficult to have fancied [Magua] the Prince of Darkness" (284); Uncas "might easily have been converted, by the imagination"—whose?—"into an exquisite and faultless representation of the warlike deity of his tribe" (248); the site of the final battle, "seen by its dim and uncertain light, appeared like the shades of the infernal regions" (335). These devices serve partly to distance Cooper from the unreality he is describing. Yet this distancing, this admission of narrative's inability to claim what it claims, admits the novel's own duplicity in converting Indian narrative to myth. Cooper thus displays what Jerome Rothenberg says of the translation of Indian oral art: "Every translation is a divergence, and the interest of translation as such is as a record of its own divergences: a comment on its failure to be source." As such, when one reviewer of *Mohicans* carped that "wild traditions" had no place in the work of a writer "so deservedly popular, for the sober voice of history," this was to ignore Cooper's awareness that the sober voice of history rests on the translation of the wild traditions of myth.[32] And as Cooper further recognized, the appropriation of myth served the nation's greatest (because least attainable) need: the need to create a history free of Indian peoples, a history that, even as it translated Indian narratives into the source of its own liberty, could claim an immediate relation to a land from which its translations necessarily distanced it.

Toward this end, however *Mohicans* satisfied a national need, it did not satisfy Cooper. Challenges, real or imaginary, to his land claims (real or imaginary) kept cropping up, prompting him to issue a series of unpopular novels (which the press twitted, bizarrely, as self-plagiarisms, prompting him to defend authorial originality with a series of libel suits). On his return from a European stay, galled to find the locals cavorting on the family picnic grounds, he published the rabid *Home As Found* (1838); in the 1840s, fearing that the tenant unrest threatening New York's hoary baronial system would spread to his neck of the woods, he churned out the even more frenzied Littlepage Trilogy. The breakneck speed with which Cooper wrote—1838 alone offered *Home As Found*, *The American Democrat*, and *The Chronicles of Cooperstown*—seems to suggest that his anxieties had outlasted Hawk-eye's antagonists, whose southern kind in 1838 were walking the Trail of Tears.

And yet, intercultural conflict floats close to the surface in these later works as well. In *Home As Found*, the dispute over a pittance of pleasure ground becomes a death struggle between faithful heirs and philistine newcomers: "The descendants of the fathers of the country [began] to make a manly stand against the looser sentiment, or the want of sentiment, that so singularly distinguishes the migratory bands. The first did begin to consider the temple in which their fathers had worshipped more hallowed than strange altars; the sods that covered their fathers' heads, more sacred than the clods that were upturned by the plough; and the places of their childhood and childish sports dearer than the highway trodden by a nameless multitude." There is an eerie resemblance between this plaint and those of Indian petitioners (though here the "migratory bands" are the villains), a resemblance Cooper strengthens with an epigraph from Bryant's "An Indian at the Burial-Place of His Fathers" (1824): "It is the spot, I came to seek / My father's ancient burial-place— / It is the spot—I know it well / Of which our old traditions tell." That fears of Indians dispossessing their dispossessors were not trivial Cooper justified in a letter he wrote to Martin Van Buren in 1840: "In a general conversation with an Indian in this village last evening, the man incidentally mentioned a fact that, it has struck me, it might be well to mention to the government. . . . He . . . told me that his brother at Green Bay had sent him word that British Agents had been sounding the tribes in that vicinity, to know if they would fight the Americans. The argument was, the Americans keep driving you off your lands, whereas the English will permit you to remain." However inflated this alarm, it lent shape to Cooper's works in this decade. Thus in *Satanstoe* (1845), the first of the Littlepage Trilogy, he employs a phrase from Indian treaties to assert his claims: "Satanstoe has the place been called . . . from time immemorial, as time is immemorial in a country in which civilized time commenced not a century and a half ago, and Satanstoe it is called to-day. I confess I am not fond of unnecessary changes, and I sincerely hope this neck of land will continue to go by its old appellation . . . as long as water shall run and grass shall grow." The half-joshing, half-tetchy remark about time immemorial, however, reveals Cooper's doubts: "Should the next twenty years do as much as the last, towards substituting an entirely new race, for the descendants of our own immediate fathers, it is scarcely too much to predict that [our] traditions will be lost in the whirl and excitement of a throng of strangers." This reference to a new "race" returns Cooper to the axis around which his thoughts revolved; for it was a new race that attacked Indian traditions and fathers. In the Trilogy's final installment, *The Redskins* (1846)—a title recalling the fact that the unruly tenants, in what must have seemed a nightmarish return of those on whose land Cooper stood, conducted their protests in Indian costume—the principal Indian character, Susquesus, draws precisely that parallel between races: "The wicked spirit [lust for land] that drove out the red-man is now about to drive off the pale-face chiefs. It is the same devil, and it is no other."[33] Going back to the aborigines did not serve, for the aborigines stayed, reminding Cooper that his claims were only claims, grounded in violence and the indefensible belief in their own necessity.

In the last months of his life, Cooper received a letter from George Copway, Ojibwa author of a volume on native history. Copway was drumming up support for a journal, and he sought a submission from his acquaintance Cooper, who he flatteringly wrote had "done more justice to our down trodden race than any other." Bedridden, Cooper dictated a reply: "My health is such, at present, as to render me capable of doing but very little with the pen. . . . Still, some little anecdote or sentiment or sketch might possibly be thrown off by the aid of an amanuensis.— In which case I promise you shall not be forgotten."[34] Cooper did not live to honor this promise. Unable to escape the Indians' presence, he spent his life recording it, that it might be forgotten.

Translating Trickster

In an 1825 article on "The Literary Spirit of Our Country," a young American poet wrote that only with the passing of the Indians could the nation possess a literature, spirit, and country all its own: "When our native Indians, who are fast perishing from the earth, shall have left forever the borders of our wide lakes and rivers, and their villages have decayed within the bosoms of our western hills, the dim light of tradition will rest upon those places, which have seen the glory of their battles, and heard the voice of their eloquence;—and our land will become, indeed, a classic ground." Thirty years later, in *The Song of Hiawatha*, Henry Wadsworth Longfellow answered his own prophecy: assimilating Indian tradition to American literature, he announced the nation's perfect claim to "our land"

and the story of it. For the past four hundred years, writers had taken down Indian stories; for the past forty, they had held (in Schoolcraft's words) that the "source of a future poetic fabric, to be erected on the frame-work of Indian words, when the Indian himself shall have passed away, exists in their mythology." But it was not until Longfellow that a prominent white poet based a work on Indian words.[35] *Hiawatha*, consequently, seemed in its time a fitting resolution to the literary use of myth: having done away with the Indians, the story went, the nation could make free with—make itself free with, and free from—the mute traces of Indian antiquities.

Literary scholars of our time have, by and large, let this story stand; engaging the poem's Indian sources only to remark that it distorts them beyond recognition, critics of the poem have permitted Longfellow an authority based on the needlessness of that which he distorts.[36] Thus Roy Harvey Pearce's thoughts on *Hiawatha* are remarkably reminiscent of his subject's 1825 essay: "The noble savage lived on in spirit precisely because he no longer lived on in the flesh." Similarly, Richard Slotkin frames his discussion by arguing that *Hiawatha* became possible only after "real Indians" had been "removed," thus preparing for "the mythicization of the Indian" (a term he uses not to analyze the stories that inform the poem, but to fit the poem to a monomyth of the frontier).[37] Like Longfellow, these scholars deem the Indians' disappearance the necessary and inevitable precondition for their appearance in literature.

Yet as an overt instance of encounter between Indian and Euro-American forms of art, *Hiawatha* would seem to warrant an intercultural approach, one that accounts not only for its mythicization of Indian stories but for its relationship to that which it mythicizes. For not only is it patently untrue, as Pearce argues, that by 1855 "the Indian as direct opponent of civilization was dead" (I have detailed numerous ways in which Indians contested the entity homogenized as "civilization," and in any event, western wars still loomed on the horizon), but Indians east of the Mississippi could challenge their displacement in a fundamental way—by telling another story. Indeed, given the scattershot ethnography of the time, that Longfellow had such a comprehensive body of stories on which to work was attributable to the fact that, as George Copway wrote in 1850, Ojibwa stories had not been subdued or subsumed: "The *traditions* handed down from father to son, were held very sacred; one half of these are not known by the white people, however far their researches may have extended."[38] Thus if Longfellow's work, like Cooper's, translates Indian stories as the absent spirit of an original literature, it is essential to contextualize this act;

for translation, as Cooper recognized, is intercultural, involving contact, conflict, and negotiation among the stories it bridges, or veils.

In this regard, it is noteworthy that the spirit that gives *Hiawatha* its name had proved both irresistible to and irresolvable by white translators: Trickster, whose Ojibwa incarnation, Manabozho, Longfellow embodied (or disfigured) in Hiawatha. Found in numerous Indian stories—Gluskabe and Manabozho were but two recorded manifestations—Trickster seemed to Euro-American interpreters even more slippery than the norm: it was always there yet tantalizingly peripheral, unabashedly physical yet so in motion as to seem more mist than matter, at the scene of every social advance yet intent on disrupting or dishonoring the rules it helped hatch.[39] Nor, as William Jones's twentieth-century collection of Manabozho stories attests, were its exploits likely to sit well with Victorian translators: Jones's Trickster defecates on baby birds, singes its anus for its failure to keep watch over a meal, fashions a vagina from a caribou spleen (which rots), punctures its testicles in an effort to extract bear grease, and, finding its grandmother (Longfellow's long-suffering Nokomis) and grandfather having sex, punishes them by burning its grandfather's rump. Equal parts brat, despot, and voluptuary, Jones's Trickster is incapable of minding— "Oh, how you make me ashamed in your trying always to do everything!" its wife scolds—and is regularly victimized by its own gleefully, recklessly raunchy appetites.[40]

At the same time, however, and for antebellum interpreters incredibly, Trickster seemed to transcend such "savage" cruelty and credulity. As Longfellow's main source, Schoolcraft, writes: "The legend of Manabozho reveals, perhaps, the idea of an incarnation. He is the great spirit-man of northern mythology. The conception of the character reveals rather a monstrosity than a deity, displaying in strong colors far more of the dark and incoherent acts of a spirit of carnality than the benevolent deeds of a god. . . . Manabozho is regarded by the Indians as a god and a benefactor, and is admired and extolled as the personification of strength and wisdom. Yet he constantly presents the paradox of being a mere mortal; is driven to low and common expedients; and never utters a sentiment wiser or better than the people among whom he appears." The missing transition between sentences two and three signals Schoolcraft's travails with Trickster: for some reason, the deity is a monster, the exalted hero a common vulgarian, the celestial spirit a rutting beast—and the divine "incarnation" a heathen abomination. Though mythographers commonly found (or sought) parallels with their savior in Trickster—it was, Schoolcraft believed, "regarded as the messenger of the Great Spirit, sent down to them in the character of a wise man, and a prophet," but "clothed with all the attributes of humanity"—they were appalled that "materialism and carnality," as in the following passage from Jones, had "corrupted and mixed" with the pure character of the Son of God: "Now, once as he was travelling along, of a sudden at the rear, 'Po!' came a sound. As he started running, 'Who was it made that noise?' he thought. . . . 'Well, now, I will try to leave behind the one that is making the sound,' he thought. Just as he was about to slacken his speed, then suddenly again, 'Po!' was the sound something made. Thereupon he became afraid. . . . 'For goodness sake! wonder who it is that may be following me! It must be a great manitou being,' he thought as he started running at the very top of his speed. . . . Then finally at every step he took it was, 'Po, po, po, po, po!'. . . . 'Oh, why, I am breaking wind! That is what the people, my uncles, shall say till the end of the world.' " Christ, though he had blessed the peacemakers, had neglected to bless the wind-breakers. Yet this was the trouble with Trickster: showing a knack for turning pratfalls to triumphs—as when it gets its head stuck in a caribou skull and names the trees into which it careens, or creates tobacco by sliding through brambles on its blistered, bloody butt—Trickster seemed to inhabit a world where morals were temporary and reversible, where fouling up and fixing up were often the same. That this was so, that the Son of God could descend to toilet talk and, conversely, that a bungler the Indians felt free to call "simpleton," "dunce," and "idiot" could be entrusted with the divine plan, led critics to conclude that Trickster was not only the output but the avatar of the Indian Mind. If, as Schoolcraft charged, the Indians had "mingled up and lost their early history, in fictions and allegories," Trickster was the apotheosis of such "mingling," a narrative miscegenete revealing the Indians' inability to draw any of the patent dichotomies on which civilization relied.[41]

Indeed, this "singular tissue of incongruities," as Schoolcraft summed up, remains both central to and decentering of critical studies, spawning a wide and disparate range of readings. Thus where Barbara Babcock-Abrahams finds Trickster "paradox personified," a being whose violations of social rules show them to be jerry-built contrivances, Franchot Ballinger argues for Trickster's normative role: "It may be that a view of Trickster as a creative rebel has been emphasized at the expense of the socially didactic function of the Trickster tradition, particularly the dramatization of Trickster as a figure deserving the ridicule heaped on him, a negative example of what can go wrong in the greater society when the individual tries to live as a society of one." What these assessments share, however—and share with their forerunners—is a need to regularize the stories, a need for consistency and authority beyond narrative and its contexts. Yet what the complexity of Trickster stories suggests, beyond obvious problems of translation, is the deeper, intercultural fact from which translation arises: the fact of diverse, conflicting, interrelated stories of which no single version is adequate or even possible. The multitude of Trickster stories, that is, announces that stories need not—cannot—be reduced to one, that the sites of story cannot be subsumed under a master narrative that is *the* story. In this respect, as Anne Doueihi writes, Trickster can be seen less as "a character *in* stories" than as a story *about* story: "Divergent readings [of Trickster stories] co-exist without being perceived as mutually exclusive or contradictory, since interpretation is always local, specific, and personal and does not pretend to present, explain, or solve the problem of the text's final, single mean-ing. . . . The features traditionally ascribed to Trickster—contradictoriness, complexity, deceptiveness, trickery—are the features of the language of the story itself." In Doueihi's shrewd analysis, the central trick of these stories is the trick of story: Trickster exposes how the multiple meanings of verbal signs may be reduced to "a" meaning and hence illustrates that any telling or reading is a situated, interested activity, not inherent in the sign. To say this is not to claim to have found the defining principle of Trickster stories or to claim that such a principle clearly differentiates them from Euro-American stories. Similar claims introduce illogic into Gerald Vizenor's analysis of "trickster discourse." Though Vizenor writes that Trickster resists the "structural binaries" of anthropology, his work abounds with binaries: "The sign is communal and the narrative is a discourse; individu-alism is isolation, a tragic mode, in the instrumental language of social science."[42] I would argue, on the contrary, that Trickster stories reveal the relative, partial, constructed nature of all stories (including those of an-thropology), the fact that stories, however authoritative they appear, do not preexist or outstrip the contexts of their production.

And as such, perhaps Trickster proved so disquieting to Euro-Ameri-cans not merely because of the nature of the stories that existed about it, but because, expressing the *co*existence of manifold, unlike, irreducible stories, it challenged the idea of absolute authority in story. This singular tissue of incongruities was incongruous because, not being singular, it showed Euro-American stories—of history toppling myth, of Indian dis-appearance, of one story supplanting all others—to be but stories among many possible. Confronting these others meant confronting the inter-

cultural; translating Trickster meant encountering the problem of translation, of encounter, itself. For translation entails what Trickster stories
suggest: the translated text is neither fully itself nor the other, or rather, it is
itself through the other. Trickster thus highlighted the fact of a nation, like
the translated text, made of stories that existed not in isolation but in
relation.

It is this that *Hiawatha* prohibits, though it is this that *Hiawatha*
requires; it is by translating its multiple stories that *Hiawatha* denies the
fact of multiple stories. A scholar of the (so-called) modern languages,
Longfellow had acknowledged this fact in his first book-length publication, an 1833 translation of a Spanish epic poem. Fearing that the "spirit of
the original" might "suffer for the imperfections of the translator," he had
printed the Spanish with the English.[43] *Hiawatha*, needless to say, does
not provide its originals; set on its own originality, it presents itself as pure
translation, the bringing into discourse of a (so-called) archaic language,
and thus as no translation. Yet, as with Cooper, Longfellow cannot conceal
the living presences at the core of his translations. Rather, bent on denying
the interaction of stories from which his poem was born, Longfellow's
translation splinters into an irreconcilable opposition: identity, the assimilation of the foreign voice, and difference, the foreignness of the unassimilable voice.[44] If Trickster reveals, or revels in, the encounter of difference, *Hiawatha* takes Indian myth as alternately, and utterly, a part of and
apart from a singular American story.

Thus on the one hand, Longfellow strives to shape Indian stories to a
unitary narrative, or narrative unity. The famous blunder by which the
poem was born—"Work at 'Manabozho;' or, as I think I shall call it,
'Hiawatha,'—that being another name for the same personage"—expresses
this. Though Longfellow was innocent of the goof, as it was Schoolcraft
who had erred,[45] his preference for Hiawatha, whom he knew from Schoolcraft as an Iroquois statesman, was steered by his attempt, as he put it, at the
"disentanglement" of Trickster's contradictions. This initial appropriative
act reflects an ideal of assimilation in a narrower sense as well; for "Hiawatha," Longfellow claimed, fulfilled the laws of poesy as "Manabozho"
did not: "Hiawatha is Iroquois. I chose it instead of Manabazho (Ojibway)
for sake of euphony."[46] One can speculate why the one word fit where the
other grated; what matters is that Longfellow's muse demanded euphony in
the first place. "Hiawatha," that is, suggests in sound what *Hiawatha* essays
in sense: the transformation of difference (as in the first canto) into a
seamless sameness:

On the Mountains of the Prairie,
On the great Red Pipe-stone Quarry,
Gitche Manito, the mighty,

. . . .

Stood erect, and called the nations,
Called the tribes of men together.

. . . .

Came the Delawares and Mohawks,
Came the Choctaws and Camanches,
Came the Shoshonies and Blackfeet,
Came the Pawnees and Omahas,
Came the Mandans and Dacotahs,
Came the Hurons and Ojibways. . . .[47]

Here the droning, much-spoofed meter replicates the canto's matter. The litany of uncouth names has a deadening effect, preparing for rebirth into homogeneity: "From the river came the warriors, / Clean and washed from all their war-paint . . ." (121). The stereotype of vengeful savages tamed by the Great White Father adumbrates artistic assimilation, as the colors of the nation merge under the poet's power to eradicate difference.

Like the poet, Hiawatha is trothed to assimilation. As a farmer, he makes the corn-spirit a "friend of man" (150); as a diplomat, he weds Minnehaha "that our tribes might be united" (185); as a lover, he offers a prettily bourgeois reconciliation of sexual spheres: "As unto the bow the cord is, / So unto the man is woman, / Though she bends him, she obeys him, / Though she draws him, yet she follows, / Useless each without the other!" (183). Even in the unlikeliest of places, as in Hiawatha's woodcraft, assimilation rules: "Give me of your bark, O Birch-Tree! . . . / Give me of your boughs, O Cedar! . . . / Give me of your roots, O Tamarack!" (162, 163, 164); merging these ingredients into a whole without "seams" (164), Hiawatha fabricates a physical counterpart to the melting pot. Further, just as this catalogue-style passage courts difference to uphold sameness, so does the catalogue style itself attempt the rhythms of archaic poetry to turn the exotic to the familiar: the "frequent repetitions" (113), built on incremental modifications rather than jarring contrasts, take on a friendliness that softens their "primitive" uncongeniality. The romance conventions with which Longfellow lards his legends similarly foster a domestic coziness: "All the birds sang loud and sweetly / Songs of happiness and heart's-ease" (191). Hiawatha's picture-writing, with its pairing of signifier and signified, sums up the immediacy of the poet's act: "Each figure had its meaning.... / Symbol and interpretation" (222). Through his own and his hero's trials, Longfellow seeks a nation cleansed of difference.

Yet this dream vanishes. As Robert Ferguson writes in one of only a few literary studies to take seriously the poem's cultural significance, *Hiawatha* ends in "utter declension and disintegration." Ferguson attributes this to anxieties in the years preceding the Civil War; I would suggest that the fall of a house divided signals an intercultural anxiety. For beneath the promise of assimilation, as Schoolcraft wrote, lurked the danger of inter-relation; fearful that his myths might be "smoothed and polished off to assume the shape of a sort of Indo-American series of tales; a cross be-tween the Anglo-Saxon and the Algonquin," Schoolcraft foresees assim-ilation yielding a "shapeless mass." Years later, in his praise of *Hiawatha*, he took a shot at those who had blurred the boundaries: "To avoid the direct issue with Indian character, it has been aimed to excite interest by taking the hero or heroine from the half-breed class. The result has been that we have had a half-breed class of poetry."[48] Translating Trickster raised the specter of intercultural mingling, for in translation, all is related to that from which it differs.

Fleeing this possibility, *Hiawatha* reverts to a second option: not the incorporation of the foreign body but its expulsion. To a certain extent, the poem reproduces structurally this division. In its final third, Hiawatha's works come undone: Chibiabos, Kwasind, and Minnehaha are claimed by the aliens his inventions had kept at bay; Nature, once tame and sunny, convulses in plague and famine; Gitche Manito retreats into the winter wasteland, deaf to Hiawatha's "cry of desolation" (263); and at last, Hia-watha must relinquish his people to the Black-robes (who "Stammered in [their] speech a little / Speaking words yet unfamiliar" [277]; babel has re-placed the pristine language of picture-writing). This binary is mirrored as well in the conflict between Hiawatha and Pau-Puk-Keewis, the latter of whom represents Longfellow's solution to the trouble of Trickster: shunt-ing Manabozho's "carnality" onto another figure, he preserves his hero's purity. In the logic of opposition that structures the climax of *Hiawatha*, Trickster must invert the hero's works; for instance, with its bewildering permutations—"Running through its various chances, / Various changes, various meanings" (234)—Pau-Puk-Keewis's game rewrites pictography, forging an antagonistic relationship between signs and their referents. The "manifold disguises" (244) he assumes in his flight from Hiawatha sim-ilarly assail the opening image, in which diverse tribes cast off their distin-guishing marks; unable to shed his precise "form and features" (244), Pau-

Puk-Keewis becomes a sign of essential difference. By the closing cantos, assimilation has wholly capitulated; though those who will replace the Indians feel "but one heart-beat in their bosoms," the Indians themselves are fated to disunity and despair: "I beheld our nation scattered. . . . / Weakened, warring with each other" (273). This divisiveness is played out in Indian story itself, in the tale of Winter and Spring (from Schoolcraft's "Peboan and Seegwun"):

> Came the sun, and said, "Behold me!
> Gheezis, the great sun, behold me!"
>   Then the old man's tongue was speechless
>
> . . . .
>
> And his body shrunk and dwindled
> As the shouting sun ascended,
> Till into the air it faded,
> Till into the ground it vanished. (269)

The European invasion follows; as in Tamenund's myth from *Mohicans*, Indian story foretells its own doom. Cecelia Tichi suggests that, at poem's end, Longfellow "conjoins the eternality of Indian legend with historical time"; but the poet's own appraisal suggests otherwise: "The contact of Saga and History is too sudden. But how could I remedy it unless I made the poem very much longer? I felt the clash and concussion, but could not prevent, nor escape it."[49] Lengthening the poem would only have primed the parody pump; it would not have changed the ultimate, dysphonic "clash and concussion," for this is necessary lest myth and history mingle.

The prospect of such mingling became particularly apparent when Longfellow met not the myths in ethnologic compilations but the "Ojibway preacher and poet," Copway, who came calling in 1849. "He left me a book of his, an autobiography," Longfellow wrote; but though Copway's books, as I will show shortly, inform a central passage in *Hiawatha*, their presence is thoroughly effaced. Helen Carr sees Copway as an "unmediated Indian source" for *Hiawatha*. I would argue that it was because Copway—a convert and literary figure, a lecturer on "the *present state* and *prospects*" of the Ojibwas—was not, as Longfellow groused, a "pure uncontaminated Indian," because he called attention to the impure, mediated nature of America's stories, that his role in *Hiawatha* was suppressed.[50]

And as such, it is in the rewriting of Copway that Longfellow's attempts to silence Indian story rise to the surface. In his account of a Copway lecture, for instance, Longfellow spirits away political presence, leaving only ornament: "A rambling talk, gracefully delivered, with a fine various voice. . . . He described very graphically the wild eagles teaching their young to fly from a nest overhanging a precipice on the Pictured Rocks of Lake Superior." This précis, like Thoreau's stifling of Polis and Cooper's of Chingachgook, dilutes Copway's careful revision of the national symbol: "Pray for us," he writes in the autobiography adorning the poet's shelves, "that *religion* and *science* may lead us on to intelligence and virtue; that we may imitate the good white man, who, like the eagle, builds its nest on the top of some high rock." Copway repeats this theme in an 1850 study of the Ojibwas, urging whites to "enlarge the arena of human freedom, and your leading the Indian may be like the noble eagle's first flight with its young to the sun."[51] Yet in *Hiawatha*, the eagle expresses merely the senseless sound of Indian story:

> Ye who love the haunts of Nature,
> . . . .
> And the thunder in the mountains,
> Whose innumerable echoes
> Flap like eagles in their eyries;—
> Listen to these wild traditions,
> To this Song of Hiawatha! (115)

These echoes could have been given voice; rambling or not, Copway sought to pierce the clamor of a one-sided history: "The pale-face has bequeathed his history's bloody page to his children after him. The Indians, on the other hand, have related the story of their wrongs to their children in the lodge, and have invariably taught them to look upon a pale-face as a hard brother." Longfellow, however, was less interested in Copway's writings than in whether he had couriered certain "precious books" to add to the poet's library; clearly, he preferred books to Copway's babble, or preferred to see Copway's books as babble, the uncomplaining vacancy of myth.[52]

For it is not merely Schoolcraft's books, but Copway's, that lie behind Hiawatha's top claim to historical presence: picture-writing. Of the pictographs listed in canto 14, those in lines 46 through 75 were based on illustrations and interpretations in Copway's *Traditional History and Characteristic Sketches of the Ojibway Nation* (1850); the remaining lines, describing totemic markers and medicine songs, follow a comparable discussion in the first volume of Schoolcraft's *Historical and Statistical Information* (1851).[53] Yet if Longfellow was surprised to discover evidence of an Ojibwa "literary" tradition, he scripts it such that it cannot meddle with his literary origin. Indian materials, he had written while shipping souvenirs to a friend, are "so frail—birch-bark, that I shall send [them] in a little box with your books": dumb objects ballasted by the written word.[54] Birch-bark, he later read in both Copway and Schoolcraft, was the material on which the Ojibwas recorded pictographs; and it is the frailty of this medium, its inability to exist without a book to translate it, that Longfellow stresses. Notably, the poem's first step toward decline occurs after the completion of picture-writing; just when Hiawatha has, seemingly, ensured that the "great traditions" (219) will not "fade and perish" (218), his invention itself decays. This erasure is replicated by Longfellow's effacement of his source. Copway, unlike Schoolcraft and other Euro-American translators, appears nowhere in the poem's notes, and thus the presence (or absence) of Indian story appears an act of pure translation, translating literally nothing, or translating nothing to literature.[55] With this act, the paradox of literary nationalism reaches an apotheosis of sorts, as the absent presence of myth accomplishes in the text what it does for the text: the transformation of Indian story into an absolute other that is American because it is not, an other that is the substance of the nation's poetry because it is the insubstantial antithesis of poetry and the nation.

And in this respect, Longfellow's grounding of literature on groundless myth participates not only in narrative but in geographic conflict. For Trickster, according to accounts collected from earliest contact to his time, was honored for the re-creation, or in some cases the creation, of the earth. Nicolas Perrot, one of the first Europeans to enter the Ojibwas' homeland, reports:

They believe that before the earth was created there was nothing but water; that upon this vast extent of water floated a great wooden raft, upon which were all the animals, of various kinds, which exist on earth; and the chief of these, they say, was the Great Hare. . . . The muskrat then jumped into the water, and boldly dived. . . . They unclosed one of his paws, then a second, then a third, and finally the fourth one, in which there was between the claws a little grain of sand. The Great Hare, who had promised to form a broad and spacious land, took this grain of sand, and let it fall upon the raft, when it began to increase; then he took a part of it, and scattered this about, which caused the mass of soil to grow larger and larger. When it had reached the size of a mountain, he started to walk around it, and it steadily increased in size to the extent of his path. . . . Since then, he has not been willing to trust any of the other animals, and continues always to increase what he has made, by moving without cessation around the earth.[56]

Similar to the stories on which Tamenund's prophecy is based, the earth-diver links creation to renewal. As such, it may be that the persistence of such stories was not only made possible by, but made possible, the Ojibwas' physical continuity. Telling of origin and endurance against mythic decline, the earth-renewal questions both the claim that all stories must become one through assimilation or annihilation and the geographic hegemony that underwrote that claim.

There is no such story in *Hiawatha*. There is no hope that "to this day must [Manabozho] be travelling along"; Hiawatha is gone "forever" (281).[57] Though Longfellow knew of the earth-diver from Schoolcraft;[58] though the cantos concerning Hiawatha's fishing and Chibiabos's death lead, in most versions available to the poet, to the deluge and world's re-creation; and though this act would seem to have befitted the heroic aspects of the character, Longfellow deletes it: translating Trickster, he refuses Trickster's translations. The effect of such attempts to construct a nation, history, and literature free of its multiple stories is evident in the (translated) words of Aurora, an Ojibwa storyteller contacted the year *Hiawatha* appeared: "I have lost my memory. The Ojibbeways have all lost their memory. The Americans have made them weak. . . . They no longer feel the same pleasure in telling the old stories, and they are being forgotten, and the traditions and fables rooted out."[59] *Hiawatha* was the most popular poem of its time, due in large part to Longfellow's reputation. But more than this, the poem succeeded because of its claim that Indian traditions had been rooted out at last. After all this time, *Hiawatha* announced, the story of the Indians was nothing but a myth.

Chapter Seven

Traditional Histories

I have written in somewhat of the spirit which will characterize a History, by an Indian, yet it does not deserve to be called Indian partiality, but only justice and the spirit of humanity.

—Elias Johnson, *Legends, Traditions and Laws of the Iroquois*

In 1856, while filling up his Indian Books, the logs he kept during the last fifteen years of his life, Henry David Thoreau came across a pamphlet entitled *Sketches of Ancient History of the Six Nations*, written in 1827 or 1828 by a Tuscarora Indian, David Cusick. "Almost entirely fabulous & puerile," Thoreau commented, "only valuable as showing how an Ind. writes history!" and, he added on second thought, "perhaps for some dim on the whole interesting and suggestive traditions." Thoreau's emphatic, befuddled reaction indicates, perhaps, his surprise at discovering not only how "an Ind. writes history," but that an Indian had written history. In his journal, Thoreau had disdained "the white man's poetry," claiming to "want the Indian's report"; yet confronted with such a report, he did not know what to make of it. Cusick, like Joe Polis, posed the curious and irksome fact that not only had Indian voices "not yet died away"—they had survived to tell their own tale, unaided by and unbeholden to the civilized poet.[1]

Thoreau's remarks, if more ambivalent than most, are typical of the response to a phenomenon that, according to the pillars of United States dominion—the geographic, ethnologic, and narrative removals of Indians—should have been impossible: the advent of Indian historians. In Cusick's case, considering how rare *Sketches* was—rare both in numbers and, as the first self-proclaimed history in English by a North American Indian, in kind—the attention, and hostility, it drew are little short of remarkable. In 1846, Schoolcraft characterized *Sketches* as "curious evidences of the way-farings and wanderings of the human intellect, unaided by letters, or the spirit of truth"; a year later, though he leaned heavily on Cusick in *Notes on the Iroquois* (1847), he contemned his source as "a mass of incongruous details," bordering on "absurdity." Shortly after, Francis Parkman, relating a version of the Iroquois founding story in *The History of the Conspiracy of Pontiac* (1851), noted: "This preposterous legend was first briefly related in the pamphlet of Cusick," who "essayed to become the historian of his people, and produced a small pamphlet, written in a language almost unintelligible, and filled with a medley of traditions in which a few grains of truth are inextricably mingled with a tangled mass of absurdities." Cusick was still serviceable in 1883, when Horatio Hale disdained his "confused and imperfect style, the English of a half-educated foreigner, his simple faith in the wildest legends, and his absurd chronology." Almost a hundred years later, the Smithsonian *Handbook of North American Indians* referred to Cusick once—and only once—to reject his account of the Iroquois League: "Cusick's chronology in this as well as other matters is extravagant."[2] It is possible to read this cautionary note, like the earlier appraisals, as a matter of setting the record straight. And yet, such a move seems overstated, if not unnecessary: what member of these writers' ideal audiences would mistake myth for truth? Indeed, to make Cusick one's gull is to risk the mockery rebounding—as in the case of Francis Parkman, unruffleable man of letters, fulminating over the maunderings of a semi-literate savage! At the least, to tackle Cusick is to keep his "preposterous legends" and "absurd chronology" alive, rather than letting them molder in obscurity as is their due.

It seems, however, that to "set the record straight," authorities felt compelled to set all other records at naught. To cite a related example, in 1826, Lewis Cass, ever a stickler for straight records, began a series of attacks on the writings (and character) of John Heckewelder, historian of the Delawares: "He was a man of moderate intellect, and of still more moderate attainments; of great credulity, and with strong personal attachments to the Indians. His entire life was passed among the Delawares, and his knowledge of the Indian history and character was derived wholly from them. . . . Every legendary story of their former power, and of their subsequent fall, such as the old men repeat to the boys, in the long winter evenings, was received by him in perfect good faith, and has been recorded with all the gravity of history. It appears never to have occurred to him, that these traditionary stories, orally repeated from generation to generation, may have finally borne very little resemblance to the events they commemorate, nor that a Delaware could sacrifice the love of truth to the love of his tribe." That Cass felt more was at stake than one missionary's methodology emerges in a stray remark: "In fact, his history, if true, would unhinge all our knowledge upon these subjects." It is unlikely Cass antici-pates this outcome. And yet, as with those grappling with Cusick, he cannot abide that Heckewelder's story—one issuing, in the missionary's words, "from the mouths of the very people I am going to speak of" and portraying the struggle of real people against European usurpers—has gained adherents: it has, Cass writes with italicized indignation, "fur-nished materials for the writers of periodical works, and even of *history*."³ Whether the Delawares' story is "true" is not the point; the point is that its very existence was seen as a threat to the truth held by Cass and others.

Indeed, if Cass's yen to discredit Heckewelder seems excessive, its source appears later in the article, when he takes on another Indian histo-rian: John Dunn Hunter, an avowed Osage captive who burst on the liter-ary scene in 1823 with *Memoirs of a Captivity among the Indians of North America*. Relatively charitable to Heckewelder, Cass pulls no punches here: "Mr John Dunn Hunter is one of the boldest imposters, that has appeared in the literary world. . . . His book . . . is a worthless fabrication, and, in this respect, beneath the dignity of criticism. . . . Our only motive for introduc-ing the work into this article is, that, by exposing so gross an imposition, the public may be put upon its guard for the future, and not give credit to tales supported neither by intrinsic nor extrinsic evidence." Hunter, like Cusick and John Tanner several years later, evoked a storm of pro-test. Schoolcraft termed his work an "utter fabrication, in which there is scarcely a grain of truth hid in a bushel of chaff," while a reviewer in 1830 made even clearer the principal objection to, and means of dismissing, the *Memoirs*: "That there was a web of truth running through the whole tissue of falsehood which he circulated, is probable; but as much of the narrative was fabulous, and as the truth and falsehood were so closely interwoven as to render it impossible to separate them, there remained no other safe course than to reject the whole of his statements." Hunter complicated the certain claims on which national and narrative hegemony relied; his his-tory could unhinge all "our" knowledge, especially since, as Schoolcraft huffed, it "abounded in misstatements and vituperation of the policy of this government respecting the Indians."⁴ The solution was to throw out the baby with the bath water; as Richard Drinnon shows, the dismantling of Hunter's work as a myth has cast doubt not only over his narrative but over his existence.⁵ If the image of the nation's historical and ethnological nabobs ranged against native pamphleteers seems bizarre, it is clear that the need to expose the Indian historian was particularly strong.

The Indian historian, meanwhile, faced problems yet more vexing.

With publication a precarious commodity, there were limits on what could be written; though Cusick managed to print his work at his own expense, most native authors were obliged to consider Euro-American editors and benefactors. Then, too, the decision to write principally for and in the forms of a predominantly Euro-American readership, to engage in "auto-ethnographic" writing (Mary Louise Pratt's term for writing that involves "partial collaboration with and appropriation of the idioms of the conqueror"), could jeopardize an author's affiliation with his/her birth culture.[6] In some cases, collaboration seems to degenerate to ventriloquism; the epigraph to this chapter, for example, though it affirms Indian creativity and veracity, was lifted almost verbatim from a white woman's history of the Iroquois.[7] Yet even this apparently egregious plagiarism points to more complex issues. Such recycling could, for example, represent an effort to master white discourse;[8] or it could suggest an author seeking, with whatever success, to reconcile traditions, Indian and Euro-American.

The point here is neither that native historians have "sold out" to the dominant culture nor that their apparent selling out cloaks "subversion." Quite the contrary, these writers reveal the inadequacy of viewing Indians as outsiders from some "dominant culture" toward which they can be either, and only, subaltern or insubordinate. This is simply the illusion of history: the illusion of one inherently authoritative story from which all others are deviations or, at best, reactions or revisions.[9] What native histories show is that there is no pristine culture—or story—of which others are outside; such texts are particularly clear, but not unique, illustrations of how stories are defined, amplified, questioned in light of their others within the intercultural field.

At the same time, there is no denying that such histories bespeak tremendous faith—or desperation. *Sketches* appeared amidst a series of Iroquois land cessions, while the text I will consider first, George Copway's *Traditional History and Characteristic Sketches of the Ojibway Nation*, came out in 1850, the year President Taylor ordered the removal of the Lake Superior Ojibwas. Indeed, these circumstances encourage one to see native histories (like all histories) as political manifestoes, efforts to make manifest claims that—since no claim is self-evident—must coexist with other claims. If so, if such stories draw strength from the rootedness they construct while rendering bearable the rootlessness they contest, it is understandable why the Iroquois and Ojibwas, like the immigrants who sought to displace them, have been such fertile producers of these tales of belonging and longing, discovery and loss. I turn to Indian histories in this final chapter to recall the variety of stories from which the nation was forged, the ways those stories complicate any exclusive or exclusionary model of American history and literature, and the reasons those stories, so often viewed and acted as irreconcilable, have become so radically entwined.

The Mythic Homeland

George Copway was familiar with rootlessness. Born in 1818 in southeastern Ontario, he converted to Christianity in 1830, thanks in large part to Peter Jones, one of the Canadian Methodists' most celebrated Ojibwa converts.[10] In 1834, the Methodists showed confidence in the young Copway by dispatching him to La Pointe, Lake Superior, where he served as an interpreter; promoted to lay preacher within a year, he spent the next decade shuttling between United States and Canadian missions. The first signs of the troubles that would dog Copway throughout his life, however, surfaced during this period. Apparently a rather flamboyant, if not grandiose, person, he alienated both his superiors and his flock; in 1846, he was expelled from the Church for allegedly dipping into tribal annuities. Yet Copway, possessed of (or by) limitless energy, overcame this setback. His United States lecturing tour led to introductions to members of New England's elite; his self-proclaimed status as a tribal chief netted him an embassy to the 1850 World Peace Conference; and his probably inflated claims to proficiency in Indian tongues convinced ethnologist E. G. Squier to submit a copy of the Delaware migration story to him for inspection.[11] Between 1847 and 1851, Copway published an autobiography, a history, a travel narrative, a short-lived, self-named periodical, and a pirated epic poem; though it would be too much to call him a literary lion, he was for the moment soaring like the eagle he claimed as his totem.

Before long, however, Copway's heady life took an Icarian nose dive. Chronically in debt after the failure of his newspaper, he pestered acquaintances for loans; ignored by the makers of Indian policy once the novelty had worn thin, he hatched a series of ill-conceived, poorly received proposals; rebuffed by Ojibwas and Methodists alike, he was increasingly isolated by his wife's abandonment—apparently due to his abusiveness— and by the deaths of three of his four children. Supporters, angered that the token they had embraced had failed to deliver, deserted him one by one: Longfellow paid a less-than-welcome tribute to Copway's impact on *Hiawatha*, clucking that Copway was "developing the Pau-Puk-Keewis element rather strongly," while Parkman sniffed that he had "no great faith" in Copway as historian: "Copway is endowed with a discursive imagination and facts grow under his hands into a preposterous shape and dimensions."[12] A drifter the last decade of his life, emerging from obscurity only when jailed for debt, Copway showed up in 1867 as a healer hawking nostrums in Detroit. He died in 1869.

His brief celebrity excepted, Copway was the prototype convert, bereft at once of birth and adoptive cultures. Indeed, his fifteen minutes of fame both exaggerated and make recoverable the tragic, representative liminality that Copway, wishing to see himself as heroic and nonpareil, resisted with such prodigal unsuccess. Longfellow's depiction of him as the Trickster figure of *Hiawatha* is ironically appropriate. Always on the move, Copway tried his hand at everything, donned a dressingroom-full of disguises, bamboozled his way into patrons' good graces only to commit the harebrained mistakes that exposed him, put the best face on affairs that were spinning out of control, was overconfident, overbearing, overextending, overshooting, overwhelmed, and finally just over. Bluffing and bumbling, Copway refused to admit that every scheme he devised to steal the spotlight depended on his adopting a persona that guaranteed his schemes would miscarry. Trickster, he found too late, can't go it alone; pl(a)ying Trickster solo, he was branded a traitor at worst, a cut-rate confidence man at best.

Copway's writings illustrate this (anti)chameleon quality: he is caught, clashing, at cultural crossroads. His autobiography, *The Life, History, and Travels of Kah-Ge-Ga-Gah-Bowh (George Copway), A Young Chief of the Ojbewa Nation, a Convert to the Christian Faith, and a Missionary to His People for Twelve Years* (1847), welds Ojibwa heritage and Christian inheritance as uneasily as his names, the parenthetical insertion affirming at once the inseparability of the two and the impossibility of their becoming one. The title shows how deeply Copway desired to gather the strands of his life: a chief and a convert, his missionary role mediates between them. Copway omits saying that he was not a missionary at this point (he had been drummed out of the ranks the year before). Then, too, it is possible he still saw himself as a missionary, a bearer of glad tidings to heathen (salvation is nigh) and Christian (witness the fruits of your labors) alike. As he beseeches the latter: "Help us, O help us to live—and teach us to die a Christian's death, that our spirits may mingle with the blessed above."[13] Such impassioned prose illustrates Copway's predicament: pledged to intercultural harmony yet uncertain whether Indian and Christian "spirits" could "mingle," he struggled to be at once what the conversionism to which he had hitched his star decreed eternally separate.

This paradox is central to Copway's *Life*—and life—as he wrestles with conflicting desires to glorify Ojibwa and Christian cultures. In early passages, he writes movingly: "It is thought great to be born in palaces, surrounded with wealth—but to be born in nature's wide domain is greater still. . . . I would much more glory in this birth-place, with the broad canopy of heaven above me, and the giant arms of the forest trees for my shelter, than to be born in palaces of marble, studded with pillars of gold!"[14] The portrait of precontact life that occupies his opening chapters seems to verify this Indian Eden: in his portrayal of hunting, fishing, worship, and so on, Copway depicts a tribe functioning in a state of innocent unity. Yet at the same time, the ethnological bent revealed in these stylized sketches may vitiate the Ojibwa utopia Copway celebrates: fixing his people in a vacuum that precedes and presupposes geographic removal, Copway's portrait of a tribal way of life is congenial to those seeking to stamp that way out.

Yet Copway's tribal idyll is not simply an impotent myth. Ethnology thrived on the Indians' silence, the inability of their mythic discourse to grasp, much less contest, the necessity of dispossession. When, therefore, Copway's myth introduces a critique of expansion, he brings myth into contact with that which made it so and restores the dialogue ethnology pronounced impossible: "In the year 1818, 18,000,000 acres of [land] were surrendered to the British government. For how much, do you ask? For $2,960 per annum! What a *great sum* for British generosity! Much of the back country still remains unsold, and I hope the scales will be removed from the eyes of my poor countrymen, that they may see the robberies perpetrated upon them, before they surrender another foot of territory." Strategically contrasted with such unscrupulous covetousness, the earlier images of precontact harmony turn to critique. Elsewhere, Copway presents an Ojibwa code of reciprocity: "Never pass by any indigent person without giving him something to eat. . . . When you kill a deer, or bear, never appropriate it to yourself alone, if others are in want; never withhold from them what the Great Spirit has blessed you with." The provenance of this canon might provoke dispute; the words "indigent person," for example, suggest the extent to which it was shaped by contact. Yet as Richard Handler and Jocelyn Linnekin point out, the dualism of "genuine" and "spurious" traditions—the former deriving from a putatively pure precontact time, the latter from a compromised, hybrid culture—is itself spurious, an artifact of the search for some Native essence; since tradition is "a process of interpretation, attributing meaning in the present" through "reference to the past," "all spurious traditions are genuine."[15] Indeed, the power of Copway's code is that it announces its affinity with the contact situation rather than presenting itself as beyond time and context; just as he trades in ethnologic currency to complicate ethnologic truisms, so does he employ market terms to tender another model of human transaction. In this light, it seems Copway is not cozying up to Uncas-crazed easterners but seeking to (re)create a tribal tradition within discourses that had ruled tribalism long gone.

If these were the final strains of Copway's autobiography, the work might be seen as a straightforward attempt, in A. LaVonne Brown Ruoff's words, at "narrating [his] life within a tribal context." Yet the *Life* is too restless for that; before long, Copway shifts key again, and his orchestration of Ojibwa solidarity is drowned out by a fanfare to the self-made man. Following on the heels of his spiritual conversion, Copway experiences an economic conversion on a hilltop overlooking Boston: "As I saw the prosperity of the white man, I said, while tears filled my eyes, 'Happy art thou, O Israel, who is like unto thee, *O people saved by the Lord!*'" This Pisgah vision of the pecuniary Promised Land is not, to be sure, free of clouds; concluding the above passage with an ode to his vanished people, Copway reveals, in Timothy Sweet's words, that "the material precondition of every pastoral landscape was the killing or at least the removal of Indians." Yet the remainder of the work seems, though far from rejoicing in this, to picture it as inevitable; Copway's single, and singular, life proves the incompatibility of individual and tribal success. Thus in the Franklinesque recital of calculation and initiative that dominates the *Life*'s second half, Copway appears determined to reduce the Ojibwa code of conduct to mockery: at best it seems a curio left in the mythic past, at worst a pretense for his sponging off acquaintances. Tutoring his poor relations on "correct views of economy," Copway becomes less tribal spokesperson than civic-minded superior; indeed, recognizing that fairy tales such as his are reserved for a favored few, he envisions the Ojibwa masses being "driven to the Pacific Ocean, there to find our graves."[16] Though the pronoun suggests Copway's bitterness, it seems that the Indians have only two choices: to genuflect before the temple of individualism, or end as a collective in exodus and holocaust.

It is possible to argue, indeed, that Copway's choice of genre itself reflects an individualist ethic. In his prefatory comments, he offers a familiar disclaimer: "The language, (except in a few short sentences,) the plan, and the arrangement are all my own; and I am wholly responsible for all the statements, and the remaining defects." This assertion of autonomy, bound up in notions of (self) property and originality, indicates, perhaps, how far Copway has strayed from the tribal code he claims as traditional. For if it is true, as Kathleen Mullen Sands argues, that native autobiographers avoid "self-aggrandizement or claim to too much authority," then Copway, for whom self-promotion was an obsession if never an art, clearly fails the test.[17]

Yet I would hesitate to flunk Copway, for a number of reasons. To begin with, not only is it possible, as with his ethnology, that he adopted Euro-American discourses to exploit them, but it is by no means certain that his discourses, whether autobiographical or ethnological, derived wholly from Euro-America. According to German traveler Johann Georg Kohl, autographs of self-fashioning were nearly ubiquitous in Ojibwa life: "The chiefs frequently have the exterior of their tents covered with pictures and writing, containing representations of their doughty deeds, their family arms, or references to their pagan beliefs and magic recipes. They have also picture-writing on their clothes, the leather side of their buffalo robes, or the blankets in which they wrap themselves. We find among them cloaks entirely covered with figures and hieroglyphics, like the dress of a magician. At times their heroic deeds are again described on these furs; and on the buffalo skins . . . there will be found long stories." In another instance, Kohl examined a tomahawk decorated with a man's "dream of life," illustrating his guardian spirit, clan totem, military triumphs, and so on.[18] To term such records "autobiographies" is, perhaps, inaccurate. Yet if one accepts Hertha Wong's expanded definition of autobiography, which embraces "nonwritten forms of personal narrative and non-Western concepts of self," it is possible to see Copway's work as a traditional/tribal "dream of life" operating restlessly within the confines of a Western/individual *Life*. If so, his work can be seen to fulfill David Brumble's description of collaborative Indian autobiographies, in which "the lineaments of ancient traditions" work "against the conventions of the dominant culture."[19]

At the same time, however, one must be cautious not to take this suggestion as an absolute—not to base Copway's "genuineness" on his adherence to "tribal" conventions. Not only are Ojibwa forms of self-making, like all Indian art, subject to questions of reconstruction and interpretation, but to dismiss Copway as a "spurious" Indian based on his apparent distance from "traditional" standards is to assume that stories, cultures, traditions exist in pure, atemporal, unadulterated form rather than as local acts in contexts of encounter. Whatever the status of Indian and Euro-American personal stories prior to their meeting, what Copway's work reveals is the complexity of intercultural autobiography; just as the *Life* questions the displacement of tribal peoples, so does it imply that the ideal of authorial autonomy—of a "self" beyond the conditions of its production—is unattainable.

The same ideal, of course, upheld Euro-American history: that of a story separate from, superior to, and superseding its intercultural matrix. It is this ideal that Copway engages in *The Traditional History and Characteristic Sketches of the Ojibway Nation*; merely implicit in the *Life*, the question of one story's relation to its others is central here. Thus, though Copway's writing a history might seem further proof of his ungenuineness—and though he appears to adopt the claim of historiographic singularity when he (wrongly) boasts that his work is "the first volume of Indian history written by an Indian"—*Traditional History* challenges the notion of an original history displacing its others. Indeed, even in the above, Copway surrounds individual act with tribal purpose: "As the first volume of Indian history written by an Indian," he hopes "it may in some degree benefit his nation."[20] Where his *Life*, in keeping with the voice of individual authority, converts tribal heritage to personal keepsake—"I have not the happiness of being able to refer to written records in narrating the history of my forefathers; but I can reveal to the world what has long been laid up in my memory"[21]—*Traditional History* emphasizes its relationship toward, reliance on, and role in furthering "traditional"—but ongoing—stories of the Ojibwa people.

Notable in this regard is Copway's approach to pictography (unmentioned in the *Life*). Ethnologists such as Schoolcraft took the pictograph as iconic evidence of mythic immobility: "It shows the Red Man, in all periods of our history, both as he *was* and as he *is*; for there is nothing more true than that, save and except the comparatively few instances where they have truly embraced experimental Christianity, there has not been, beyond a few customs, such as dress and other externals, any appreciable and permanent change in the Indian character since Columbus first dropped anchor at the Island of Guanahana." *Traditional History*, by contrast, devotes a chapter to pictography as a flexible form of tribal memory: "The records of the Ojibways have a two-fold meaning; the hieroglyphic symbols of material objects represent the transmission of a tradition from one generation to another" (127). To illustrate this, Copway glosses for the uninitiated a catalogue of pictographs (the same that Longfellow took as the sign of myth's evanescence). Starting with concrete nouns (man, sun), he moves to abstract ones (death, worship), then combines them to form narratives (fight-man bad spirit) before concluding with a string that represents an invitation to a medicine-lodge ceremony (134–37). This roster functions, on the one hand, to proclaim the Ojibwas' ability to record events, to set down, as one observer put it, "where they came from, where they are heading, and what they plan to do."[22] Rather than being limited to static images, pictography conveys the "whole story" (136) of the tribe. Moreover, by invoking the medicine-lodge or Midewiwin society, a possibly syncretic religious movement that used birch-bark scrolls (one recalls Longfellow's disdain for this material) to record medicine formulae, Copway invites comparison between his act and those of the Mide priests, who, he says, renew the "sacred records" of the tribe to prevent them from "decaying" (130). Entering his text into the sacred record, Copway renders ambiguous the relationship between individual story and its tradition. (Further, as a convert, he complicates Schoolcraft's claim that pictography belongs solely to those mired in myth.) As such, he suggests, as did another Ojibwa storyteller whose words were translated by Kohl, that "there were so many stories in the world, that he did not know where to begin"—that any "beginning" is inseparable from the tradition it revives, reenacts, or recreates.[23]

Yet Copway recognizes that to rehabilitate Ojibwa storytelling is not enough; an original history might still erupt into time and sweep stale traditions aside. What he attempts, rather, is to synthesize Ojibwa and Euro-American stories, to suggest in the manner of the Trickster stories he had likely experienced that despite their initial and current differences, "a great number of legends, stories, and historical tales" (95) have joined to originate an intercultural tradition of storytelling. And if this is so, if Indian and Euro-American stories mutually arise from the sites of their interaction, then Indian claims—the country's "traditions"—can neither be erased nor appropriated by the nation's origin.[24]

In his opening chapter, Copway tests this model. For example, he conveys Ojibwa claims through the literary romanticism that had coopted such claims as the silent foundation of its own origin: "[Lake Superior] is the most remarkable of all lakes, not merely on account of its size, but on account of the picturesque scenery around it, and the almost innumerable traditions related of it. . . . When I look upon the land of the Ojibways, I cannot but be convinced of the fact that in no other portion of the world can there be a territory more favored by Heaven" (6, 10). Similarly, he melds images of sylvan freedom and patriotic republicanism: "I love my country; and will any of my readers condemn a child of the forest for loving his country and his nation?" (15). The doubleness of these passages—the land of the Ojibways is favored by the Christian God; the child of the forest claims the nation as his—perhaps reflects Copway's trouble straddling diverse allegiances. Yet his clumsiness, if such it is, unsettles the idea of a single, inherently valid story: in his sentences, diverse elements neither cancel nor control their others. Copway, it seems, is trying to reproduce—or produce—a land embracing sons of the forest, connoisseurs of the picturesque, worshipers of Heaven, and tellers of traditions—all lovers of "their" country.

Having detailed the characteristics of the Ojibwa homeland, Copway turns to its stories. Again balancing traditions, he adopts the skepticism of Western historiography—"with these traditions there are rules to follow by which to determine whether they are true or false" (19)—yet bases his judgments on the very authorities western historiography rejected: "[One must] notice whether the traditions are approved by the oldest chiefs and wise men. Such are most likely to be true" (19). Moreover, Copway scorns the distinction between a transient orality and a permanent literacy: "Many think we cannot keep the words of tradition longer than one hundred years," he scoffs. "We have the tradition of the flood; the organization of the medicine worship of the Indians" (138). Such references to the flood—Manabozho's, one assumes—and the Midewiwin would not have impressed the historical profession. Yet the force of Copway's methodology lies in its suggestion that "truth" is local, not absolute: that diverse stories generate diverse grounds of validation. Thus, though he accepts the axiom that Indian and Euro-American stories differ, he disputes the corollary that the two are simple opponents, the former needing to be viewed through, and fated to be vanquished by, the latter.

Copway's attempt to forge an intercultural tradition culminates in the chapter in which he collects a series of Ojibwa tales. Here, conscious that he is trespassing on the territory of writers such as Schoolcraft, Copway seeks to establish his credentials. His means of doing so, however, appear at odds with the profession in which he claims a role: opening his discussion with the taxonomic observation that Indian stories "are of three distinct classes, namely, the Amusing, the Historical, and the Moral," and apologizing that "I can at present have only time and space to give specimens of the second of these" (97), he challenges the grounds of ethnology, the opposition of "historical" and "mythical." Yet uncomfortably, if not surprisingly, Copway reproduces certain requirements of the genre. "The Star and the Lily," for instance, opens with a frame typical of fairy tales: "There was once a time when this world was filled with happy people, when all nations were as one, and the crimson tide of war had not begun to roll. . . . It was at such a time, when earth was a paradise and man worthily its possessor, that the Indians were the sole inhabitants of the American wilderness" (98). As in the *Life*, this sequestration of Indians in a prelapsarian world seems to prepare for their becoming mere "specimens" of the scientist he invokes, with apparent sincerity if not with accuracy, as "H. R. Schoolcraft, Esq." (96).

Yet if Copway and Schoolcraft are both telling fairy tales, they are not telling them the same way. In Schoolcraft, Indian stories are torn from context, from the conditions of their production, from ongoing concerns. Indeed, the hermits and outcasts who people his myths seem symbols of this limbo state: "There lived a celebrated hunter" in "a wild, lonesome place"; "an old man was sitting alone in his lodge"; "a solitary lodge stood on the banks of a remote lake" are typical Schoolcraft frames.[25] To Schoolcraft, Ojibwa tradition had no tradition, no heritage; severing each actor, story, and storyteller from contextual ties, he portrays myth's overthrow as mere necessity, not as the result of specific factors in the contact situation.

One can only guess whether such *isolatoes* were characteristic of Ojibwa story. If they were, however, it might be that the recluses Schoolcraft took as signs of myth's innately solipsistic nature represented the results of, and the Ojibwas' commentary on, the devastation of a tribal collective under colonialism. Thus in William Jones's Trickster myths, Manabozho may be a desperado, but the tales form a chorus to condemn its actions: its disregard for social edicts—it gorges on its companions' fish, refuses to hunt for its children, and so on—elicit only scoldings for its failure to "giv[e] heed to anything one tries to tell" it and its refusal to "behave." For all its vaunted independence, Manabozho is most indebted to others when it tries to be least: having offended another spirit-being by proclaiming itself "the only manitou existing," for instance, it must call on the weasel for help. Manabozho's heroism, conversely, inheres not in deeds of swashbuckling derring-do but in bungling discoveries of social rituals; even the godlike stunt of earth-renewal suggests a social imperative: "So, therefore, have I now finished the creation of everything from which the people will derive life."[26] Tributes not to hedonistic freedom but to humble fraternity, Jones's stories suggest, at least, a countertradition to Schoolcraft's depiction of the Ojibwas as random particles doomed to decay.

Copway's lone-wolf life, of course, might seem to prove Schoolcraft's point. Yet just as *Traditional History* insists on the interdependence of stories, so do its stories invoke a tradition of interdependence. Thus, though the first words of "The Two Cousins" appear to introduce a tale of exile—"There lived amongst the hills of the north"—the sentence defies expectations, ending with the words, "two most intimate friends" (113). Those who live outside the tribe, such as the hero of "The Thunder's Nest," are nonetheless identified by it: "There lived on the northern shore of Lake Superior, an Indian warrior, who from his childhood had been noted for being a wise and sedate man" (109). Even more tellingly, though "The Star and the Lily" opens with a Schoolcraftian touch—an old man alone in a lodge—it knits an institutional fabric around this solitary figure: "An old chieftain sat in his wigwam quietly smoking his favourite pipe, when a crowd of Indian boys and girls suddenly entered, and with numerous offerings of tobacco, begged him to tell them a story" (97). These social observances find their counterpart in the chief's story, which tells of a people so tightly integrated that the principal actor is a collective entity identified as "they." The lone individual in the story, a star, is desperate for community: it "had fallen in love with mankind" and "was desirous to dwell with them." The people, acting as always in concert, unite to "welcome the stranger to earth. They went and presented it a pipe of peace," and "were rejoiced to find that it took it" (100). As in the telling of the story, which unfolds within a network of reciprocal acts, this generosity is rewarded, the star metamorphosing into lilies that Copway says he himself has picked.

Copway's stories are, needless to say, idealizations. But then, so are Schoolcraft's; and it becomes possible to see his as such when read through Copway's. Schoolcraft prescribes separatism: his myths show pariahs unable to mingle with their tribe, his theories prohibit myth from mingling with history. Conversely, Copway advocates integration. Indeed, the star-human story, whatever its roots in precontact tradition, functions here in an intercultural context; a "bright fugitive" (101) from a distant place, the star presages the foreigners who, offering the fair flower of civilization, had realized little but devastation. Copway's tales thus make Schoolcraft's confront their suppressed history, or the desires their history seeks to naturalize. Ojibwa stories, Copway's tales reveal, arise from specific sites, are spoken by specific speakers, and serve specific purposes, but these contexts have been denied by those who render the stories as if they came from nowhere. Having brought the "crimson tide of war," the invaders have read the atomism they caused as the essential feature of the stories and the people who told them.

Yet however powerful this reading, Copway is unwilling to admit that it is absolute. Rather, by launching his critique from within the Schoolcraft tradition, offering another story inside the discourse that denied the possibility of others, he both describes and displays how multiple stories interact. In this respect, Copway offers the intimate revision of Schoolcraft for which Tanner's narrative, given the chronology of the texts, could merely prepare; Copway not only revises ethnology overtly, by contextualizing it, but brings into contact with ethnology the stories that ethnology deemed wholly separate from and superseded by its own. And as such, Copway presents Ojibwa storytelling, in which multiple stories interact within a tradition, not just as one method among many but as a model of story. Where Schoolcraft believes that stories of a "golden age" "flit through the Indian mind as a dream, and furnis[h] him rather the source of a pleasing secret retrospection than any spring to present and future exertions," Copway seeks to make "The Star and the Lily," his story of a golden age, manifest both in and for a renewed nation.[27]

It should be said, however, that a number of factors complicate this project. To begin with, Copway is far better able to evoke than assert the mingling of stories; thus he leaves his "mythic" tales unintegrated with an ensuing "historical" chronicle. William Warren, a younger Ojibwa historian whose work Copway knew, connects "myth" and "history" with a confidence that eludes his elder. Though he has "confined himself altogether to history," Warren writes, he has obtained it "from the lips of their old men and chiefs who are the repositories of the traditions of the tribe." (Warren, moreover, occasionally drops his obeisant references to Schoolcraft, "the learned author on Indians," to point out the ethnologist's philological and mythological errors; only one with "a most intimate acquaintance with [the Ojibwas] as a people, and individually with their old story tellers"—as opposed to an armchair scholar reliant on "imperfect interpreters"—can avoid mistaking specious, humorous, or corrupt tales for ancient standards.)[28] By contrast, when Copway takes the direct approach, his prose suffers convulsions: "The history of the tradition of the stars," he writes, "according to Indian tradition, would be a history indeed" (152–53). It is possible that Copway was trying to show in such passages how intimately stories were linked. Yet it is also possible that he did not know what he wanted to say, or that he could not say it without the words that made nonsense of what he wanted to say.

Further, when Copway could not say what he wanted, he was willing to allow others to say it for—or against—him. As much as one-third of his history (according to Donald Smith's count) consists of excerpts poached from, among others, such hostile parties as Cass. Perhaps Copway was simply following the nineteenth-century practice of cobbling together one's own words and the words of one's sources; or perhaps he meant some new pattern to emerge. That pattern, however, remains inscrutable. While it is misleading to write, as James Clifton does, that the *History* "was for the most part copied word for word" from others—the implication being that an alloyed text is not "genuine"—it is fair to say that the transplanted material, far from making a good match, often rebels against its host.[29] The chapter containing "Star," for example, bears the dubious epigraph: "'Tis a story, / Handed from ages down; a nurse's tale, / Which children open-eyed and mouthed devour, / And thus as garrulous ignorance re- lates, / We learn it, and believe" (95). It could be that George Copway, Esq. felt, or wanted to look, superior to myth; he was capable of peppering his text with epithets on "fanciful stories" (96) or even "absurdities" (138). The lasting impression, however, is that, ever querulous of his erudition, he felt that the mere act of quoting authorities lent his text a scholarly air, and that he could not find, was in too much of a rush to find, or did not bother to find quotations that would not sabotage the foundation he had laid.

On the other hand, Copway's conceptual difficulties and reliance on scaffolding pale beside, though they participate in, an aspect of *Traditional History* hard to square with his efforts at mediation: in the end, he comes out for Removal. From the time of his American debut, Copway had circulated a plan for a western territory where assorted tribes would fuse into a coalition of Christian farmers: "I want to make the great family of the Indians ONE, should I live long enough—*one* in interest, *one* in feel- ing, *one* while they live, and *one* in a better world after death" (282). It appears, however, that for the people to be united, they must be divided: "Each would labour for the other's good—a spirit of rivalry would soon be seen were a premium to be given to those who should raise the largest amount of agricultural produce" (283). Here Copway falls back on an opposition his dash can hardly heal: on the one hand, a paradisal collectiv- ism; on the other, a bracing competition. In this light, Copway's stories take on a less rosy blush: just as the Ojibwa code of his *Life* appears to herald the rising arc of individualism, perhaps "Star" prepares for a new home—a home, however, physically and ideologically distinct from the home of that tale.

That Copway came to embrace the prevailing Indian policy of his day may seem to invalidate his intercultural vision. His biographers, in fact, have dismissed his plan as mere "vanity," a ploy for his name to live on in the reservation he christened Kahgega.[30] Yet however fair this assessment, Copway's text suggests a more complex motive for his founding of an Indian Canaan. In *Traditional History*, Copway struggles to be in two places most saw as irreconcilable: the "mythic" homeland of "Star" and the "historical" homeland of the West. Thus, just as his myths offer a tradition of rootedness in order to project that placement into a new place, so do his politics prophesy a recovery of wholeness through loss. Seeking a world for himself and his people both traditional and original, Copway came to believe that the return must be a removal; to exist in history, the fabled land of Kahgega must exist outside it.

Yet whatever Copway's aims, he found himself instrumental in gaining for the western Ojibwas what his one-time backer Peter Jones advocated for the eastern bands: titles conferred not "individually" but "on the whole tribe," "securing their reserved lands to them and their posterity forever." Stumping Washington like a veteran lobbyist, Copway helped persuade Millard Fillmore to halt the removal plans of 1850; in 1854, at the Treaty of La Pointe—the station where, twenty years earlier, Copway had embarked on his checkered career—the Ojibwas secured reservations on ancestral lands in Michigan, Wisconsin, and Minnesota.[31] An act of earth renewal of which Manabozho might have been proud, this was the perfect occasion for Copway's ticker-tape return; only by this time, he had resumed his wanderings. Ironically, it was Copway who—individually—began a gradual but final drift toward the West, while the Ojibwas remained, a collective body in their traditional homeland.

Ritual History

To turn from George Copway to David Cusick is to leave one of the nineteenth century's most notorious native authors for one of its most obscure. In 1981, a bibliography of Indian writers had only this to say of him: "David Cusick, from New York, died about 1840"; no more has emerged since. One can catch glimpses of Cusick's life in the careers of family members. His father, Nicholas, was a bodyguard to Lafayette during the Revolutionary War, a signatory to Iroquois land cessions, and an interpreter to Baptist missionary Elkanah Holmes; his brother, James—"a very talented man" according to George Catlin, who painted his portrait in the 1830s—took over the Baptist ministry to the Tuscaroras in 1838, and in 1846 led the faithful to Kansas. William Beauchamp, a scholar of the Iroquois who reprinted *Sketches of Ancient History* in 1892, writes that Cusick "had a fair education, and was thought a good doctor by both whites and Indians"; but what sort of education he had, and what sort of doctor he was, Beauchamp does not say.[32] If not for the history he wrote, Cusick might have been lost to written history.

That he wrote such a work—and the work he wrote—doubtless reflects his people's long and bitter acquaintance with loss. Adopted by the Iroquois after their 1713 revolt against North Carolina was betrayed by one of their own, the Tuscaroras, according to white authorities such as Lewis Henry Morgan, were relegated to a nebulous position: "They were admitted into the League as the Sixth nation, and were ever afterwards regarded as a constituent member of the confederacy, although never admitted to a full equality. . . . The Tuscaroras were partially scattered among the other nations, although they continued to preserve their nationality. . . . In the councils of the League, they had no national designation." This anomalous status suggests, perhaps, why during the American Revolution the Tuscaroras adopted a course damaging both to the League and to themselves. Encouraged by missionary Samuel Kirkland to take up arms for the colonies, the Tuscaroras found their isolation complete: as Indians, they suffered John Sullivan's retaliatory strikes, while as patriots, they were targeted by the Mohawks' Loyalist leader, Joseph Brant. In the chaotic postwar period, the tribe was split again: some followed the Loyalist Iroquois to Ontario, while those left behind fought to retain their home—a reservation that, even after the lease of North Carolina lands enabled them to buy additional territory, totaled less than ten square miles.[33]

No sooner had they settled in, moreover, than another challenge arose: a second wave of missionaries. A Baptist church was organized in 1806 with Nicholas Cusick as an elder; in 1820, he described its fruits: "We have a school, and a small church, sixteen members only, but sincere." The same year, however, a neighboring missionary identified a reason for the gospel's halting progress: "The pagan party of late have made violent struggles, and as their last resort they determined to break the tribe up by persuading such a number to move into Canada that the remainder would not be of importance for a missionary establishment."[34] Estranged from the League, hemmed in by whites, and divided among themselves, the small Tuscarora community might well have seemed to be fading into—or because of—myth.

Interestingly, in his preface, Cusick seems to agree: "I determined to commence the work," he writes, "but found the history involved with fables" (1). That Cusick should frame *Sketches* in this way may seem odd. At best, one might say that he was obliged to curry favor with white readers, or that, like Copway in his cut-and-paste mode, he had simply picked up the idea that "history" was supposed to debunk "fable." (Considering that he is self-effacing to a fault, aghast that someone "so small educated" [1] should essay so mighty a work, his concession could be but a verbal tic.) Less charitably, one might say that Cusick was not simply parroting his readers' beliefs but parading them.

Yet given what follows, Cusick's findings must have confounded those readers. *Sketches* begins: "Among the ancients there were two worlds in existence. The lower world was in a great darkness; the possession of the great monster; but the upper world was inhabited by mankind; and there was a woman conceived and would have the twin born" (1). Presenting this "fable"—the first in a sequence of stories of origin, migration, warfare, and confederation—as "history," Cusick renders equivocal the opposition he has echoed; indeed, the opening fable, with its doublings and twinnings, initiates a project in which oppositionalism itself will break down, as putative opposites become "involved" with one another. The pejorative sense of "involved"—the sense in which historians charged Cusick with "tangling" myth and history in a shapeless "mass"—yields to a positive, or better, a necessary sense: history and fable, *Sketches* suggests, are so fully involved as to make their separation, their very definitions, unsure.

Thus on the one hand, *Sketches* is dedicated to revising notions of Indian story as vanished, not present; or it is dedicated to revising notions of past and present as neatly separable. In this regard, the origin story with which *Sketches* begins cannot be said to be original (or even a beginning): "When the monsters were assembled, and they made consultation, one of them was appointed in haste to search the great deep, in order to procure some earth, if it could be obtained; accordingly the monster descends, which succeeds, and returns to the place. Another requisition was presented, who would be capable to secure the woman from the terrors of the great water, but none was able to comply except a large turtle came forward and made proposal to them to endure her lasting weight, which was accepted. The woman was yet descending from a great distance. The turtle executes upon the spot, and a small quantity of earth was varnished on the back part of the turtle" (2). Cusick's creation is at once surprising and predictable, spontaneous and well ordered, volatile and stable; the peculiarities of his prose—tense shifts, clauses strung with conjunctions—may reveal his troubles with English or writing, but at the same time they capture the paradoxical inevitability and excitement of an event that has happened, and will happen, and is happening once more. Accentuating the vitality of Iroquois story by connecting moments of its (re)enactment, Cusick rejects its status as ethnologic artifact superseded by history. Both paradigmatic and prophetic, his creation figures renewal as re-union.

Indeed, if it is true, as William Fenton writes, that the Iroquois Creation establishes the possibility and conditions for "restoring society" and "all ceremonial associations of renewal," *Sketches* as a whole can be seen as an updated origin story, one that revisits, revises, and revives the world's making to empower the Tuscaroras to remake their world.[35] Each of *Sketches'* three sections recalls a formative period, a re-creation grounded by the original/traditional act. Part one recounts the labors of the Good Mind, who "formed two images of the dust of the ground in his own likeness, male and female, and by his breathing into their nostrils he gave them the living souls, and named them Ea-gwe-howe, i. e., a real people" (3); part two picks up the trials of the Eagwehowe in a world in transition, where they are assailed by Stonish Giants, Flying Heads, and other horrors; part three finds the survivors a united body who, under the tutelage of "*Tarenyawagon*, i. e. the Holder of the Heavens," "entered into a resolution to preserve the chain of alliance which should not be extinguished in any manner" (11, 12). Each section, then, celebrates a major achievement: creation, reconciliation, confederation.[36] Each gain, moreover, is offset by loss, and vice versa: the Good Mind's twin is bested, but claims "equal power over the souls of mankind after death" (5); the interspecies battles escalate until the combatants "had utterly destroyed each other," but "a body of people" escape (11); the Tuscaroras are divided from their relatives, but call on the cognate roots of their speech to "send expresses" to "their brethren, the Five Nations" (37). A notable case of this balancing occurs in Cusick's telling of the Iroquois foundational story, where the chief who is, literally, a viper in the people's nest becomes their greatest peacemaker: "A war broke out among the Five Nations; during the unhappy differences the Atotarho was the most hostile chief, resided at the fort Onondaga; his head and body was ornamented with black snakes;—his dishes and spoons were made of skulls of the enemy; after a while he requested the people to change his dress, the people immediately drove away the snakes—a mass of wampum were collected and the chief was soon dressed in a large belt of wampum; he become a law giver, and renewed the chain of alliance of the Five Nations and framed their internal government" (16–17). Again, Cusick's idiosyncracies fuse the ancient and the urgent, conveying the mutually sustaining interplay of disaster and triumph, injury and healing, decrepitude and rejuvenation.

Intriguingly, the same rhythms animate versions of the ritual that contained and extended the foundational story: the Condolence. Thus in Tuscarora ethnologist J. N. B. Hewitt's rendering, the orator opens the ceremonial process of reconfederation by invoking the primal act of creation: "Oh, my offspring, lo, verily, this present day, such as is this day in kind and aspect, He Himself, He the Finisher of our Faculties, He the Master of All [Dehayenhyaawa′′gih] (He the Sky remember), has made." The orator reminds the audience, however, of "the being that is faceless because its lineaments were unknown to our ancestors, the Great Destroyer that it is, which every day and every night roams about with its weapon couched, yea, uplifted, at the very tops of our heads," and that has "snatched away from thee one in whom thou didst trust for words of wisdom and comfort." Following this prologue, the orator performs a series of ritual actions—wiping away tears, removing obstructions from ears and throat, tempering sickness of heart, and so on—to prepare for a hopeful, if not absolute, affirmation: "Now, we gather again the scattered Fire-brands . . . and now, indeed, do we rekindle the (Council) Fire for thee. And now, in fact, verily, the smoke shall rise again, and that smoke . . . will be fine, and it will even pierce the sky."[37] In Hewitt's text, the energies that quicken *Sketches*, energies of corrosion and restoration, relapse and redemption, focus in the Condolence. Perhaps, then, one can see Cusick's work not simply as a telling but as a performance of the "interview of consolation," as he terms it (14): binding the forces of atomism with a reconstitutive act of remembrance, Cusick calls on the enduring value of the League to transform a tale of loss into a ritual of renewal.

To propose a ritual history was, clearly, to challenge oppositions that persist to this day: the stasis, orality, and repetition of ritual versus the progress, textuality, and originality of history. Yet like Copway, Cusick is not content to rehearse his people's stories or announce their persistence. Of equal importance, by refusing to partition ritual and history along racial lines, he offers the poetics of *Sketches*—in which present and past, origin and tradition, incantation and transformation are intimately "involved"— as an ideal for the stories of the nation itself.

Toward this end, one of the most notable aspects of *Sketches* is its accommodation of diverse stories. What might seem a gimmick of track-

ing traditional moments along a European horizon—the arrival of Columbus—allows the two to overlap: "After decisive contests the warriors gained
the victory; and it was supposed that the Ronnongwetowanea tribe has
ever since ceased to exist. (This fate happened probably about two thousand five hundred winters before Columbus discovered the America.)" (9).
Whereas Copway faltered in the face of the technical challenges of inte-
grating stories, Cusick declines to present any in isolation; coupling originary Euro-American and Iroquois events, he makes each necessary to the
other. Those who objected to Cusick's "absurd chronology" were thus
bridling not only at his muffs but at his method: "By putting the frame-
work of a suppositional chronology to the traditions," Schoolcraft asserted,
Cusick "entered on quicksands where stouter feet have sunk."[38] Had the
dates simply been imprecise, this would have been bad enough; the fact
that Cusick dates stories through one another—that, as Russell Judkins
writes in an important study of *Sketches*, he attempts to "coordinate Iroquois and Euro-American knowledge systems, to have them share and
exchange world views"—undermines any story's solitary claim.[39]

More subtly, but no less "absurdly," Cusick permits stories to perme-
ate one another, to join not only in the placement of events but in their
status as events. At the simplest—though to the Tuscaroras' missionaries,
who blanched that "revealed religion" had become "intermingled with
their ancient superstition," intolerably[40]—he incorporates notions and passages from the Bible in his pagan account, as when the Good Mind forms
the human race "in his own likeness" (3), or when the people, enjoying pre-
Babel rapport, are found "yet in one language" (11). In a more comprehensive sense, Cusick's stories intertwine with the versions of events familiar to
a Euro-American audience to form a condensed, evocative interpretation
of the encounters in which Indians and Euro-Americans were mutually
involved. Thus, the plagues that so reduced Cusick's people find expression in the discovery of "a strange animal": "The warrior was confused at
not being able to kill the animal; he hastened to retire from the spot, but
when a few paces he was taken with the pestilence which was influenced by
the creature, and suddenly died; another warrior was at sight and directly
fled to carry the intelligence, but also died at a short distance, and the
others returned to the camp; but the pestilence soon prevailed" (22). Elsewhere, Cusick sketches a conflict reminiscent of colonial wars: "The Emperor built many forts throughout his dominions and almost penetrated
the lake Erie; this produced an excitement, the people of the north felt that
they would soon be deprived of the country on the south side of the Great

Lakes they determined to defend their country against any infringement of foreign people; long bloody wars ensued which perhaps lasted about one hundred years . . . at last the northern nations gained the conquest and all the towns and forts were totally destroyed and left them in the heap of ruins" (10–11). More generally, but just as urgently, he touches on his people's experience of reservation life: "Finding themselves circled by the monstrous serpent, some of them endeavored to pass out at the gate, and others attempted to climb over the serpent, but were unable; the people remained in this situation for several days; the warriors had made oppositions to dispel the monster, but were fruitless, and the people were distressed of their confinement" (21).[41] A less spectacular but more insidious threat surfaces when "a mischievous person named Shotyerronsgwea, while visiting the people at first distinguished himself of a good character and in mean time gained the confidence of the people; by doing this he was fairly concealed from being discovered of his real designs, and in a short time began to injure the people. . . . And the next he ventured to break the harmony of the nation and created dissensions among the people. At this the chiefs were so offended that the Shotyeronsgwea was banished from the village" (9). It is possible to read this tale as an account of antimissionary sentiment, culminating (as it had in the 1820s) in the expulsion of the troublemaker. Whether Cusick took sides during these conflicts is unknown; if his calling the intruder "the greatest mischievous person that ever existed" (10) places his sympathies with the antimission unit, his familiarity with the Bible argues otherwise: "By Some this may seem an incredible story," he writes of his people's crossing the Mississippi on a vine. "Why more so than that the Israelites should cross the Red Sea on dry land" (13 n). This note suggests, however, that familiarity had bred contempt. The missionaries not only "break the harmony" of the tribe by fostering opposed sides (itself a simplification of conversion, as Cusick knew, having produced a text that must have pained Kirkland's brethren despite his family's impeccable service); at the same time, they oppose their unimpeachable scripture to the tribe's "incredible" stories. Thus, by including such a man in his story, Cusick practices what the ministers preach against—the intermingling of religions—while requiting those who invest their stories with inherent authority.

If this is the case, however, then one should not insist on definitive readings of Cusick's stories; or one should not insist on defining "definitive" in conventional terms. The preceding readings might be legitimate, or not; *Sketches* might delineate any number of events, or none—by which I mean not that it is fantastic, but that its delineation of events calls into question what constitutes an event and its delineation. As I have said, Cusick's text—though it claims to proceed in a straight line and though no event is literally reproduced—is structured by an ebb and flow of conflict, resolution, respite. Thus, just as *Sketches* presents stories as compatriots rather than competitors, so does it present story itself as a progression that is also a repetition. To specify what Cusick borrows, or duplicates, or critiques is, then, to ask what any borrowing, duplicating, and critiquing upset; the fuzziness that inflamed Cusick's critics indicates not so much his failure to distinguish events as his unwillingness to accept any one event, or version of events, as sacrosanct. Unlike antebellum history—which opposed its original, nonreplicable nature to the traditional, rote nature of myth, the one true explication of the event to the false representations of all others—*Sketches* refuses to read story as unprecedented or independent; it refuses to accept absolute constructions of events, for it reads events as alloys of the unique and the exemplary, and it refuses to accept itself as the negation of one story's presence, for it reads presence as an overlay of stories. This does not mean that Cusick views his stories as unreal (he subtitles his work a "real account"); more properly and profoundly, his text reenvisions the real, asking if it can be fixed, absolute, singular. And if it cannot, then to oppose true to false, original to traditional—Indian to Euro-American—is a logical impossibility, for all stories depend on their involvement with the others from which they differ, but without which they could not exist.

This vision remains active on the final page of Cusick's work, in which the anticipated meeting of stories is articulated at last: "In the reign Atotarho XIII, in the year 1492, Columbus discovered the America" (38). Save for a flurry of battles, *Sketches* ends here, where Euro-American story begins. This terminal date is, as I suggested, only apparent; then again, since *Sketches* is an "ancient" history, Cusick was perhaps content to leave the "modern" period to others. Yet considering how others had told the tale, his decision to bow out is puzzling. Though Judkins believes that it is here that Cusick "correlates the two historical experiences," "affirming the validity of each" by "the fact of the existence of the other," it is also possible that, whether intimidated by the weight of testimony against him or unwilling to enumerate the details of conquest, he despairs of joining the two.[42] If so, perhaps his sense that Indian story has shaded into myth appears in a prophetic message: "The whites would in some future day take possession of the Big Island, and it was impossible to prevent it; the red children would melt away like snow before the heat" (31). This prediction, however, is belied by a prophecy of revitalization: "The defender ceased from visiting the people in bodily form, but appeared to the prophet. In a dream he foretells the whites would cross the Big Waters and bring some liquors, and buy up the red people's lands; he advises them not to comply with the wishes of the whites, lest they should ruin themselves and displease their Maker; they would destroy the tree of peace and extinguish the Great Council Fire at Onondaga, which was so long preserved to promote their national sovereignty" (37). Here as throughout, *Sketches* envisions an equilibrium between loss and gain: the forecast of doom and foretaste of regeneration are, like the text's many advances and retreats, a necessarily balanced pair. In this light, Cusick's use of a simile that had come to stand both as the summit of Indian figural language and, as in "Peboan and Seegwun," the summary of their fate—"the red children would melt away like snow before the heat"—suggests that this prophecy, like his opening thoughts on fable, is a reminder that there are multiple ways to read any story; for seasonal change, Cusick knew if others had forgotten, was recurrent rather than absolute. Thus, his choice of an ending seems a final, ambiguous commentary on, or enactment of, stories that are deeply, tragically, yet necessarily involved. What *Sketches* leaves one with is not simply a plea for diverse stories to coexist but an illustration that they must—for they are too patently interdependent to exist at all any other way.

Conclusion

When I say that I am not, have never been, nor offered myself, as an authority on things Amerindian, I do not wish to have it understood that I may not, at times, have succeeded in being an Indian.

—Mary Austin, *The American Rhythm*

Reflecting on the allure of Native American studies to non-Indian scholars, Angela Cavender Wilson paints a highly unflattering portrait of those who do offer themselves as authorities on things Amerindian: "American Indian history is a field dominated by white, male historians who rarely ask or care what the Indians they study have to say about their work. Under the guise of academic freedom they have maintained their comfortable chairs in archives across the country. . . . Very few have attempted to find out how Native people would interpret, analyze, or question the documents they confront, nor have they asked if the Native people they are studying have their own versions or stories of their past."[1] While this may be an exaggeration, and while I find problematic the suggestion that "the Indians they [historians] study" are identical with or manifestly accessible through their descendants, Wilson's argument is weighty: academia may indeed be yet another image-making industry that denies Indians self-representation. One need not adopt Mary Austin's outrageous assumption of Indian-ness in *The American Rhythm* (1923) to fall into the arrogant claim that one is authorized to speak for the Indians or the delusive belief that one has rescued their voices from the void when one has only been talking to oneself.

If this characterization seems unduly harsh, I should add that it is a *self*-characterization. Replace Wilson's "historian" with "literary critic," and you have me: I am a white, male academic; I have not solicited what contemporary Native people have to say about my work; and I believe I am free to conduct a study like this, even in ways unacceptable to others.[2] Yet I also believe, in Talal Asad's words, that "for criticism to be responsible, it must always be addressed to someone who can contest it."[3] Thus throughout this study, I have sought to make clear the provisional nature of my readings, not only because I find contact provisional but because I wish to be read with the same resistance and revision I perceive in America's literature. At this point, then, I would like to pose one more revision: not of any particular reading but of the idea, or at least my enactment, of interculturalism itself.

For have I, in fact, read interculturally? Much suggests I have not: I have used only written, and mostly white-authored, texts; I have taken what these texts seem to set down as their norm *as* a norm, and have read Indian "voices" mainly as posing options *to* this norm; indeed, I have perhaps seen Indian voices as posing options to the norm because to see them in this way was characteristic of that norm—and because I belong to, or at least am powerfully affected by, the norm it was my intention to critique. Of itself, my reliance on a limited and limiting paradigm is not particularly troubling; no criticism can (or should) hope to cover everything. Yet as an intercultural critic—one who claims that diverse traditions underlie American literatures—I must ask whether in all my readings, in interculturalism itself, there lies only the tradition of Euro-America.

How, one wonders, did encounter really appear to David Cusick (or the basket-maker of *Walden*, Cannasatego, Jane Johnston Schoolcraft)? Granted, Cusick seems concerned with myth and history: he seems to oppose them when he writes that Indian story is "involved with fables," to connect them when he mates the reigns of the Atotarhos with the impending arrival of Columbus. Granted as well, I have tried to see the terms "myth" and "history" in his terms, to suggest that for him, story was more like ritual, or ceremony, or something else entirely. But it is this something else entirely that has no voice in my pages. (It is possible, after all, that I have been able, or inclined, to see myth and history as "stories" only because history saw them as such.) I am baffled that Cusick ends with two columns in transliterated Mohawk and Tuscarora (38), or that, after recounting a battle, he takes up a seemingly unrelated subject: "The Skunantoh or Deer was the most useful game of the Five Nations; the animal can run considerable distance in a day" (34). Perhaps if I had learned his language or contacted speakers of it, I would have seen that for him the paradigm I employ is meaningless, and that my paradigm prevents me from exploring the one I should. But I did not learn his language or contact its speakers, and I am left with a reading that, however provisional, may not make sufficient provision for Cusick himself.

There is little more trifling than self-indulgent hand-wringing, so let me clarify the purpose of these reflections. Throughout this study, I have stressed the translations—the conversions—of textualization; and though I believe that criticism itself is involved in the processes of interculturalism, this means that criticism is also shaped by, participates in, the practices of conversionism. The question for the future, then, is not whether any paradigm can be applied to the literature (for any can), nor whether it should; the question is for whom, and for what purposes, it can or should. The question, in short, is how to construct a responsible criticism when the someone who can contest it no longer exists, has left no words (in some cases, no descendants) to speak out against the critic, or has left words, and descendants, ensnared in the conversionist discourses of the past, the present, the critical act. If an intercultural literary criticism holds possibilities for seeing beyond any one culture's terms, seeing how those terms may damage other cultures—seeing that among those terms are "one," "other," and "cultures"—the critic must be willing to go beyond interculturalism, to see it as another potentially dangerous term. Cusick's terms might be equally so. But we will never know until we hear his story.

Notes

Introduction

1. D. H. Lawrence, *Studies in Classic American Literature* (1923) (New York: Penguin, 1977), 41, 40–41.

2. Gary B. Nash, *Red, White, and Black: The Peoples of Early America* (Englewood Cliffs, N.J.: Prentice-Hall, 1974), 3. Another accessible introduction to ethnohistory is Colin G. Calloway, *New Worlds for All: Indians, Europeans, and the Remaking of Early America* (Baltimore: Johns Hopkins University Press, 1997). For Native American literary criticism, see Helen Jaskoski, ed., *Early Native American Writing: New Critical Essays* (Cambridge: Cambridge University Press, 1996); and Arnold Krupat, ed., *New Voices in Native American Literary Criticism* (Washington, D.C.: Smithsonian Institution Press, 1993).

3. Jarold Ramsey, "Thoreau's Last Words—and America's First Literatures," in *Redefining American Literary History*, ed. A. LaVonne Brown Ruoff and Jerry W. Ward, Jr. (New York: Modern Language Association of America, 1990), 52; Roy Harvey Pearce, *Savagism and Civilization: A Study of the Indian and the American Mind* (1953) (Berkeley: University of California Press, 1988), xvii, 5; Richard Drinnon, *Facing West: The Metaphysics of Indian-Hating and Empire-Building* (New York: Schocken, 1990), xxvii–xxviii; Robert F. Berkhofer, Jr., *The White Man's Indian: Images of the American Indian from Columbus to the Present* (New York: Vintage, 1978), xv.

4. Pearce, *Savagism and Civilization*, 250; Lucy Maddox, *Removals: Nineteenth-Century American Literature and the Politics of Indian Affairs* (New York: Oxford University Press, 1991), 174, 139; Susan Scheckel, *The Insistence of the Indian: Race and Nationalism in Nineteenth-Century American Culture* (Princeton: Princeton University Press, 1998), 3, 9. The pervasiveness of the image approach is suggested by the following sample: S. Elizabeth Bird, ed., *Dressing in Feathers: The Construction of the Indian in American Popular Culture* (Boulder, Colo.: Westview Press, 1996); Philip J. Deloria, *Playing Indian* (New Haven: Yale University Press, 1998); Klaus Lubbers, *Born for the Shade: Stereotypes of the Native American in United States Literature and the Visual Arts, 1776–1894* (Amsterdam: Rodopi, 1994); and Gordon M. Sayre, *Les Sauvages Américains: Representations of Native Americans in French and English Colonial Literature* (Chapel Hill: University of North

Carolina Press, 1997). Cheryl Walker's *Indian Nation: Native American Literature and Nineteenth-Century Nationalisms* (Durham: Duke University Press, 1997) plays off the image study, asking not how the nation made images of Indians but how Indians made images of the nation. For a critique of the ways in which theories of American literature exclude non-white peoples generally, see Russell J. Reising, *The Unusable Past: Theory and the Study of American Literature* (New York: Methuen Press, 1986). One of the few works to consider the Indians' *presence* in American literature is Eric J. Sundquist's "The Indian Gallery: Antebellum Literature and the Containment of the American Indian," in *American Literature, Culture, and Ideology: Essays in Memory of Henry Nash Smith*, ed. Beverly R. Voloshin (New York: Peter Lang, 1990), 37–64.

    5. Betsy Erkkila, "Ethnicity, Literary Theory, and the Grounds of Resistance," *American Quarterly* 47 (1995): 586.

    6. Roy Harvey Pearce, "From the History of Ideas to Ethnohistory," *Journal of Ethnic Studies* 2 (1974): 90.

    7. Richard White, *The Middle Ground: Indians, Empires, and Republics in the Great Lakes Region, 1650–1815* (Cambridge: Cambridge University Press, 1991), xi.

    8. Alfonso Ortiz, "Indian/White Relations: A View from the Other Side of the 'Frontier,'" in *Indians in American History: An Introduction*, ed. Frederick E. Hoxie (Arlington Heights, Ill.: Harlan Davidson, 1988), 9; Arnold Krupat, *Ethnocriticism: Ethnography, History, Literature* (Berkeley: University of California Press, 1992), 15, 26; Thomas Biolsi, "The American Indian and the Problem of Culture," *American Indian Quarterly* 13 (1984): 262.

    9. See, for example, A. Irving Hallowell, "The Backwash of the Frontier: The Impact of the Indian on American Culture," in *The Frontier in Perspective*, ed. Walker D. Wyman and Clifton B. Krocher (Madison: University of Wisconsin Press, 1957), 229–58.

    10. See "The 'Iroquois Influence' Thesis—Pro and Con," *William and Mary Quarterly* 53 (1996): 587–636; James Axtell, "The Unkindest Cut, or Who Invented Scalping? A Case Study," in his *The European and the Indian: Essays in the Ethnohistory of Colonial North America* (New York: Oxford University Press, 1981), 16–35; and Ward Churchill, "A Little Matter of Genocide: Sam Gill's *Mother Earth*, Colonialism and the Expropriation of Indigenous Spiritual Tradition in Academia," in his *Fantasies of the Master Race: Literature, Cinema and the Colonization of American Indians*, ed. M. Annette Jaimes (Monroe, Maine: Common Courage, 1992), 187–213. See also Robert Berkhofer's argument that the "contributions" model is static and ethnocentric ("Native Americans and United States History," in *The Reinterpretation of American History and Culture*, ed. William H. Cartwright and Richard L. Watson [Washington, D.C.: National Council for the Social Studies, 1973], 37–52). An illustration is Jack Weatherford's naive *Native Roots: How the Indians Enriched America* (New York: Crown, 1991), which waxes sentimental over what the Indians have "given to us" (128).

11. Andrew Wiget, "Reading Against the Grain: Origin Stories and American Literary History," *American Literary History* 3 (1991): 210; Arnold Krupat, *The Voice in the Margin: Native American Literature and the Canon* (Berkeley: University of California Press, 1989), 216. Other valuable multicultural/comparative/cosmopolitan approaches include Eric Anderson, "Manifest Dentistry, or Teaching Oral Narrative in *McTeague* and Old Man Coyote," in *Tricksterism in Turn-of-the-Century American Literature: A Multicultural Perspective*, ed. Elizabeth Ammons and Annette White-Parks (Hanover, N.H.: University Press of New England, 1994), 61–78; Annette Kolodny, "Letting Go Our Grand Obsessions: Notes toward a New Literary History of the American Frontiers," *American Literature* 64 (1992): 1–18; Paul Lauter, "The Literatures of America—A Comparative Discipline," in his *Canons and Contexts* (New York: Oxford University Press, 1991), 48–96; and Dana D. Nelson, "Reading the Written Selves of Colonial America: Franklin, Occom, Equiano, and Palou/Serra," *Resources for American Literary Study* 19 (1993): 246–59.

12. As Werner Sollors points out, to consider ethnicity the defining feature of a text is to obscure both the complexity of ethnic heritage and "the ethnic innovations and cultural mergers that took place in America" ("A Critique of Pure Pluralism," in *Reconstructing American Literary History*, ed. Sacvan Bercovitch [Cambridge: Harvard University Press, 1986], 256). For a consideration of this issue in Indian-authored texts, see Wolfgang Hochbruck, "Cultural Authenticity and the Construction of Pan-Indian Metanarrative," in *Cultural Difference and the Literary Text: Pluralism and the Limits of Authenticity in North American Literatures*, ed. Winfried Siemerling and Katrin Schwenk (Iowa City: University of Iowa Press, 1996), 18–28.

13. Barry O'Connell, introduction to *On Our Own Ground: The Complete Writings of William Apess, a Pequot*, ed. O'Connell (Amherst: University of Massachusetts Press, 1992), lv.

14. William Walton, in John Eliot, *A Late and Further Manifestation of the Progress of the Gospel amongst the Indians in New-England* (London: M. S., 1655), 20. Throughout this study, as in the quotation from Walton, I have preserved primary sources' spelling, punctuation, and typography, however antiquated or idiosyncratic. I have made no silent corrections of obvious typographical errors, but I have avoided the obtrusive and obnoxious "sic" as well; I have provided bracketed emendations only when their absence might lead to misreading.

15. Archaeological analyses, indeed, often fold back into textual ones. Thus Laurier Turgeon argues that material evidence helps correct for how "written records . . . systematically filter information," yet in interpreting the meanings copper kettles had for Micmac Indians, Turgeon relies largely on European written records ("The Tale of the Kettle: Odyssey of an Intercultural Object," *Ethnohistory* 44 [1997]: 3).

16. Among the handful of Indians whose written works survive from colonial times is one of Eliot's interpreters: James (the) Printer, who helped prepare the

missionary's Algonquian Bible, acted as Metacom's (King Philip's) scribe in negotiating the release of Mary Rowlandson, and may have set type for the second edition of Rowlandson's captivity narrative. See Walter T. Meserve, "English Works
of Seventeenth-Century Indians," *American Quarterly* 8 (1956): 268–70; and Jill
Lepore, *The Name of War: King Philip's War and the Origins of American Identity*
(New York: Knopf, 1998), 34, 145–49. On the theoretical implications of texts
jointly authored by European missionaries and native converts, see Louise M.
Burkhart, "The Amanuenses Have Appropriated the Text: Interpreting a Nahuatl
Song of Santiago," in *On the Translation of Native American Literatures*, ed. Brian
Swann (Washington, D.C.: Smithsonian Institution Press, 1992), 339–55.

  17. On issues of ethnographic interpretation, see James Clifford and George
E. Marcus, eds., *Writing Culture: The Poetics and Politics of Ethnography* (Berkeley:
University of California Press, 1986). The problems of ethnohistorical analysis are
evident in a fascinating work that appeared in the pages of *Ethnohistory*: a tran-
scribed theological debate between Jesuit missionaries and Ojibwa Indians. The
editors, Denys Delâge and Helen Hornbeck Tanner, note that "the translations
involved in this document are complex"—it was apparently written down by a
bilingual Ojibwa interpreter, then reconstructed months later by a priest who had
taken part in the debate—but they nonetheless feel that the encounter is "clearly
presented," that the Indians' opinions are "conveyed with great care" by those who
recorded them, and that the similarity of themes in seventeenth-century written
accounts to those in this nineteenth-century debate shows a "continuity in the
ideology of North American Indian philosophers" ("The Ojibwa-Jesuit Debate at
Walpole Island, 1844," *Ethnohistory* 41 [1994]: 299, 295, 299). In effect, the editors
separate the fact of translation from its realization in the translated text—clearly an
untenable distinction. Regrettably, literary critics have tended to ignore the textual
issues presented by ethnohistorical writings; instead, in their own search for Indian
"voices," they have used such writings to sidestep the textuality of primary sources.
To cite one example, Hilary Wyss cautions that the "reliability" of seventeenth-
century Indian conversion narratives is "suspect." Yet she is thoroughly incautious
in using ethnohistorical texts to reconstruct "traditional [Indian] society" and "the
Native perspective"; and as such, these modern texts allow her to assert the extratextual value of the conversion accounts: they "offer a significant opportunity to
look at the words, however mediated, of Native American converts" ("'Things
That Do Accompany Salvation': Colonialism, Conversion, and Cultural Exchange in Experience Mayhew's *Indian Converts*," *Early American Literature* 33
[1998]: 53, 47, 50, 54).

  18. Fredric Jameson, *The Political Unconscious: Narrative as a Socially Symbolic
Act* (Ithaca: Cornell University Press, 1981), 85; Henry Louis Gates, Jr., "Critical
Fanonism," *Critical Inquiry* 17 (1991): 466.

  19. David Murray, *Forked Tongues: Speech, Writing and Representation in
North American Indian Texts* (Bloomington: Indiana University Press, 1991), 3.

20. Pearce, *Savagism and Civilization*, 127.

21. Françoise Lionnet, "'Logiques Métisses': Cultural Appropriation and Postcolonial Representations," *College Literature* 19 (1992): 102.

22. Ramón Gutiérrez, *When Jesus Came, the Corn Mothers Went Away: Marriage, Sexuality, and Power in New Mexico, 1500–1846* (Stanford: Stanford University Press, 1991), xvii.

Chapter 1. Indian Conversions

1. Henry A. S. Dearborn, *A Sketch of the Life of the Apostle Eliot* (Roxbury, Mass.: Norfolk County Journal Press, 1850), 9; *Report of the Commissioners Relating to the Condition of the Indians in Massachusetts* (1849), quoted in Laura E. Conkey, Ethel Boissevain, and Ives Goddard, "Indians of Southern New England and Long Island: Late Period," in *Handbook of North American Indians*, vol. 15, *Northeast*, ed. Bruce G. Trigger (Washington, D.C.: Smithsonian Institution Press, 1978), 180; Dearborn, *Sketch of the Life*, 28.

2. When using transliterated Indian names, I have removed hyphens, an older convention that tends to emphasize their "primitiveness."

3. Dearborn, *Sketch of the Life*, 29; George Copway, in *Sketch of the Life*, 31. See Copway, "The American Indians," *American Review* 9 (1849): 631–37; and Dearborn, "Journals of Henry A. S. Dearborn: A Record of Councils with the Seneca and Tuscarora Indians at Buffalo and Cattaraugus in the Years 1838 and 1839," *Publications of the Buffalo Historical Society* 7 (1904): 33–225.

4. Lawrence, *Studies in Classic American Literature*, 57; Victor Turner, "Betwixt and Between: The Liminal Period in *Rites de Passage*," in his *The Forest of Symbols: Aspects of Ndembu Ritual* (Ithaca: Cornell University Press, 1967), 97, 99.

5. On Eliot, see Neal Salisbury, "Red Puritans: The 'Praying Indians' of Massachusetts Bay and John Eliot," *William and Mary Quarterly* 31 (1974): 27–54.

6. Eliot, *Late and Further Manifestation*, 1, 2; Berkhofer, *White Man's Indian*, 151; George E. Tinker, *Missionary Conquest: The Gospel and Native American Cultural Genocide* (Minneapolis: Fortress Press, 1993), 4. See also Robert F. Berkhofer, Jr., *Salvation and the Savage: An Analysis of Protestant Missions and American Indian Response, 1787–1862* (Lexington: University of Kentucky Press, 1965).

7. R. Pierce Beaver, "Protestant Churches and the Indians," in *Handbook of North American Indians*, vol. 4, *History of Indian-White Relations*, ed. Wilcomb E. Washburn (Washington, D.C.: Smithsonian Institution Press, 1988), 430; Forrest G. Wood, *The Arrogance of Faith: Christianity and Race in America from the Colonial Era to the Twentieth Century* (New York: Knopf, 1990), 142.

8. Richard W. Cogley, "John Eliot and the Origins of the American Indians," *Early American Literature* 21 (1987): 210–25.

9. Thomas Shepard, *The Clear Sunshine of the Gospel Breaking Forth upon

the Indians in New England (1648), in *The Works of Thomas Shepard* (Boston: Doctrinal Tract and Book Society, 1853; New York: AMS Press, 1967), 3:455; Increase Mather, *An Earnest Exhortation to the Inhabitants of New-England* (Boston: John Foster, 1676), 19; *New Englands First Fruits* (London: R. O. and G. D., 1643), 10 (incorrectly paginated 18).

10. Eliot, in Shepard, *Clear Sunshine*, 470; Francis Jennings, *The Invasion of America: Indians, Colonialism, and the Cant of Conquest* (New York: Norton, 1975), 232; Salisbury, "Red Puritans," 34. For a more sympathetic portrait, see Richard W. Cogley, *John Eliot's Mission to the Indians Before King Philip's War* (Cambridge: Harvard University Press, 1999).

11. John Eliot, *A Brief Narrative of the Progress of the Gospel amongst the Indians in New-England* (1670), 10; Cotton Mather, *Magnalia Christi Americana; Or, the Ecclesiastical History of New-England; from its First Planting, in the Year 1620, unto the Year of Our Lord 1698* (1702) (Hartford: Silas Andrus, 1855), 1:581; Solomon Stoddard, *Question Whether God is Not Angry with the Country for Doing So Little towards the Conversion of the Indians?* (Boston: B. Green, 1723), 12.

12. *New Englands First Fruits*, 6; Isaac McCoy, *Remarks on the Practicability of Indian Reform, Embracing Their Colonization* (Boston: Lincoln and Edmands, 1827), 43 n; Mary Rowlandson, *The Narrative of the Captivity and Restoration of Mrs. Mary Rowlandson* (1682) (Boston: Houghton Mifflin, 1930), 57.

13. James Axtell, "Some Thoughts on the Ethnohistory of Missions," in his *After Columbus: Essays in the Ethnohistory of Colonial North America* (New York: Oxford University Press, 1988), 50, 54, 55, 54, 55; David Zeisberger, *Diary of David Zeisberger, a Moravian Missionary among the Indians of Ohio*, trans. and ed. Eugene F. Bliss (Cincinnati: Robert Clarke, 1885; St. Clair Shores, Mich.: Scholarly Press, 1972), 1:28.

14. Most ethnohistorical studies are similarly uncritical in reconstructing converts' motives and beliefs. See Elise M. Brenner, "To Pray or to Be Prey: That Is the Question. Strategies for Cultural Autonomy of Massachusetts Praying Town Indians," *Ethnohistory* 27 (1980): 135–52; Cogley, *John Eliot's Mission*, 33–37, 56–58, 243–44; Robert James Naeher, "Dialogue in the Wilderness: John Eliot and the Indian Exploration of Puritanism as a Source of Meaning, Comfort, and Ethnic Survival," *New England Quarterly* 62 (1989): 346–68; and Harold W. Van Lonkhuyzen, "A Reappraisal of the Praying Indians: Acculturation, Conversion, and Identity at Natick, Massachusetts, 1646–1730," *New England Quarterly* 63 (1990): 396–428.

15. For Eliot's prohibitions, see Shepard, *Clear Sunshine*, 459–60.

16. Eliot, *Late and Further Manifestation*, 15.

17. Roger Williams, *A Key into the Language of America* (1643), ed. John J. Teunissen and Evelyn J. Hinz (Detroit: Wayne State University Press, 1973), 191; Eliot, *Late and Further Manifestation*, 9; John Eliot, *John Eliot's Indian Dialogues* (1671), ed. Henry W. Bowden and James P. Ronda (Westport, Conn.: Greenwood Press, 1980), 103.

18. Benjamin Franklin to Peter Collinson, 9 May 1753, in *The Papers of Benjamin Franklin*, ed. Leonard W. Labaree (New Haven: Yale University Press, 1959–), 4:482; Annette Kolodny, *The Land Before Her: Fantasy and Experience of the American Frontiers, 1630–1860* (Chapel Hill: University of North Carolina Press, 1984), 72, 73; Susan Walsh, " 'With Them Was My Home': Native American Autobiography and *A Narrative of the Life of Mrs. Mary Jemison*," *American Literature* 64 (1992): 49, 51; Scheckel, *Insistence of the Indian*, 73; June Namias, introduction to James E. Seaver, *A Narrative of the Life of Mrs. Mary Jemison*, ed. Namias (Norman: University of Oklahoma Press, 1992), 44–45, 44. Ethnohistorians have been more successful in delineating the intercultural nature of captivity than have literary critics; see, for example, James Axtell, "The White Indians of Colonial America," in his *European and the Indian*, 168–206; and A. Irving Hallowell, "American Indians, White and Black: The Phenomenon of Transculturalization," *Current Anthropology* 4 (1963): 519–31. For a work of literary scholarship that considers captivity a "complex practice in which various indigenous and European traditions . . . converged," see Pauline Turner Strong, *Captive Selves, Captivating Others: The Politics and Poetics of Colonial American Captivity Narratives* (Boulder, Colo.: Westview Press, 1999), 3.

19. James E. Seaver, *A Narrative of the Life of Mrs. Mary Jemison* (1824) (Syracuse: Syracuse University Press, 1990), xxvi, xxvii, xxviii, xxx, 33, 27, 31, 51, 32, 76, 130, 145.

20. George Catlin, *Letters and Notes on the Manners, Customs, and Condition of the North American Indians* (London: George Catlin, 1841), 1:3, 2:223; Thomas L. McKenney, *Memoirs, Official and Personal* (New York: Paine and Burgess, 1846), 2:83, 113; "Catlin's North American Indians," *United States Magazine and Democratic Review* 11 (1842): 44; Catlin, *Letters and Notes* 2:223.

21. Williams, *Key into the Language*, 87; Patrick Frazier, *The Mohicans of Stockbridge* (Lincoln: University of Nebraska Press, 1992), 240; Alden T. Vaughan and Edward W. Clark, "Cups of Common Calamity: Puritan Captivity Narratives as Literature and History," in *Puritans among the Indians: Accounts of Captivity and Redemption, 1676–1724*, ed. Vaughan and Clark (Cambridge: Harvard University Press, 1981), 16; Joshua David Bellin, "Apostle of Removal: John Eliot in the Nineteenth Century," *New England Quarterly* 69 (1996): 3.

22. Martin Moore, *Memoirs of the Life and Character of Rev. John Eliot, Apostle of the N. A. Indians* (Boston: T. Bedlington, 1822), 165. On the missionizing spirit of the early nineteenth century, see also Henry Warner Bowden, *American Indians and Christian Missions: Studies in Cultural Conflict* (Chicago: University of Chicago Press, 1981), 164–97; and Joseph Conforti, "Jonathan Edwards's Most Popular Work: 'The Life of David Brainerd' and Nineteenth-Century Evangelical Culture," *Church History* 54 (1985): 188–201.

23. Philip Freneau, "The Indian Convert" (1797), in *Poems of Philip Freneau: Poet of the American Revolution*, ed. Fred Lewis Pattee (Princeton: Princeton University Press, 1907), 3:190; "Cooper's Novels," *North American Review* 23 (1826),

195–96; George Bancroft, *History of the United States from the Discovery of the American Continent*, 22nd ed. (Boston: Little, Brown, 1873), vol. 3 (1839), 302–03; Lewis Cass, "Removal of the Indians," *North American Review* 30 (1830): 105; Convers Francis, *Life of John Eliot, the Apostle to the Indians*, vol. 5 of *The Library of American Biography*, ed. Jared Sparks (Boston: Hilliard, Gray, 1836), 295.

24. Russell Thornton notes that the Cherokees numbered about 22,000 in 1835, up from an 1808 low of 13,000 (*American Indian Holocaust and Survival: A Population History Since 1492* [Norman: University of Oklahoma Press, 1987], 114–18). Yet as Brian Dippie shows, such increases were routinely denied by the makers of Indian policy (*The Vanishing American: White Attitudes and U.S. Indian Policy* [Middletown, Conn.: Wesleyan University Press, 1982]).

25. Elias Boudinot, "An Address to the Whites Delivered in the First Presbyterian Church, on the 26th of May, 1826," in *Cherokee Editor: The Writings of Elias Boudinot*, ed. Theda Perdue (Knoxville: University of Tennessee Press, 1983), 73; Rufus Anderson, ed., *Memoir of Catharine Brown, a Christian Indian, of the Cherokee Nation* (1825), 3rd ed. (Boston: Crocker and Brewster, 1828), 76; Theda Perdue, "Rising from the Ashes: The *Cherokee Phoenix* as an Ethnohistorical Source," *Ethnohistory* 24 (1977): 216; Ronald Satz, "Cherokee Traditionalism, Protestant Evangelism, and the Trail of Tears," *Tennessee Historical Quarterly* 44 (1985): 395. See also William G. McLoughlin, *Cherokees and Missionaries, 1789–1839* (New Haven: Yale University Press, 1984).

26. The fact that most Cherokees were not speakers or readers of English, a substantial plurality being literate solely in the syllabary designed by Sequoyah, suggests the shortcomings of a study (such as mine) reliant on English documents. On this point, see Perdue, "Rising from the Ashes"; and Theda Perdue, "Traditionalism in the Cherokee Nation: Resistance to the Constitution of 1827," *Georgia Historical Quarterly* 66 (1982): 159–70.

27. John Ross to John C. Calhoun, 11 February 1824, in *The Papers of Chief John Ross*, vol. 1, 1807–1839, ed. Gary E. Moulton (Norman: University of Oklahoma Press, 1985), 65–66; Cass, "Removal of the Indians," 83; Wilson Lumpkin, *The Removal of the Cherokee Indians from Georgia* (New York: Dodd, Mead, 1907; New York: Augustus M. Kelley, 1971), 1:165; McKenney, *Memoirs* 2:112–13. On the Cherokee challenge to American authority and identity, see Walter H. Conser, Jr., "John Ross and the Cherokee Resistance Campaign, 1833–1838," *Journal of Southern History* 44 (1978): 191–212; and Priscilla Wald, *Constituting Americans: Cultural Anxiety and Narrative Form* (Durham: Duke University Press, 1995), 20–40.

28. Wayne Franklin, *The New World of James Fenimore Cooper* (Chicago: University of Chicago Press, 1982), 123; Nathaniel Hawthorne, "Life of Eliot," *American Magazine of Useful Knowledge* 2.12 (August 1836): 496; Nathaniel Hawthorne, "The May-Pole of Merry Mount" (1836), in his *Twice-Told Tales*, vol. 9 of *The Centenary Edition of the Works of Nathaniel Hawthorne*, ed. William Charvat et al. (Columbus: Ohio State University Press, 1974), 57; F. O. Matthiessen, *American Renaissance: Art and Expression in the Age of Emerson and Whitman* (London:

Oxford University Press, 1941), 276; Nathaniel Hawthorne, "Sketches from Memory" (1835), in his *Mosses from an Old Manse*, vol. 10 of *Centenary Edition* (1974), 429; Nathaniel Hawthorne, *The Scarlet Letter* (1850), vol. 1 of *Centenary Edition* (1962), 114.

29. Robert Montgomery Bird, *Nick of the Woods or the Jibbenainosay: A Tale of Kentucky* (1837), ed. Curtis Dahl (Albany: New College and University Press, 1967), 34. All further citations in this chapter appear in parentheses in the text.

30. James Fenimore Cooper, *The Wept of Wish-Ton-Wish: A Tale* (1829) (New York: Frank F. Lovell, n. d.), 18.

31. James C. Bryant, "The Fallen World in *Nick of the Woods*," *American Literature* 38 (1966): 364.

32. Mary Kelley, introduction to Catharine Maria Sedgwick, *Hope Leslie; Or, Early Times in the Massachusetts* (1827), ed. Kelley (New Brunswick: Rutgers University Press, 1987), xxxi. All further citations appear in parentheses in the text.

33. Sedgwick's text is, in any event, the only such work to attract sustained attention. An anonymous pamphlet, *Boston Two Hundred Years Ago, or the Romantic Story of Miss Ann Carter, Daughter of One of the First Settlers[,] and the Celebrated Indian Chief Thundersquall* (Boston, 1830), not only presents physical love between its title characters—"their lips met, he threw his arms around her, he strained her to his bosom" (14)—but writes of their union: "Many who reside in this city, are descended from this stock, and the pure blood [!] which courses through their veins, claims consanguinity with Thundersquall" (15). Published in the year of the Indian Removal Act, this work raises the tantalizing thought of a popular counter-tradition that awaits discovery.

34. Sandra A. Zagarell, "Expanding 'America': Lydia Sigourney's *Sketch of Connecticut*, Catharine Sedgwick's *Hope Leslie*," *Tulsa Studies in Women's Literature* 6 (1987): 235; Christopher Castiglia, "In Praise of Extra-Vagant Women: *Hope Leslie* and the Captivity Romance," *Legacy* 6.2 (Fall 1989): 5. See also Castiglia's *Bound and Determined: Captivity, Culture-Crossing, and White Womanhood from Mary Rowlandson to Patty Hearst* (Chicago: University of Chicago Press, 1996), which enlarges the discussion of Sedgwick (159–79) while arguing for the radicalness of the captivity tradition as a whole.

35. In a later story, "The Catholic Iroquois," Sedgwick presents an Indian convert deeply devoted to her faith. Yet devotion does not save her; ordered by her father to renounce Christianity, she makes "the sign of the cross" and submits to death (*Tales and Sketches* [Philadelphia: Carey, Lea, and Blanchard, 1835], 64).

36. On Sedgwick's inability to sustain contact between Indians and whites, see also Philip Gould, *Covenant and Republic: Historical Romance and the Politics of Puritanism* (Cambridge: Cambridge University Press, 1996), 61–90; and Maddox, *Removals*, 103–10.

37. Douglas Ford, "Inscribing the 'Impartial Observer' in Sedgwick's *Hope Leslie*," *Legacy* 14 (1997): 90.

38. James Fenimore Cooper, *The Deerslayer* (1841), ed. Donald E. Pease (New

York: Penguin, 1987), 191, 193. Hetty performs double duty for Cooper when, writing that "Indian traditions" had "mingl[ed] with the christian lore [she] received in childhood" (366), he suggests that only the half-wit can become a spiritual half-breed.

39. Hawthorne, *Scarlet Letter*, 165, 183.

40. Nehemiah Adams, *The Life of John Eliot: With an Account of the Early Missionary Efforts among the Indians of New England* (Boston: Massachusetts Sabbath School Society, 1847), 254, 26, 26–27, 278.

41. William Ellis, *Polynesian Researches, During a Residence of Nearly Six Years in the South Sea Islands* (1829; London: Dawsons, 1967), 1:vi, vii; review of *Typee*, *London Critic*, 28 March 1846, in Watson G. Branch, ed., *Melville: The Critical Heritage* (London: Routledge, 1974), 57; George Long Duyckinck to Mrs. Edward Baker, 14 April 1846, in Jay Leyda, ed., *The Melville Log: A Documentary Life of Herman Melville, 1819–1891* (New York: Gordian, 1951; rpt. with supplement, 1969), 1:211. For the passages deleted from the American Revised edition, see Herman Melville, *Typee: A Peep at Polynesian Life*, ed. Harrison Hayford, Hershel Parker, and G. Thomas Tanselle, vol. 1 of *The Writings of Herman Melville* (Evanston, Ill.: Northwestern University Press, 1968), 309 n. 15–16.

42. See, for example, Richard Chase, *Herman Melville: A Critical Study* (New York: Macmillan, 1949), 9–15; Lawrence, *Studies in Classic American Literature*, 139–52; and Milton R. Stern, *The Fine Hammered Steel of Herman Melville* (Urbana: University of Illinois Press, 1957), 34–65.

43. Gorman Beauchamp, "Melville and the Tradition of Primitive Utopia," *Journal of General Education* 33 (1981): 13; T. Walter Herbert, Jr., *Marquesan Encounters: Melville and the Meaning of Civilization* (Cambridge: Harvard University Press, 1980), 159; Mitchell Robert Breitwieser, "False Sympathy in Melville's *Typee*," *American Quarterly* 34 (1982): 397. For a brief intercultural reading of *Typee*, see Greg Dening, *Islands and Beaches: Discourse on a Silent Land: Marquesas 1774–1880* (Honolulu: University Press of Hawaii, 1980), 147–49.

44. Herman Melville, *Typee: A Peep at Polynesian Life* (1846), ed. George Woodcock (New York: Penguin, 1972), 37. All further citations appear in parentheses in the text.

45. On the imperial context/subtext of *Typee*, see Malini Johar Schueller, "Indians, Polynesians, and Empire Making: The Case of Herman Melville," in *Genealogy and Literature*, ed. Lee Quinby (Minneapolis: University of Minnesota Press, 1995), 48–67.

46. Christopher Herbert, *Culture and Anomie: Ethnographic Imagination in the Nineteenth Century* (Chicago: University of Chicago Press, 1991), 155. See also Mark Hanley's argument that the missionaries Tommo scorns were, like him, outspoken in their attacks on imperialism (*Beyond a Christian Commonwealth: The Protestant Quarrel with the American Republic, 1830–1860* [Chapel Hill: University of North Carolina Press, 1994], 75–84).

47. Leonard Cassuto, "'What an Object He Would Have Made of Me!': Tattooing and the Racial Freak in Melville's *Typee*," in *Freakery: Cultural Spectacles of the Extraordinary Body*, ed. Rosemarie Garland Thomson (New York: New York University Press, 1996), 235; Samuel Otter, *Melville's Anatomies* (Berkeley: University of California Press, 1999), 47.

48. William Oland Bourne, "Typee: The Traducers of Missions" (1846), in *Critical Essays on Herman Melville's "Typee,"* ed. Milton R. Stern (Boston: G. K. Hall, 1982), 42; Herman Melville, *Moby-Dick; or, The Whale* (1851), ed. Harold Beaver (New York: Penguin, 1986), 183–84. *Moby-Dick* parodies Eliot relentlessly, as in the cook's sermon to the sharks (401–2) and the rescue of Tashtego from the sinking "wigwam" (441) of the whale's head (450–51).

Chapter 2. The Charm of the Indian

1. Mather, "The Life of the Renowned John Eliot," in *Magnalia Christi Americana* 1:558, 559; William Wood, *New England's Prospect* (1634), ed. Alden T. Vaughan (Amherst: University of Massachusetts Press, 1977), 88.

2. Jane Tompkins, "'Indians': Textualism, Morality, and the Problem of History," in *"Race," Writing, and Difference*, ed. Henry Louis Gates, Jr. (Chicago: University of Chicago Press, 1985–1986), 63, 72; James Axtell, "The Ethnohistory of Native America," in *Rethinking American Indian History*, ed. Donald L. Fixico (Albuquerque: University of New Mexico Press, 1997), 15.

3. Hayden White, "The Noble Savage Theme as Fetish," in *First Images of America: The Impact of the New World on the Old*, ed. Fredi Chiappeli (Berkeley: University of California Press, 1976), 1:121; Arthur O. Lovejoy and George Boas, eds., *A Documentary History of Primitivism and Related Ideas in Antiquity* (Baltimore: Johns Hopkins University Press, 1935), 16. Introductions to the literature of the Noble Savage include Hoxie Neale Fairchild, *The Noble Savage: A Study in Romantic Primitivism* (New York: Columbia University Press, 1928); Anthony Pagden, "The Savage Critic: Some European Images of the Primitive," *Yearbook of English Studies* 13 (1983): 32–45; and Pearce, *Savagism and Civilization*, 136–50, 169–95.

4. Lovejoy and Boas, *Documentary History*, 17; White, "Noble Savage Theme," 124; Richard Slotkin, *Regeneration Through Violence: The Mythology of the American Frontier, 1600–1860* (Middletown, Conn.: Wesleyan University Press, 1973), 356–57. For an opposing view of the genesis and cultural significance of Noble Savagism, see William Brandon, *New Worlds for Old: Reports from the New World and Their Effect on the Development of Social Thought in Europe, 1500–1800* (Athens: Ohio University Press, 1986).

5. See Louise K. Barnett, *The Ignoble Savage: American Literary Racism, 1790–1890* (Westport, Conn.: Greenwood Press, 1975).

6. Christopher Columbus, *Four Voyages to the New World*, trans. and ed. R. H. Major (London: Hakluyt Society, 1847; Gloucester, Mass.: Peter Smith, 1978), 7; Stephen Greenblatt, *Marvelous Possessions: The Wonder of the New World* (Chicago: University of Chicago Press, 1991), 110; Columbus, *Four Voyages*, 17.

7. Eric Cheyfitz, *The Poetics of Imperialism: Translation and Colonization from "The Tempest" to "Tarzan"* (New York: Oxford University Press, 1991), 156. On the tendency of critics to conceptualize material interchange within and between Indian and European groups in European terms only, see Christopher L. Miller and George R. Hamell, "A New Perspective on Indian-White Contact: Cultural Symbols and Colonial Trade," *Journal of American History* 73 (1986): 311–28.

8. Michel de Montaigne, "Of Cannibals" (1578–1580), in *The Complete Works of Montaigne*, trans. Donald M. Frame (Stanford: Stanford University Press, 1958), 153, 158–59, 158, 159. I gratefully acknowledge Cheyfitz's impact on my reading of "Cannibals" (*Poetics of Imperialism*, 142–57).

9. See William M. Hamlin, *The Image of America in Montaigne, Spenser, and Shakespeare: Renaissance Ethnography and Literary Reflection* (New York: St. Martin's Press, 1995), 37–43.

10. Lawrence Buell, "American Pastoral Ideology Reappraised," *American Literary History* 1 (1989): 5–6.

11. Daniel Denton, *A Brief Description of New-York: Formerly Called New-Netherlands*, March of America Facsimile Series, no. 26 (London, 1670; Ann Arbor: University Microfilms, 1966), 11; Adriaen Van der Donk, *A Description of the New Netherlands* (1656), ed. Thomas F. O'Donnell (Syracuse: Syracuse University Press, 1968), 74; Thomas Morton, *New English Canaan* (1637), ed. Charles Francis Adams, Jr. (Boston: Prince Society, 1883; New York: Burt Franklin, 1967), 176–77. For theories of Indian reciprocity, see Neal Salisbury, *Manitou and Providence: Indians, Europeans, and the Making of New England, 1500–1643* (New York: Oxford University Press, 1982), 10–11, 85–86, 237–38; and Calvin Martin, *Keepers of the Game: Indian-Animal Relationships and the Fur Trade* (Berkeley: University of California Press, 1978). For arguments against such theories, see the essays in Shepard Krech III, ed., *Indians, Animals, and the Fur Trade: A Critique of "Keepers of the Game"* (Athens: University of Georgia Press, 1981).

12. Hendrick Aupaumut, "Indian History," in Electa F. Jones, *Stockbridge, Past and Present; Or, Records of an Old Mission Station* (Springfield, Mass.: Samuel Bowles, 1854), 18.

13. Marcel Mauss, *The Gift: Forms and Functions of Exchange in Archaic Societies* (1950), trans. Ian Cunnison (Glencoe, Ill.: Free Press, 1954), 2, 4, 35.

14. John Lawson, *A New Voyage to Carolina* (1709), ed. Hugh Talmage Lefler (Chapel Hill: University of North Carolina Press, 1967), 184; Robert A. Brightman, *Grateful Prey: Rock Cree Human-Animal Relationships* (Berkeley: University of California Press, 1993), 189.

15. Roger Williams, *A Key into the Language of America* (1643), ed. John J. Teunissen and Evelyn J. Hinz (Detroit: Wayne State University Press, 1973), 90. All further citations in this chapter appear in parentheses in the text.

16. John Winthrop, "A Model of Christian Charity" (1630), in *The Puritans in America: A Narrative Anthology*, ed. Alan Heimert and Andrew Delbanco (Cambridge: Harvard University Press, 1985), 86–87, 88, 91; Stephen Innes, *Creating the Commonwealth: The Economic Culture of Puritan New England* (New York: Norton, 1995), 71, 72; Winthrop, "Model of Christian Charity," 82. On Puritan economic culture, see also Darrett B. Rutman, *Winthrop's Boston: Portrait of a Puritan Town, 1630–1649* (Chapel Hill: University of North Carolina Press, 1965), 68–97, 241–59. On the encounter of English and Narragansett economic cultures, see Joshua Micah Marshall, "'A Melancholy People': Anglo-Indian Relations in Early Warwick, Rhode Island, 1642–1675," *New England Quarterly* 68 (1995): 402–28.

17. Krupat, *Voice in the Margin*, 133.

18. Jack L. Davis, "Roger Williams among the Narragansett Indians," *New England Quarterly* 43 (1970): 602. See also Donald A. Grinde and Bruce E. Johansen, *Exemplar of Liberty: Native America and the Evolution of Democracy* (Los Angeles: University of California Press, 1991), 73–91.

19. See Gordon Brotherston, "A Controversial Guide to the Language of America, 1643," in *1642: Literature and Power in the Seventeenth Century*, ed. Francis Barker et al. (Essex: University of Essex, 1981), 84–100; and Eric Wertheimer, "'To Spell out Each Other': Roger Williams, Perry Miller, and the Indian," *Arizona Quarterly* 50.2 (Summer 1994): 1–18.

20. Wood, *New England's Prospect*, 88; Sacvan Bercovitch, *The Rites of Assent: Transformations in the Symbolic Construction of America* (London: Routledge, 1993), 31; Anne Keary, "Retelling the History of the Settlement of Providence: Speech, Writing, and Cultural Interaction on Narragansett Bay," *New England Quarterly* 69 (1996): 269; Raymond Williams, *Marxism and Literature* (Oxford: Oxford University Press, 1977), 121.

21. Thomas Cole, "Essay on American Scenery" (1836), in *Thomas Cole: The Collected Essays and Prose Sketches*, ed. Marshall Tymn (St. Paul: John Colet, 1980), 6, 4, 5. See also Perry Miller, "The Romantic Dilemma in American Nationalism and the Concept of Nature," in his *Nature's Nation* (Cambridge: Harvard University Press, 1967), 197–207.

22. Michel-Guillaume St. Jean de Crèvecoeur, *Journey into Northern Pennsylvania and the State of New York* (1801), trans. Clarissa Spencer Bostelmann (Ann Arbor: University of Michigan Press, 1964), 52; Jean-Jacques Rousseau, "A Discourse on the Origin of Inequality" (1755), in *The Social Contract and Discourses*, trans. G. D. H. Cole (New York: Everyman's Library, 1973), 50.

23. Philip Freneau, "Tomo Cheeki, the Creek Indian in Philadelphia," *The Time-Piece and Literary Companion* 1.4 (20 March 1797): 14; 1.27 (12 May 1797), 106; Rousseau, "Discourse," 32, 99.

24. Tomochichi, who visited England in the 1730s, is said to have remarked that "the English lived worse than the Creeks who were a more innocent people" (quoted in David H. Corkran, *The Creek Frontier, 1540–1783* [Norman: University of Oklahoma Press, 1967], 87). There is no record of his having toured Philadelphia, but Freneau would have known of him through the many British poems and plays he inspired (Benjamin Bissell, *The American Indian in English Literature of the Eighteenth Century* [New Haven: Yale University Press, 1925; New York: Archon Press, 1968], 63–68).

25. Benjamin Hawkins to James McHenry, 24 April 1797, in *Letters, Journals and Writings of Benjamin Hawkins*, vol. 1, 1796–1801, ed. C. L. Grant (Savannah: Beehive Press, 1980), 107; Hawkins to David Henley, 5 June 1798, in *Letters of Hawkins* 1:197. See also Kathryn E. Holland Braund, *Deerskins and Duffels: The Creek Indian Trade with Anglo-America, 1685–1815* (Lincoln: University of Nebraska Press, 1993), 121–38, 164–86; and Florette Henri, *The Southern Indians and Benjamin Hawkins, 1796–1816* (Norman: University of Oklahoma Press, 1986), 83–134.

26. James Adair, *Adair's History of the American Indians* (1775), ed. Samuel Cole Williams (Johnson City, Tenn.: Watauga, 1930), 462–63.

27. Philip Freneau, "Reflections on My Journey from the Tullassee Towns to the Settlements on the River Hudson," *New York Daily Advertiser* (8 September 1790), n. p.

28. Ralph Waldo Emerson, "Historical Discourse, at Concord, on the Second Centennial Anniversary of the Incorporation of the Town, September 12, 1835," in *The Complete Works of Ralph Waldo Emerson* (Boston: Houghton Mifflin, 1903–1904; New York: AMS Press, 1968), 11:53; Catharine Maria Sedgwick, "Autobiography" (manuscript, 1853, 1860), in *The Power of Her Sympathy: The Autobiography and Journal of Catharine Maria Sedgwick*, ed. Mary Kelley (Boston: Northeastern University Press, 1993), 49.

29. Boudinot, "Address to the Whites," 72. See also William G. McLoughlin, *Cherokee Renascence in the New Republic* (Princeton: Princeton University Press, 1986), 277–301; and Theda Perdue, "Cherokee Planters: The Development of Plantation Slavery Before Removal," in *The Cherokee Nation: A Troubled History*, ed. Duane H. King (Knoxville: University of Tennessee Press, 1979), 110–28. The economies of the other "civilized tribes" are far less well documented; see J. Leitch Wright, Jr., *Creeks and Seminoles: The Destruction and Regeneration of the Muscogulge People* (Lincoln: University of Nebraska Press, 1986), 224.

30. Cass, "Removal of the Indians," 71, 74.

31. Cass, "Removal of the Indians," 73; Edward Everett, "Address Delivered at Bloody Brook, in South Deerfield, September 30, 1835," in his *Orations and Speeches, on Various Occasions* (Boston: American Stationers' Company, 1836), 590–91.

32. See Thomas D. Birch and Fred Metting, "The Economic Design of

Walden," *New England Quarterly* 65 (1992): 587–602; and Judith P. Saunders, "Economic Metaphor Redefined: The Transcendental Capitalist at Walden," *American Transcendental Quarterly* 36 (1977): 4–7.

33. Pearce, *Savagism and Civilization*, 146; Bird, *Nick of the Woods*, 32; Lewis Cass, "Heckewelder on the American Indians," *North American Review* 26 (1828): 375, 376; Timothy Flint, "Hope Leslie," *Western Monthly Review* 1 (1827): 295.

34. Review of *Walden*, *Boston Atlas*, 1854, quoted in Walter Harding, *The Days of Henry Thoreau: A Biography* (New York: Dover, 1982), 335; reviews of *Walden*, quoted in Bradley P. Dean and Gary Scharnhorst, "The Contemporary Reception of *Walden*," *Studies in the American Renaissance*, ed. Joel Myerson (Charlottesville: University Press of Virginia, 1990), 300, 302, 299, 305, 301; Robert F. Sayre, *Thoreau and the American Indians* (Princeton: Princeton University Press, 1977), 60. The reviews quoted by Dean and Scharnhorst are from *Salem Register*, 10 August 1854; *New Bedford Mercury*, 12 August 1854; *Boston Daily Bee*, 9 August 1854; *New York Morning Express*, 24 August 1854; and *Boston Commonwealth*, 12 August 1854.

35. Estwick Evans, *A Pedestrious Tour, of Four Thousand Miles, Through the Western States, and Territories, during the Winter and Spring of 1818* (1819), in *Early Western Travels, 1748–1846*, ed. Reuben Gold Thwaites (Cleveland: Arthur H. Clark, 1904), 8:101, 102, 103; Henry Nash Smith, *Virgin Land: The American West as Symbol and Myth* (Cambridge: Harvard University Press, 1978), 52.

36. Charles Lane, "Life in the Woods," *The Dial* 4.4 (April 1844): 416, 422.

37. Lane, "Life in the Woods," 422.

38. Henry David Thoreau, *"Walden or, Life in the Woods" [1854] and "On the Duty of Civil Disobedience"* (New York: New American Library, 1960), 121, 130. All further citations in this chapter appear in parentheses in the text.

39. For the original passage (slightly altered by Thoreau), see William Bartram, *Travels of William Bartram* (1791), ed. Mark Van Doren (New York: Dover, 1955), 399.

40. Alexander McGillivray, 1791, quoted in John Witthoft, *Green Corn Ceremonialism in the Eastern Woodlands*, Occasional Contributions from the Museum of Anthropology of the University of Michigan, no. 13 (Ann Arbor: University of Michigan Press, 1949), 56; Benjamin Hawkins, *A Sketch of the Creek Country* (manuscript, 1790), quoted in Witthoft, *Green Corn Ceremonialism*, 61; John Howard Payne, "The Green Corn Dance" (1835), ed. John R. Swanton, *Chronicles of Oklahoma* 10 (1932): 175, 183, 194, 195. For a Removal-era account of Creek reciprocity written by a biracial trader, see George Stiggins, *Creek Indian History: A Historical Narrative of the Genealogy, Traditions and Downfall of the Ispocoga or Creek Indian Tribe of Indians*, ed. Virginia Pounds Brown (1836 [?]) (Birmingham: Birmingham Public Library, 1989), 51–53.

41. Henry David Thoreau, *The Journal of Henry D. Thoreau*, ed. Bradford Torrey and Francis H. Allen (Boston: Houghton Mifflin, 1906; New York: Dover, 1962), 1:129–30 (undated). I have used this edition when the Princeton edition was

unavailable to me; in such cases, volume and page numbers refer to the Dover two-volume reprint of the fourteen-volume *Journal*.

42. Leonard N. Neufeldt, *The Economist: Henry Thoreau and Enterprise* (New York: Oxford University Press, 1989), 54; Elizabeth I. Hanson, *Thoreau's Indian of the Mind* (Lewiston, N.Y.: Edwin Mellen, 1991), 22.

43. As Randall Moon points out, Indian writers contested such blindness; see "William Apess and Writing White," *Studies in American Indian Literatures* 3.4 (Winter 1993): 45–54.

44. Henry David Thoreau, *Journal*, vol. 3, 1848–1851, ed. Robert Sattelmeyer, Mark R. Patterson, and William Rossi (Princeton: Princeton University Press, 1990), 130–31 (after 31 October 1850).

45. Thoreau, *Journal* 3:130 (after 31 October 1850). Thoreau had read the *Key* by 1849; see Robert Sattelmeyer, *Thoreau's Reading: A Study in Intellectual History, with Bibliographical Catalogue* (Princeton: Princeton University Press, 1988), 291.

46. Russell G. Handsman and Ann McMullen, "An Introduction to Woodsplint Basketry and Its Interpretation," in *A Key into the Language of Woodsplint Baskets*, ed. Handsman and McMullen (Washington, Conn.: American Indian Archaeological Institute, 1987), 33. See also Daniel R. Mandell, *Behind the Frontier: Indians in Eighteenth-Century Eastern Massachusetts* (Lincoln: University of Nebraska Press, 1996), 199–200; and Ann McMullen, "Many Motives: Change in Northeastern Native Basketry Making," in *The Art of Native American Basketry: A Living Legacy*, ed. Frank W. Porter III (Westport, Conn.: Greenwood Press, 1990), 45–78.

47. Thoreau, *Journal* 3:177 (after 10 January 1851), 3:93 (after 16 July 1850); Michael T. Gilmore, *American Romanticism and the Marketplace* (Chicago: University of Chicago Press, 1985), 44; Thoreau, *Journal of Henry D. Thoreau*, ed. Torrey and Allen, 1:249 (23 August 1851).

48. On Thoreau's views of Nature, see James McIntosh, *Thoreau as Romantic Naturalist: His Shifting Stance Toward Nature* (Ithaca: Cornell University Press, 1974); on his ambivalence toward trade, see Leo Stoller, *After Walden: Thoreau's Changing Views on Economic Man* (Stanford: Stanford University Press, 1957); and Richard F. Teichgraeber III, *Sublime Thoughts/Penny Wisdom: Situating Emerson and Thoreau in the American Market* (Baltimore: Johns Hopkins University Press, 1995), 44–74; and on his struggles in the literary marketplace, see Steven Fink, *Prophet in the Marketplace: Thoreau's Development as a Professional Writer* (Princeton: Princeton University Press, 1992).

49. Leo Marx, *The Machine in the Garden: Technology and the Pastoral Ideal in America* (New York: Oxford University Press, 1964), 246, 23; Edwin Fussell, *Frontier: American Literature and the American West* (Princeton: Princeton University Press, 1965), 213–14; Lawrence Buell, *New England Literary Culture: From Revolution Through Renaissance* (Cambridge: Cambridge University Press, 1986), 324; Marx, *Machine in the Garden*, 226; Sherman Paul, *The Shores of America: Thoreau's Inward Exploration* (Urbana: University of Illinois Press, 1958), 230.

50. Marx, *Machine in the Garden*, 246. Even when Indians appear in Thoreau studies, they serve only as symbols of his anxieties and desires. Nicholas Bromell considers the Indians of Concord "exterminated" by Thoreau's time (88) and hence focuses only on the after-image of the Indian in Thoreau's *Week* (*By the Sweat of the Brow: Literature and Labor in Antebellum America* [Chicago: University of Chicago Press, 1993], 87–92); Michael Newbury terms the basket-maker episode a "parable" of publication ("Healthful Employment: Hawthorne, Thoreau, and Middle-Class Fitness," *American Quarterly* 47 [1995], 706); and David M. Robinson finds the Indians of the bean field significant only as they reveal Thoreau's views of labor ("'Unchronicled Nations': Agrarian Purpose and Thoreau's Ecological Knowing," *Nineteenth-Century Literature* 48 [1993]: 326–40).

Chapter 3. Radical Faiths

1. *Speeches Delivered by Several Indian Chiefs* (New York: Samuel Wood, 1810), 9–10.

2. *Speeches by Indian Chiefs*, 13–15, 16.

3. Catlin, *Letters and Notes* 2:106; Thomas L. McKenney and James Hall, *The Indian Tribes of North America, with Biographical Sketches and Anecdotes of the Principal Chiefs* (1836–1844), ed. Frederick Webb Hodge (Edinburgh: John Grant, 1933–1934), 1:6.

4. See Samuel G. Drake, *The Book of the Indians* (1833), 9th ed. (Boston: Benjamin B. Mussey, 1845), bk. 5, 98–100; Minnie Myrtle (Anna Cummings Johnson), *The Iroquois; Or, the Bright Side of Indian Character* (New York: D. Appleton, 1855), 166–69; William L. Stone, *The Life and Times of Sa-go-ye-wat-ha or Red Jacket* (New York: Wiley and Putnam, 1841), 187–94; and B. B. Thatcher, *Indian Biography* (New York: A. L. Fowle, 1832; Glorieta, N.M.: Rio Grande, 1973), 2:290–94.

5. For a corrective, see Robert A. Brightman, "Toward a History of Indian Religion: Religious Change in Native Societies," in *New Directions in American Indian History*, ed. Colin G. Calloway (Norman: University of Oklahoma Press, 1988), 223–49.

6. Joel W. Martin, "Before and Beyond the Sioux Ghost Dance: Native American Prophetic Movements and the Study of Religion," *Journal of the American Academy of Religion* 59 (1991): 678. Catharine L. Albanese's *Nature Religion in America: From the Algonkian Indians to the New Age* (Chicago: University of Chicago Press, 1990) is an example of the "first-chapter-only" approach. Slightly different in structure but identical in principle is Peter W. Williams's *America's Religions: Traditions and Cultures* (New York: Macmillan, 1990), which promises to explore Indian religions "in all their own complexity" (2) but, after the first chapter, returns to them only to note their alteration by Christianity. For critiques, see Robert S. Michaelsen, "Red Man's Religion/White Man's Religious His-

tory," *Journal of the American Academy of Religion* 51 (1983): 667–84; and Ingo W. Schröder, "From Parkman to Postcolonial Theory: What's New in the Ethnohistory of Missions?" *Ethnohistory* 46 (1999): 809–15.

7. See Sam D. Gill, *Mother Earth: An American Story* (Chicago: University of Chicago Press, 1987).

8. John Webster Grant, *Moon of Wintertime: Missionaries and the Indians of Canada in Encounter Since 1534* (Toronto: University of Toronto Press, 1984), 248, 262.

9. See, for example, William B. Hart, "'The Kindness of the Blessed Virgin': Faith, Succour, and the Cult of Mary among Christian Hurons and Iroquois in Seventeenth-Century New France," in *Spiritual Encounters: Interactions between Christianity and Native Religions in Colonial America*, ed. Nicholas Griffiths and Fernando Cervantes (Lincoln: University of Nebraska Press, 1999), 65–90; Kenneth Morrison, "Towards a History of Intimate Encounters: Algonkian Folklore, Jesuit Missionaries, and Kiwakwe, the Cannibal Giant," *American Indian Culture and Research Journal* 3.4 (1979): 51–80; and John Steckley, "The Warrior and the Lineage: Jesuit Use of Iroquoian Images to Communicate Christianity," *Ethnohistory* 39 (1992): 478–509.

10. I draw on a variety of sources for this sketch, including Ann Douglas, *The Feminization of American Culture* (New York: Doubleday, 1977), 17–43; Nathan O. Hatch, *The Democratization of American Christianity* (New Haven: Yale University Press, 1989); and Joseph Haroutunian, *Piety Versus Moralism: The Passing of the New England Theology* (New York: Henry Holt, 1932).

11. Increase Mather, in C. Mather, *Magnalia Christi Americana* 1:571; John Greenleaf Whittier, *The Supernaturalism of New England* (1847), ed. Edward Wagenknecht (Norman: University of Oklahoma Press, 1969), 32; Nathaniel Hawthorne, "Whittier's *Supernaturalism of New England*" (1847), in his *Miscellaneous Prose and Verse*, ed. Thomas Woodson, Claude M. Simpson, and L. Neal Smith, vol. 23 of *Centenary Edition* (1994), 243.

12. Williams, *Key into the Language*, 192; Samson Occom, "A Short Narrative of My Life" (manuscript, 1768), in *The Elders Wrote: An Anthology of Early Prose by North American Indians 1768–1931*, ed. Bernd Peyer (Berlin: Dietrich Reimer, 1982), 12; Lawson, *New Voyage to Carolina*, 219. On the problems of reconstructing oral religions, see Carlo Ginzburg, *The Cheese and the Worms: The Cosmos of a Sixteenth-Century Miller*, trans. John and Anne Tedeschi (Baltimore: Johns Hopkins University Press, 1980).

13. See, for example, Alfred A. Cave, "The Delaware Prophet Neolin: A Reappraisal," *Ethnohistory* 46 (1999): 265–90; John Webster Grant, "Missionaries and Messiahs in the Northwest," *Studies in Religion* 9 (1980): 125–36; and Joseph B. Herring, "Kenekuk, the Kickapoo Prophet: Acculturation without Assimilation," *American Indian Quarterly* 9 (1985): 295–307.

14. James P. Ronda, "'We Are Well As We Are': An Indian Critique of

Seventeenth-Century Christian Missions," *William and Mary Quarterly* 34 (1977): 67.

15. John Eliot, in Henry Whitfield, *The Light Appearing More and More toward the Perfect Day* (1651), *Collections of the Massachusetts Historical Society*, 3rd ser., no. 4 (1833): 129; Shepard, *Clear Sunshine*, 485; John Eliot and Thomas Mayhew, *Tears of Repentance; Or, a Further Narrative of the Progress of the Gospel amongst the Indians in New-England* (1653), *Collections of the Massachusetts Historical Society*, 3rd ser., no. 4 (1833): 215; John Eliot, *A Further Accompt of the Progresse of the Gospel amongst the Indians in New-England* (London: M. Simmons, 1659), 12, 13. The significance of the mourning analogy is amplified by an episode in Shepard's *Clear Sunshine* that suggests it was not a mere analogy, that Eliot's converts may have fused Algonquian funerary practices with Christian ones (487–88).

16. John Wilson, *The Day-Breaking, If Not the Sun-Rising, of the Gospel with the Indians in New England* (1647), in *Old South Leaflets*, vol. 6 (New York: Burt Franklin, 197-?), 384; Eliot and Mayhew, *Tears of Repentance*, 205; Eliot, *Further Accompt*, 9; Henry Whitfield, "To the Christian Reader," in *Strength out of Weaknesse; Or a Glorious Manifestation of the Further Progresse of the Gospel among the Indians in New-England* (London: M. Simmons, 1652), n. p.

17. David Murray, "Spreading the Word: Missionaries, Conversion and Circulation in the Northeast," in *Spiritual Encounters*, ed. Griffiths and Cervantes, 44; Eliot and Mayhew, *Tears of Repentance*, 223; Geoffrey F. Nuttall, *The Holy Spirit in Puritan Faith and Experience* (Oxford: Blackwell, 1946), 33.

18. Shepard, *Clear Sunshine*, 467; Eliot, quoted in *Strength out of Weaknesse*, 13, 14; John Endecott, quoted in *Strength out of Weaknesse*, 33; John Wilson, quoted in *Strength out of Weaknesse*, 18, 19.

19. Whitfield, *Light Appearing*, 113.

20. Williams, *Key into the Language*, 193; Eliot, *Indian Dialogues*, 87; Ronda, " 'We Are Well As We Are,' " 76.

21. See Gregory Evans Dowd, *A Spirited Resistance: The North American Indian Struggle for Identity, 1745–1815* (Baltimore: Johns Hopkins University Press, 1992), 23–46.

22. John Sergeant, quoted in Samuel Hopkins, *Historical Memoirs Relating to the Housatonic Indians* (1753) (New York: William Abbatt, 1911), 100; David Zeisberger, "Zeisberger's Diary of a Journey to the Ohio, Sept. 20—Nov. 16, 1767," *Ohio Archaeological and Historical Publications* 21 (1912): 25; Jonathan Edwards, *The Life of David Brainerd* (1749), ed. Norman Pettit, vol. 7 of *The Works of Jonathan Edwards* (New Haven: Yale University Press, 1985), 329, 330, 392; William Ellery Channing, "Spiritual Freedom" (1830), in *The Works of William Ellery Channing* (Boston: American Unitarian Association, 1903), 4:72, 86.

23. See Richard W. Pointer, " 'Poor Indians' and the 'Poor in Spirit': The Indian Impact on David Brainerd," *New England Quarterly* 67 (1994): 403–26.

24. White, *Middle Ground*, 337.

25. Anthony F. C. Wallace's classic study of the Handsome Lake revival, *The Death and Rebirth of the Seneca* (New York: Vintage, 1969), is problematic on a number of counts. It suffers from the ethnohistorical tendency to trust written documents unreservedly, as when it quotes Mary Jemison's narrative without mentioning James Seaver (33); it psychoanalyzes long-dead Indians, and in ways that never transcend musty notions of infantile egotism (92–93); it perpetuates stereotypes about "underdeveloped" and "superior" cultures (184); and it adheres to a simplistic opposition of "conservative" (pagan) versus "progressive" (Christian) Indians (202). It remains, however, the fullest study of, and hence an invaluable tool in researching, the subject.

26. Arthur C. Parker, *The Code of Handsome Lake, the Seneca Prophet* (Albany: University of the State of New York, 1913; Ontario: Iroqrafts, 1990), 68. Moments such as this illustrate the inadequacy of seeing Handsome Lake's movement as an instance of "accommodation" rather than "resistance" to Christianity (Martin, "Before and Beyond the Ghost Dance," 682); the two are not irreconcilable. Whatever his views on religious difference, it is fascinating that—in a rare recorded instance of Indian proselytizing—Handsome Lake dictated a letter to Thomas Jefferson urging the President to heed his message: "The Lord has confidence in your people as well as ours, provided we can settle all our Business. He will take care of us first, and you afterwards if you will Take Notice of the voice of the Angels" (quoted in Wallace, *Death and Rebirth of the Seneca*, 268). Given the context of this letter, however—the prophet was seeking Jefferson's support against speculators—it seems likely he cared less for the presidential soul than the presidential seal.

27. Asher Wright, "Seneca Indians by Asher Wright" (1859), ed. W. N. Fenton, *Ethnohistory* 4 (1957): 304–5.

28. Halliday Jackson, "Halliday Jackson's Journal to the Seneca Indians, 1798–1800," ed. Anthony F. C. Wallace, *Pennsylvania History* 19 (1952): 146–47, 142.

29. Jackson, "Journal," 332, 333; Halliday Jackson, *Civilization of the Indian Natives* (Philadelphia: Marcus T. C. Gould, 1830), 45. The visions appear in Jackson, "Journal," 341–44.

30. Henry Simmons, in Jackson, "Journal," 345, 348; Jackson, *Civilization of the Indian Natives*, 83. Seneca religion's continuing effect on Quaker discourse can be seen in a letter of Lucretia Mott: "The pagans adhere . . . to the sacred festivals of their fathers, and are not disposed to exchange them for the 'bread and wine' &c., of the Christian party. We had an interesting conference with them, during which their differences were presented; but we declined to decide between them, as, if attempted, we might be found equally discountenancing each form, and recommending our Quaker non-conformity. But, as that was not our mission, we commended them to the 'Great Spirit,' believing that those who danced religiously, might be as nearly perfect, as were those who communed in some other

chosen form" ("Letter from Lucretia Mott," *The Liberator* 17.40 [6 October 1848]: 159).

31. Lewis Henry Morgan, *League of the Iroquois* (1851; Secaucus, N.J.: Citadel, 1975), 150.

32. Morgan, *League of the Iroquois*, 169, 182, 226, 229, 230. Morgan cites several other Parker translations (175–76 n. 2, 219 n. 1, 232 n. 1); none, however, is as central or extended as this. All other of Morgan's footnotes refer to classical or European sources; all other of his translated passages cite no translator.

33. Morgan, *League of the Iroquois*, 246.

34. Morgan, *League of the Iroquois*, 233 n. 1; Seaver, *Narrative of Mrs. Mary Jemison*, 145–46; J. B. Patterson, *Black Hawk: An Autobiography* (1833), ed. Donald Jackson (Urbana: University of Illinois Press, 1955), 93; Alexander Long, "A Small Postscript of the Ways and Maners of the Indians Called Charikees" (manuscript, 1725), ed. David H. Corkran, *Southern Indian Studies* 21 (1969): 19.

35. Lydia Maria Child, *The Progress of Religious Ideas, Through Successive Ages* (New York: C. S. Francis, 1855), 2:184, 3:450; Child to Lucy Osgood, 1869, in *Letters of Lydia Maria Child*, ed. John Greenleaf Whittier (Boston: Houghton Mifflin, 1882), 202; Lydia Maria Child, "The Intermingling of Religions," *Atlantic Monthly* 28 (1871): 395.

36. Lydia Maria Child, *"Hobomok" [1824] and Other Writings on Indians*, ed. Carolyn L. Karcher (New Brunswick, N.J.: Rutgers University Press, 1986), 69, 133; Lydia Maria Child, *Aspirations of the World: A Chain of Opals* (Boston: Roberts Brothers, 1878), 1–2. Whatever her knowledge of specialized works, Child was aware of Hannah Adams's *A Dictionary of All Religions and Religious Denominations* (1784), one of many compilations to consider Indian religions ([New York: James Eastburn, 1817; Atlanta: Scholars Press, 1992], 138).

37. Lydia Maria Child, *The First Settlers of New-England or, Conquest of the Pequods, Narragansetts and Pokanokets. As Related by a Mother to Her Children* (Boston: Munroe and Francis, 1829), 65, 43.

38. I follow Barry O'Connell in the spelling of "Apess" (*On Our Own Ground: The Complete Writings of William Apess, a Pequot*, ed. O'Connell [Amherst: University of Massachusetts Press, 1992], xiv n. 2). All further citations to Apess's writings appear in parentheses in the text. O'Connell, who has led the resurgence of interest in Apess, assesses his life, culture, and standing in "William Apess and the Survival of the Pequot People," in *Algonkians of New England: Past and Present*, Proceedings of the Dublin Seminar on New England Folklife (Boston: Boston University, 1991), 89–100; and "'Once More Let Us Consider': William Apess in the Writing of New England Native American History," in *After King Philip's War: Presence and Persistence in Indian New England*, ed. Colin G. Calloway (Hanover, N.H.: University Press of New England, 1997), 162–77. On Apess's life, see also Kim McQuaid, "William Apes, Pequot: An Indian Reformer in the Jackson Era," *New England Quarterly* 50 (1977): 605–25; Donald M. Niel-

sen, "The Mashpee Indian Revolt of 1833," *New England Quarterly* 58 (1985): 400–20; and Bernd C. Peyer, *The Tutor'd Mind: Indian Missionary-Writers in Antebellum America* (Amherst: University of Massachusetts Press, 1997), 117–65.

39. Hatch, *Democratization of American Christianity*, 10; William S. Simmons, "Red Yankees: Narragansett Conversion in the Great Awakening," *American Ethnologist* 10 (1983): 265.

40. Timothy Dwight, *Travels in New England and New York* (1821–1822) (Cambridge: Belknap Press of Harvard University Press, 1969), 3:14. See also Jack Campisi, "The Emergence of the Mashantucket Pequot Tribe, 1637–1975," in *The Pequots of Southern New England: The Fall and Rise of an American Indian Nation*, ed. Laurence M. Hauptman and James D. Wherry (Norman: University of Oklahoma Press, 1990), 117–40.

41. Thoreau, *Walden*, 73; Lydia Maria Child, *Letters from New-York* (New York: Charles S. Francis, 1843), 109–110; Child, *Hobomok*, 76; "An Indian Talk," *Free Enquirer*, 2nd ser., no. 3.27 (30 April 1831): 214; Samuel Kirkland, *The Journal of Samuel Kirkland: Eighteenth-Century Missionary to the Iroquois, Government Agent, Father of Hamilton College*, ed. Walter Pilkington (Clinton, N.Y.: Hamilton College, 1980), 23–24.

42. Thoreau, *Walden*, 73; Krupat, *Ethnocriticism*, 225 n. 24; Murray, *Forked Tongues*, 60.

43. See James Axtell, "The Power of Print in the Eastern Woodlands," in his *After Columbus*, 86–99. Peter Wogan suggests, however, that European reports are likely exaggerated and thus of little value in determining Indians' understandings of writing. See "Perceptions of European Literacy in Early Contact Situations," *Ethnohistory* 41 (1994): 407–27.

44. Krupat, *Voice in the Margin*, 145, 148; Murray, *Forked Tongues*, 58. Other studies that stress the complexity of Apess's persona include Carolyn Haynes, "'A Mark for Them All to . . . Hiss at': The Formation of Methodist and Pequot Identity in the Conversion Narrative of William Apess," *Early American Literature* 31.1 (1996): 25–44; Karim M. Tiro, "Denominated 'SAVAGE': Methodism, Writing, and Identity in the Works of William Apess, a Pequot," *American Quarterly* 48 (1996): 653–79; and Walker, *Indian Nation*, 41–59, 164–81.

Interlude

1. Thoreau, *Journal of Henry D. Thoreau*, ed. Torrey and Allen, 1:129 (undated); Hawthorne, *The American Notebooks*, ed. Claude M. Simpson, vol. 8 of *Centenary Edition* (1972), 169 (6 December 1837).

2. Michel de Certeau, *The Writing of History*, trans. Tom Conley (New York: Columbia University Press, 1988), 2, 3.

3. Richard Slotkin, "Myth and the Production of History," in *Ideology and*

Classic American Literature, ed. Sacvan Bercovitch and Myra Jehlen (Cambridge: Cambridge University Press, 1986), 72, 74; Roland Barthes, *Mythologies*, trans. Annette Lavers (New York: Hill and Wang, 1972), 142; Slotkin, "Myth and the Production of History," 73.

4. See William G. Doty, *Mythography: The Study of Myths and Rituals* (Tuscaloosa: University of Alabama Press, 1986).

5. Mircea Eliade, *Myth and Reality*, trans. Willard R. Trask (New York: Harper and Row, 1963), 138. While I was revising this work for publication, I received a mailing that underscores how uncritically the word "myth" is applied: an advertisement for a Time-Life series on American Indians that claims to be "for those who seek more than myth." Here, of course, "myth" connotes falsehood; the series is going to tell the truth about Indians. Yet one wonders how much truth it can tell when it can so blithely use as a synonym for "lie" the word that most non-Indian readers associate with (and many Indian peoples use for) Indian stories.

6. Ivan Strenski, *Four Theories of Myth in Twentieth-Century History: Cassirer, Eliade, Lévi-Strauss and Malinowski* (Iowa City: University of Iowa Press, 1987), 6. Historians have not left unexplored the ideological nature of their texts; see, for example, Robert F. Berkhofer, Jr., *Beyond the Great Story: History as Text and Discourse* (Cambridge: Belknap Press of Harvard University Press, 1995); and Hayden White, *Metahistory: The Historical Imagination in Nineteenth-Century Europe* (Baltimore: Johns Hopkins University Press, 1973). For all their impact on the profession's view of itself, however, such works have done little to alter its view of myth.

7. To call history a "story" is, of course, to distinguish a type of narrative from a sense of time—something historians generally fail to do, thereby letting their "histories" seem less studies of "history" than conjurations of it. I use "history" and "myth" principally as narrative; and I use "story" to avoid opprobrious labels ("fiction") and, in the case of myth, potentially invalid ones ("prose" and "poetry"). Some scholars contrast myths (sacred stories) with tales (secular stories); yet as these designations appear to vary widely, I attempt no taxonomy of my own.

8. Paula Gunn Allen, *The Sacred Hoop: Recovering the Feminine in American Indian Traditions* (Boston: Beacon Press, 1992), 105.

9. Raymond J. DeMallie, " 'These Have No Ears': Narrative and the Ethnohistorical Method," *Ethnohistory* 40 (1993): 516.

10. Betty Louise Bell, "Letter to the Editor," *PMLA* 110 (1995): 411. On the New Indian History, see also Robert F. Berkhofer, Jr., "Cultural Pluralism Versus Ethnocentrism in the New Indian History," in *The American Indian and the Problem of History*, ed. Calvin Martin (New York: Oxford University Press, 1987), 35–45; Daniel K. Richter, "Whose Indian History?" *William and Mary Quarterly* 50 (1993): 379–93; and Richard White, "Using the Past: History and Native American Studies," in *Studying Native America: Problems and Prospects*, ed. Russell

Thornton (Madison: University of Wisconsin Press, 1998), 217–43. For work in this field, see Jay Miller, Colin G. Calloway, and Richard A. Sattler, comps., *Writings in Indian History, 1985–1990* (Norman: University of Oklahoma Press, 1995), 165–74.

11. Robert H. Lowie, "Oral Traditions and History," *American Anthropologist*, new ser., 17 (1915): 598.

12. See Glenn J. Farris, "Recognizing Indian Folk History as Real History: A Fort Ross Example," *American Indian Quarterly* 13 (1984): 471–80; Bernard L. Fontana, "American Indian Oral History: An Anthropologist's Note," *History and Theory* 8 (1969): 366–70; Jay Miller, "Tsimshian Ethno-Ethnohistory: A 'Real' Indigenous Chronology," *Ethnohistory* 45 (1998): 657–74; and Clifford E. Trafzer, "Grandmother, Grandfather, and the First History of the Americas," in *New Voices in Native American Literary Criticism*, ed. Krupat, 474–87.

13. Bernard S. Cohn, "Toward a Rapprochement," *Journal of Interdisciplinary History* 12 (1981): 247; Fred Eggan, "From History to Myth: A Hopi Example," in *Studies in Southwestern Ethnolinguistics: Meaning and History in the Languages of the American Southwest*, ed. Dell H. Hymes (Paris: Mouton, 1967), 52; Ramsey, "Thoreau's Last Words," in *Redefining American Literary History*, ed. Ruoff and Ward, 58.

14. Karl Kroeber, "The Wolf Comes: Indian Poetry and Linguistic Criticism," in *Smoothing the Ground: Essays on Native American Oral Literature*, ed. Brian Swann (Berkeley: University of California Press, 1983), 106; Elizabeth C. Fine, *The Folklore Text: From Performance to Print* (Bloomington: Indiana University Press, 1984), 114–33; Robert A. Georges, "Toward an Understanding of Storytelling Events," *Journal of American Folklore* 82 (1969): 317.

15. Richard Schechner, *Between Theater and Anthropology* (Philadelphia: University of Pennsylvania Press, 1985), 50. In what follows, I am indebted to the tripartite scheme of Alan Dundes in "Texture, Text, and Context," *Southern Folklore Quarterly* 28 (1964): 251–65.

16. See Raoul N. Smith, "The Interest in Language and Languages in Colonial and Federal America," *Proceedings of the American Philosophical Society* 123 (1979): 29–46.

17. Bancroft, *History of the United States* 3:259, 258, 255; Dell Hymes, *"In Vain I Tried to Tell You": Essays in Native American Ethnopoetics* (Philadelphia: University of Pennsylvania Press, 1981), 333; Judith Berman, "Oolachan-Woman's Robe: Fish, Blankets, Masks, and Meaning in Boas's Kwakw'ala Texts," in *On the Translation of Native American Literatures*, ed. Swann, 156.

18. William N. Clements, "'Tokens of Literary Faculty': Native American Literature and Euroamerican Translation in the Early Nineteenth Century," in *On the Translation of Native American Literatures*, 40. On the ongoing politics of translating Indian stories, see Susan Hegeman, "Native American 'Texts' and the Problem of Authenticity," *American Quarterly* 41 (1989): 265–83.

19. Georges, "Understanding of Storytelling Events," 324.

20. Victor Turner, "Are There Universals of Performance in Myth, Ritual, and Drama?" in *By Means of Performance: Intercultural Studies of Theatre and Ritual*, ed. Richard Schechner and Willa Appel (Cambridge: Cambridge University Press, 1990), 16; Michel Foucault, *Madness and Civilization: A History of Insanity in the Age of Reason*, trans. Richard Howard (New York: Vintage, 1988), x.

Chapter 4. Stories of the Land

1. Thomas Harriot, *A Briefe and True Report of the New Found Land of Virginia* (1588) (Frankfurt: Theodor de Bry, 1590; New York: Dover, 1972), 25, 26–27.

2. Gananath Obeyesekere, *The Apotheosis of Captain Cook: European Mythmaking in the Pacific* (Princeton: Princeton University Press, 1992), 3; Stephen Greenblatt, "Invisible Bullets: Renaissance Authority and Its Subversion," *Glyph* 8 (1981): 51; Cheyfitz, *Poetics of Imperialism*, 78.

3. Carolyn Porter, "Are We Being Historical Yet?" *South Atlantic Quarterly* 87 (1988): 769–70. For a reading of encounter narratives that seeks to embrace both European and indigenous viewpoints, see Marshall Sahlins, *Historical Metaphors and Mythical Realities: Structure in the Early History of the Sandwich Islands Kingdom* (Ann Arbor: University of Michigan Press, 1981).

4. Anthony Kemp, *The Estrangement of the Past: A Study in the Origins of Modern Historical Consciousness* (New York: Oxford University Press, 1991), 106. Among the numerous works written on Enlightenment historiography, Frank Manuel's study of myth theories, *The Eighteenth Century Confronts the Gods* (Cambridge: Harvard University Press, 1959), stands out.

5. David Hume, *The History of England from the Invasion of Julius Caesar to the Revolution in 1688* (1754) (Indianapolis: Liberty Classics, 1983), 1:4; Henry St. John, Lord Bolingbroke, *Letters on the Study and Use of History* (1752), in *Lord Bolingbroke: Historical Writings*, ed. Isaac Kramnick (Chicago: University of Chicago Press, 1972), 50; Voltaire, "Histoire," in *Encyclopédie, ou Dictionnaire Raisonné des Sciences, des Arts et des Métiers*, comp. Denis Diderot (Paris: 1751–1776; Elmsford, N.Y.: Pergamon, 1969), 2:335. The Voltaire passage was translated from the French by Jennifer Saitz and Lisa Maria Noudehou.

6. Bernard Fontenelle, "Of the Origin of Fables" (1724), in *The Rise of Modern Mythology, 1680–1860*, ed. Burton Feldman and Robert D. Richardson, Jr. (Bloomington: Indiana University Press, 1972), 18.

7. Antoine Banier, *The Mythology and Fables of the Ancients, Explain'd from History* (London: A. Millar, 1739; New York: Garland, 1976), 1:2; Pierre de Charlevoix, *Journal of a Voyage to North-America* (London: R. and J. Dodsley, 1761; Ann Arbor: University Microfilms, 1966), 1:304, 2:141; Joseph François Lafitau, *Customs of the American Indians Compared with the Customs of Primitive Times* (1724), ed.

and trans. William N. Fenton and Elizabeth L. Moore (Toronto: Champlain Society, 1974), 81; Nicolas Perrot, "Memoir on the Manners, Customs, and Religion of the Savages of North America" (manuscript, 1680–1718), in *The Indian Tribes of the Upper Mississippi Valley and Region of the Great Lakes*, ed. and trans. Emma Helen Blair (Cleveland: Arthur H. Clark, 1911), 1:31; David Zeisberger, "History of the Northern American Indians" (1779–1780), ed. Archer Butler Hulbert and William Nathaniel Schwarze, *Ohio Archaeological and Historical Quarterly* 19 (1910): 132.

8. John Locke, *Two Treatises of Government* (1690), ed. Peter Laslett (Cambridge: Cambridge University Press, 1994), 286, 289, 290, 294. Justifications for Indian dispossession are summarized in Wilcomb E. Washburn, *Red Man's Land/ White Man's Law: A Study of the Past and Present Status of the American Indian* (New York: Scribner's, 1971), 27–58.

9. However apt "communalism" is as a description of Indian peoples' relationships to the land, it is likely that diverse populations—or any one—engaged in diverse practices; countless variants are documented (and these may reflect either writers' misprisions or local modifications due to the European presence). Consider, for example, the Delawares. While William Penn found them "exact Observers of Property" (*His Own Account of the Lenni Lenape or Delaware Indians* [1683], ed. Albert Cook Myers [Moylan, Pa.: Albert Cook Myers, 1937], 34), John Heckewelder felt that they considered land "given jointly to all" (*History, Manners, and Customs of the Indian Nations Who Once Inhabited Pennsylvania and the Neighbouring States* [1819] [Philadelphia: Historical Society of Pennsylvania, 1876; Bowie, Md.: Heritage, 1990], 101). Frank Speck sought to resolve this by positing "family hunting territories," tracts jointly used yet individually owned ("The Family Hunting Band as the Basis of Algonkian Social Organization," *American Anthropologist* 17 [1915]: 289–305). Anthony Wallace, however, argues that "owner" is a mistranslation of a word for the "representative of the occupying social unit" ("Woman, Land, and Society: Three Aspects of Aboriginal Delaware Life," *Pennsylvania Archaeologist* 17 [1947]: 4). As a final wrinkle, Harvey Feit suggests that Speck projected private ownership into the past to legitimize the modern Delawares' claims for restitution ("The Construction of Algonquian Hunting Territories: Private Property as Moral Lesson, Policy Advocacy, and Ethnographic Error," in *Colonial Situations: Essays on the Contextualization of Ethnographic Knowledge*, ed. George W. Stocking, Jr. [Madison: University of Wisconsin Press, 1991], 109–34).

10. For example, *Mourt's Relation: A Journal of the Pilgrims of Plymouth* (1622), ed. Jordan D. Fiore (Plymouth, Mass.: Plymouth Rock Foundation, 1985): "They are not industrious, neither have art, science, skill or faculty to use either the land or the commodities of it; but all spoils, rots, and is marred for want for manuring, gathering, ordering, &c. As the ancient patriarchs, therefore, removed from straiter places into more roomy, where the land lay idle and waste, and none used

it, though there dwelt inhabitants by them, . . . so is it lawful now to take a land which none useth, and make use of it" (79).

11. Robert Beverley, *The History and Present State of Virginia* (1705), ed. Louis B. Wright (Chapel Hill: University of North Carolina Press, 1947), 225, 17, 225; Dwight, *Travels* 3:18. This distinction served Removal as well; despite evidence of Cherokee private landholding, the Commissioner of Indian Affairs announced that "common property and civilization cannot co-exist" (T. Hartley Crawford, "Report of 1838," in *The American Indian and the United States: A Documentary History*, ed. Wilcomb E. Washburn [New York: Random House, 1973], 1:36).

12. Thomas Jefferson, *Notes on the State of Virginia* (1787), ed. William Peden (New York: Norton, 1982), 85; Christopher Looby, *Voicing America: Language, Literary Form, and the Origins of the United States* (Chicago: University of Chicago Press, 1996), 17. A number of critics have noted the fact of multiple, competing narratives in the early republic; Edward Watts, for example, considers those of "European cultures leftover from the colonial period" and of "new groups" who arrived "after the Revolution" (*Writing and Postcolonialism in the Early Republic* [Charlottesville: University Press of Virginia, 1998], 37). Indian narratives, however, have gone largely unremarked. For an exception, see Jared Gardner, "Alien Nation: Edgar Huntly's Savage Awakening," *American Literature* 66 (1994): 429–61.

13. Charles Brockden Brown, *Address to the Government of the United States on the Cession of Louisiana to the French* (Philadelphia: John Conrad, 1803), 49, 46.

14. On postwar Indian conflicts, see Colin G. Calloway, *The American Revolution in Indian Country: Crisis and Diversity in Native American Communities* (Cambridge: Cambridge University Press, 1995), 272–91; and Wiley Sword, *President Washington's Indian War: The Struggle for the Old Northwest, 1790–1795* (Norman: University of Oklahoma Press, 1985).

15. Cheyfitz, *Poetics of Imperialism*, 55, 54. Other discussions include William Cronon, *Changes in the Land: Indians, Colonists, and the Ecology of New England* (New York: Hill and Wang, 1983); and R. Douglas Hurt, *Indian Agriculture in America, Prehistory to the Present* (Lawrence: University Press of Kansas, 1987), 27–41.

16. Angela Cavender Wilson, "Power of the Spoken Word: Native Oral Traditions in American Indian History," in *Rethinking American Indian History*, ed. Fixico, 113. See also Geoffrey Kimball, "Koasati Narrator and Narrative," in *New Voices in Native American Literary Criticism*, ed. Krupat, 3–36; and Joel Scherzer, "Strategies in Text and Context: The Hot Pepper Story," in *Recovering the Word: Essays on Native American Literature*, ed. Brian Swann and Arnold Krupat (Berkeley: University of California Press, 1987), 151–97.

17. Albert B. Lord, *The Singer of Tales* (Cambridge: Harvard University Press, 1960), 100, 101.

18. Appraisals of Jefferson's Indian policies are mixed; contrast Bernard Shee-han, *Seeds of Extinction: Jeffersonian Philanthropy and the American Indian* (Chapel Hill: University of North Carolina Press, 1973); and Drinnon, *Facing West*, 78–103.

19. See John Ettwein, "Remarks upon the Traditions, &c. of the Indians of North America" (1788), *Bulletin of the Historical Society of Pennsylvania* 1 (1845): 29–44.

20. Jefferson to Meriwether Lewis, 20 June 1803, in Donald Jackson, ed., *Letters of the Lewis and Clark Expedition with Related Documents, 1783–1854* (Urbana: University of Illinois Press, 1962), 62; James P. Ronda, *Lewis and Clark among the Indians* (Lincoln: University of Nebraska Press, 1984), 4.

21. Jefferson to William Henry Harrison, 27 February 1803, in Logan Esarey, ed., *Governors Messages and Letters: Messages and Letters of William Henry Harrison* (Indianapolis: Indiana Historical Commission, 1922), 1:71; Jefferson, "Congressional Address" (1803), in *A Compilation of the Messages and Papers of the Presidents*, comp. James D. Richardson (New York: Bureau of National Literature, 1897), 1:340; United Indians to United States Congress, 18 December 1786, in *American State Papers: Indian Affairs* (Washington, D.C.: Gales and Seaton, 1832), 1:8; Alexander McGillivray to James White, 8 April 1787, *State Papers* 1:18.

22. Northwestern tribes to United States, 16 August 1793, *State Papers* 1:356.

23. Jefferson to Captain Hendrick, 21 December 1808, in *The Writings of Thomas Jefferson*, ed. H. A. Washington (Washington, D.C.: Taylor and Maury, 1854), 8:225, 226, 227.

24. See Alan Taylor, "Captain Hendrick Aupaumut: The Dilemmas of an Intercultural Broker," *Ethnohistory* 43 (1996): 431–57; and, for his own account, Hendrick Aupaumut, "A Narrative of an Embassy to the Western Indians" (1791), ed. B. H. Coates, *Memoirs of the Historical Society of Pennsylvania* 2 (1827): 63–131.

25. Jefferson to Hendrick, in *Writings of Jefferson* 8:226, 227.

26. Jefferson, *Notes on Virginia*, 101, 151, 98.

27. Jefferson to Handsome Lake, 3 November 1802, in *Writings of Jefferson* 8:187–88; Jackson, *Civilization of the Indian Natives*, 43; Code of Handsome Lake, in Elias Johnson, *Legends, Traditions and Laws, of the Iroquois, or Six Nations, and History of the Tuscarora Indians* (Lockport, N.Y.: Union, 1881), 194; Tecumseh, quoted in William Henry Harrison to William Eustis, 6 August 1810, in *Governors Messages and Letters* 1:457; Tecumseh, quoted in McKenney and Hall, *Indian Tribes of North America* 1:89.

28. Abeel [Cornplanter] to United States, 2 August 1783, in *Early American Indian Documents: Treaties and Laws, 1607–1789*, vol. 18, *Revolution and Confederation*, ed. Colin G. Calloway (Bethesda, Md.: University Publications of America, 1994), 284. See also Barbara Graymont, *The Iroquois in the American Revolution* (Syracuse: Syracuse University Press, 1972), 259–91.

29. Pearce, *Savagism and Civilization*, 139. See, however, Alfred Owen Aldridge on "Remarks" as a satire of "religious proselytizing and economic imperial-

ism" ("Franklin's Deistical Indians," *Proceedings of the American Philosophical Society* 94 [1950]: 398).

30. Benjamin Franklin, "Remarks Concerning the Savages of North-America" (1783), in *Benjamin Franklin: Writings*, ed. J. A. Leo Lemay (New York: Library of America, 1987), 969, 970; Noah Webster, "On the Education of Youth in America," in his *A Collection of Essays and Fugitive Writings* (1790; Delmar, N.Y.: Scholars' Facsimiles and Reprints, 1977), 23; Benjamin Rush, "Of the Mode of Education Proper in a Republic" (1798), in his *Essays Literary, Moral and Philosophical*, ed. Michael Meranze (Schenectady, N.Y.: Union College Press, 1988), 5, 9; Franklin, "Remarks Concerning the Savages," 970.

31. Franklin, "Remarks Concerning the Savages," 971–72.

32. Iroquois to Pennsylvania, 1736, in Carl Van Doren and Julian P. Boyd, eds., *Indian Treaties Printed by Benjamin Franklin 1736–1762* (Philadelphia: Historical Society of Pennsylvania, 1938), 7; Franklin, "Remarks Concerning the Savages," 970; Cannasatego to Pennsylvania, 26 June 1744, in *Indian Treaties*, 51.

33. Treaty of 1753, in *Indian Treaties*, 125, 128; Matthew Dennis, *Cultivating a Landscape of Peace: Iroquois-European Encounters in Seventeenth-Century America* (Ithaca: Cornell University Press, 1993), 85. See also Michael M. Pomedli, "Eighteenth-Century Treaties: Amended Iroquois Condolence Rituals," *American Indian Quarterly* 19 (1995): 319–39. A passage from Aupaumut similarly shows the likeness of the Condolence to the originary stories of Franklin's nation: "It is a happy thing that we should maintain a Union. But to us it is not a new thing. For our good Ancestors, (who used to have compassion to each other,) many, many years ago, have agreed to this. And we, who are of their desendance, should not hisitate, or, as it were, ask one another whether we should like it. But we must always remind each other how our ancestors did agree on this Subject, that we may never forgo that" ("Embassy to the Western Indians," 101).

34. Bruce E. Johansen and Donald A. Grinde, Jr., "The Debate Regarding Native American Precedents for Democracy: A Recent Historiography," *American Indian Culture and Research Journal* 14.1 (1990): 71. See also Johansen's *Forgotten Founders: How the American Indian Helped Shape Democracy* (Cambridge: Harvard Common Press, 1982).

35. Benjamin Franklin to James Parker, 20 March 1751, in *The Papers of Benjamin Franklin*, ed. Leonard W. Labaree (New Haven: Yale University Press, 1959–), 4:118–19; Donald A. Grinde, Jr., "Iroquois Political Theory and the Roots of American Democracy," in Oren Lyons et al., *Exiled in the Land of the Free: Democracy, Indian Nations, and the U.S. Constitution* (Santa Fe: Clear Light, 1992), 280. Elisabeth Tooker terms the Iroquois Founders theory a "myth" in "The United States Constitution and the Iroquois League," *Ethnohistory* 35 (1988): 305–36. As Frederick Hoxie notes, the debate has become increasingly illogical, with both sides arguing roughly the same thing: that Indian history matters only if it is part of white history. See "Ethnohistory for a Tribal World," *Ethnohistory* 44 (1997): 602–3.

36. Peter Hulme, *Colonial Encounters: Europe and the Native Caribbean, 1492–1797* (London: Routledge, 1986), 15.

37. Francis Jennings, for example, traces the destruction of the Susquehannocks to a network of colonial intrigue embracing Indians and whites; see "Glory, Death, and Transfiguration: The Susquehannock Indians in the Seventeenth Century," *Proceedings of the American Philosophical Society* 112 (1968): 15–53. The standard account of the Susquehannocks' end is presented in Elisabeth Tooker, "The Demise of the Susquehannocks: A 17th-Century Mystery," *Pennsylvania Archaeologist* 54.3–4 (Sept.-Dec. 1984): 1–10.

38. Benjamin Franklin, *A Narrative of the Late Massacres* (1764), in *Papers of Franklin* 11:47.

39. Franklin, *Late Massacres*, 65, 50, 64; Benjamin Franklin, "Speech in the Convention at the Conclusion of Its Deliberations" (1787), in *Benjamin Franklin: Writings*, 1141. For a harsher indictment of Franklin, see Carla J. Mulford, "*Caritas* and Capital: Franklin's *Narrative of the Late Massacres*," in *Reappraising Benjamin Franklin: A Bicentennial Perspective*, ed. J. A. Leo Lemay (Newark: University of Delaware Press, 1993), 347–58.

40. R. S. Cotterill, *The Southern Indians: The Story of the Civilized Tribes Before Removal* (Norman: University of Oklahoma Press, 1954), 57, 153; Benjamin Hawkins to George Washington, 10 February 1792, in Clarence Edwin Carter, ed., *The Territorial Papers of the United States* (Washington, D.C.: U.S. Government Printing Office, 1934; New York: AMS Press, 1973), 2:368. See also Calloway, *American Revolution in Indian Country*, 182–271; James H. O'Donnell III, "The Southern Indians and the War for American Independence, 1775–1783," in *Four Centuries of Southern Indians*, ed. Charles M. Hudson (Athens: University of Georgia Press, 1975), 46–64; and Randolph C. Downes, "Creek-American Relations, 1790–1795," *Journal of Southern History* 8 (1942): 350–73.

41. "Travels, Through North and South Carolina," *Massachusetts Magazine* 4 (1792): 686; William Bartram, *Travels of William Bartram* (1791), ed. Mark Van Doren (New York: Dover, 1955), 381. All further citations to the *Travels* appear in parentheses in the text.

42. Bissell, *American Indian in English Literature*, 46. On Bartram as Noble Savagist, see also N. Bryllion Fagin, *William Bartram: Interpreter of the American Landscape* (Baltimore: Johns Hopkins University Press, 1933), 53; Patricia Medeiros, "Three Travelers: Carver, Bartram, and Woolman," in *American Literature, 1764–1789: The Revolutionary Years*, ed. Everett Emerson (Madison: University of Wisconsin Press, 1977), 195–211; Pearce, *Savagism and Civilization*, 143; and Larzer Ziff, *Writing in the New Nation: Prose, Print, and Politics in the Early United States* (New Haven: Yale University Press, 1991), 158. For an alternative reading, see Eve Kornfeld, "Encountering 'The Other': American Intellectuals and Indians in the 1790s," *William and Mary Quarterly* 52 (1995): 287–314.

43. Wald, *Constituting Americans*, 113.

44. Christopher Looby, "The Constitution of Nature: Taxonomy as Politics in Jefferson, Peale, and Bartram," *Early American Literature* 22 (1987): 257. Also reading Bartram in light of Revolutionary-era disquietude is Douglas Anderson, "Bartram's *Travels* and the Politics of Nature," *Early American Literature* 25 (1990): 3–17.

45. Mary Louise Pratt, *Imperial Eyes: Travel Writing and Transculturation* (London: Routledge, 1992), 33; Mary Louise Pratt, "Scratches on the Face of the Country; Or, What Mr. Barrow Saw in the Land of the Bushmen," in *"Race," Writing, and Difference*, ed. Gates, 144; Pratt, *Imperial Eyes*, 7.

46. Pamela Regis, *Describing Early America: Bartram, Jefferson, Crèvecoeur, and the Rhetoric of Natural History* (DeKalb: Northern Illinois University Press, 1992), 76.

47. Though he traces Bartram's distrust of naturalism to a different source, Charles H. Adams's "Reading Ecologically: Language and Play in Bartram's *Travels*," *Southern Quarterly* 32.4 (Summer 1994): 65–74, is a brilliant discussion of the multiple discourses of the *Travels*.

48. William Bartram, "Observations on the Creek and Cherokee Indians, 1789," *Transactions of the American Ethnological Society* 3 (1853): 20.

49. Harriot, for instance, writes: "Most thinges they sawe with vs, as Mathematicall instruments, sea compasses, the vertue of the loadstone in drawing yron, a perspectiue glasse whereby was shewed manie strange sightes, burning glasses, wildefire woorkes, gunnes, bookes, writing and reading, spring clocks that seeme to goe of themselues, and manie other thinges that wee had, were so straunge vnto them, and so farre exceeded their capacities to comprehend the reason and meanes how they should be made and done, that they thought they were rather the works of gods then of men, or at the leastwise they had bin giuen and taught vs of the gods" (*Briefe and True Report*, 27).

50. Beverley, *History and Present State of Virginia*, 17; "Bartram's Travels," *The Monthly Review, or, Literary Journal*, 2nd ser., no. 10 (Feb. 1793): 132.

51. See Gary C. Goodwin, *Cherokees in Transition: A Study of Changing Culture and Environment Prior to 1775*, University of Chicago Department of Geography, Research Paper no. 181 (Chicago: University of Chicago Press, 1977); and Wright, *Creeks and Seminoles*, 21–27, 101–53.

52. See Annette Kolodny, *The Lay of the Land: Metaphor as Experience and History in American Life and Letters* (Chapel Hill: University of North Carolina Press, 1975).

53. Hawkins to William Panton, 28 January 1799, in *Letters of Hawkins* 1:240.

54. See the Creek stories of the origin of corn in John R. Swanton, *Myths and Tales of the Southeastern Indians* (Washington, D.C.: U.S. Government Printing Office, 1929), 9–17; and the Cherokee stories of the enchanted lake and lost settlement in James Mooney, *Myths of the Cherokee* (Washington, D.C.: U.S. Government Printing Office, 1900; St. Clair Shores, Mich.: Scholarly Press, 1970),

321–23, 431–42. Since these stories of the inaccessible homeland were recorded well after the 1830s, however, they almost surely reflect the western removals.

55. Bruce Greenfield, *Narrating Discovery: The Romantic Explorer in American Literature, 1790–1855* (New York: Columbia University Press, 1992), 95. Greenfield, interestingly, finds that the comparable narrative of Bartram's father, John, likewise "registers the inhabited character of the lands through which he traveled" (75).

Chapter 5. Mind out of Time

1. Joseph-Marie Dégerando, *The Observation of Savage Peoples* (1800), trans. F. C. T. Moore (Berkeley: University of California Press, 1969), 61–62, 67, 68, 70.

2. Dégerando, *Observation of Savage Peoples*, 94, 99.

3. Herbert, *Culture and Anomie*, 195; Lee Clark Mitchell, *Witnesses to a Vanishing America: The Nineteenth-Century Response* (Princeton: Princeton University Press, 1981), 219.

4. Johannes Fabian, *Time and the Other: How Anthropology Makes Its Object* (New York: Columbia University Press, 1983), 31 (italicized in original); Dégerando, *Observation of Savage Peoples*, 63; Catlin, *Letters and Notes* 1:3, 239; Morgan, *League of the Iroquois*, 59.

5. Mitchell, *Witnesses to a Vanishing America*, 219. Bernard McGrane attempts a radical critique of the profession in *Beyond Anthropology: Society and the Other* (New York: Columbia University Press, 1989); yet by focusing on how anthropology "systematically constructs" its others (4) while ignoring how those others construct anthropology, he furthers what he critiques. While my study was in press, a work that approaches antebellum ethnology in ways similar to mine appeared; see Scott Michaelsen's provocative *The Limits of Multiculturalism: Interrogating the Origins of American Anthropology* (Minneapolis: University of Minnesota Press, 1999).

6. Studies of ethnology include Robert E. Bieder, *Science Encounters the Indian, 1820–1880: The Early Years of American Ethnology* (Norman: University of Oklahoma Press, 1986); and Curtis M. Hinsley, Jr., *Savages and Scientists: The Smithsonian Institution and the Development of American Anthropology, 1846–1910* (Washington, D.C.: Smithsonian Institution Press, 1981). On Schoolcraft, see Bieder, *Science Encounters the Indian*, 146–93; and Richard G. Bremer, *Indian Agent and Wilderness Scholar: The Life of Henry Rowe Schoolcraft* (Mount Pleasant: Central Michigan University Press, 1987).

7. Morgan, *League of the Iroquois*, 4.

8. Robert D. Richardson, Jr., *Myth and Literature in the American Renaissance* (Bloomington: Indiana University Press, 1978), 10; Banier, *Mythology of the Ancients* 1:27. The *Oxford English Dictionary* contains no record of the word "myth"

(in its present sense as a noun meaning "a purely fictitious narrative" or "an untrue or popular tale") prior to 1830; the initial senses of the word—a verb meaning "to show," "to mark," or "to measure"—had become obsolete centuries earlier.

9. Henry Rowe Schoolcraft, *Notes on the Iroquois* (Albany, 1847; New York: AMS Press, 1975), 56, 57; Henry Rowe Schoolcraft, *Historical and Statistical Information Respecting the History, Condition and Prospects of the Indian Tribes of the United States* (Philadelphia: Lippincott and Grambo, 1851–1857; New York: Paladin, 1969), vol. 1 (1851), 66. I am indebted in what follows to Pearce's *Savagism and Civilization*, a comment in which initially suggested to me the significance of Schoolcraft's theories: "First the savage was put back in history; then he was put out of it" (127).

10. Anna Brownell Jameson, *Winter Studies and Summer Rambles in Canada* (1838) (New York: Wiley and Putnam, 1839), 2:160; Henry Rowe Schoolcraft, *Personal Memoirs of a Residence of Thirty Years with the Indian Tribes on the American Frontiers* (Philadelphia: Lippincott, 1851), 107–08, 109.

11. Schoolcraft, *Personal Memoirs*, 109; Henry Rowe Schoolcraft, *Travels in the Central Portions of the Mississippi Valley* (New York: Collins and Hannay, 1825; Millwood, N.Y.: Kraus, 1975), 404; Henry Rowe Schoolcraft, "The Unchangeable Character of the Indian Mind" (1827), in his *The Literary Voyager or Muzzeniegum*, ed. Philip P. Mason (East Lansing: Michigan State University Press, 1962), 108, 109.

12. Henry Rowe Schoolcraft, *Schoolcraft's Indian Legends*, ed. Mentor L. Williams (East Lansing: Michigan State University Press, 1991), 4, 5, 10. This volume contains *Algic Researches* (1839) as well as myths from other Schoolcraft works. All further citations in this chapter appear in parentheses in the text.

13. Schoolcraft, *Personal Memoirs*, 655.

14. Just as my purpose is not to provide a pedigree of ethnologic thought, I do not mean to track the ethnologic concept of "race." Most scholars believe that before the nineteenth century, scientists adhered to a biblical concept of human unity and thus attributed variation not to "race" but to environment; see Ronald L. Meek, *Social Science and the Ignoble Savage* (Cambridge: Cambridge University Press, 1982); Anthony Pagden, *The Fall of Natural Man: The American Indian and the Origins of Comparative Ethnology* (Cambridge: Cambridge University Press, 1982); and Alden T. Vaughan, "From White Man to Redskin: Changing Anglo-American Perceptions of the American Indian," *American Historical Review* 87 (1982): 917–53. For dissenting views, see Ronald Sanders, *Lost Tribes and Promised Lands: The Origins of American Racism* (Boston: Little, Brown, 1978); and G. E. Thomas, "Puritans, Indians, and the Concept of Race," *New England Quarterly* 48 (1975): 3–27. While I find this debate important, for it contextualizes what is often essentialized, I follow Drinnon's view that if racism is the practice of "treating, feeling, and viewing physically dissimilar peoples" as "less than persons," then racism goes hand in hand with the colonization of America (*Facing West*, 51).

15. Peter S. Duponceau to Heckewelder, in Heckewelder, *History, Manners, and Customs,* 387, 418; Ephraim George Squier, *The Serpent Symbol, and the Worship of the Reciprocal Principles of Nature in America* (New York: George Putnam, 1851), 18. On ethnology's fellow sciences, see Jacob W. Gruber, "Ethnographic Salvage and the Shaping of Anthropology," *American Anthropologist,* new ser., 72 (1970): 1289–99; Mary P. Haas, "Grammar or Lexicon? The American Indian Side of the Question from Duponceau to Powell," *International Journal of American Linguistics* 35 (1969): 239–55; and Reginald Horsman, "Scientific Racism and the American Indian in the Mid-Nineteenth Century," *American Quarterly* 27 (1975): 152–68.

16. Johann Gottfried von Herder, *Outlines of a Philosophy of the History of Man* (1784–1791) (1800; New York: Bergman, 1966), 314; Leopold von Ranke, "On Progress in History" (1854), in *The Theory and Practice of History,* ed. Georg G. Iggers and Konrad von Moltke, trans. Wilma A. Iggers and Moltke (Indianapolis: Bobbs-Merrill, 1973), 52; Bancroft, *History of the United States* 3:304, 305. On antebellum history, see David Levin, *History as Romantic Art: Bancroft, Prescott, Motley, and Parkman* (1959; New York: AMS Press, 1967).

17. Samuel George Morton, *Crania Americana; Or, A Comparative View of the Skulls of Various Aboriginal Nations of North and South America* (Philadelphia: J. Dobson, 1839), 82.

18. Henry Rowe Schoolcraft, *An Address, Delivered Before the Was-Ah-Ho-De-Ne-Son-Ne or New Confederacy of the Iroquois, Aug. 14, 1846* (Rochester: Jerome and Brother, 1846), 29. See also James Ruppert, "Henry Rowe Schoolcraft: The Indian Expert and American Literature," *Platte Valley Review* 19 (1991): 99–128.

19. Daniel Brinton, *The Myths of the New World: A Treatise on the Symbolism and Mythology of the Red Race of America,* 2nd ed. (New York: Henry Holt, 1876; New York: Greenwood Press, 1969), 41; Stith Thompson, *Tales of the North American Indians* (1929; Bloomington: Indiana University Press, 1966), xv; Elémire Zolla, *The Writer and the Shaman: A Morphology of the American Indian,* trans. Raymond Rosenthal (New York: Harcourt, 1973), 150. For attempts to explain Schoolcraft's methodology, see Richard Bauman, "Representing Native American Oral Narrative: The Textual Practices of Henry Rowe Schoolcraft," *Pragmatics* 5 (1995): 167–83; and William M. Clements, "Schoolcraft as Textmaker," *Journal of American Folklore* 103 (1990): 177–92.

20. Lucien Lévy-Bruhl, *How Natives Think* (1923), trans. Lilian A. Clare (Princeton: Princeton University Press, 1985), 38, 108; Ernst Cassirer, *Language and Myth,* trans. Susanne K. Langer (New York: Dover, 1946), 98; Ernst Cassirer, *The Philosophy of Symbolic Forms,* vol. 2, *Mythical Thought* (1925), trans. Ralph Manheim (New Haven: Yale University Press, 1955), 24; Benjamin Lee Whorf, "Language, Mind, and Reality" (1942), in *Language, Thought, and Reality: Selected Writings of Benjamin Lee Whorf,* ed. John B. Carroll (Cambridge: M.I.T. Press, 1956), 252, 256; Claude Lévi-Strauss, *The Savage Mind* (1962), trans. George Wei-

denfeld (Chicago: University of Chicago Press, 1966), 19; Schoolcraft to Cass, 1830, quoted in Bremer, *Indian Agent and Wilderness Scholar*, 189.

21. Kenneth M. Roemer, "Native American Oral Literatures: Context and Continuity," in *Smoothing the Ground*, ed. Swann, 39; Lord, *Singer of Tales*, 138, 94, 4.

22. The view of myth as juvenile literature did originate at this time; see Thomas Bulfinch, *The Age of Fable* (1855) (London: J. M. Dent, 1912). Schoolcraft's myths reemerged in Cornelius Matthews's anthology for children, *The Indian Fairy Book* (1867; rpt. as *The Enchanted Moccasins and Other Legends of the American Indians* [New York: G. P. Putnam's Sons, 1877; New York: AMS Press, 1970]).

23. Schoolcraft attributes two tales to Chusco, an Ottawa shaman and convert (*Indian Legends*, 146, 190). This storyteller, however, had recently died, and was thus unable to verify or deny Schoolcraft's translations, and unavailable to others who might encroach on his turf.

24. James Clifford, "On Ethnographic Allegory," in *Writing Culture*, ed. Clifford and Marcus, 112, 113; Scott Michaelsen, "Ely S. Parker and Amerindian Voices in Ethnography," *American Literary History* 8 (1996): 617; Richard Bauman, "The Nationalization and Internationalization of Folklore: The Case of Schoolcraft's 'Gitshee Gauzinee,'" *Western Folklore* 52 (1993): 267, 268.

25. Brian Dippie, *Catlin and His Contemporaries: The Politics of Patronage* (Lincoln: University of Nebraska Press, 1990), 334.

26. Gordon M. Sayre's "Abridging between Two Worlds: John Tanner as American Indian Autobiographer," *American Literary History* 11 (1999): 480–99, argues that, as with Mary Jemison's narrative, critics have labeled Tanner's work a "captivity" instead of an Indian autobiography due to lingering racial biases. On Tanner's relationship with Schoolcraft, see Maxine Benson, "Schoolcraft, James, and the 'White Indian,'" *Michigan History* 54 (1970): 311–28.

27. Schoolcraft, *Personal Memoirs*, 601, 315, 343. Schoolcraft snubs the Tanner *Narrative* in his masterwork, remarking only of a Tanner-James translation of the Gospels that "neither the Doctor nor his pundit were, or professed to be, vital Christians" at the time—that, indeed, Tanner was fully submerged "in the depths of Indian prejudices and superstitions"—and thus that "it cannot excite surprise that the translation is often so wide of the true meaning, as to render the book worthless" ("Literature of the Indian Languages," in his *Historical and Statistical Information* 4 [1854], 536–37).

28. This list is from Benson, "Schoolcraft, James, and the 'White Indian.'" Bremer ignores Tanner completely, identifying him only, and incorrectly, as "an old enemy" of Schoolcraft (*Indian Agent and Wilderness Scholar*, 291). Benson also suggests as a motive Schoolcraft's belief that Tanner was responsible for the 1846 murder of his brother; but this charge—likely mistaken—cannot explain the attacks of the 1830s. Tanner, for his part, vanished after the murder, lending unfortunate credence to Schoolcraft's accusation and to his theory of the white Indian's inability to endure civilization.

29. Edwin James, ed., *A Narrative of the Captivity and Adventures of John Tanner, (U.S. Interpreter at the Saut de Ste. Marie,) during Thirty Years Residence among the Indians in the Interior of North America* (New York: Carvill, 1830), 4, 7.

30. James, *Narrative of John Tanner*, 8, 35, 39, 45, 71. The episodes listed appear on 77, 111, and 164.

31. James, *Narrative of John Tanner*, 4, 5; Tanner to Charles Lee, 1846, quoted in Benson, "Schoolcraft, James, and the 'White Indian,'" 320.

32. Sayre, "Abridging between Two Worlds," 493.

33. On the title page of the copy of the Tanner *Narrative* I consulted (in the University of Pittsburgh's Darlington Room), an anonymous penciled inscription reads: "I saw John Tanner at the Sault-de St. Marie in August 1841." Though a mere line evidencing Tanner's existence, a note such as this is hard to imagine on any title page of *Algic Researches*.

34. John T. Fierst, "Strange Eloquence: Another Look at *The Captivity and Adventures of John Tanner*," in *Reading beyond Words: Contexts for Native History*, ed. Jennifer S. H. Brown and Elizabeth Vibert (Peterborough, Ont.: Broadview Press, 1996), 230.

35. James, *Narrative of John Tanner*, 14, 13; Henry Rowe Schoolcraft, "Travellers among the Aborigines," *North American Review* 27 (1828): 101. James' critique of Schoolcraft appears in *Narrative of John Tanner*, 8 n.

36. Lewis Cass, "Indian Treaties," *North American Review* 24 (1827): 391; Schoolcraft, *Personal Memoirs*, 601. The Cass episode appears in James, *Narrative of John Tanner*, 245.

37. Sayre, "Abridging Between Two Worlds," 494; Schoolcraft, *Personal Memoirs*, 316; James, *Narrative of John Tanner*, 171–72.

38. In *Travels in the Central Portions of the Mississippi Valley* (1825), Schoolcraft does credit a "fragment" of narrative, and two "specimens" of poetry, to "the polite attainments and literary taste" of Jane (426 n); the implication is that her white training qualifies her to translate the dumb materials of her Indian bloodline. Information on Jane is scant, and research on her virtually nonexistent (Michaelsen devotes several valuable pages to her in *Limits of Multiculturalism*, 41–45). For a speculative but fascinating reconstruction of the cultures in which Jane lived, see Jacqueline Peterson's exploration of the ways in which Ojibwa women (including Jane's mother) may have "interpreted and used the presence of white men and their sources of . . . power within a tribally sanctioned context" ("Women Dreaming: The Religiopsychology of Indian-White Marriages and the Rise of a Metis Culture," in *Western Women: Their Land, Their Lives*, ed. Lillian Schlissel, Vicki L. Ruiz, and Janice Monk [Albuquerque: University of New Mexico Press, 1988], 49–68; quote on 63).

39. Jameson, *Winter Studies* 2:247–48.

40. Jameson, *Winter Studies* 2:246. To confuse matters further, a version of the Winter-Spring story appeared in Thomas McKenney's *Sketches of a Tour to the*

Lakes (Baltimore, 1827; Minneapolis: Ross and Haines, 1959), 369–70; yet though he credits the telling to Jane's mother, he attributes its translation to Jane's sister and father. Moreover, this rendering is so close to Jameson's that one wonders whether McKenney's book, and not Jane, was Jameson's source.

41. Dwight, *Travels* 4:131–32.

42. James Kenny, "Journal of James Kenny, 1761–1763," ed. John W. Jordan, *Pennsylvania Magazine of History and Biography* 37 (1913): 175.

43. [Tenskwatawa], "Origin Legend" (transcription, 1824), in C. C. Trowbridge, *Shawnese Traditions: C. C. Trowbridge's Account*, ed. Vernon Kinietz and Erminie W. Voegelin, Occasional Contributions from the Museum of Anthropology of the University of Michigan, no. 9 (Ann Arbor: University of Michigan Press, 1939), 1, 3; William Henry Harrison to Henry Dearborn, 1 September 1808, in *Governors Messages and Letters*, ed. Esarey, 1:302; [Tenskwatawa], "Origin Legend," 56.

44. In Dwight's case, for instance, it cannot be by accident that a minister who disputes that humans "sprang from different original stocks" records a myth of multiple origins (*Travels* 3:128). Failure to consider such factors weakens Dowd's *Spirited Resistance*; and William G. McLoughlin and Walter H. Conser, Jr.'s "'The First Man Was Red': Cherokee Responses to the Debate over Indian Origins," *American Quarterly* 41 (1989): 243–64.

45. Schoolcraft, *Historical and Statistical Information* 1:412; review of *Algic Researches*, quoted in Schoolcraft, *Personal Memoirs*, 653; Henry Rowe Schoolcraft, "Incentives to the Study of the Ancient Period of American History," *New York Historical Society Proceedings* 4 (1846): suppl., 33.

46. Fabian, *Time and the Other*, 144.

47. Henry Rowe Schoolcraft, *Narrative Journal of Travels Through the Northwestern Regions of the United States* (1821), ed. Mentor Williams (East Lansing: Michigan State University Press, 1992), 265–66; Henry Rowe Schoolcraft, "Account of the Native Copper on the Southern Shore of Lake Superior," *American Journal of Science and Arts* 3 (1821): 215.

Chapter 6. Myth and the State

1. Schoolcraft, *Address Before the Was-Ah-Ho-De-Ne-Son-Ne*, 5–6; John G. Palfrey, "Yamoyden," *North American Review* 12 (1821): 477, 484; R. C. Sands, "Domestic Literature," *Atlantic Magazine* 1 (1824): 133; "York Town, a Historical Romance," *American Quarterly Review* 2 (1827): 30, 45.

2. See G. Harrison Orians, "The Romance Ferment After *Waverley*," *American Literature* 3 (1932): 408–31; and William Ellery Sedgwick, "The Materials for an American Literature: A Critical Problem of the Early Nineteenth Century," *Harvard Studies and Notes in Philology and Literature* 17 (1935): 141–62.

3. Benjamin T. Spencer, *The Quest for Nationality: An American Literary Campaign* (Syracuse: Syracuse University Press, 1957), 1, 104.

4. Ralph Waldo Emerson, *Nature* (1836), in his *Complete Works* 1:3; Friedrich Schlegel, "Talk on Mythology" (1800), in *Rise of Modern Mythology*, ed. Feldman and Richardson, 309; Emerson, *Nature*, 29, 35, 30.

5. Ralph Waldo Emerson, "Quotation and Originality" (1868), in his *Complete Works* 8:178, 200.

6. "Memorials of the Cherokee Indians" (1830), rpt. in Krupat, *Ethnocriticism*, 170, 172; Henry David Thoreau, "Walking" (1862), in *The Natural History Essays* (Salt Lake City: Peregrine Smith, 1984), 121; Henry David Thoreau, *The Maine Woods* (1864), ed. Joseph J. Moldenhauer (Princeton: Princeton University Press, 1972), 172.

7. Ralph Waldo Emerson, "The Poet" (1844), in his *Complete Works* 3:21; Charles G. Leland, *Algonquin Legends* (Boston: Houghton Mifflin, 1884; New York: Dover, 1992), 65, 62. The tale of the monster moose appears in *Algonquin Legends*, 65; and in Frank G. Speck, "Penobscot Tales and Religious Beliefs," *Journal of American Folk-Lore* 48 (1935): 43–44. Leland himself, according to Thomas Parkhill, distorted and suppressed sources in order to present his tales as distinctively "American"; see " 'Of Glooskap's Birth, and of His Brother Malsum, the Wolf': The Story of Charles Godfrey Leland's 'Purely American Creation,' " *American Indian Culture and Research Journal* 16.1 (1992): 45–69.

8. Richardson, *Myth and Literature in American Renaissance*, 90.

9. On Thoreau's academic interest in Indian myth, see Suzanne D. Rose, "Following the Trail of Footsteps: From the Indian Notebooks to *Walden*," *New England Quarterly* 67 (1994): 77–91.

10. Thoreau, *Maine Woods*, 136–37. See also Linda Frost, " 'The Red Face of Man,' the Penobscot Indian, and a Conflict of Interest in Thoreau's *Maine Woods*," *Emerson Society Quarterly* 39 (1993): 21–47; and Bruce Greenfield, "Thoreau's Discovery of America: A Nineteenth-Century First Contact," *Emerson Society Quarterly* 32 (1986): 80–95.

11. William Gilmore Simms, "Literature and Art among the American Aborigines" (1845), in his *Views and Reviews in American Literature, History and Fiction*, ed. C. Hugh Holman (Cambridge: Belknap Press of Harvard University Press, 1962), 132.

12. Robert Clark, "The Last of the Iroquois: History and Myth in James Fenimore Cooper's *The Last of the Mohicans*," *Poetics Today* 3.4 (Autumn 1982): 120, 130; Helen Carr, *Inventing the American Primitive: Politics, Gender, and the Representation of Native American Literary Traditions, 1789–1936* (New York: New York University Press, 1996), 107, 102. For other readings that connect literary nationalism to expansion, see Teresa A. Goddu, *Gothic America: Narrative, History, and Nation* (New York: Columbia University Press, 1997), 55–58; and Wald, *Constituting Americans*, 109–17.

13. Thoreau, *Maine Woods*, 213.

14. James Fenimore Cooper, *The Pioneers* (1823), ed. Donald A. Ringe (New York: Penguin, 1988), 345. On Cooper's landholding, see L. H. Butterfield, "Cooper's Inheritance: The Otsego Country and Its Founders," *New York History* 35 (1954): 374–411.

15. Richard Slotkin, introduction to James Fenimore Cooper, *The Last of the Mohicans* (1826), ed. Slotkin (New York: Penguin, 1986), xx. All further citations appear in parentheses in the text.

16. Schoolcraft, *Indian Legends*, 18; "York Town, a Historical Romance" 46; Cooper to New York Bread and Cheese Club, 30 May 1826, in *The Letters and Journals of James Fenimore Cooper*, ed. James Franklin Beard (Cambridge: Belknap Press of Harvard University Press, 1960–1968), 1:140; Cooper to William Swain, 27 September–10 October 1840, in *Letters and Journals of Cooper* 4:73–74. For antebellum thought on the romance, see Nina Baym, *Novels, Readers, and Reviewers: Responses to Fiction in Antebellum America* (Ithaca: Cornell University Press, 1984), 224–48.

17. Thomas Philbrick, "*The Last of the Mohicans* and the Sounds of Discord," *American Literature* 43 (1971): 31.

18. Heckewelder, *History, Manners, and Customs*, 80, 78, 80. See also Francis Jennings, "The Scandalous Indian Policy of William Penn's Sons: Deeds and Documents of the Walking Purchase," *Pennsylvania History* 37 (1970): 19–39; and C. A. Weslager, *The Delaware Indian Westward Migration* (Wallingford, Pa.: Middle Atlantic Press, 1978).

19. James Logan and Nutimus, 1735, quoted in Anthony F. C. Wallace, *King of the Delawares: Teedyuscung, 1700–1763* (Syracuse: Syracuse University Press, 1990), 21.

20. Most writers find Cooper's historiography execrable. See Robert Clark, *History and Myth in American Fiction, 1823–52* (New York: St. Martin's Press, 1984), 79–95; Ian K. Steele, *Betrayals: Fort William Henry and the "Massacre"* (New York: Oxford University Press, 1990), 157–70; and Paul A. W. Wallace, "John Heckewelder's Indians and the Fenimore Cooper Tradition," *Proceedings of the American Philosophical Society* 96 (1952): 447–56.

21. Stephen Railton, *Fenimore Cooper: A Study of His Life and Imagination* (Princeton: Princeton University Press, 1978); Mark R. Patterson, *Authority, Autonomy, and Representation in American Literature, 1776–1865* (Princeton: Princeton University Press, 1988), 86; Eric Cheyfitz, "Savage Law: The Plot against American Indians in *Johnson and Graham's Lessee v. M'Intosh* and *The Pioneers*," in *Cultures of United States Imperialism*, ed. Amy Kaplan and Donald E. Pease (Durham: Duke University Press, 1993), 118.

22. On filial rhetoric in the Removal Era, see Michael Paul Rogin, *Fathers and Children: Andrew Jackson and the Subjugation of the American Indian* (New York: Knopf, 1975).

23. Thomas Jefferson, "Second Inaugural Address" (1805), in *Compilation of the Messages and Papers of the Presidents*, comp. Richardson, 1:368; Cass, "Indian

Treaties," 391; Wilson Lumpkin, quoted in "House Debate on the Indian Removal Question, May 15, 26, 1830," in *American Indian and the United States*, ed. Washburn, 2:1073-74.

24. "Memorials of the Cherokee Indians," in Krupat, *Ethnocriticism*, 164-65; Boudinot, "Address to the Whites," 69; Susan Fenimore Cooper, *Pages and Pictures, from the Writings of James Fenimore Cooper* (New York: W. A. Townsend, 1861), 130.

25. Steven Blakemore, "Strange Tongues: Cooper's Fiction of Language in *The Last of the Mohicans*," *Early American Literature* 19 (1984): 39.

26. Forrest G. Robinson writes that Magua's "devious oratorical strategies are identical to those of the utterly unprincipled demagogues who were, Cooper was convinced, the special plague of popular American democracy" ("Uncertain Borders: Race, Sex, and Civilization in *The Last of the Mohicans*," *Arizona Quarterly* 47 [1991]: 24). To say this, however, is to blur the racial difference on which Cooper, no less than Magua, insists.

27. See Henry S. Manley, "Red Jacket's Last Campaign," *New York History* 31 (1954): 149-68.

28. Deeds of 23 June 1683 and 15 June 1692, quoted in Edwin P. Kilroe, *Saint Tammany and the Origin of the Society of Tammany or Columbian Order in the City of New York* (New York: M. B. Brown, 1913), 16, 17. See Alan Leander MacGregor, "Tammany: The Indian as Rhetorical Surrogate," *American Quarterly* 35 (1983): 391-407. MacGregor recognizes that the "rhetorical" Indian was used "against the real Indians" during the early national period (403); but he concludes that by Cooper's time, Indians had become merely rhetorical, not real.

29. Heckewelder, *History, Manners, and Customs*, 345. Cooper's political patron, DeWitt Clinton, reported a similar story: "Their antient men . . . weep like infants, when they speak of the fallen condition of the nation. They, however, derive some consolation from a prophecy of antient origin and universal currency among them, that the man of America will, at some future time, regain his antient ascendancy, and expel the man of Europe from this western hemisphere" (*Discourse Delivered Before the New-York Historical Society, at Their Anniversary Meeting, 6th December, 1811* [New York: James Eastburn, 1812], 48).

30. Donald Darnell, "Uncas as Hero: The *Ubi Sunt* Formula in *The Last of the Mohicans*," *American Literature* 37 (1965): 263.

31. On the equation of Indian speech with Indian backwardness, see Dennis Allen, " 'By All the Truth of Signs': James Fenimore Cooper's *The Last of the Mohicans*," *Studies in American Fiction* 9 (1981): 159-79; and Murray, *Forked Tongues*, 14-33.

32. Jerome Rothenberg, " 'We Explain Nothing, We Believe Nothing': American Indian Poetry and the Problematics of Translation," in *On the Translation of Native American Literatures*, ed. Swann, 68; "Cooper's Novels," *North American Review* 23 (1826): 167.

33. James Fenimore Cooper, *Home As Found* (1838) (New York: Capricorn, 1961), 166; William Cullen Bryant, epigraph in Cooper, *Home As Found*, 137; Cooper to Martin Van Buren, 15 March 1840, in *Letters and Journals of Cooper* 4:25; James Fenimore Cooper, *Satanstoe, or The Littlepage Manuscripts: A Tale of the Colony* (1845), ed. Kay Seymour House and Constance Ayers Denne (Albany: State University of New York Press, 1990), 10, 7; James Fenimore Cooper, *The Redskins or Indian and Injin, Being the Conclusion of the Littlepage Manuscripts* (1846) (New York: Frank F. Lovell, n. d.), 422.

34. George Copway to Cooper, 12 June 1851, in *Letters and Journals of Cooper* 6:275; Cooper to Copway, 17 June 1851, in *Letters and Journals of Cooper* 6:275.

35. Henry Wadsworth Longfellow, "The Literary Spirit of Our Country," *United States Literary Gazette* 2.1 (1 April 1825): 27; Henry Rowe Schoolcraft, "Poetic Development of the Indian Mind," in his *Historical and Statistical Information* 3 (1853), 328. Wilbur Lang Schramm notes that, though many epic poems on Indian subjects preceded *Hiawatha*, Longfellow's was the first "based on Indian legend rather than on Indian history" ("*Hiawatha* and Its Predecessors," *Philological Quarterly* 11 [1932]: 341). There had also been a few short stories based on Indian "legend," such as William Gilmore Simms, "The Arm-Chair of Tustenuggee. A Tradition of the Catawba," in his *The Wigwam and the Cabin (Life in America)* (George Clark, 1845; Ridgewood, N.J.: Gregg, 1968), 130-59.

36. Anthropologists have long been interested in *Hiawatha*'s sources; see Rose M. Davis, "How Indian Is Hiawatha?" *Midwest Folklore* 7 (1957): 5-25; and Stith Thompson, "The Indian Legend of Hiawatha," *PMLA* 37 (1922): 128-40.

37. Pearce, *Savagism and Civilization*, 194; Slotkin, *Regeneration Through Violence*, 356-57.

38. Pearce, *Savagism and Civilization*, 192; George Copway, *The Life, History, and Travels of Kah-Ge-Ga-Gah-Bowh (George Copway)*, 2nd ed. (Philadelphia: James Harmstead, 1847), 43.

39. Most tales refer to the Ojibwa Trickster as male; but since this may reflect the biases of translators, and since gender, like all social categories, is suspect in Trickster stories, I use the impersonal pronoun. Also, though the Ojibwa Trickster's name appears variously, I use Schoolcraft's orthography—"Manabozho"—simply because Longfellow did. For useful introductions to Trickster literature, see Jarold Ramsey, "Coyote and Friends: An Experiment in Interpretive Bricolage," in his *Reading the Fire: Essays in the Traditional Literatures of the Far West* (Lincoln: University of Nebraska Press, 1983), 24-46; and Andrew Wiget, "His Life in His Tale: The Native American Trickster and the Literature of Possibility," in *Redefining American Literary History*, ed. Ruoff and Ward, 83-96.

40. William Jones, *Ojibwa Texts*, ed. Truman Michelson, Publications of the American Ethnological Society, vol. 7 (Leiden: E. J. Brill, 1917), pt. 1, 361. The episodes listed appear in *Ojibwa Texts*, pt. 1, 41-43, 101-9, 139-45, 311-15, 451-55.

41. Schoolcraft, *Indian Legends*, 23, 80, 65, 80; Jones, *Ojibwa Texts*, pt. 1, 113–

15, 169, 181, 179; Schoolcraft, *Notes on the Iroquois*, 263. The episodes from Jones appear in *Ojibwa Texts*, pt. 1, 123–25, 177–79.

42. Schoolcraft, *Indian Legends*, 80; Barbara Babcock-Abrahams, "'A Tolerated Margin of Mess': The Trickster and His Tales Reconsidered," *Journal of the Folklore Institute* 11 (1975): 148; Franchot Ballinger, "Living Sideways: Social Themes and Social Relationships in Native American Trickster Tales," *American Indian Quarterly* 13.1 (Winter 1989): 15; Anne Doueihi, "Trickster: On Inhabiting the Space between Discourse and Story," *Soundings* 67 (1984): 284, 297, 308; Gerald Vizenor, "Trickster Discourse: Comic Holotropes and Language Games," in *Narrative Chance: Postmodern Discourse on Native American Indian Literatures*, ed. Vizenor (Albuquerque: University of New Mexico Press, 1989), 194, 204.

43. Henry Wadsworth Longfellow, preface to "Coplas de Manrique" (1833), in *The Poetical Works of Henry Wadsworth Longfellow* (Boston: Houghton Mifflin, 1886), 6:181.

44. As Arnold Krupat notes, modern translators continue to approach Indian texts in this way; see "Identity and Difference in the Criticism of Native American Literature," *Diacritics* 13.2 (Summer 1983): 2–13.

45. Henry Wadsworth Longfellow, in Samuel Longfellow, ed., *Life of Henry Wadsworth Longfellow, with Extracts from His Journals and Correspondence* (Boston: Ticknor, 1886), 2:248 (28 June 1854). On the Manabozho/Hiawatha mix-up, see Ernest J. Moyne, "Manabozho, Tarenyawagon, and Hiawatha," *Southern Folklore Quarterly* 29 (1965): 195–203.

46. Longfellow, in *Life* 2:250 (28 September 1854); Henry Wadsworth Longfellow to Ferdinand Freiligrath, 11 January 1856, in *The Letters of Henry Wadsworth Longfellow*, ed. Andrew Hillen (Cambridge: Belknap Press of Harvard University Press, 1966–1982), 3:517.

47. Henry Wadsworth Longfellow, *The Song of Hiawatha* (1855), in his *Poetical Works* 2:116, 117, 118. All further citations are identified by page (rather than line) number and appear in parentheses in the text.

48. Robert A. Ferguson, "Longfellow's Political Fears: Civic Authority and the Role of the Artist in *Hiawatha* and *Miles Standish*," *American Literature* 50 (1978): 195; Schoolcraft, *Personal Memoirs*, 575; Henry Rowe Schoolcraft, *The Indian in His Wigwam, or Characteristics of the Red Race of America* (New York: W. H. Graham, 1848; New York: AMS Press, 1978), 224; Schoolcraft to Longfellow, 19 December 1855, in Samuel Longfellow, ed., *Final Memorials of Henry Wadsworth Longfellow* (Boston: Ticknor, 1887), 45–46.

49. Cecelia Tichi, "Longfellow's Motives for the Structure of 'Hiawatha,'" *American Literature* 42 (1971): 553; Longfellow to Freiligrath, 29 January 1857, in *Letters of Longfellow* 4:11.

50. Longfellow, in *Life* 2:135 (26 February 1849); Carr, *Inventing the American Primitive*, 136; Copway, *Life, History, and Travels*, vii; Longfellow, quoted in Ernest J. Moyne, "Longfellow and Kah-Ge-Ga-Gah-Bowh," in *Henry W. Long-*

fellow Reconsidered, ed. J. Chesley Mathews (Hartford: Transcendental Press, 1970), 51.

51. Longfellow, in *Life* 2:137 (12, 14 April 1849); Copway, *Life, History, and Travels*, viii; George Copway, *The Traditional History and Characteristic Sketches of the Ojibway Nation* (London: Charles Gilpin, 1850), 280–81. Copway was a member of the Ojibwa Eagle clan; moreover, he might have sensed or sought a bond between the eagle and the Thunder Bird of Ojibwa story. One such story appears in *Traditional History*, 108–12.

52. George Copway, "The American Indians," *American Review* 9 (1849): 631; Longfellow to Freiligrath, 16 July 1851, in *Letters of Longfellow* 3:302.

53. Carr, in *Inventing the American Primitive*, 136–37, reveals Longfellow's debt to Copway; however, she suggests that Copway was the poet's lone source on pictography. Conversely, Virginia Jackson discusses only Schoolcraft's part, not Copway's ("Longfellow's Tradition; or, Picture-Writing a Nation," *Modern Language Quarterly* 59 [1998]: 471–96). For Copway's pictographs, see *Traditional History* (1850), 134–36; for Schoolcraft's, see "Indian Pictography," in his *Historical and Statistical Information* 1 (1851), 333–430. Given the chronology, it is possible that Copway was one of Schoolcraft's sources as well.

54. Longfellow to Freiligrath, 15 March 1843, in *Letters of Longfellow* 2:516.

55. Longfellow does list John Tanner as a source; if in fact Tanner was responsible for any or all of Schoolcraft's translations, this suggests an even more tangled path to *Hiawatha*. Having vanished a decade before the publication of Longfellow's poem, however, Tanner was safely distant as Copway was not.

56. Perrot, "Memoir," in *Indian Tribes*, ed. Blair, 31–32, 35–36.

57. Jones, *Ojibwa Texts*, pt. 1, 501.

58. See Schoolcraft, *Indian Legends*, 75–77.

59. Johann Georg Kohl, *Kitchi-Gami: Life among the Lake Superior Ojibway*, trans. Lascelles Wraxall (1859; St. Paul: Minnesota Historical Society, 1985), 367.

Chapter 7. Traditional Histories

1. Henry David Thoreau, quoted in Sayre, *Thoreau and the Indians*, 128; Henry David Thoreau, *Journal*, vol. 1, 1837–1844, ed. Elizabeth Hall Witherell, William L. Howarth, Robert Sattelmeyer, and Thomas Blanding (Princeton: Princeton University Press, 1981), 321 (18 August 1841); Thoreau, *Maine Woods*, 137.

2. Schoolcraft, *Address Before the Was-Ah-Ho-De-Ne-Son-Ne*, 21; Schoolcraft, *Notes on the Iroquois*, 63; Francis Parkman, *The Conspiracy of Pontiac and the Indian War After the Conquest of Canada* (1851) (Boston: Little, Brown, 1907), 1:16 n. 1, 1:18 n. 1; Horatio Hale, *The Iroquois Book of Rites*, Brinton's Library of Aboriginal American Literature, no. 2 (Philadelphia: D. G. Brinton, 1883), 12; Elisabeth Tooker, "The League of the Iroquois: Its History, Politics, and Ritual," in *Hand-*

book of North American Indians, ed. Trigger, 15:420. On the continuing debate be-tween Iroquois and Euro-American historians, see Barbara A. Mann and Jerry L. Fields, "A Sign in the Sky: Dating the League of the Haudenosaunee," *American Indian Culture and Research Journal* 21.2 (1997): 105–63.

3. Cass, "Indians of North America," *North American Review* 22 (1826): 65, 66; Heckewelder, *History, Manners, and Customs*, xxiii; Cass, "Indians of North America," 67.

4. Cass, "Indians of North America," 101; Schoolcraft, *Personal Memoirs*, 238; "Tanner's Indian Narrative," *American Quarterly Review* 8 (1830): 113; School-craft, *Personal Memoirs*, 83.

5. See Richard Drinnon, *White Savage: The Case of John Dunn Hunter* (New York: Schocken, 1972).

6. Pratt, *Imperial Eyes*, 7.

7. "I have written in something of the spirit which would characterize the history written by an Indian, yet it does not deserve to be called Indian partiality, but only justice and the spirit of humanity" (Minnie Myrtle [Anna Cummings Johnson], *The Iroquois; Or, the Bright Side of Indian Character* [New York: D. Ap-pleton, 1855], 31). The quote that Elias Johnson provides from Handsome Lake (note 27 of my fourth chapter) was also secondhand, taken from Morgan's *League of the Iroquois*, 239–40. Since, however, the passage is Ely Parker's, Johnson may have felt authorized to reproduce it.

8. For example, in the appendix to the first edition of *A Son of the Forest*, Apess excerpts Euro-American works to prove that the Indians, as the descen-dants of the Lost Tribes of Israel, are the children not of doom but of destiny (*On Our Own Ground*, 52–97). On the significance of this move, see Laura J. Murray, "The Aesthetic of Dispossession: Washington Irving and Ideologies of (De)Colo-nization," *American Literary History* 8 (1996): 205–27.

9. Moreover, as Barry O'Connell points out, the contrast of "resistant" Indians with "sell-outs" ignores the paradoxes of a colonized people's self-repre-sentation: "To be 'Indian' . . . was necessarily to be a 'fake' whose fakery met white ideas of the authentic. Successful Indians . . . were the best fakes, those most able to manipulate Euro-Americans' notions about Indians" ("Transgressors or Non-Entities: Reading Native Americans in and out of American Literature," paper presented at the American Studies Association Convention, Boston, 4–7 Novem-ber 1993, 16). These comments should be kept in mind during my discussion of George Copway, who, O'Connell points out, has been caricatured as a "traitor to his people, or an abandoner of 'traditional' Indian ways, or an unnatural or false Indian" (19).

10. On Copway, see Donald B. Smith, "The Life of George Copway or Kah-ge-ga-gah-bowh (1818–1869)—and a Review of His Writings," *Journal of Cana-dian Studies* 23.3 (Fall 1988): 5–38. Smith explores the contact of Ojibwa and Christian cultures in his biography of Copway's patron, Peter Jones; see *Sacred*

Feathers: The Reverend Peter Jones (Kahkewaquonaby) and the Mississauga Indians (Lincoln: University of Nebraska Press, 1987). Peyer offers an intriguing discussion of Copway that appeared too late for my study to benefit substantially from it; see *Tutor'd Mind*, 224–77.

11. See E. G. Squier, "Historical and Mythological Traditions of the Algonquins: With a Translation of the 'Walum-Olum,' or Bark Record of the Linni-Lenape," *American Review* 9 (1849): 173–93.

12. Longfellow to Freiligrath, 14 December 1858, in *Letters of Longfellow* 4:109; Francis Parkman to E. G. Squier, 18 November 1849, in *Letters of Francis Parkman*, ed. Wilbur R. Jacobs (Norman: University of Oklahoma Press, 1960), 1:66.

13. George Copway, *The Life, History, and Travels of Kah-Ge-Ga-Gah-Bowh (George Copway)*, 2nd ed. (Philadelphia: James Harmstead, 1847), viii.

14. Copway, *Life, History, and Travels*, 17.

15. Copway, *Life, History, and Travels*, 20–21, 33; Richard Handler and Jocelyn Linnekin, "Tradition, Genuine or Spurious," *Journal of American Folklore* 97 (1984): 287, 288. On the complexity of nativist re-creations of tribal life, see Roger M. Keesing, "Creating the Past: Custom and Identity in the Contemporary Pacific," *The Contemporary Pacific* 1 (1989): 19–42.

16. A. LaVonne Brown Ruoff, "Three Nineteenth-Century American Indian Autobiographers," in *Redefining American Literary History*, ed. Ruoff and Ward, 257; Copway, *Life, History, and Travels*, 95; Timothy Sweet, "Pastoral Landscape with Indians: George Copway and the Political Unconscious of the American Pastoral," *Prospects* 18 (1993): 9; Copway, *Life, History, and Travels*, 126, 155.

17. Copway, *Life, History, and Travels*, 9; Kathleen Mullen Sands, "American Indian Autobiography," in *Studies in American Indian Literature: Critical Essays and Course Designs*, ed. Paula Gunn Allen (New York: Modern Language Association of America, 1983), 59.

18. Kohl, *Kitchi-Gami*, 144, 296. On pictography, see Frances Densmore, *Chippewa Customs*, Smithsonian Institution Bureau of American Ethnology, Bull. 86 (Washington, D.C.: U.S. Government Printing Office, 1929; St. Paul: Minnesota Historical Society, 1979), 174–83.

19. Hertha Dawn Wong, *Sending My Heart Back across the Years: Tradition and Innovation in Native American Autobiography* (New York: Oxford University Press, 1992), 5; H. David Brumble III, *American Indian Autobiography* (Berkeley: University of California Press, 1988), 47. Copway's *Life, History, and Travels* may, in fact, qualify as a collaborative work, for his wife, Elizabeth Howell, seems to have acted, though in unknown degree, as his editor. On the complexities of such texts, see Arnold Krupat, *For Those Who Come After: A Study of Native American Autobiography* (Berkeley: University of California Press, 1985).

20. George Copway, *The Traditional History and Characteristic Sketches of the*

Ojibway Nation (London: Charles Gilpin, 1850), ix–x. All further citations appear in parentheses in the text.

21. Copway, *Life, History, and Travels*, 13.

22. Schoolcraft, "Indian Pictography," in *Historical and Statistical Information* 1:340; Joseph Nicollet, *The Journals of Joseph N. Nicollet, A Scientist on the Mississippi Headwaters, with Notes on Indian Life, 1836–37*, trans. André Fertey, ed. Martha Coleman Bray (St. Paul: Minnesota Historical Society, 1970), 266.

23. Kohl, *Kitchi-Gami*, 194.

24. On the ways in which Indian writers combined Euro-American "literary models" and Indian "oral traditions," see William M. Clements, "'This Voluminous Unwritten Book of Ours': Early Native American Writers and the Oral Tradition," in *Early Native American Writing*, ed. Jaskoski, 122–35; quote on 123.

25. Schoolcraft, *Indian Legends*, 27, 39, 92.

26. Jones, *Ojibwa Texts*, pt. 1, 69, 249, 197, 409. The episodes listed appear on 49–51 and 51–73.

27. Schoolcraft, *Indian Legends*, 22.

28. William W. Warren, *History of the Ojibway Nation* (1885; Minneapolis: Ross and Haines, 1957), 26, 35, 57, 56. Schoolcraft was equally underhanded in his praise of Warren, writing of the latter's essay: "The following traditions are given, as being entitled to the highest respect, but without endorsing the opinions incidentally expressed, or the particular archæological dates" (headnote to Warren, "Oral Traditions Respecting the History of the Ojibwa Nation," in *Historical and Statistical Information* 2 [1852], 135). Copway avoids Schoolcraft's scorn, but also his notice; he appears in Schoolcraft's magnum opus only once, and then only as co-translator of the Gospel of Luke ("Literature of the Indian Languages," in *Historical and Statistical Information* 4:532). On Copway's fellow historians, see D. Peter MacLeod, "The Anishinabeg Point of View: The History of the Great Lakes Region to 1800 in Nineteenth-Century Mississauga, Odawa, and Ojibwa Historiography," *Canadian Historical Review* 73 (1992): 194–210.

29. Smith, "Life of Copway," 23; James A. Clifton, "The Tribal History—An Obsolete Paradigm," *American Indian Culture and Research Journal* 3.4 (1979): 93.

30. Smith, "Life of Copway," 19.

31. Peter Jones, *History of the Ojibway Indians: With Especial Reference to Their Conversion to Christianity* (London: A. W. Bennett, 1861), 243. On Copway's activism, see Dale T. Knobel, "Know-Nothings and Indians: Strange Bedfellows?" *Western Historical Quarterly* 15 (1984): 175–98.

32. Daniel F. Littlefield, Jr., and James W. Parins, *A Biobibliography of Native American Writers, 1772–1924*, Native American Bibliography Series, no. 2 (Metuchen, N.J.: Scarecrow Press, 1981), 230; Catlin, *Letters and Notes* 2:104; W. M. Beauchamp, *The Iroquois Trail, or Foot-Prints of the Six Nations, in Customs, Traditions, and History. In Which Are Included David Cusick's "Sketches of Ancient History of the Six Nations" [1827?]* (Fayetteville, N.Y.: H. C. Beauchamp, 1892;

New York: AMS Press, 1976), 41. All further citations to *Sketches* appear in parentheses in the text.

33. Morgan, *League of the Iroquois*, 44, 45, 99. See also Graymont, *Iroquois in the American Revolution*, 285–93; and David Landy, "Tuscarora Tribalism and National Identity," *Ethnohistory* 5 (1958): 250–84.

34. Nicholas Cusic[k], quoted in Jedidiah Morse, *A Report to the Secretary of War of the United States, on Indian Affairs* (New Haven: S. Converse, 1822; New York: Augustus M. Kelley, 1970), app., 5; Jabez Hyde, "A Teacher among the Senecas" (1820), *Publications of the Buffalo Historical Society* 6 (1903): 249. On religious factionalism among the Tuscaroras, see Barbara Graymont, "The Tuscarora New Year Festival," *New York History* 50 (1969): 143–63.

35. William N. Fenton, "'This Island, the World on the Turtle's Back,'" *Journal of American Folklore* 75 (1962): 298.

36. Cusick's sections parallel the phases of Indian story identified by Andrew Wiget: Origin Period (gods create the world); Transformation Period (supernaturals modify the world); and Legendary/Historical Period (humans establish social precedents). See *Native American Literature* (Boston: Twayne, 1985), 3–5. *Sketches*, however, does not seem to present these phases as separable or evolutionary.

37. J. N. B. Hewitt, "The Requickening Address of the Iroquois Condolence Council," ed. William N. Fenton, *Journal of the Washington Academy of Sciences* 34 (1944): 70, 76.

38. Schoolcraft, *Historical and Statistical Information* 5 (1855), 631. Schoolcraft, who reprints *Sketches* in this volume (632–46), had, however, moderated his judgment of Cusick by the 1850s; in a statement remarkable for him or any ethnologist, he writes that "history may be said to be indebted to [Cusick] for telling his own story of these things in his own way" (*Historical and Statistical Information* 1:125). For a fine reading of the Schoolcraft-Cusick connection, see Scott Michaelsen, "Resketching Anglo-Amerindian Identity Politics," in *Border Theory: The Limits of Cultural Politics*, ed. Michaelsen and David Johnson (Minneapolis: University of Minnesota Press, 1997), 221–52.

39. Russell A. Judkins, "David Cusick's Ancient History of the Six Nations: A Neglected Classic," in *Iroquois Studies: A Guide to the Documentary and Ethnographic Resources from Western New York and the Genesee Valley*, ed. Judkins (Genesco: State University of New York Press, 1987), 26.

40. Kirkland, *Journal of Samuel Kirkland*, 363.

41. Though the serpent story likely belonged to a traditional repertoire—it appears in numerous antebellum texts, including Seaver, *Narrative of Mrs. Mary Jemison*, 143—its adaptation to intercultural affairs is further suggested by a story told to Henry A. S. Dearborn (proposer of the Eliot monument) in the 1830s: "There was a tradition among the Senecas, that their nation was at one period established in a large village on a high hill. . . . After many years of a prosperous & peaceful occupation of this hill, an enormous serpent came out of the lake & so

vast was his size & length that he was enabled to entirely surround its base, so as to preclude a passage. . . . The distress at length became so great for the want of provisions, that it was found the whole tribe would die of hunger" ("Journals of Henry A. S. Dearborn," *Publications of the Buffalo Historical Society* 7 [1904]: 80–81). Given the context—Dearborn was acting as a commissioner for the purchase of Seneca lands—the story, which ends with the defeat of the serpent, seems particularly pointed.

42. Judkins, "David Cusick's Ancient History," 35 (italicized in original).

Conclusion

1. Angela Cavender Wilson, "American Indian History or Non-Indian Perceptions of American Indian History?" in *Natives and Academics: Researching and Writing about American Indians*, ed. Devon A. Mihesuah (Lincoln: University of Nebraska Press, 1998), 23.

2. On the appropriation of Indians by literary critics, see Daniel F. Littlefield, Jr., "American Indians, American Scholars, and the American Literary Canon," *American Studies* 33 (Fall 1992): 95–111; and Jana Sequoya-Magdaleno, "Telling the Différance: Representations of Identity in the Discourse of Indianness," in *The Ethnic Canon: Histories, Institutions, and Interventions*, ed. David Palumbo Liu (Minneapolis: University of Minnesota Press, 1995), 88–116.

3. Talal Asad, "The Concept of Cultural Translation in British Social Anthropology," in *Writing Culture*, ed. Clifford and Marcus, 156.

Index

Acknowledgments

I would like to thank all the people whose lives and works are discussed in these pages. I hope I have treated them with the seriousness they deserve.

I have other, more immediate debts for the years this book has been forming, changing, settling, and unsettling. First are those I owe my graduate school teachers: Betsy Erkkila, who guided me from start to finish; Eric Cheyfitz, whose writings and, later, presence revolutionized my thinking; and Lisa New, who has been an inspiring model, a keen critic, and an unabashed fan. In graduate school, I also met people who both intellectually (50-Book, ASG, Teaching Forvms) and socially (cocktails, Walsh's, the Jersey Shore) kept me going: Bronwyn Beistle, Jill Cunningham-Crowther, Fred DeNaples, Jackie Labbe, Lisa Maria Noudehou, John Pollack, and Laura Renick-Butera. I neither see nor talk to these friends as much as I should, but their presence—their smarts, ease, and humor—has shaped everything I've written.

In the years after graduate school, numerous colleagues and students have contributed to my development. In particular I thank Fred Adams, Linda Jordan, Mike Keener, Tim Landy, Bill Lenz, Dave Leschock, Chris Orr, Ed Palm, Kathy Pivak, Amy Smith, and Barb Vandermer. I would also be remiss if I didn't mention my cousin Vincent Rocchio, a model of scholarly dedication and iconoclasm. It's just too bad he's in film studies and doesn't read books.

My final substantial intellectual debt is to the readers of this book in manuscript. There have been four, two of whom I know only through their readings, and two of whom I've had the good fortune to meet (via email, at least): Barry O'Connell and Priscilla Wald. All have made my work immeasurably better by being what scholars should be: honest, rigorous, knowing, and humble. More particularly, Barry O'Connell has shown great enthusiasm for the project and has led me to believe he's learned from it—a real compliment, considering how much I've learned from him.

I would also like to thank the people at the University of Pennsylvania Press who shepherded this book from manuscript to publication, especially

Jerry Singerman, Noreen O'Connor, Gail Kienitz, and Bridie Chapman. Thanks to them, and to the many others involved.

Earlier versions of parts of this book have been previously published. Portions of Chapter 1 appeared as "Apostle of Removal: John Eliot in the Nineteenth Century," *New England Quarterly* 69 (March 1996), copyright *The New England Quarterly*, reproduced by permission of the publisher. Portions of Chapters 2 and 4 appeared as "Wicked Instruments: William Bartram and the Dispossession of the Southern Indians," *Arizona Quarterly* 51.3 (1995), reprinted by permission of the Regents of the University of Arizona. I am thankful for permission to reprint, and for the initial chance to test my work in the scholarly community.

Finally, I would like to acknowledge the people who, though not directly involved in my academic work, have made the real difference. My grandparents, to whom this book is dedicated, are no longer alive, but I can't forget them, here or elsewhere. My parents, Judith and Marvin Bellin, gave me Classic Comics when I was young, and the real things when I was older; it's nice to be able to give a book back to them. My siblings, Sam and Becka, have encouraged me and tolerated most of my pontificating. Lilly, to whom I hope to pass on the love of literature one day, has more important things on her mind as of this writing, such as walking and finding Spot and giving Mommy tummy-kisses. And my wife, Christine Saitz, has given me strength to follow my chosen path, laughter when the going gets rough, and an example of caring to remind me why we're here. I thank her for indulging my passions, and for being the greatest of them.